The literary turn in interpreting Old Testament narratives has brought great insight. Yet, important methodological gaps remain. In this enlightening study, Konstantin Nazarov shows the importance of focalization, demonstrating its value in his reading of Ruth and filling a methodological gap. This important study deserves to be widely read and studied.

David G. Firth, PhD
Old Testament Tutor and Academic Dean,
Trinity College Bristol, UK

This work can indeed be considered as innovative. The author sets himself a rather difficult task: to expand the boundaries of the application of narratological theory and to consider the concept of focalization, which is traditionally used to study contemporary fictional texts in relation to the Old Testament narratives. He also further studies the very idea of focalization, laying a theoretical foundation for this heuristic concept. To do so, he first gives a broader definition of the concept of focalization. Then, based on the latest developments in narratology, he creates a methodology that allows applying the concept of focalization to any texts, including the Old Testament narratives. Worth noting is the author's desire to show the applicability of his model on a fairly large corpus of narratological material. Thus, the book will be useful both for those who engage in research in general narratology and those who wish to expand their horizons in the field of research of biblical narratives. The work will undoubtedly contribute to the development of dialogue between these disciplines and will affect further research on this topic.

Wolf Schmid, PhD
Professor Emeritus of Slavic Literary Studies,
University of Hamburg, Germany

Focalization in the Old Testament Narratives with Specific Examples from the Book of Ruth

Konstantin Nazarov

MONOGRAPHS

© 2021 Konstantin Nazarov

Published 2021 by Langham Monographs
An imprint of Langham Publishing
www.langhampublishing.org

Langham Publishing and its imprints are a ministry of Langham Partnership

Langham Partnership
PO Box 296, Carlisle, Cumbria, CA3 9WZ, UK
www.langham.org

ISBNs:
978-1-83973-215-7 Print
978-1-83973-510-3 ePub
978-1-83973-511-0 Mobi
978-1-83973-512-7 PDF

Konstantin Nazarov has asserted his right under the Copyright, Designs and Patents Act, 1988 to be identified as the Author of this work.

All rights reserved. No part of this publication may be reproduced, stored in a retrieval system or transmitted, in any form or by any means, electronic, mechanical, photocopying, recording or otherwise, without the prior written permission of the publisher or the Copyright Licensing Agency.

Requests to reuse content from Langham Publishing are processed through PLSclear. Please visit www.plsclear.com to complete your request.

Scripture quotations are from The Holy Bible, English Standard Version® (ESV®), copyright © 2001 by Crossway, a publishing ministry of Good News Publishers. Used by permission. All rights reserved.

British Library Cataloguing-in-Publication Data
A catalogue record for this book is available from the British Library

ISBN: 978-1-83973-215-7

Cover & Book Design: projectluz.com

Langham Partnership actively supports theological dialogue and an author's right to publish but does not necessarily endorse the views and opinions set forth here or in works referenced within this publication, nor can we guarantee technical and grammatical correctness. Langham Partnership does not accept any responsibility or liability to persons or property as a consequence of the reading, use or interpretation of its published content.

Contents

Acknowledgements xiii
Abstract.. xv
Abbreviations xvii
Introduction 1
    The Purpose of the Research.. 1
    Why Focalization? 1
    The Review of the Present Research................................... 4
    The Book of Ruth... 5
    Expected Contributions 7
Chapter 1 9
    What Is Focalization?
    1.1. Overview of Genette's Book 9
    1.2. Regrettable Confusion 11
    1.3. Definition of the Term 14
    1.4. Examples of Zero Focalization 15
    1.5. Examples of Internal Focalization 16
    1.6. Examples of External Focalization 21
    1.7. Boundaries between Different Types of Focalization ... 21
    1.8. Shifts in Focalization 23
    1.9. Conclusion 24
Chapter 2 25
    Focalization in Old Testament Narratology
    2.1. Robert Alter 25
    2.2. Shimon Bar-Efrat... 27
    2.3. Adele Berlin... 30
    2.4. Meir Sternberg 33
    2.5. Jean Louis Ska 37
    2.6. Jerome Walsh 40
    2.7. Gary Yamasaki 45
    2.8. Conclusion 55
Chapter 3 57
    Evolution of the Notion of Focalization
    3.1. Mieke Bal (1981).. 57

  3.2. Boris Uspensky (1970) / Shlomith Rimmon-Kenan (1983) 61
    3.2.1. Uspensky (1970) 61
    3.2.2. Rimmon-Kenan (1983) 64
  3.3. Preliminary Conclusions..67
  3.4. Minor Development of the Concept of Focalization in
    1990s and 2000s 68
    3.4.1. William F. Edmiston (1991)...69
    3.4.2. Patrick O'Neill (1994) 70
    3.4.3. Ruth Ronen (1994)..71
    3.4.4. Manfred Jahn (1996, 1999, 2005) 72
    3.4.5. Essays on Fiction and Perspective (2004) 74
    3.4.6. Point of View, Perspective, Focalization (2009) 77
    3.4.7. Living Book of Narratology (2011)..................................79
  3.5. Wolf Schmid (2005, 2010)..81
  3.6. Valeri Tjupa (2016) 87
  3.7. Methodology of Studying Focalization in Old Testament
    Narratives 93
    3.7.1. From Genette to Schmid 93
    3.7.2. The Outline of the Research...95

Chapter 4 97
Focalization on the Level of Selection of Narrative Information
  4.1. Allocation of Episodes in the Book of Ruth 98
  4.2. Intentionality of Events..100
    4.2.1. The Imperatives and the Convictions of the
      Narrator of the Book of Ruth..101
    4.2.2. The First Event of the Book of Ruth...............................103
    4.2.3. The Second Event of the Book of Ruth..........................109
    4.2.4. The Third Event of the Book of Ruth.............................121
    4.2.5. The Fourth Event of the Book of Ruth...........................127
    4.2.6. Conclusion 131
  4.3. The Eventfulness of the Prologue and the Denouement of
    the Story..133
    4.3.1. Prologue – the Event Preceding the Story Proper 133
    4.3.2. The Eventfulness of the Denouement............................135
  4.4. The Eventfulness of the Episodes of the Main Story................136
    4.4.1. Relevance...137
    4.4.2. Unpredictability..139
    4.4.3. Persistence 142
    4.4.4. Irreversibility 142
    4.4.5. Non-Iterativity 143

4.4.6. Conclusion 144
4.5. Conclusion of Chapter 4 145

Chapter 5 147
Focalization on the Level of Composition
5.1. The Woman Was Left Alone (1:1–22) 150
    5.1.1. Historical Perspective in the Prologue (1:1) 150
    5.1.2. Restriction of Perspective in the Prologue 153
    5.1.3. The Beginning of the Journey (1:6–7) 154
    5.1.4. Dialogue between Naomi and Her Daughters-in-Law (1:8–14) 156
    5.1.5. The Decisions of Orpah and Ruth (1:14) 162
    5.1.6. Dialogue between Naomi and Ruth (1:15–18) ..164
    5.1.7. Arrival to Bethlehem (1:19–21) 166
    5.1.8. Summary of Return (1:22) 167
5.2. Boaz, a Relative (2:1–19) 168
    5.2.1. Introduction of Boaz (2:1) 169
    5.2.2. Dialogue between Ruth and Naomi (2:2) 171
    5.2.3. Intrusion: Summary of Ruth's Gleaning before Meeting with Boaz (2:3) 172
    5.2.4. The Arrival of Boaz (2:4) 173
    5.2.5. Dialogue between Boaz and Foreman (2:5–7) .175
    5.2.6. Dialogue between Boaz and Ruth (2:8–13) 178
    5.2.7. Mealtime (2:14) 181
    5.2.8. Boaz's Commands to His Servants (2:15–17) ...182
    5.2.9. Ruth Reports to Naomi about Her Day (2:18–19) 184
5.3. Boaz, a Redeemer (2:20–3:11) 185
    5.3.1. The Horizon of Ruth Expands (2:20–23) 185
    5.3.2. Naomi Suggests a Plan (3:1–5) 188
    5.3.3. Ruth Fulfills Naomi's Plan (3:6–7) 192
    5.3.4. Exchange at the Threshing Floor (3:8–13) 194
5.4. Pelony Almony, a Closer Relative (3:12–4:12) 202
    5.4.1. The Readers' Horizon is Expanded for the Second Time (3:11–13) 202
    5.4.2. Early Wake (3:14–15) 204
    5.4.3. The Dialogue between Ruth and Naomi (3:16–18) 205
    5.4.4. Boaz Convenes a Legal Assembly (4:1–2) 208
    5.4.5. Legal Discussion (4:3–8) 211
    5.4.6. Decisions and Blessings (4:9–12) 215
5.5. Obed as Predecessor of David (4:17b–22) 218
    5.5.1. Marriage, Conception and Birth of the Son (4:13) 218

    5.5.2. Naomi and the Women of Bethlehem (4:14–17a) 218
    5.5.3. Epilogue (4:17–22) 220
  5.6. Conclusion: Narrative Strategy of the Book of Ruth 225

Chapter 6 231
Focalization on the Level of Presentation
  6.1. General Considerations 233
  6.2. Narrative Function 240
    6.2.1. Ruth 1:11–12 240
    6.2.2. Ruth 1:20–21 241
    6.2.3. Ruth 2:8–9 241
    6.2.4. Ruth 2:14 243
    6.2.5. Ruth 2:16 243
    6.2.6. Ruth 2:21 244
    6.2.7. Ruth 3:3–4 244
    6.2.8. Ruth 3:17 246
    6.2.9. Ruth 4:3–4 246
    6.2.10. Ruth 4:7 247
  6.3. Evaluative Function 247
    6.3.1. Ruth 1:6 247
    6.3.2. Ruth 1:8 248
    6.3.3. Ruth 1:13b 248
    6.3.4. Ruth 1:14 248
    6.3.5. Ruth 1:15 250
    6.3.6. Ruth 2:10 250
    6.3.7. Ruth 2:11–12 250
    6.3.8. Ruth 2:13 251
    6.3.9. Ruth 2:20 (with 2:10) 252
    6.3.10. Ruth 3:9–10 252
    6.3.11. Ruth 4:9–10 253
    6.3.12. Ruth 4:11–12 254
    6.3.13. Ruth 4:14–15 255
  6.4. Referential Function 255
    6.4.1. Ruth 1:7 255
    6.4.2. Ruth 1:22 256
    6.4.3. Ruth 2:6 257
    6.4.4. Ruth 2:7 257
    6.4.5. Ruth 2:17–18 258
    6.4.6. Ruth 2:19 258
    6.4.7. Ruth 3:2 259
    6.4.8. Ruth 3:6 259

  6.4.9. Ruth 3:13 259
  6.4.10. Ruth 3:14 260
  6.4.11. Ruth 3:16 261
  6.4.12. Ruth 3:18 261
  6.4.13. Ruth 4:1 261
  6.4.14. Ruth 4:5 263
  6.4.15. Ruth 4:17 263
  6.4.16. Ruth 4:17–22 264
 6.5. Conclusion 264

Chapter 7 267
 Conclusion
 The Results of the Research 267
 Original Contribution 271
 Doors for Further Study 272

Glossary 275

Bibliography 281

List of Tables

Table 1. Subjective and objective nature of focalizations 65

Table 2. Facets (manifestations) of focalization in respect to subject 66

Table 3. Facets (manifestations) of focalization in respect to focalized object 66

Table 4. Points of connection between Bal and Genette 69

Table 5. Distribution of different forms of Hebrew verbs in Ruth in
        realtion to types of focalization 235

Acknowledgements

This research would have been impossible without the many people who supported me in its successful completion. First of all, I express my sincere gratitude to my tutor Prof. Dr. David Firth, who offered me a great honor by accepting me as one of his PhD students. Throughout the years he always encouraged and helped me to improve my skills. During individual consultations in his office and in colloquiums, Dr. Firth was instrumental in proposing directions to my work and finding new and fresh ideas in this relatively new field of biblical studies.

I also would like to pay my respect to Prof. Dr. Paul Kissling, who was my tutor when I was working on my MA/MDiv degree and who fostered my decision to undertake PhD studies, and to Prof. Dr. Valeri Tjupa, who provided good advice while I wrote my dissertation.

I convey my warm thanks to Rex and Sue Wolfe for excellent work on proofreading my work and encouragement which they have given me during all these years.

I express my sincere gratitude to all the supporters and staff of Langham Partnership for their faithful financial and academic support during all these years. In particular I want to thank Dr. Yan Show and Liz MacGregor for helping me to overcome the challenges of academic research.

Several key people demonstrated great patience while I was doing this study. My heartfelt thanks go to Max and Marilyn Goins for the support they offered to our family, and to Phil Casey, who was sensitive to my situation and did not bother me with new projects but waited patiently until I finished my last paragraph.

My sincere appreciation goes to TCM International Institute, where I was working as adjunct professor, and personally to Prof. Dr. Tony Twist and to Prof. Dr. Peter Penner. Thank you for your trust and useful guidelines.

Many thanks to my friends and partners in ministry Alexey and Marina and to our little home church for assistance and prayers.

Finally, I am immensely grateful to my lovely wife Irina, who did much to cover the shortfall of my attention to our four kids – Elisha, Anisya, Semion, and Kira. Indeed, all our friends and neighbors know that you are אֵשֶׁת חַיִל.

Abstract

The works in the field of general narratology that have been written since the concept was first introduced by Gérard Genette in 1972 demonstrate a great dynamic in the development of narratology. Unfortunately, the refinements of Genette's theory often suffer from an inconsistency of definitions and remain heuristic, which does not allow the dissemination of the achievements to other types of texts (for example, Old Testament narratives). In the field of biblical narratology the concept of focalization (especially its recent development) was largely overlooked, and the attempts to study the Old Testament narratives in relation to the notion of focalization are generally not accompanied by careful examination of the subject.

The purpose of the present research is the consideration of the narratological concept of focalization with regard to the book of Ruth. To this end, the research examines if recent narrative theories suggest a universal methodology of exploring focalization that can be equally applicable to any narrative texts (including Old Testament narratives) and explores the question "what are the specifics of applying this methodology to the Old Testament narratives?"

To answer the question above, the research considers Wolf Schmid's ideal genetic model of narrative constitution and Valeri Tjupa's theory of eventfulness and narrative world pictures as universal models for studying focalization. With some modifications and refinements these ideas are transformed into a methodology of studying focalization in the Old Testament narratives.

The application of the method to the book of Ruth shows that on the level of selection of narrative information, the narrator selects sixteen episodes that constitute four narratological events that became the basis of the plot. Then, on the level of composition by the means of reported speech and the play of horizons, those episodes and events were placed in a certain order. Finally, on the level of presentation, these events were presented mainly in the scope of internal focalization, which as demonstrated in the work correlates with the use of the *qatal* form of the Hebrew verb.

Since Schmid's ideal genetic model of narrative constitution claims to be universal, the method of studying focalization can be equally applied to other Old Testament narratives. Tjupa's theory of eventfulness and narrative world pictures can help to emphasize narratological events and to blueprint the thread of the narrative and logic of selectivity for those Old Testament narratives that do not have clear division into episodes and events. A subject of special interest is the question does the hypothesis about correlation between constructions with the *qatal* form of the Hebrew verb and internal focalization remain true to other Old Testament narratives.

Abbreviations

CF	character-focalizer
CO	character-objects
EF	external focalizer
IF	internal focalizer
NF	narrator-focalizer

Introduction

The Purpose of the Research

The fact that the Old Testament narratives with all their seemingly simple structure are not so ordinary was expressed by many prominent biblical scholars. Subtlety of ancient authors was often emphasized and became a subject of consideration for a number of books and monographs in the field of so-called "literary approach to the Bible." Yet most of the time analysis of the texts was exclusively empirical and conclusions had a heuristic nature, presenting a set of recommendations applicable only to certain situations.

The desire to find all-embracing typology leads to the need of employing existing theoretical concepts, terminology, and models of general narratology and examining them on the subject of their appropriateness for describing Old Testament narratives. In the center of the present work is the notion of focalization that was introduced first by Gérard Genette in 1972 and then developed and revised over subsequent decades. The object of analysis is the Old Testament book of Ruth. Consequently, the purpose of the present research is consideration of the narratological concept of focalization with regard to the book of Ruth.

Why Focalization?

Focalization was chosen among other narratological concepts because contemporary narratology considers it to be one of the major tools used by the narrator to convey information to the readers. The significance of the concept is repeatedly highlighted by many scholars. It would not be a mistake to say that in any contemporary introduction to narrative theory (or narratology), a chapter or at least a section about the notion of focalization is mandatory. For example, the contributor of *Cambridge Companion to Narrative*, Manfred Jahn, begins the chapter on focalization by stressing the central place the concept occupies in modern narrative theory:

> If narratology – the structural theory and analysis of narrative texts – were to be divided into just two major parts, then narration and focalization would be very suitable candidates. Narration is the telling of a story in a way that simultaneously respects the needs and enlists the co-operation of its audience; focalization is the submission of (potentially limitless) narrative information to a perspectival filter.[1]

Mieke Bal, the first critic of Genette's theory, also underlines the importance of the concept itself arguing that focalization

> ... has an overarching position with respect to the other aspects [of narrative]. The significance of certain aspects cannot be viewed unless it is linked to focalization. Moreover, focalization is ... the most important, most penetrating, and most subtle means of manipulation.[2]

Yet another famous scholar Shlomith Rimmon-Kenan, to whose work many modern researchers refer and who also considerably amended Genette's ideas, also explains the importance of Genette's insight:

> Most studies of point of view ... treat two related but different questions as if they were interchangeable. Briefly formulated, these questions are "who sees?" v. "who speaks?" Obviously, a person (and, by analogy, a narrative agent) is capable of both speaking and seeing, and even of doing both things at the same time – a state of affairs which facilitates the confusion between the two activities. Moreover, it is almost impossible to speak without betraying some personal "point of view," if only through the very language used. But a person (and, by analogy,

---

1. Jahn, "Focalization," in *Cambridge Companion*, 94.
2. Bal and van Boheemen, *Narratology*, 176.

a narrative agent) is also capable of undertaking to tell what another person sees or has seen. Thus, speaking and seeing, narration and focalization, may, but need not, be attributed to the same agent. The distinction between the two activities is a theoretical necessity, and only on its basis can the interrelations between them be studied with precision.³

In one of the most recent studies on focalization, Manfred Jahn speaks about the progressivity of the notion of focalization in spite of all critiques of Genette's theory:

> It [Genette's theory] establishes and strengthens the distinction between "who speaks" and "who sees"; it avoids the category error (famously perpetrated by Booth and others) of confusing focal characters with narrators; and it allows full combinatorial freedom in the sense that all types and features of focalization are allowed to co-occur (at least in principle) with all other aspects of narration.⁴

Finally, according to H. Porter Abbot, focalization enriches our comprehension and aesthetic effect from reading:

> Focalizing can contribute richly to how we think and feel as we read. Just as we pick up various intensities of thought and feeling from the voice that we hear, so also do we pick up thought and feeling from the eyes we see through. And just as the voice we hear can be either a character in the narrative or a narrator positioned outside of it, so also our focalizer can be a character within or a narrator without.⁵

In short, today comprehensive analysis of a narrative text is almost impossible without consideration of the notion of focalization.

Old Testament scholars, while long overdue, are increasingly turning to the consideration of the concept of focalization. This becomes particularly evident since the issue of focalization started to appear on the pages of the books

---

3. Rimmon-Kenan, *Narrative Fiction*, 73–74.
4. Jahn, "Focalization," in *Routledge Encyclopedia*, 176.
5. Abbott, *Cambridge Introduction*, 67.

that are not intended for a specialized audience. Among those intended for a general audience is the book of Daniel Marguerat, Marcel Durrer, and Yvan Bourquin *How to Read Bible Stories: An Introduction to Narrative Criticism*,[6] which fairly accurately conveys the idea of Genette's concept. The second is the book of Steven D. Mathewson *The Art of Preaching Old Testament Narratives*,[7] which is intended for preachers. The author considers that the concept of focalization is well worthy of a separate section.

Nevertheless, the research on the application of the concept to the Old Testament narratives is far from complete. This is evidenced, for example, by the fact that at the Special Session on Perspective Criticism featured by the Canadian Society of Biblical Studies in June 2014, the members of the Perspective Criticism Community compiled a list of aspects of point-of-view studies in need of further work. A separate paragraph in this list is devoted to the concept of focalization. List proposers admit that "while considerable work has been done on the related concept of 'focalization' . . . a methodology of focalization analysis illuminating the interpretive significance of choosing one focalization strategy over another needs further development."[8] This demonstrates the relevance of further study of the concept of focalization in the Old Testament narratives.

The Review of the Present Research

In view of the importance of this concept I found it necessary to devote the first chapter of this work to understanding the essence of Genette's concept by looking at different examples of externally, internally, and zero focalized texts that are found in the works of Genette and other narratologists. This helped to see clearly strengths and limitations of the concept and understand the need for its further development.

The second chapter of this work is focused on the review of works that employ focalization or related concepts (like perspective or point-of-view) in the study of Old Testament narratives. Unfortunately, the research shows that in the field of biblical narratology the concept of focalization was highly

---

6. Marguerat, Durrer, and Bourquin, *How to Read*.
7. Mathewson, *Art of Preaching*.
8. See "Researchers Needed," *Perspective Criticism*.

overlooked. While biblical scholars also found the idea of perspective to be a useful tool to interpret biblical narratives, their attempts to study the Old Testament texts in relation to the notion of focalization are generally not accompanied by careful examination of the subject. For example, the majority of these works do not clearly distinguish between the terms "focalization" and "point-of-view."[9]

The works that have been written during recent decades demonstrate great dynamic in the development of the concept of focalization. Therefore, the third chapter of my research is devoted to the evolution of the concept of focalization from 1972 until present. Unfortunately, the refinements of Genette's theory were not always successful; most of the time the attempt ends up with formulation of a new concept of perspective in the narrative. It also shows that, generally speaking, any narratologist meets with two challenges when studying focalization. First, the works on focalization often suffer from inconsistency of definitions. Second, most of the time the research remains heuristic, which does not allow the dissemination of the achievements to other types of texts. The latter problems are addressed by the end of the third chapter where I propose to study focalization on the basis of Schmid's ideal genetic model of narrative constitution.

The rest of the work is devoted to the study of focalization in the book of Ruth according to Schmid's model. Chapter 4 considers focalization on the level of selection of narrative information. Chapter 5 deals with composition of selected events. And chapter 6 examines one of the aspects of presentation of the narrative.

The Book of Ruth

The book of Ruth was chosen as an object of narratological analysis partly because of size, which makes it suitable for illustrative purposes, and partly because of the narrative excellence of the story. Containing only four chapters (totaling eighty-five verses), this book nevertheless is a complete short story

---

9. While Berlin uses only the term "point of view" and does not even mention "focalization" as category, Culpepper does not see the difference between these two terms. See Berlin, *Poetics and Interpretation*, 43–82; Culpepper, *Anatomy of the Fourth Gospel*, 20. The same with Jean Louis Ska, *Our Fathers*, 65.

that possesses all the necessary attributes of good narrative, such as fascinating plot, developed characters, and deep meaning.

Besides, in recent years the book of Ruth has become the focus of attention among Old Testament scholars. For the period of 2015–2016 two commentaries on the book of Ruth by Daniel Hawk[10] and by Jeremy Schipper[11] were published. Both works have been consulted in carrying out this study. In the introduction to his commentary Schipper points out that "space does not allow for a full exploration of the poetics of Ruth's narrative"[12] and therefore confines himself only to limited observations on selective representation and narrative ambiguity in the book of Ruth. The present study of focalization in some way starts from these issues and continues the discussion initiated by Schipper in his commentary.

Studying the book of Ruth in respect to focalization has proven to be a challenge. Existing studies of focalization tend to consider mainly descriptive narrative passages where the point of view and spatial aspect of focalization is best exemplified. However, the book of Ruth is organized as dialogic narratives, and some standard methods of studying focalization are not always applicable to it. But since most of the Old Testament narratives are composed the same way, this challenge turns into important tasks that may affect the study of focalization in all the corpus of the Old Testament narratives.

Concerning the text of the book of Ruth, I used primarily the text of Biblia Hebraica Stuttgartensia (BHS).[13] However, the Hebrew text in quotations is placed without cantillation marks in order to increase its readability. The primary translation used in this work is the English Standard Version (ESV), although occasionally I point to inconsistencies of this translation with the original text of the book. I have also followed the numbering of chapters and verses in the ESV.

---

10. Hawk, *Ruth*.
11. Schipper, *Ruth*.
12. Schipper, 23.
13. *Biblia Hebraica Stuttgartensia: With Werkgroep Informatica, Vrije Universiteit Morphology; Bible. O.T. Hebrew. Werkgroep Informatica, Vrije Universiteit.* Logos Bible Software, 2006.

Expected Contributions

As will be shown, this work attempts to make original contributions in three areas of study. First is the area of general narratology. This area considers subsequent transformations that Genette's typology underwent during the last few decades and through them to build methodology for studying focalization. The second is the area of biblical narratology, where I will attempt to apply highly theoretical concepts of general narratology to biblical text. Third is the area of Hebrew syntax: the last chapter of the work endeavors to demonstrate correlation between the form of the Hebrew verb and the type of focalization.

CHAPTER 1

What Is Focalization?

The notion of focalization was originally introduced by French narratologist Gérard Genette in the book *Figures III* in 1972 along with other concepts that together constitute an entirely new holistic approach to analysis of narrative text.[1] Most studies of focalization mistakenly try to explain and use the concept without respecting the entire theory of narrative that is introduced by Genette in his book. As a result those studies too quickly come to the conclusion that focalization has very limited use for the analysis of narrative texts. Therefore, for an accurate understanding of the notion, I prefer to begin this study by examining the notion of focalization among the other concepts of Genette's work.

1.1. Overview of Genette's Book

Genette starts his book with several definitions. First, he differentiates between story, narrative text, and the act of narration. The relationship between these three aspects of narrative reality constitutes for Genette an analysis of narrative discourse. Then Genette proposes that every narrative, being a linguistic production, could be metaphorically interpreted as "the expansion of a verb."[2] This assumption permitted him to analyze narrative discourse "according to categories borrowed from the grammar of the verb."[3] In particular he chooses

---

1. Genette, *Figures III*; later this book was translated into English and published under the title *Narrative Discourse: An Essay in Method*.
2. Genette, *Narrative Discourse*, 30.
3. Genette, 30.

three categories or three determinations that determine the verb, tense, mood, and voice, and then metaphorically (with some expansion) applies them to the narrative text. These determinations characterize relationships between story and narrative, narrative and narration, and narration and story.

According to Genette, the relationship between story and narrative can be adequately explained by studying such characteristics as order, duration, and frequency of narrative events in comparison to those of the real story. In other words, the relationship between story and narrative can be studied under the category of *tense*.

The category of *voice* explains the relationship between narration and story, and narration and narrative. It is connected with the so-called narrative agent, the one who actually gives an account of the facts of the narrative (or the one who speaks).

The narrative agent may hold a different temporal position and therefore can speak about past, present, or future events (or to be, according to Genette, a subsequent, prior, simultaneous, or interpolated narrator).[4] One narrative agent can give his responsibility to the other so there could be different levels on narration (as Genette puts it, narrative agents staying on different narrative levels: extradiegetic, diegetic, and metadiegetic).[5]

The narrative agent may stay within the story as one of the characters or outside of the story, in other words, may have different degrees of presence (or to be heterodiegetic and homodiegetic).[6] Finally, the narrative agent may play different functions (narrative, directing, communicating, emotive, and ideological). Therefore, the category of voice covers the problems of point of view in the narrative and answers the question of how the process of narration is revealed in the narrative.

However, according to Genette, identification of the one who speaks (or narrative agent) has to be supplemented with two characteristics of narration: form and degree of representation. These two characteristics determine what Genette calls the mood of the narrative (which shows the relation between narrative and story). The degree of the representation depends on inclusion of details; representation can be more or less distanced, to use Genette's

---

4. Genette, 216–23.
5. Genette, 227–31.
6. Genette, 245–52.

metaphor. The form of representation is described by perspective, which Genette calls focalization. Distance is quantitative modulation ("how much?") and focalization is qualitative modulation ("by what channel?").[7]

Genette proposes then that different determinations within the scope of one narrative are not necessarily dependent upon each other, which permits the study of perspective (the one who sees) in isolation from voice (the one who speaks). Practically it means that in the narrative, the one who narrates does not implicitly express their perception, but can convey perception (for example, perspective) of someone else. This conclusion brings Genette to criticize the then prevailing concept of narrative point of view.

1.2. Regrettable Confusion

Study of the subjectivity of narrative discourse had been one of the key issues in narratology for about a hundred years before the emergence of the concept of focalization. According to Wallace Martin, the "theoretical framework used by most English and American critics in discussing point of view was fully developed by 1960"[8] and systematic study of point of view became "the most frequently discussed aspect of narrative method."[9] According to Scholes, who looks at the development of point of view in historical perspective,

> The period of the rise of the novel as a literary form has also been the period of really great experimentation with, and development of, techniques in the management of point of view . . . This remarkable development is largely the result of the problems and opportunities presented to narrative artists seeking to achieve an effective combination of empirical and fictional techniques of narration.[10]

After indicating that his predecessors have already made considerable progress in the question of narrative perspective, Genette evaluates existing classifications of narrative point of view proposed by such scholars as Percy Lubbock, George Blin, Cleanth Brooks, Robert Penn Warren, F. K. Stanzel,

---

7. Genette, *Narrative Discourse Revisited*, 43.
8. Martin, *Recent Theories*, 134.
9. Martin, 133.
10. Scholes, Phelan, and Kellogg, *Nature of Narrative*, 241–42.

Norman Friedman, Wayne Booth, and Bertil Romberg. His study leads him to the conclusion that all these typologies "suffer from regrettable confusion."[11]

The reason for that confusion was that the concept of point of view was initially the product of nineteenth- and twentieth-century novelists (not literary critics) who attempted to "overcome the limitations of authorial and first-person narration"[12] in order to make their stories as realistic as possible. It is no wonder that writers proposed to achieve this purpose as writers, not as critics, and used for it familiar terms. Accordingly, one can limit the influence of the author and make the story more realistic:[13]

1. By suppressing narratorial use of the pronoun "I."
2. By eliminating commentary and substituting it with dramatic presentation when possible.
3. By accessing the mind of only one character and using the visual perspective of that character.

Such were writing tools that the authors beginning from Henry James experimented with in order to bring their narrative closer to life experience. Therefore, classifications, which initially were conducted by the writers and for the writers, reflected the writer's train of thought and were heuristic in their nature (e.g. first-person narration vs. third-person narration).

Genette approaches the problem of point of view theoretically (not as writer but as literary critic) and finds point 3 in the above list problematic. The problem of "point of view" as a characteristic of narrative text lies in its definition. What do we mean by "point of view"? There are at least two different understandings of this term. When we speak about someone's point of view, we may mean either perspective or opinion, which already creates confusion. Martin asserts that "access to consciousness" has two meanings: a third-person narrator can look into a character's mind or look through it. In the first case, the narrator is the perceiver and the character's mind is perceived.[14] And Wolf Schmid adds to this question:

---

11. Genette, *Narrative Discourse*, 186.
12. Martin, *Recent Theories*, 133.
13. See Martin, 133.
14. Martin, 143.

Access to a character's interior and the taking on of the character's perceptual perspective, no matter how often they are mixed in theories of perspective (as indicated above), are two entirely separate things. In the first case, the character or, more specifically, his or her consciousness, is the object of the narrator's perception; in the second, it is the subject or the prism of perception through which the narrator sees the narrated world.[15]

Any attempt to explain all the complexities of the narrative text with variation of one simple characteristic like point of view inevitably brings one to confusion. More than that, the fact that the narrating agent does not necessarily express their opinion or speak about their vision, makes the problem even more complicated. Initially Genette's idea of focalization was directed toward the resolution of this particular confusion. First, he showed that earlier typologies of point of view would classify both situations as third-person narration while obviously "speaking" (narration) and "seeing" (vision or opinion) belong to different categories. He then convincingly proved that the problem cannot be solved without the distinguishing of and separate analysis of the mood (who perceives) and voice (who speaks).

According to Genette, the fundamental principle underlying the analysis of narrative should not be the identity of the voice or perceiver, whether character, narrator, or hypothetical observer, but the purely visual/perceptual aspect: to what degree the information that the narrator shares with the reader is restricted. The range of information is measured according to the "ratio of knowledge between the narrator and the character."[16]

This restriction of information might be called in old-fashioned style "vision," "field," or "point of view," but Genette uses the abstract term "focalization" in order "to avoid the too specifically visual connotations of the terms."[17]

---

15. Schmid, *Narratology*, 104.
16. Scholes, Phelan, and Kellogg, *Nature of Narrative*, 318. The knowledge of the narrator has nothing to do with the position of the narrator, as it is wrongly suggested by Prince, who says,
   zero focalization obtains when the story is presented in terms of a nonlocatable, indeterminate position; internal focalization obtains when the story is presented in terms of the knowledge, feelings, or perceptions of a single character or several different ones; external focalization obtains when the story is presented in terms of a focal point in the world of the events recounted but outside any of the character.
   See Prince, *Narratology*, 123.
17. Genette, *Narrative Discourse*, 189.

1.3. Definition of the Term

The above considerations are crystallized into the definition of focalization in Genette's second book:

> Focalization is "a restriction of field" – actually, that is, a selection of narrative information with respect to what was traditionally called omniscience . . . [or] . . . completeness of information . . . The instrument of this possible selection is a situated focus, a sort of information-conveying pipe that allows passage only of information that is authorized by the situation.[18]

For practical purposes, I will substitute the term "field of knowledge" with the more appropriate term "horizon of knowledge" or simply "horizon" used by Bakhtin.[19] Accordingly, the narrator can choose one of three ways to restrict and convey information to the readers.

Zero Focalization. Information can be channeled without any restriction – that is when the narrator knows and says more than any given character knows (narrator > character) and "exercises the privilege of moving freely about the story world to comment first on this scene and this character and then on that scene and that character."[20] In this case the reader obtains information about the narrative world that is not accessible to any character; the horizon of the narrator is wider than the horizon of the characters. The text in this instance is "zero focalized" or not focalized (not restricted).

Internal Focalization Information is restricted to the cognition of one of the characters. The narrator's horizon equals the character's horizon (narrator = character) because the narrator restricts himself to the character's perspective. In this case, the reader perceives the narrative world through the mind of this character. So, respectively, this type of focalization is called "internal" focalization and the text is considered to be internally focalized.

External Focalization. Finally, the scene of the narrative can be presented to the reader just as it is, without any additional information about mind or motives of its inhabitants (narrator < character). Information is restricted to a behaviorist report and the reader "sees" the narrative world externally.

---

18. Genette, *Narrative Discourse Revisited*, 74.

19. Russian word for "horizon" is "krugozor" (кругозор). See Bakhtin "Автор и герой в эстетической деятельности," 104–74.

20. Scholes, Phelan, and Kellogg, *Nature of Narrative*, 318.

"The narrator is restricted to reporting the character's observable behavior."[21] Focalization is accordingly called "external" and the text is considered to be externally focalized.

In order to comprehend the notion of focalization as it was understood by Genette, one must consider, as appropriate, as many case studies as he and other scholars use in order to illustrate the concept. One meets here with the obvious difficulty that because a lot of practical examples of focalization are given by Genette in passing, it is difficult to understand and apply the notion to the narratives beyond the scope of modern European literature. Therefore, in the next section I seek to discuss Genette's examples in greater detail and consider additional examples from other scholars who, following the same rationale, were looking for examples to demonstrate Genette's theory in practice.

1.4. Examples of Zero Focalization

According to Monika Fludernik's understanding of the term, zero focalization is found in the narratives where the narrator is "above the action," "unrestricted and unlimited."[22] Practically, this is evident when the narrator can freely shift between various locations and various time periods of the narrative world, as much as being able to look into the mind of any characters.

Since Genette does not give any particular examples of this type of focalization besides saying that zero focalization is the prerogative of "classical narrative," literary scholars after him tried to bridge this gap and find concrete examples of non-focalized narratives. An example given by Scholes shows how easy it is for an omniscient narrator to shift from the mind of one character to another, telling what each of them thinks about the marriage of Sir Casaubon:

> One morning, some weeks after her arrival at Lowick, Dorothea – but why always Dorothea? Was her point of view the only possible one with regard to this marriage? Protest against all our interest, all our effort at understanding being given to the young skins that look blooming in spite of trouble; for these too

---

21. Scholes, Phelan, and Kellogg, 318.
22. Fludernik, *Introduction to Narratology*, 38.

will get faded, and will know the older and more eating griefs which we are helping to neglect. In spite of the blinking eyes and white moles objectionable to Celia, and the want of muscular curve which was morally painful to Sir James, Mr. Casaubon had an intense consciousness within him, and was spiritually a-hungered like the rest of us.[23]

Herman gives an excerpt from James A. Michener's modern novel *Hawaii* to illustrate the style of zero focalization as the ability of the narrator to make shifts in time and space:

Across a million years, down more than ten million years [the island] existed silently in the unknown sea and then died, leaving only a fringe of coral where the birds rest and where gigantic seals of the changing ocean play. Ceaseless life and death, endless expenditure of beauty and capacity, tireless ebb and flow and rising and subsidence of the ocean. Night comes and the burning day, and the island waits, and no man arrives. The days perish and the nights, and the aching beauty of lush valleys and waterfalls vanishes, and no man will ever see them.[24]

The narrator had access to something that is not "accessible to ordinary humans"[25] – the ability that is enhanced by the final phrase "no man will ever see . . ." In all the above examples, the perspective was unrestricted or unlimited, in contrast to the following examples with limitations of internal and external focalizations.

1.5. Examples of Internal Focalization

Internal focalization is probably one of the most interesting ways of manipulation of perspective in the narrative. It is also one of the most confusing ideas. Recalling Pouillon, Genette points to the paradox that,

---

23. Eliot and Maertz, *Middlemarch*, 242, quoted in Scholes, Phelan, and Kellogg, *Nature of Narrative*, 318.
24. Michener, *Hawaii*, quoted in Jahn, "Focalization," in *Cambridge Companion*, 97.
25. Jahn, "Focalization," in *Cambridge Companion*, 98.

in "vision with," the character is seen not in his innerness, for then we would have to emerge from the innerness whereas instead we are absorbed into it, but is seen in the image he develops of others, and to some extent through that image. In sum, we apprehend him as we apprehend ourselves in our immediate awareness of things, our attitudes with respect to what surrounds us – what surrounds us and is not within us. Consequently we can say in conclusion: vision as an image of others is not a result of vision "with" the main character, it is itself that vision "with."[26]

In the following examples, the text presents information that is accessible (limited, focalized) to one character of the story. Genette himself illustrates this type of focalization with two novels of Henry James – *The Ambassadors* and *What Maisie Knew*. He remarks in passing that the latter novel illustrates internal focalization better, which is an important point for the present research. Consider the following excerpt from *The Ambassadors*:

> The ordered English garden, in the freshness of the day, was delightful to Strether, who liked the sound, under his feet, of the tight fine gravel, packed with the chronic damp, and who had the idlest eye for the deep smoothness of turf and the clean curves of paths.[27]

Information in this passage is definitely focalized internally; the reader perceives the freshness of the day and sees the garden through Strether's eyes. Though one can find a great number of such passages in the novel, the text is not always internally focalized. There are passages that report dialogues and are written from the perspective of a detached onlooker. But internally (in regard to Stretcher) focalized passages that are imbedded in the narrative here and there induce a general sense of fixed internal focalization and dialogues do not necessarily spoil this impression.

The novel *What Maisie Knew* by the same author, according to Genette, illustrates internal focalization better. The principal reason, I think, is that in this novel the reader can immediately identify internally focalized passages when the narrator restricts the field by imposing the language of a child to

---

26. Genette, *Narrative Discourse*, 193.
27. James, *Ambassadors*, 26.

convey the point of view of Maisie. The same style of child's vision is used in James Joyce's novel *A Portrait of the Artist*. The following excerpt from the novel is used by Rimmon-Kenan to illustrate internally focalized passages:

> Once upon a time and a very good time it was there was a moocow coming down along the road and this moocow that was coming down along the road met a nicens little boy named baby tuckoo... His father told him that story: his father looked at him through a glass: he had a hairy face. He was baby tuckoo. The moocow came down the road where Betty Byrne lived: she sold lemon platt.[28]

In order to describe the elements of the narrative world, Joyce operates by the ideas that are simple enough to be part of the child's perception. For example, the word "glass" is used instead of the word "glasses," "hairy face" is the way a child would probably describe the unshaven face of his father. In other words, the restriction here is linguistic in nature: it is the restriction of vocabulary. Very basic vocabulary testifies about the age of the character. This type of internal focalization can be found in the biblical narrative of Ruth, as will be shown later.

Another good example of internal focalization is provided by H. Porter Abbott. In the following excerpt from Flaubert's *Madam Bovary*, the one who sees is not the narrator of the story, but Rodolphe, one of the characters, "who is at that moment walking beside Emma, planning his campaign of seduction."[29]

> She nudged him with her elbow.
> "What does that mean?" he wondered, glancing at her out of the corner of his eye as they moved on.
> Her face, seen in profile, was so calm that it gave him no hint. It stood out against the light, framed in the oval of her bonnet, whose pale ribbons were like streaming reeds. Her eyes with their long curving lashes looked straight ahead: they were fully open, but seemed a little narrowed because of the blood that was pulsing gently under the fine skin of her cheekbones. The rosy

---

28. Joyce, *Portrait of the Artist*, quoted in Rimmon-Kenan, *Narrative Fiction*, 74.
29. Abbott, *Cambridge Introduction*, 66–67.

flesh between her nostrils was all but transparent in the light. She was inclining her head to one side, and the pearly tips of her white teeth showed between her lips.

"Is she laughing at me?" Rodolphe wondered.

But Emma's nudge had been no more than a warning, for Monsieur Lheureux was walking along beside them, now and then addressing them as though to begin conversation.

Compared with the previous example, here the restriction has more to do with the visual aspect. The reader is looking through Rodolphe's eyes and sees anatomic details of Emma. The specificity of details that are captured by Rodolphe testifies about the intensity of Rodolphe's feeling. In other words, the details described by the narrator are the details that concern character. This conclusion also will be used when considering the book of Ruth.

However, visual restriction is not the only type of focalization that is possible. In the book *Narrative Discourse Revisited*, Genette explains that focalization may not be unique to the vision of the character, but could well be applied to any type of the perception:

> There would have been no point in taking great pains to replace *point of view* with *focalization* if I was only going to fall right back into the same old rut; so obviously we must replace *who sees?* with the broader question of *who perceives?*[30]

Non-visual perception is found in the excerpt from Ernest Hemingway's *For Whom the Bell Tolls*, which is given as an example of internal focalization by Jahn:

> He lay flat on the brown, pine-needled floor of the forest, his chin on his folded arms, and high overhead the wind blew in the tops of the pine trees. The mountainside sloped gently where he lay; but below it was steep and he could see the dark of the oiled road winding through the pass. There was a stream alongside the road and far down he saw a mill beside the stream and the falling water of the dam, white in the summer sunlight.[31]

---

30. Genette, *Narrative Discourse Revisited*, 64.

31. Hemingway, *For Whom the Bell Tolls*, 6, quoted in Jahn, "Focalization," in *Cambridge Companion*, 98.

According to Jahn, the character not only sees, but also feels and hears. His perception modes are not only indicated by explicit phrases such as "he could see" but more subtly also by the "pine-needled floor," the "gently" sloping ground, the wind blowing "high overhead."[32] This expands considerably the scope of application of the notion of focalization which is specifically important for the Old Testament narratives due to their rather modest list of visual methods of representation.

All the above examples illustrate what Genette calls "fixed internal focalization." In addition, Genette distinguishes two other types of focalization, which he calls variable and multiple focalizations. Fixed focalization is the restriction of information according to the perception of only one character of the story. However, when focalization in the narrative shifts from one focal character to another, it becomes "variable." Genette mentions that this method is often used by Stendhal but does not offer any specific examples, mentioning only that in Stendhal's books focalization tends to shift from one character to another "rapidly and subtly."[33] The following extract from *The Red and the Black*, which describes the scene of the first meeting of Madame de Rênal and Julien and moves between their perspectives, seems to be a good example of what Genette means by variable focalization:

> Madame de Rênal was silent, bewildered; they were standing very close, looking at each other. Julien had never seen anyone so beautifully dressed, especially a woman with such a dazzling complexion, speaking to him in so sweet a voice. Madame de Rênal looked at the heavy tears on the young peasant's cheeks, which had been at first so exceedingly pale, and which were now so rosy.[34]

Finally, by "multiple focalization" Genette means situations where "the same event may be evoked several times according to the point of view of several . . . characters."[35] Besides the illustration from the film *Rashomon* given by Genette, multiple examples from the Bible can be cited. One of them is the story of the death of Saul repeated twice, the first time by the narrator (1

---

32. Jahn, "Focalization," in *Cambridge Companion*, 98.
33. Genette, *Narrative Discourse Revisited*, 64.
34. Stendhal, *Red and the Black*, 30.
35. Genette, *Narrative Discourse*, 190.

Sam 31:3–6) and second time by the Amalekite (2 Sam 1:1–10). As will be shown in this work, the rudiments of multiple focalization can also be found in the book of Ruth.

1.6. Examples of External Focalization

Genette mentions Hammet, Hemingway, and several other authors who presented their characters without displaying their thoughts or feelings, at least for a part of the story.[36] Jahn introduces the example from Hemingway's *The Killers* as "prototypical case":[37]

> The door of Henry's lunch-room opened and two men came in. They sat down at the counter.
> "What's yours?" George asked them.
> "I don't know," one of the men said. "What do you want to eat, Al?" "I don't know," said Al. "I don't know what I want to eat."
> Outside it was getting dark. The street-light came on outside the window. The two men at the counter read the menu.[38]

According to Jahn, one can be certain that a passage is externally focalized, if information is presented as it would be recorded by a "virtual camera." The books of Hammet and Hemingway are almost entirely written in such manner and mostly consist of dialogues, which are from time to time interrupted by a description of appearance of the characters, or details of the narrative world, or stage directions. The similarity of this technique with the book of Ruth will allow me to come to the conclusion that on the whole, the narrative of Ruth is also externally focalized with several inserts of internal focalization.

1.7. Boundaries between Different Types of Focalization

In the rest of the chapter on focalization, Genette makes additional notes concerning the boundary lines between different types of focalization. First,

---

36. Genette, 190.
37. Jahn, "Focalization," in *Cambridge Companion*, 98.
38. Hemingway, "Killers" 215, quoted in Jahn, "Focalization," in *Cambridge Companion*, 98–99.

he points out that the entire narrative is not necessarily the subject of only one type of focalization and that shifts in focalization can be very short.[39] This note is important for the present research, for, as we will see, the sections of internal focalization in the book of Ruth are short indeed.

In addition, Genette admits that the borderline between different types of focalization is sometimes blurred. The same passage can be classified internally as well as externally focalized, depending on the chosen focal character. The narrator's words can be regarded as non-focalized and focalized, depending on the meaning of omniscience. The narrator's words are non-focalized just because the narrator knows everything. Yet the narrator does not have to say everything ("he who can do most can do least") and it is actually impossible to say everything, which means that even the words of the narrator are focalized (restricted). Internal focalization is also "rarely applied in a totally rigorous way" with the exception of interior monologue or experimental narratives like Robbe-Grillet's *La Jalousie*, where "the central character is limited absolutely to and strictly inferred from his focal position alone."[40]

Two examples from Stendhal illustrate this idea. In the first example as Genette suggests, only the last couple of words turn out to be really internally focalized – they describe what the hero sees.

> Without hesitation, although ready to yield up his soul with disgust, Fabrizio flung himself from his horse and took the hand of the corpse which he shook vigorously; then he stood still as though paralysed. He felt that he had not the strength to mount again. What horrified him more than anything was that open eye.[41]

In the second example the whole passage is focalized internally: "A bullet, entering on one side of the nose, had gone out at the opposite temple, and disfigured the corpse in a hideous fashion. It lay with one eye still open."[42]

---

39. Genette, *Narrative Discourse*, 191.
40. Genette, 192.
41. Stendhal, *Charterhouse of Parma*, quoted in Genette, *Narrative Discourse*, 192.
42. Stendhal, quoted in Genette, 192–93.

1.8. Shifts in Focalization

Nevertheless, in many situations it is possible to identify the boundary (find shifts) of focalization. According to Genette, a specific example of such shift is found in Jules Verne's *Around the World in Eighty Days*. Genette makes only passing reference to it, but for practical purposes I will repeat the example in more detail because later it will serve as a model for further implications while studying the book of Ruth.

In chapter 12 of the book, "Phileas Fogg is looked at first from the outside, through the puzzled gaze of his contemporaries, and how his inhuman mysteriousness will be maintained until the episode that will reveal his generosity."[43]

The chapter reports some details of the long and exhausting trip of three travellers – General Cromarty, Phileas Fogg, and Passepartout – across the Indian forests on the elephant. Phileas Fogg and Sir Francis Cromarty are horribly jostled by the swift trotting of the elephant, but endure the discomfort with true British phlegm. However, when after two hours the guide stops the elephant, and gives him an hour for rest, Sir Francis Cromarty finds himself broken while "Mr. Fogg seemed as fresh as if straight out of bed."

> "He's made of iron!" said the Brigadier-General, looking at him with admiration.
> "Wrought iron," answered Passepartout, as he prepared a simple lunch.[44]

Later, the travellers meet with a procession of Brahmins who plan to sacrifice a woman. Fogg, who is greatly limited with time, decides to save the woman. According to Genette, the following dialogue with the General uncovers Fogg's true nature:

> "Save the woman, Mr. Fogg!"
> "I have yet twelve hours to spare; I can devote them to that."
> "Why, you are a man of heart!"
> "Sometimes," replied Phileas Fogg, quietly; "when I have the time."

---

43. Berlin, *Poetics and Interpretation*, 91.

44. The new translation of Verne's book is used here, because traditional translation loses the point of the scene. See Verne and Butcher, *Around the World in Eighty Days*.

Now, according to Genette, the first episode focalizes Fogg externally – two of his companions noticed that Fogg seems (to them) "fresh and straight." They talk to each other and come to the conclusion that Fogg has a strong personality (this interpretation depends on our understanding of the metaphor). The author uses dialogue between two characters in order to picture the substance of the third man. Of course, the conclusion of Cromarty happens to be just his personal opinion based on his own observations of Fogg's behavior. This means that the reader then gets to know both the outer appearance of Fogg and the evaluative (ideological) conclusion from the point of view of the general. In the second scene, according to Genette, Fogg is focalized internally. Again (together with Cromarty and other people) the reader watches Fogg's behavior. In this case he just verbally states his intentions that come to be the basis for Cromarty's conclusion about Fogg's inner character (namely, generosity).

From this example we can infer that characters' behavior and words that are essentially externally focalized elements can constitute a sufficient ground for determining their inner selves. This means that in the course of the narrative, the opinions of one character about another verbalized in direct speech can be considered as internal focalization.

1.9. Conclusion

The examples given above seem to be quite enough to understand what Genette originally meant under the term "focalization." They show that Genette provided only general trends and that each particular example requires further consideration and an intuitive approach. Inconsistency of the theory, its general and non-specific character and difficulties in applying its conclusions to other narratives had led to significant rethinking (though not always improvement) of the concept by other scholars. The critique of Genette's concept of focalization and, accordingly, major developments of the concept in recent years will be considered in chapter 3 of this work. But before doing so, I will demonstrate in chapter 2 that such an established concept was not properly reflected in the works on the Old Testament narratology.

CHAPTER 2

Focalization in Old Testament Narratology

For several recent decades biblical narratology developed intensely. This development, usually, had to do with adaptation of concepts of general narratology to biblical texts. However, the notion of focalization, for some reason, has been highly overlooked by OT scholars. This chapter analyzes key works on OT narratology, beginning with Robert Alter, and underscores the problems that derive from this significant omission.

2.1. Robert Alter

The rise of narrative criticism of the Bible is usually attributed to Robert Alter and to his book *The Art of Biblical Narrative*, which was published in 1981. Though the literary approach to the Bible was not originated by Alter and was widely used long before him,[1] the "incredible, and continuing, success of Alter's work"[2] proliferated interest in biblical narratology, evinced in many subsequent publications on the same issue. Yet, considered fresh and new, Alter's work overlooked the concept of focalization that emerged in literary theory almost a decade earlier. By saying this, I am not suggesting that Alter overlooked the whole idea of restriction of information in biblical narratives. For example, chapter 8 "Narration and Knowledge" is committed to

---
1. Weitzman, "Before and After," 191–210. According to Weitzman, "Interest in the Bible 'as literature' has a long intellectual pedigree that can be traced back to the eighteenth century, which itself looked back to the ancient Greek scholar Longinus as an antecedent."
2. Weitzman, "Before and After," 196.

the study of omniscience and ignorance (what he calls "fictional experiment in knowledge"[3] and what I will call "horizons") in the story of Joseph. In the process of interpretation of the story, he asserts that the biblical narrator, despite his omniscience, is "highly selective about sharing this omniscience with his readers."[4] According to Alter, the style of composition of biblical narrators is different from Victorian novels (which Genette considered to be zero focalized) because they do not want their readers to become like God.[5]

> His typically monotheistic decision is to lead us to know as flesh-and-blood knows: character is revealed primarily through speech, action, gesture, with all the ambiguities that entails; motive is frequently, though not invariably, left in a penumbra of doubt; often we are able to draw plausible inferences about the personages and their destinies, but much remains a matter of conjecture or even of teasing multiple possibilities.[6]

In the same chapter we hear the echoes of the idea of purposeful ordering of narrative information in "meaningful pattern in the events through a variety of technical procedures"[7] and the idea that significance of the event or the personage can be measured by distance from divine knowledge.[8]

However, all these ideas remain on the level of heuristic discovery; rules of interpretation inherent in literary theory are not fully implemented in Alter's work. It seems odd since one of the main theses of the book is the fictional character of biblical narratives, which Alter characterizes as "the beginning of prose fiction." Obviously it is possible to take a heuristic approach, even with apparent success. But the study of the text that does not take into account theorized and generalized methods will always be adhered to the particular narrative section and will always have difficulties in comparative studies.

It is not difficult to guess that Genette, with his concept of focalization, is also not mentioned in the book. The absence of any records of Genette's work or references to his typology in Alter's book can be attributed to the rather

---

3. Alter, *Art of Biblical Narrative*, 159.
4. Alter, 158.
5. Comp. Alter, 158.
6. Alter, 158.
7. Alter, 158.
8. Alter, 158–59.

late English translation of *Figures*.⁹ But, as I show in the following sections, the monographs on a literary approach to the Bible that were published in subsequent years continue to overlook the notion of focalization as well.

2.2. Shimon Bar-Efrat

Shimon Bar-Efrat, in his book *Narrative Art in the Bible*,[10] asserts that the aim of the book is to present "... a way of reading which is based on the employment of tools and principles current in the study of literature, and it combines summary and methodical survey with the observation of new aspects."[11] Bar-Efrat claims that anyone who wants to study biblical narratives as they are (as opposed to historical critics who are interested in the way biblical narratives come into existence) must use

> the avenue of literary analysis, for it is impossible to appreciate the nature of biblical narrative fully, understand the network of its component elements or penetrate into its inner world without having recourse to the methods and tools of literary scholarship.[12]

The goal of the author is to explore methods, structures, and forms of biblical narratives that constitute firm ground upon which ensuing interpretation will rest.[13] Therefore, the book examines the questions of narrator and modes of narration, shaping of the characters, the structure of the plot, time and space, and details of style. But as typical for the works on literary criticism of the Bible of that time, the author does not pursue subordinating himself to any existing literary theory reiterating old heuristic approaches.

In the chapter on narrator, Bar-Efrat analyzes different narrative modes, by examining the viewpoint from which the narrator observes the events in the narrative world.[14] He chooses five opposite modes that he considers to be the most important for biblical narratives:

---

9. Genette, *Narrative Discourse*.

10. Bar-Efrat, *Narrative Art*. In fact, the book was first published in Hebrew in 1979 (i.e. one year earlier than Alter's work), but became popular only after its publication in English in 1989.

11. Bar-Efrat, *Narrative Art*, 7.

12. Bar-Efrat, 9.

13. Bar-Efrat, 11.

14. Bar-Efrat, 14.

1. Narrator with unlimited knowledge vs. Narrator with limited knowledge.
2. Narrator who intrudes into the story vs. Silent and self-effacing narrator.
3. Narrator with remote perspective vs. Narrator with minimum mediation.
4. Narrator with the view "from above" vs. Narrator with the viewpoint of a character.
5. Neutral or objective narrator vs. Narrator with definite attitude.

It can be definitely said that the above typology of point of view suffers from the inaccuracy that Genette highlighted in his book, for different modes of Bar-Efrat's typology belong to different, unrelated, independent variables. The first point describes the mode of knowledge, the second describes the mode of presence, third is the mode of spatial distance, fourth is the mode of subjectivity, and the fifth one is the mode of ideology. As for Genette, he offered a simpler but more inclusive model. Nevertheless, just the mere fact of occurrence of typology of point of view in the monograph on OT narratology should already be regarded as a remarkable step and merits our greater consideration.

Among the strengths of Bar-Efrat's typology is an indication of different degree of awareness of the narrator from his total omniscience to a restricted view. Separation between a situation when the narrator is looking at the mind of the character and when the narrator takes a character's point of view is also noteworthy. Thus, the typology of Bar-Efrat consists of all three types of focalization that we find in Genette's book except that they have different names and that they are not linked to each other by one single principle (like the ratio of narrator's knowledge that he shares with the reader in relation to the horizon of characters). This turns typology into a chaotic and inconsistent set of oppositions that may look good separately, but are incompatible together. The first opposition is based on knowledge; the second is on the presence or absence of the narrator in the text. The third opposition reflects the distance between narrator and narrated events, and the fourth one distinguishes different spatial positions of the narrator. Finally, the fifth opposition is about presence or absence of an ideological point of view in the words of narrator. While all these narrative modes certainly appear in biblical narratives,

Bar-Efrat's typology (in contrast to the typology of Genette) lacks symmetry and theoretical justification.

Besides, Bar-Efrat is often confused over the meaning of point of view. For example, explaining the idea of omniscient narrator, he makes the following statement, from which it is unclear what he means by point of view:

> Language limits the author to describing events consecutively, thus creating the impression that the narrator is now here and then there, looking first into one man's heart and then into another's, constantly transferring the point of view from one place to another.[15]

Literal reading of this passage leads to the conclusion that the point of view, according to Bar-Efrat, is everything that comes to the attention of the narrator. Therefore, if the story talks about the city of Bethlehem, then about a field, and then about a threshing floor, and then again about the city of Bethlehem, the point of view, according to Bar-Efrat, changes four times. Genette, in contrast, proposes to separate the one who speaks and the one who perceives and to define the type of focalization on the basis of perception. As we will see in this chapter, such significant theoretical limitations are typical of most works on biblical narratology.

The author considers that the awareness of the narrator in most secret conversations and intimate details of a character's behavior and even his presence as a witness of meetings in heaven betrays his omniscience. However, narratologically it is not always so: zero focalization, according to Genette, derives from different reasons. That said, there are some conclusions of the author that I would totally agree with. For example, in the following section of the same chapter he discusses the narrator's omniscience that is reflected in the narrator's ability to penetrate the characters' minds and display their knowledge, emotions, and volition.[16]

To sum up, the book of Bar-Efrat has both excellent findings as well as some misconceptions. The major problem, as I see it, involves the absence of a coherent theory of point of view. Nevertheless, recognition of the need

---

15. Bar-Efrat, 17.
16. Bar-Efrat, 19–23.

of that theory and the attempt to create typology of point of view should be commended.

2.3. Adele Berlin

The book of Adele Berlin *Poetics and Interpretation of Biblical Narratives*,[17] written in 1983, deserves our special attention. No, Berlin does not mention Genette's contribution – it had been almost a decade since publication of *Narrative Discourse* in French and two years after its publication in English, but Genette's ideas remained ignored by biblical scholarship. Yet, the distinguishing feature of Berlin's work is its high appreciation of theoretical poetics. According to Berlin, "poetics . . . is an inductive science that seeks to abstract the general principles of literature from many different manifestations of those principles as they occur in actual literary texts."[18] Only after discovery of general principles can one move to interpretation of concrete texts for "if we know how texts mean, we are in a better position to discover, what a particular text means."[19]

As history of interpretation shows, Bible interpreters traditionally hold a different approach. Even those schools of interpretation that claimed to use a literary approach to the Bible (beginning from midrashic school of interpretation), tended to give to the passages or construction under consideration a semantic instead of poetic explanation by paying greater attention to its meaning instead of its function.

> The search for meaning led to some observations that had poetic significance, but their significance qua poetics was not developed. This is true even in the relatively modern literary approaches, subsumed under terms such as rhetorical criticism, total-interpretation, etc., which study words, phrases, motifs, and various other patternings in a given text. At their best, these approaches represent fine literary criticism, explicating the surface patterning and the underlying meaning of specific passages. They have given us a new appreciation for the intricacy

---

17. Berlin, *Poetics and Interpretation*.
18. Berlin, 15.
19. Berlin, 17.

and integrity of the text. But they fall short of being poetics, for they neither aim for nor discover general rules of composition.[20]

In order to remedy some of these omissions, in chapter 3 Berlin recourses to the study of point of view, taking for the basis two current typologies of point of view proposed by Seymour Chatman and Boris Uspensky. After a brief review of these typologies, she applies them to the study of point of view in the biblical narrative of Ruth (which makes her work even more important to this present study). Her research, therefore, is less heuristic and more theoretically grounded.

Uspensky's typology will be treated separately due to the great influence of this typology on the development of Genette's concept of focalization.[21] In the meantime, it should be noted that while Berlin calls the typology of Uspensky a "highly developed scheme"[22] and "theoretical ground-work,"[23] it should be admitted that while being respected among literary scholars, this typology represents a series of heuristic findings in the field of point of view. Therefore, Berlin's treatment of point of view in the book of Ruth is essentially a series of excellent findings grouped around five planes of point of view (according to Uspensky). In this present work I will certainly use and make the best of Berlin's contribution while trying to systematize all her findings into a coherent typology of focalization.

Before engaging in the discussion of the contribution of the next OT scholar, I would like to give critical assessment of the metaphor of camera eye, extensively used by Berlin and by other biblical scholars. Berlin compares biblical narratives with film narratives (due to its scenic nature) and the narrator in biblical narratives with camera eye: "we see the story through what he presents."[24] Despite its apparent simplicity, this frequent comparison is not legitimate because of the fact that film and literary text are supposed to be perceived as two different kinds of narratives, each with its own specific ways

---

20. Berlin, 18.

21. For the purpose of the present research, I will look only to how Berlin utilizes Uspensky's typology, because, as Berlin notes, it is more "suited for the identification of point of view" (see Berlin, *Poetics and Interpretation*, 44) while the typology of Chatman was used only for studying "interest point of view" which goes out of the boundaries of my consideration.

22. Berlin, *Poetics and Interpretation*, 47.

23. Berlin, 55.

24. Berlin, 44.

of conveying information. Unless the narrative is purposefully written for visual perception, this collation seems to be mistaken. As Genette remarks, "unlike the director of a movie, the novelist is not compelled to put his camera somewhere; he has no camera."[25]

Most likely, with the metaphor of camera eye Berlin and other scholars try to introduce the idea of restriction of information. But the term "camera eye," more than any other metaphor, suffers from strong visual connotation – something that Genette seeks to avoid by introducing the new term "focalization."[26] It may be one of the reasons why after the introduction of the ideological point of view, Berlin does not use it extensively in her study of the book of Ruth, while at the same time discussing shifts in spatial point of view in great detail.

Generally, the work of Berlin signifies a considerable step that biblical narratology made from heuristic to a theoretically grounded approach. However, Berlin could not completely move beyond traditional, purely semantic methods for biblical narratology, as she says:

> I do not seek a theory that can be applied to all narrative, but only a theory of biblical narrative. Before we can understand general poetics we must understand specific poetics. This specific poetics should be derived from the literature that it seeks to describe, not imported from some other, perhaps quite alien, literature. General theory can suggest what we are to look for, but it cannot tell us what we will find.[27]

While it is probably impossible to free oneself from all intuitive, heuristic findings, the approach adopted in this work will still be different from Berlin's in this very matter – the biblical narrative of Ruth will be approached didactically, from general narratological axioms to specifics of biblical text.

---

25. Genette, *Narrative Discourse Revisited*, 73.
26. Genette, *Narrative Discourse*, 189.
27. Berlin, *Poetics and Interpretation*, 19.

2.4. Meir Sternberg

Meir Sternberg's book *Poetics of Biblical Narratives*[28] in sophisticated style relates essential ideas about the organization of perspectives in Old Testament narratives. From the very beginning of the book, the author admits the need for a theoretical framework suitable to study perspective in Old Testament narratives – something that he could not find in a so-called literary approach to the Bible:

> Nor is it that the literary approach, whatever it may mean and however it may operate, has failed to yield good or at least stimulating results. On the contrary, the small and uneven corpus thus far produced has done more to illuminate the text (and enliven the field) than traditional research many times its size and duration. Rather, the practice suffers from the deficiencies of the underlying theoretical framework, so that both are exposed to serious and often gratuitous objections.[29]

In fact, Sternberg is so much dissatisfied with works on poetics of Old Testament narratives done to date that he, in his own words, constantly keeps quarreling with them on the pages of his book:

> That such a hodgepodge of vulgarized truisms and plain nonsense should masquerade as a theory of literature, indeed as the distillation and consensus of literary study, might suggest a parody in the manner of F. C. Crews's *The Pooh Perplex*.[30]

For him the challenge of biblical narratology is inconsistency of theory, the absence of continuity between theory and practice.[31] However, the theory that should be expected after such claims never emerges on the pages of his book. One can find only seeds of the concept which resembles very much the concept of Genette, even though Sternberg never mentions Genette in this book. He states, for example, that discourse "operates with three basic relationships that constitute the point of view: between narrator and characters, narrator

---

28. Sternberg, *Poetics*.
29. Sternberg, 3.
30. Sternberg, 4–5.
31. Sternberg, 6.

and reader, reader and characters."[32] There is even a tendency to judge the measure of subjectivity of the character in relation to the omniscience of the narrator. The readers, according to Sternberg, can make judgments about characters' perspectives only

> ... by making inferences about the different perspectives in relation to one another and above all to the supreme authority that figures as the contextual measure of their validity. A judgment cannot be located along a scale of reliability, nor a description pronounced objective or subjective, nor a character stamped as ignorant or knowing, nor a reading follow an ironic or straight line – except by reference to the contextual norm embodied in the all-authoritative narrator.[33]

Sternberg considers that biblical narratives have a lot of specific and unusual ways to express point of view, the most notable of which is the special position of God in relation to both narrator and characters. God is a character, but separated from other characters; God is not the narrator, but is endowed with the same omniscience. According to Sternberg, all theoretical taxonomies fail to recognize these phenomena.[34]

Sternberg then proposes a kind of taxonomy – a fourfold structure of point of view – which is based on two oppositions: (1) God vs. Narrator and (2) Narrator and Reader vs. God and Characters:

> The lines of demarcation are thus redrawn to establish a novel fourfold pattern, involving two assorted and roughly symmetrical couples: the elevated superhumans on the one hand and the erring humans on the other. God existentially inside while perspectivally above the world, the reader wedded in some degree to his fellow men: this structure of point of view acts as a constant reminder of their respective positions in the scheme of things. From this unpromising premise, and not so much

---

32. Sternberg, 130.
33. Sternberg, 130.
34. Sternberg, 131.

despite as because of its theological bearing, there also springs an intricate, flexible, and challenging art of perspective . . .[35]

According to Sternberg, God differs from narrator in three ways or "perspectival distinctions" – aesthetic interest, rhetorical complication, and expressive opposition. Aesthetic interest is "the whole aesthetic dimension of the narrative, that is, whatever might separate it from 'pure' historico-theological discourse that straightforwardly presents the divine outlook and lays down the law" what he calls "degree-zero of writing."[36] Practically this includes "regulating principles" like indirect speech or conclusions; "major strategies" like gapping, repetition, external portrayal, dialogue chains; the form of point of view itself; and "occasional devices" like insertion in the form of poetry, parable, or epigram.

The difference between God and narrator in rhetoric is even more strict than in aesthetic. God operates more with deeds than with words, and when he speaks his words are few and they often include performatives, forecasts, commands, admonitions – things that have to be obeyed, fulfilled. Whereas the narrator operates with words only and "chooses to wield them as a net rather than as a stick: he persuades where God would and does prescribe."[37]

Expressive modes of the narrator are "rhetorical questions, figurative language, imperatives and other forms of command, vocatives, references to the first and second person, oaths, emotionalisms, verbal irony."[38] All these are human types of speech, while God is not speaking in human voice at all in order to avoid "the proverbial effects of familiarity."[39] He goes without vulgarism and uses prophetic language; his questions are always rhetorical and information-seeking.

Narrator and reader differ from God and characters in several ways. Narrator and reader operate outside of the represented world while God and the characters operate within the represented world. Each one of them has their sphere of communication. While the narrator is expressive, God tends to be non-expressive. The narrator tends to be neutral in his judgment, while

---

35. Sternberg, 131.
36. Sternberg, 154.
37. Sternberg, 157.
38. Sternberg, 158.
39. Sternberg, 131.

God's words are always expressive and conspicuous. While God evaluates, the narrator tends to persuade.[40]

The reader, according to Sternberg, is given more privileged position in relation to characters when he shares the knowledge of the narrator which corresponds with Genette's zero focalization. Whether Sternberg explores figurally or externally focalized texts is not clear. Weak reference to that could be reasonings about plot, which, in Sternberg's view, is built according to three basic strategies which may be called reader-elevating, character-elevating, and even-handed (neutral). Characters' divergence – "in interest, interpretation, world view, scenario, hope and fear – keeps the action going, just as their convergence makes for its resolution."[41]

If the essence of Sternberg's work were to be expressed conceptually (with the use of categories of general narratology), he regards the question of perspective mainly as cognitive phenomena. He sees the development of the plot in the Old Testament narratives as the way of characters from ignorance to knowledge – a poetical device that he considers "one of the great archetypes of literature . . . Hebraic innovation, for which the Greeks got all the credit."[42]

As examples above show, Sternberg has done significant work in clarification of roles and interrelations among narrator, characters, God and reader in the Old Testament narratives. His conclusions seem to correspond (although partially) to Genette's idea of focalization which is based on comparative analysis of the information shared with the reader with restricted knowledge of characters. But the main weaknesses of Sternberg's "taxonomy" is that lack of system or specificity. He obviously fails to propose simple and workable typology that can adequately explain all his heuristic observations. The book is rather a number of stated principles than workable typology operating by simple measurable values. The concept of focalization posed by Genette partly fills this gap. Moreover, as I will show in the next chapter, as the concept continued to evolve, Genette's ideas were enhanced to a more holistic theory with additional types of perspective that eventually have much more to offer to the study of narrative.

---

40. Sternberg, 160.
41. Sternberg, 172.
42. Sternberg, 176.

Unfortunately, the special position of God in biblical narratives is not of interest to our discussion, simply because Ruth is one of those Old Testament narratives where God is not present as a character. Nevertheless, in the course of my research, Sternberg's conclusions may be beneficial because of common consensus that God is still present in the book of Ruth, though behind the scenes.

2.5. Jean Louis Ska

The little book of Jean Louis Ska *Our Fathers Have Told Us: Introduction to the Analysis of Hebrew Narratives*[43] written in 1990 and then reprinted in 2000 is the first work on biblical narratology that employs Genette's concept to study focalization in OT narratives. Just the fact of using a highly theoretical literary concept to study biblical narrative marks a very important breakthrough in the history of biblical narratology. So, let us examine the work of Ska with more precision.

In the first part of the chapter on point of view,[44] Ska describes the idea of focalization as Genette has proposed it. He also shows the points of connection between Genette and other narratologists, including Sternberg, whose book on poetics of biblical narratives I already assessed. Three comments should be made in regard to the theoretical reasoning of Ska. First, in his study of focalization he limits himself to Genette's initial ideas, not taking into account the development of narratological thought since then. Second, he leaves all contentious issues of Genette's model beyond the scope of discussion. Third, following Lubbock and Sternberg, he mistakenly links zero focalization with the narrator's point of view, internal focalization with character's point of view, and external focalization with reader's point of view.

The next section is devoted to focalization in biblical narratives, specifically to the indicators of focalization. Ska mentions two stylistic indicators of point of view:

(1) Expressions like וַיֹּאמֶר אֶל־לִבּוֹ ("and he said in his heart") that work as a signal to interior monologue. Here he adds two other words: בְּקִרְבָּהּ ("to herself") and אָמַר ("to say") which "can be

---

43. Ska, *Our Fathers*.
44. Ska, 65–67.

translated 'to think,' or 'to say to oneself,' when the speaker is obviously alone."[45]

(2) Particle וְהִנֵּה ("and behold") which "often (but not always!) . . . indicates a shift from the omniscient narrator's point of view to the perspective of one of the characters."[46]

Ska also adds that verbs of perception such as "to see," "to hear," and "to know" "can be important indicators of specific 'focalizations.' But here, as elsewhere in biblical exegesis, the context is decisive."[47] With this observation Ska concludes the theoretical part, leaving beyond the scope of the discussion the most important issue – a definition of focalization. Indeed, like many scholars after Genette, Ska primarily focuses on classification of focalization instead of addressing the core of the phenomena. As a result, in his presentation, focalization is no different than the traditional idea of point of view. According to Genette, focalization means restriction, and a passage is called focalized because it presents the circumstances of the story partially. All following inaccuracies in Ska's conclusions come from this initial omission.

The first example is taken from Moses's call narrative (Exod 3:1–6).[48] Even the analysis of the very first verse of the passage calls into question the decision of the author about type of focalization.

וּמֹשֶׁה הָיָה רֹעֶה אֶת־צֹאן יִתְרוֹ חֹתְנוֹ כֹּהֵן מִדְיָן וַיִּנְהַג אֶת־הַצֹּאן אַחַר הַמִּדְבָּר וַיָּבֹא אֶל־הַר הָאֱלֹהִים חֹרֵבָה׃

Now Moses was keeping the flock of his father-in-law, Jethro, the priest of Midian, and he led his flock to the west side of the wilderness and came to Horeb, the mountain of God. (Exod 3:1)

According to Ska, verse 1 is externally focalized. This means (according to Genette's typology) that the narrator in this verse says less than the character knows. But what exactly does this suggest? As I demonstrated in the first chapter, in the examples given by Genette and other scholars, externally focalized passages are akin to the record of the chronicle; they record the events as they go, continually and never indefinitely. So, the passage under

---

45. Ska, 68.
46. Ska, 68.
47. Ska, 68.
48. Ska, 69.

consideration, be it externally focalized, would have more descriptive details in it focused more on the process of shepherding than on family relations and geography. Moreover, in a purely externally focalized passage, the narrator would probably refrain even from using the name of the character to create enigma, for such is the nature of external focalization.[49] The given passage is closer to zero focalization because the narrator provides the reader with two specific details. First, he speaks about Moses's family while for external representation of the scene, one does not need to know that Moses's father-in-law was a Midian priest. Second, the narrator informs the readers that the mountain that Moses approached was the mountain of God – information that even Moses could not be aware of. Therefore, verses 1 and 2 – "And the angel of the LORD appeared to him in a flame of fire out of the midst of a bush" – are both zero focalized, as is pertinently captured by Ska.

Ska is also absolutely right to define the following sentence as internally focalized:

וַיַּרְא וְהִנֵּה הַסְּנֶה בֹּעֵר בָּאֵשׁ וְהַסְּנֶה אֵינֶנּוּ אֻכָּל

> He looked, and behold, the bush was burning, yet it was not consumed. (Exod 3:2b)

The presence of particle וְהִנֵּה "behold" and perceptual verb וַיַּרְא "to look" together with understanding that Moses was not aware that the burning bush was theophany points to internal focalization.

Correct interpretation of verse 3 as internally focalized interior monologue gives way to another questionable conclusion. The following sentence:

וַיַּרְא יהוה כִּי סָר לִרְאוֹת

> When the LORD saw that he turned aside to see . . . (Exod. 3:4)

is described as zero focalized because

> the camera moves to God's side and from his perspective observes Moses coming . . . God's "perspective" observed from the narrator's "viewpoint," since the narrator sees that God sees ["zero focalisation"] . . .[50]

---

49. Dialogues would be another example of external focalization. However, focalization in dialogue in many ways depends on the nature of the speeches.

50. Ska, *Our Fathers*, 69.

This explanation seems somewhat tangled and confusing. Every word of the narrative belongs to the narrator, but it does not mean that all the narrative is zero focalized. Besides, it does not appear that such interpretation brings any clarity to the subject. In this particular example it would be more beneficial to point out that the verb of perception רָאָה ("to see") points to internal focalization as regard to God. Moreover the verb סוּר ("to turn aside") is rather unusual and reflects God's perspective (God saw Moses going one direction and then deviated from that line). Particle כִּי is also an important marker of internal focalization, as I will show later. But let's put first things first.

It seems that Ska is trying to find points of connection between focalization theory and the traditional point of view approach. In fact, in the next chapter he even goes on and introduces Uspensky's typology of point of view. His conclusions are not always correct, but it is completely legitimate to merge both concepts as it was done by Rimmon-Kenan.[51] Why Ska, being aware of the work of Rimmon-Kenan, does not employ it in his book remains a mystery.

2.6. Jerome Walsh

Jerome Walsh's book *Old Testament Narrative: A Guide to Interpretation*[52] was initially printed in 2009 almost thirty years since the publication of the English edition of *Narrative Discourse*. Yet, the following quotation from Walsh demonstrates an ongoing tendency to confuse the concept of point of view and the concept of focalization. Like many others, Walsh considers "focalization" to be just another term which has the same meaning as "point of view":

> For several decades, point of view has been a topic of intense interest for theoreticians of narrative. Its nature and varieties have been explored in several different ways. For our purposes, however, this scholarly discussion is far too abstruse and technical; we are interested in a practical exploration of how point of view, in a simple and basic sense, works in narrative. Those who are interested in learning more about the theoretical

---

51. Rimmon-Kenan, *Narrative Fiction*. First edition was published in 1983.
52. Walsh, *Old Testament Narrative*.

complexities of point of view (or "focalization," as it is called in some recent writing) will profit from the treatments of Adele Berlin and Jean Louis Ska.[53]

Following Berlin and Ska, Walsh explains the idea of point of view in narrative with the dangerous metaphor of camera eye. It is dangerous because it can cause the interpreter to slide to the optical understanding of point of view. This tendency becomes obvious as Walsh starts to unfold this metaphor. He says that a real camera has two aspects of positioning – angle and distance. Metaphorically, then, the point of view in narrative, according to Walsh, also has angle and distance as two of its aspects. From here on, Walsh, in essence, outlines his typology, while he never names it this way.

There are several "angles" that the narrator can take. The first one is the angle of omniscience. If the narrator wants the readers to see the story from this angle, he shares all that information with the narratee. Risking to slide into optical connotations, Walsh provides the following illustration: "One might imagine this as a point of view 'from above,' where everything in the story world is visible and nothing is hidden."[54] But soon he leaves this slippery path of ocularization, by exemplifying angle as an introductory note of the narrator that sets the theme of the narrative section, thus helping the reader to take the right position in regard to unfolding events.[55]

The second position of the "camera" is the position of a neutral observer: "the reader sees and hears only what any neutral observer would see and hear."[56] In this position of the "camera," the reader is not aware of inner thoughts and feelings of the characters or distant events that happen simultaneously. This position "invites us to ask questions about the unspecified motives of characters."[57]

Finally, the third position of the metaphoric "camera" is identical to one of the characters. Walsh calls it "involved point of view."[58] Discussing this type of

---

53. Walsh, 44.
54. Walsh, 45.
55. As an example of this type of angle Walsh uses the story of Abraham and Isaac in Gen 22, where "the narrator tells us right from the start that 'God tested Abraham.'" (22:1). See Walsh, *Old Testament Narrative*, 45.
56. Walsh, *Old Testament Narrative*, 45.
57. Walsh, 46.
58. Walsh, 46.

"camera" position, Walsh makes a traditional mistake when he says, "In this case, the reader sees and hears things as that character does and may have some insight into that character's inner life . . ."[59] As has been said, this very mistake became a starting point of Genette's concept of focalization. To see as the character sees and to explore the mind of the character are essentially two different activities. In fact, the tendency to confuse the one who sees and the one who speaks is the major problem of Walsh's whole treatment on point of view.

From one side, it may seem that Walsh stands firmly on the cognitive position of Genette's focalization concept. One can see the progress even in his description of camera metaphor, for unlike previous scholars, who used this metaphor, he speaks more about restriction and selection on narrative information (i.e. camera eye in his work is indeed no more than a metaphor). A shift toward cognitive understanding of point of view is one of the characteristic features of Walsh's work. In this tendency we can observe tentative convergence with Genette's concepts. An omniscient narrator, according to Walsh, does not need "to share all of that information with the narratee (and the reader) . . ."[60] (the case of either internal or external focalization). But occasionally the narrator opens their competence before the reader and "shares with us information that no character could have"[61] (the case of zero focalization). Narrative situations, that Walsh names "neutral external," are consistent with Genette's external focalization. Finally, "involved point of view" in essence constitutes Genette's concept of internal focalization. In fact, Genette's impact on the work of Walsh is so significant that sometimes it almost comes to the point of absolute verbal resemblance like in the following excerpt:

> One of the common features of an omniscient point of view is a sense of distance from the characters, because we know more than any of them [the characters] and, therefore, cannot share their limited perspectives.[62]

---

59. Walsh, 46.
60. Walsh, 44.
61. Walsh, 45.
62. Walsh, 45.

However, when it comes to examples (case study passage is taken from 1 Kings 3:16–28), one can find a lot of noticeable differences between the methodology of Genette and Walsh. Start, for example, from the idea that in the conversation of two characters,[63] the point of view always shifts to the listening/watching one. But as soon as the parties' roles are reversed and the second character starts to speak or act, the point of view shifts to the first character, and the reader starts to share the point of view of the first character. This idea probably came to the mind of the author from the obvious fact taken, I suppose, from real life. But even in real life when one interlocutor is speaking or acting, the other one does not necessarily become a listener or a watcher. The intention of the author to describe the construction of point of view in dialogue is understandable – OT narratives use dialogues often. However, this anthropological observation has to find its place in the holistic theory of focalization; only then it can help to explore point of view or focalization in dialogic scenes. I doubt that approach is viable in the form it is amended to by Walsh, for the whole mechanism and the whole idea of point of view in narrative is of a different nature.

Another side of Walsh's analysis that is common for the discussions of point of view is the descent of the interpreter to the level of the narrative world, while Genette's approach presupposes that the interpreter of the text should stay above the narrative world, together with the narrator, on the level of discourse. This attitude completely changes the entire research process because the interpreter starts to work with text instead of imagining the place of metaphorical camera or even themselves as an invisible spirit within the story world. Running ahead, I will demonstrate the practical difference between Walsh's manner of interpretation and the cognitive approach to interpretation of the passage from 1 Kings 3:16–28.

Walsh considers that "the story begins with a neutral external point of view in 3:16"[64] while in the footnote adds that "there may be an element of omniscience in the narrator's information that these women were prostitutes" and that this depends on whether Solomon knew about their profession or

---

63. Walsh rightly observes that biblical scenes normally involve two characters (or at least two sides).

64. Walsh, *Old Testament Narrative*, 45.

not.[65] But on what grounds does the author use Solomon as a measure of point of view? Unless there are firm evidences of external perspectival view (external focalization), the text is presented with omniscient perspective (zero focalized). I would rather argue that information about the profession of these two women comes from outside of the text and thus the passage has to be considered zero focalized. After all, information about the profession of these women is not essential for the story. What is essential is the reputation that goes together with prostitution. Pious readers normally relate to prostitutes with little or no respect; therefore, by naming this occupation the narrator immediately paints a word portrait. And the question of the story now is whether a person with such reputation can be honest, practice true love, and gain respect. The sentence is certainly zero focalized.[66]

Further considering the passage Walsh comes to the conclusion that at one point of the story focalization shifts to internal:

> But that changes immediately, as "first woman" tells her tale to Solomon and then becomes embroiled in an argument with "other woman." The lengthy speech and subsequent altercation focus our attention directly on the women and the case they are presenting. In other words, we stand with Solomon, and our point of view approximates his. We see what he sees; we hear what he hears; and we, like him, are stymied by the problem. When he voices (internally?) the insolubility of the dilemma in 3:23, he voices our bafflement as well, and our point of view is almost completely identified with his.[67]

However, Walsh's reasoning seems unconvincing for he suggests a sort of psychological interpretation of the passage where identification of perspectives will always be a matter of opinion. Genette's theory, on the other hand, suggests approaching narrative texts with a neutral scale. In the passage considered above, the "altercation" of the woman can be only externally focalized because the narrator does not reveal to the reader which of the women is saying the truth. The women know who is right, the readers do not. The

---

65. Walsh, 45n49.

66. As I said, my interpretation of the passage is running ahead, for I refer to the upgraded typology of Genette.

67. Walsh, *Old Testament Narrative*, 46.

horizon of women is wider than the horizon of the readers; therefore, the passage is externally focalized.[68]

We must now return to the overall assessment of the book and its method. The chapter on point of view consists of many wonderful observations, but it also consists of much cloudy speculation. The whole text cries out for one unambiguous typology, which would provide solid ground for interpretation.

But Walsh himself admits the imperfection of his approach and as practical steps to explore point of view in biblical stories suggests not to approach the story analytically and not to look for techniques of the narrator. Instead, he suggests first to read the story and get an impression of it and only then consider the point of view by asking the following questions: Where am I visualizing this from? What am I focusing my gaze on? How close am I to what I am looking at?

But what if the story (as it is with most stories) is not written for us to visualize it (like most biblical stories)? To this question Walsh does not give a sufficient answer.

2.7. Gary Yamasaki

Gary Yamasaki is known as the founder, moderator, and main contributor to a newly formed internet project named "Perspective criticism." On the website, perspective criticism is introduced as "new methodology for analyzing the point-of-view crafting in biblical narratives."[69] The content of the website, however, far exceeds the scope of biblical narratives and the visitor can also find articles that describe shift in point of view in movies and non-biblical texts.

My focus in this section are three books of Yamasaki – *Watching a Biblical Narrative: Point of View in Biblical Exegesis*; *Perspective Criticism: Point of View*; and *Evaluative Guidance in Biblical Narrative and Insights from Filmmaking for Analyzing Biblical Narrative* – written in 2007, 2012, and 2016 respectively.

---

68. Walsh rightly considers that the narrator restricts information this way in order for the reader to understand the challenge King Solomon faced, but the passage is still externally focalized.

69. "Welcome to Perspective Criticism" https://perspectivecriticism.com.

Yamasaki starts *Watching a Biblical Narrative* with the discussion of "a distinct evolution in the way that fiction writers conceived of the positioning of the narrator – or author – in relation to the story world."[70] In eighteenth-century novels, the author is always present in the text by using first-person narration and "the reader cannot help but perceive the elements of the story as being filtered through the point of view of the [omniscient] author."[71] In the nineteenth century in the third-person novel, the author supplies the commentary to the reader, which "contributes to a sense of the author's presence in the story."[72]

However, in the novel *Emma* by Jane Austen, Yamasaki points to an apparent anomaly, for the book begins with the commentaries from the author's point of view in the introductory part but then

> ... transfer[s] this task of providing introductory matters over to Emma, a character in the story. This means, of course, that this introductory material is no longer being presented only from the point of view of the author, but also being presented from the point of view of Emma.[73]

The narrator takes the reader into the mind of the character by using the expressions like "she thought," "she feared," "she considers" and so engenders in the reader a sense of sympathy for the character.

Then Yamasaki mentions James, who made one more step to make the author disappear from the novel, while the purpose was not to dismiss the author but, according to Booth, "to achieve an intense illusion of reality."[74]

Discussion continues by examining the ideas of Booth, Lubbock, Uspensky, Genette, Chatman, and Stanzel. With Genette, he does not consider his ideas as being helpful because "Genette sets very narrow parameters with regard to which narrative dynamics relate to point of view and which do not."[75] I would agree with this statement and, in fact, the next chapter of my research

---

70. Yamasaki, *Watching a Biblical Narrative*, 11.
71. Yamasaki, 12.
72. Yamasaki, 14.
73. Yamasaki, 17–18.
74. Yamasaki, 24.
75. Yamasaki, 35.

deals with the development (expanding) of the concept of focalization in recent decades.

Further in this book, Yamasaki discusses monographs on biblical studies that in one way or another have had an impact on the study of point of view in biblical narratives and even provide the methodology of examining point of view in biblical narratives. Methodology includes three steps: (1) Selecting narrative text, (2) determination of the person of the narrator, and (3) verse-by-verse search for textual indicators of point of view.

On the third step, he proposes to look for indicators of point of view using Uspensky's five planes of point of view. For example, to discern spatial point of view he suggests to examine spatial deixis, the degree to which a character is followed, degree of details, order in a noun phrase in a coordinate structure, possessive noun phrases, and subject of a clause. To study the temporal plane of point of view, according to Yamasaki, one has to look for temporal deixis, the order and pacing of events, verb tenses, and extended discourses. The psychological point of view is expressed by *verba sentiendi*, the particle "behold" and naming. The phraseological plane is reflected in individual speech characteristics of the characters. The ideological plane of point of view of the narrator or characters can be found in explicit statements, epistemic modality, narration of characters' internal views, direct discourse, and actions of the character. And, finally, Yamasaki expands Uspensky's model to one more plane – informational – which is based on information accessible to the narrator, characters, and the reader.

While theoretically this method looks very impressive, its practical application in the next book *Perspective Criticism* is less helpful. In this book Yamasaki suggests to start the study of point of view of the narrative from the spatial plane of point of view because he considers it "the most accessible entry into the complex world of point of view." But what is spatial point of view from the point of view of Yamasaki? (pardon the pun). He defines it on the basis of cinematic storytelling as a picture of the story world that is presented before the reader. Therefore, to identify the spatial point of view in a given passage, one has to explain how the picture of the story world is represented. According to Yamasaki, there are only two major ways to represent the story world: "drawing the reader into a position in proximity to a particular character, or pulling the reader back into a position at a distance from the character."[76] Yamasaki, then, argues that there are several literary techniques that help the reader to identify the distance between them and the character. However, the technique is more to do with movies than literary narratives. Yamasaki's conclusions are true for movies, where the camera and its position are an obligatory element of representation. But in the literary work, as has been said by Genette, "unlike the director of a movie, the novelist is not compelled to put his camera somewhere; he has no camera."[77] But Yamasaki ignores this warning and examining the passage from 2 Kings 5:1–19a, he suggests to his readers to start "imagining the events of this passage being filmed."[78] Therefore, he considers that in verses 2–3 "the camera is situated in the house of Naaman":

> Now the Syrians on one of their raids had carried off a little girl from the land of Israel, and she worked in the service of Naaman's wife. She said to her mistress, "Would that my lord were with the prophet who is in Samaria! He would cure him of his leprosy." (2 Kgs 5:2–3)

Here Yamasaki, from what I can see, makes two mistakes. First, as has been stated already, the scenic nature of biblical narrative does not necessarily suggest that they have to be read as film scripts. Second, even if one imagines the scene as being filmed, there is no ground to assert that the camera is situated in the house of Naaman. There are no details in the passage that would say anything about the house. Indeed, as regards the spatial representation, the only certainty may be that the scene is presented from the point of view of a detached observer, as basically in most scenes of biblical narratives.

This example is not unique. According to Yamasaki, spatial location in verses 4–5a is the palace of the king of Aram, while the passage says nothing about the palace:

> So Naaman went in and told his lord, "Thus and so spoke the girl from the land of Israel." And the king of Syria said, "Go now, and I will send a letter to the king of Israel." (2 Kings 5:4–5a)

---

76. Yamasaki, *Perspective Criticism*, 19.
77. Genette, *Narrative Discourse Revisited*, 74.
78. Yamasaki, *Perspective Criticism*, 21.

Thinking about spatial point of view in this manner, Yamasaki suggests that "the camera follows Naaman as he moves" from the king's palace to another location, then situates at the entrance of Elisha's house, then at the road from Elisha's house, and finally at the Jordan River. But first of all, as Genette pointed out, "narrator does not have a camera." And yet, Yamasaki constantly involves this filmic device to describe narrative texts. His conclusions would be useful to write a screenplay but not to find the spatial point of view of the narrator or one of the characters.

Continuing on, talking about readers' distance from characters, Yamasaki also considers the "empathy hierarchy" – the idea offered by Susumu Kuno. According to Kuno, "the readers are being led to empathize with the character that is being given syntactic prominence," that is, "being placed close to the head of a clause."[79] However, the example provided in this section does not actually bring new light to the question. Yamasaki examines the story of young Saul and a servant searching for lost donkeys (1 Sam 9:3–14) which ends with emphatic "behold":

וַיַּעֲלוּ הָעִיר הֵמָּה בָּאִים בְּתוֹךְ הָעִיר וְהִנֵּה שְׁמוּאֵל יֹצֵא לִקְרָאתָם לַעֲלוֹת הַבָּמָה׃

> So they went up to the city. As they were entering the city, they saw Samuel coming out toward them on his way up to the high place. (1 Sam 9:14)

But the construction וְהִנֵּה + Noun is very common for biblical Hebrew and it has long been argued that these types of contractions reflect the change in psychological as well as spatial point of view. In fact, this illustration reflects real shift in spatial point of view, for it shows Samuel as he is seen by Saul in contrast to the misleading idea of empathy.

It is true that the place of the noun in biblical Hebrew sentences sometimes plays an important role in comprehending the idea of the narrator. But whether it reflects the empathy or spatial point of view is questionable. Let us consider two examples from the book of Ruth where the noun placement may reflect some ideas of the narrator.

---

79. Yamasaki, 24.

וּֽלְנָעֳמִ֞י מידע מוֹדַ֣ע לְאִישָׁ֗הּ אִ֚ישׁ גִּבּ֣וֹר חַ֔יִל מִמִּשְׁפַּ֖חַת אֱלִימֶ֑לֶךְ וּשְׁמ֖וֹ בֹּֽעַז׃

> Now Naomi had a relative of her husband's, a worthy man of the clan of Elimelech, whose name was Boaz. (Ruth 2:1)

According to Wilch, who draws this conclusion from the book of Waltke and O'Connor, when ן is attached to a noun rather than a verb in the beginning of a sentence,

> the narrator is presenting parenthetical, explanatory information that is essential for full appreciation of the following new episode, namely, the proleptic introduction of a major new character.[80]

Let me consider another example from the book of Ruth:

וּבֹ֨עַז עָלָ֣ה הַשַּׁעַר֮ וַיֵּ֣שֶׁב שָׁם֒ וְהִנֵּ֨ה הַגֹּאֵ֤ל עֹבֵר֙ אֲשֶׁ֣ר דִּבֶּר־בֹּ֔עַז וַיֹּ֛אמֶר ס֥וּרָה שְׁבָה־פֹּ֖ה פְּלֹנִ֣י אַלְמֹנִ֑י וַיָּ֖סַר וַיֵּשֵֽׁב׃

> Now Boaz had gone up to the gate and sat down there. And behold, the redeemer, of whom Boaz had spoken, came by. So Boaz said, "Turn aside, friend; sit down here." And he turned aside and sat down. (Ruth 4:1)

In this example, placing a noun at the beginning of the sentence introduces a new scene and refocuses attention of the reader from Naomi and Ruth to Boaz,[81] for the denouement of the story is now dependent on him. Obviously, in both cases the reason for placing a noun at the beginning of a sentence is not connected with shift in spatial point of view as Yamasaki suggests.[82]

Degree of details as the way to show distance from the character is relevant to the topic of spatial point of view, but as Yamasaki rightly observes, "biblical narratives are generally sparse when it comes to details."[83]

---

80. Wilch, *Ruth*, Concordia Commentary, 188.

81. See Wilch, 306.

82. As I will show later, this position of the noun can still be important for determining focalization, if focalization is understood as selection of narrative information.

83. Yamasaki, *Perspective Criticism*, 30. Even though Yamasaki considers that biblical narratives still provide enough examples of shifts in spatial perspective on the basis of different degrees of details, his own example of Acts 9:1–9 shows weaknesses and pointless of this conclusion; Yamasaki, *Perspective Criticism*.

Probably the only section of the chapter on spatial point of view that is relevant to the topic is the discussion of the narrator creating a big picture of the scene by sequential survey, bird's-eye view, and silent scene. The only OT example Yamasaki provides in this section is Numbers 11:31 where the distance from the Israelites' camp is designated by the mentioning of the area that was covered by the quails:

> Then a wind from the LORD sprang up, and it brought quail from the sea and let them fall beside the camp, about a day's journey on this side and a day's journey on the other side, around the camp, and about two cubits above the ground. (Num 11:31)

Unfortunately, the discussion of spatial point of view in biblical narrative in the work of Yamasaki is not the only one that shows methodological problems. Following Uspensky, he says that an inside view of the character in written narratives can be introduced by *verba sentiendi*. However, I wish to see not only illustration of psychological point of view but also the analysis of how this point of view affects comprehension of narrative.

For example, when Yamasaki illustrates psychological point of view in Esther 1:10–12, it seems important to underline that the feeling of characters can be presented from two positions: from the position of omniscient narrator (which is the case here) or from the position of the character themselves.[84] It would be good to note that biblical narrators rarely present the inner world of the characters from the character's position – usually the reader is presented with a mix of narrator's view and characters' views. The use of the particle הִנֵּה is probably one of those few instances of clear presentation of internal view of the character.

In general, it is better and more convenient to speak about the psychological point of view in terms of focalization than in terms of point of view theory because the psychological point of view is obviously a restricted point of view

---

84. As Uspensky asserts,
   Generally speaking, human behavior may be described in two basically distinct ways. First, it may be described from the point of view of an outside observer whose position in the work may be either clearly defined or unspecified, and who describes only the behavior which is visible to an onlooker. Second, behavior may be described from the point of view of the person himself or from the point of view of an omniscient observer who is permitted to penetrate the consciousness of that person.

See Uspensky, *Poetics of Composition*, 83.

in respect to omniscience; it reflects horizon of the character in relation to horizon of the narrator and horizon of the reader. In order to speak about restriction, Yamasaki has to resort to "informational plane of point of view."

The analysis of the example of 1 Kings 10, which Yamasaki uses, could be much more interesting and, in fact, clearer, if it is examined for focalization instead of planes of point of view. Yamasaki considers only the beginning of the story, where the omniscient narrator is talking about the horizon of the Queen of Sheba: "Now when the queen of Sheba heard of the fame of Solomon concerning the name of the LORD, she came to test him with hard questions" (1 Kgs 10:1). However, the context of the passage shows the constant growth of the horizon of Sheba.

> And when the queen of Sheba had seen all the wisdom of Solomon, the house that he had built, the food of his table, the seating of his officials, and the attendance of his servants, their clothing, his cupbearers, and his burnt offerings that he offered at the house of the LORD, there was no more breath in her.
>
> And she said to the king, "The report was true that I heard in my own land of your words and of your wisdom, but I did not believe the reports until I came and my own eyes had seen it. (1 Kgs 10:4–7a)

It is noteworthy that right after this passage in 1 Kings 10:7b, the narrator uses particle הִנֵּה in order to express an internal view of Sheba: "And behold, the half was not told me. Your wisdom and prosperity surpass the report that I heard" (1 Kgs 10:7b). Therefore, the passage is given in scope of internal focalization, while in verses 2 and 3 focalization shifts to zero, for it presents narratorial evaluation of Sheba's visit.

Therefore, the passage could be well described without the involvement of the informational plane of point of view, which seems excessive when focalization is defined as selection of narrative information. Nevertheless, the chapter remains valuable because of its practical examples. According to Yamasaki, there are several means the narrator can use to manipulate the amount of the information given to the reader. They can use narratorial commentary (as we will see in Ruth 2:1), or fracture the chronology of the narrative (present in Ruth to some degree), or use "experiencing language" which proves to be the expression of Uspensky's psychological point of view through phraseology. He also lists three narrative plots that use convergence and divergence of characters' and readers' knowledge: investigation, con (i.e. swindle or conspiracy), and irony. It seems, however, that Genette's theory gives a more elegant treatment of changes in informational awareness of characters and of the reader because it uses fewer categories to explain the same narrative phenomena and is more dynamic in discerning various degrees of divergence. I will discuss this subject in chapter 5 of this work, which deals with the play of horizons.

The chapter on temporal plane of point of view gives the impression that Yamasaki is not talking about point of view, but about different methods of representation of time in narrative. He himself admits this, saying in the conclusion that "temporal matters are very important in the analysis of a narrative passage, though not that important in the analysis of point of view in the passage."[85]

Close reading of the book shows that Yamasaki misunderstood Uspensky's idea of temporal point of view. Uspensky defines temporal point of view as the position of the narrator in relation to his story, while Yamasaki explores the methods used by the narrator in order to manipulate the reader's encounter of the events.[86] Uspensky makes helpful reference to the research of Vladimir Vinogragdov, who shows that the account of time can be carried out differently from the position of different characters, for each one of them can have their own "concept of time":

> Thus, the narrator may change his positions, borrowing the time sense of first one character, then another – or he may assume his own temporal position and use his own authorial time, which may not coincide with the individual time sense of any of the characters.[87]

Nevertheless, analysis of the matters of time made by Yamasaki is quite helpful for other areas of my research. For example, as Yamasaki points out himself, the study of the matter of time in narrative helps to understand how the narrator manipulates the amount of narrative information (which is the question of

---

85. Yamasaki, *Perspective Criticism*, 90.

86. See, for example, his interpretation of using historical present in the New Testament narratives in Yamasaki, *Perspective Criticism*, 72.

87. Uspensky, *Poetics of Composition*, 66.

focalization or horizons of the narrator, characters, and the reader). Ordering of the events in the narrative (which I, following Schmid, will call linearization), according to Yamasaki, makes significant impact on the reader[88] – I will call this impact by the traditional word "suspense." Yamasaki does not overlook pacing of the events. He considers that the "willingness to sacrifice detail reflects the event has a low degree of importance in the development of the story."[89] Importance points to the ideology of the narrator but not always. Sometimes, fast pacing serves to bring the reader from one scene to another.

In the midst of all this reasoning, Yamasaki, however, fails to talk about temporal plane of point of view. In this work I will show that the analysis of temporal plane of point of view plays an important role in understanding how the text of the book of Ruth is focalized, what the intentions of the narrator are, and what the narrative strategy of the book is.

Chapters 6 and 7 are committed to phraseological and ideological planes of point of view, are much shorter, and have fewer examples than the other chapters of the book. With phraseological plane it is quite understandable, for as Yamasaki reasonably notes, speech characteristics of characters are "only occasionally coming into play in biblical narrators' crafting of their narratives."[90] Yamasaki does not provide any examples from the Old Testament where the narrator would use this plane of point of view. However, as I will show later, the narrator of the book of Ruth does use phraseology if not as speech characteristic of the character (even though some think this is also a possibility), but to underline certain more important ideas.

As for the next chapter, Yamasaki considers ideology on the macro-level (for the whole narrative) and ideology on the micro-level (for just one passage or one character). He argues that ideology on the macro-level does not actually bring any helpful insights by itself but only in relation with ideology on the micro-level. I would agree with this argument. However, Yamasaki does not say anything about the method of defining the ideology of the narrative on the macro-level. I would suggest that careful examination of the beginning and the end (the last words) of the narrative often contains macro-level

---

88. Yamasaki, *Perspective Criticism*, 76.
89. Yamasaki, 78.
90. Yamasaki, 91.

ideology. The evidence of this method will be submitted in the chapters dealing with the book of Ruth.

It can be concluded that Yamasaki's attempt to explore point of view in biblical narratives doubtless marks an important step in development of what he calls "perspective criticism" of the Bible. Some of his conclusions (like informational plane of point of view) are directly related to the topic of this work, even though Yamasaki does not tie them with focalization. Most of the other conclusions, unfortunately, require further refining; this applies in particular to his reasoning on spatial and temporal points of view.

2.8. Conclusion

The review of works on the Old Testament narratology shows that for many years the idea of focalization was largely overlooked by most Old Testament scholars. The works that did name the concept used it without due research of the core of the concept. As a result, focalization in works on biblical narratology is often used as mere substitution of the older term point of view. Analysis of examples used by Old Testament scholars shows that focalization often better explains relationships between narrator, character, and reader and contributes to a better understanding of Old Testament stories. This is not to mention new approaches to focalization that have been developed since first publication of Genette's book. In the outlined works on Old Testament narratology these refinements are not considered at all. This logically leads us to the next chapter on development of the concept during recent decades.

CHAPTER 3

Evolution of the Notion of Focalization

As may be observed, every time I speak about focalization I invariably supplement my words with additional "as it was proposed by Genette." This suggests that in the field of narratology there are other understandings of the term as well. The notion of focalization from its very roots was the matter of collision of opinions. From the first publication of Genette's book, almost every article about focalization or chapter on focalization in any book starts with a historical review of the development of the concept and often finishes either with refinements of the existing concepts or with a proposal of a whole new concept. Consequently, the number of definitions of the term "focalization" has been growing together with the number of works on the issue. The search for more appropriate typology continues until today.[1] This means that I too cannot avoid this path, though my desire is not to propose new and better typology or reformulate existing models. In this chapter I aim, rather, to look at the very heart of the idea. Out of the scope of different typologies I will then find the most practical and simplest systematic tools that could clearly describe the narrative strategy of the book of Ruth and enrich understanding of biblical texts.

3.1. Mieke Bal (1981)

The first scholar who criticized and at the same time overhauled Genette's idea of focalization was Mieke Bal. Well known is the written debate between

---

1. See, for example, Meister and Schönert, "DNS of Mediacy."

Genette and Bal, which later even impelled Genette to write the second book[2] to clarify his theory. As for Bal, she unfolds her theory of focalization in a number of publications. The most notable of them are (1) her article "The Laughing Mice,"[3] which was later included in her book on narratology[4] and (2) the chapter on narration and focalization from the book on narrative theory.[5]

In subsequent years Bal's ideas were carefully scrutinized so that interpretations and refinements of her views sometimes seem even more elaborate than her own reasoning. Therefore, in this section I will speak about Bal's reformulation of Genette's concept using not only her own works but the works of other scholars who examined Bal's ideas.

Bal shares the opinion that typologies of point of view existing at that time " . . . [did] not make an explicit distinction between, on the one hand, the vision through which the elements are presented and, on the other, the identity of the voice that is verbalizing that vision."[6] According to Bal, this distinction is important because " . . . when no distinction is made between these two different agents, it is difficult, if not impossible, to describe adequately the technique of a text in which something is seen – and that vision is narrated."[7] At the same time, Bal points to an inconsistency of Genette's typology. She considers that in Genette's model, the difference between zero and internal focalization is the difference in subjects of focalization. In zero focalized passages, the one who sees is the omniscient narrator, while in internally focalized passages the one who sees is the character. However, the difference between internal and external focalization is the difference in the object of vision. In internally focalized passages the character sees, while in externally focalized passages the character is seen.[8] The only coherent element in Genette's typology, according to Bal, is the narrator's knowledge, which decreases from zero to external focalization. Yet Bal considers that this variable does not concern point of view or focalization. Considering these

---

2. Genette, *Narrative Discourse Revisited*.
3. Bal, "Laughing Mice," 202–10.
4. Bal, *Narratology*. See also Bal and van Boheemen, *Narratology*.
5. Bal, "Narration and Focalization."
6. Bal, *Narratology*, 101.
7. Bal, 101.
8. Edmiston, *Hindsight and Insight*, 151.

confusions erroneous, Bal then introduces her own concept of focalization within the complex theory of narrative.

According to William F. Edmiston's careful analysis of Bal's theory, the most important contribution of Bal's typology is differentiation between the subject and object of focalization.[9] The subject of focalization is called the focalizer and defined as the point from which the elements are viewed.[10] This point can be placed inside or outside of the story world. If the focalizer is placed inside of the story world, it is called internal; if it is placed outside of the story, it is called external. Usually, the external focalizer is bound to the narrator of the story and accordingly called the narrator-focalizer (NF); the internal focalizer is usually associated with one of the characters and therefore called the character-focalizer (CF). If the object of focalization is a character (i.e. has consciousness), it can be perceptible and imperceptible and can be characterized from without or from within.

Bal considers that the narrative emerges as a result of three successive levels, ("instances"): action, focalization, and narration. This is how Edmiston defines each of these instances:

> (1) narration – a text consists of linguistic signs produced by a subject, the narrator; (2) focalization – the vision is the content of the narrator's words, presented in a certain order and from one or more points of view by a second subject, the focalizer, whose identity may or may not coincide with that of the narrator; (3) action – the story, object of the vision, consists of chronologically ordered actions performed by the actors or characters; an actor's identity may coincide with that of the other two subjects, which is usually the case in autobiography.[11]

The focalizer is the one who transforms the story into fabula and the narrator is the one who transforms the fabula into narration. Therefore, the focalizer as well as narrator is granted with linguistic-communicative powers – the point of Bal's theory that was subsequently criticized by William F. Bronzwaer, who considers that "the focalizer is not endowed with narrative powers but simply

---

9. Edmiston, 151.
10. Bal, *Narratology*, 104.
11. Edmiston, *Hindsight and Insight*, 151–52. See also Bronzwaer, "Mieke Bal's Concept," 193–201.

introduced in his role as focalizer by the narrator."[12] He also disagrees with widening the process of focalization from spatio-temporal to psychological activity (such as thinking, deliberating, judging, and remembering) for, he argues, these activities are of an entirely different nature.

Can Bal's innovations be considered as an evolution of Genette's concept? I argue rather not. By introducing these new, foreign to Genette, ideas, Bal in fact "redefines the very nature of focalization."[13] While Genette's typology was related to the restriction of the narrator's knowledge, Bal defines focalization as the relationship between focalizer, focalized object, and the vision (the picture which is actually seen by the focalizer). As has been stressed by Genette himself,

> The Balian theory of focalizations develops according to its own logic, based on her innovation (establishment of an *instance of focalization* composed of a focalizer, a focalized, and even, "recipients of the focalizing"), whose usefulness escapes me and whose effects perplex me.[14]

In fact, some scholars consider that Bal's model does not only not develop Genette's theory but constitutes a return to the traditional though developed idea of external and internal point of view.[15] However, after examining Bal's theory, and even more so after reading critical notes to her theory, I came to the conclusion that point of view and focalization are not two links in the chain of evolution, but two different concepts that complement each other. As I will show later, the development of the concept was primarily directed toward convergence and interaction of two concepts within narrative text. This prompted me to continue my search for a model that would allow combining concepts of Genette and Bal into one holistic typology.

---

12. Bronzwaer, "Mieke Bal's Concept," 194–96.
13. Edmiston, *Hindsight and Insight*, 150.
14. Genette, *Narrative Discourse Revisited*, 76.
15. Schmid, *Narratology*, 95.

3.2. Boris Uspensky (1970) / Shlomith Rimmon-Kenan (1983)

With the book of Shlomith Rimmon-Kenan, the concept of focalization takes a new turn. Rimmon-Kenan takes the concept of focalization as it is stated by Bal and combines it with the ideas of five planes of point of view, the typology that was proposed by Russian philologist and semiotician Boris Uspensky. Since Uspensky's work, which Schmid calls "a decisive contribution to the modeling of point of view,"[16] heavily impacted the study of biblical narratology as much as general narratology, I want to take time to briefly introduce his concept before turning to the analysis of Rimmon-Kenan's typology.

3.2.1. Uspensky (1970)

The Russian edition of Uspensky's book *Поэтика композиции* was published in 1970, two years prior to Genette's work.[17] Soon it was translated into French, English,[18] and German so Genette had opportunity to read and even cite Uspensky.[19] Therefore, for the purposes of the present work it seems absolutely necessary to look at Uspensky's typology of five planes of point of view.

According to Uspensky, poetics is designed to find compositional structure of the artistic text. This compositional structure can be discerned by examination of points of view that are embedded in the text by its author:

> The structure of the artistic text may be described by investigating various points of view (different authorial positions from which the narration or description is conducted) and by investigating the relations between these points of view (their concurrence and non-concurrence) and the possible shifts from one point of view to another, which in turn are connected with the study of the function of the different points of view in the text.[20]

Thus Uspensky proposes to take holistic text and identify its structure by studying five planes of point of view that are named after five major semantic fields: ideological, phraseological, spatial, temporal, and psychological.

---

16. Schmid, 95.
17. Uspensky, *Поэтика Композиции*.
18. Uspensky, *Poetics of Composition*.
19. Genette, *Narrative Discourse*, 189.
20. Uspensky, *Poetics of Composition*, 5.

The ideological or appraisal plane becomes apparent when the narrator or characters evaluate what they like or dislike in themselves, in other characters, or in the outer world. It helps to build a basic system of worldview in the narrative universe. This system of ideas shapes the "deep compositional structure" of the narrative and as such should be opposed to its "surface compositional structure," which may be traced on the psychological, spatio-temporal, or phraseological levels.

Examination of the ideological plane of point of view should be isolated from so-called characterization. Characterization helps to discover what character is in the world of the narrative, what are the features of their personality. A character's ideological point of view being uncovered shows "what the world is to the character and what the character is to himself."[21] It helps to understand the self-consciousness of the character.

The ideological plane of point of view can be revealed to the reader explicitly as, for example, in this biblical passage: "But the thing that David had done displeased the LORD" (2 Sam 11:27). In such cases God is pictured as the highest authority, whose ideological appraisal the narrator conveys. As I will show later, the ideological point of view can be equally conveyed by major and even minor characters or group of characters.

The ideological point of view is usually developed along with the course of the plot by specific linguistic means like fixed epithets and naming, logic of sentence, and correlation between author's and character's speech, naming, modal auxiliaries, and so on.[22]

The phraseologial plane becomes apparent "in those cases where the author uses different diction to describe different characters or where he makes use of one form or another of reported or substituted speech in his description."[23] By doing it, the narrator expresses the point of view of the character whose manner of speech they imitate. Changes of authorial position on the phraseological plane of point of view are specifically evident in the act of naming[24] but not limited to it. In fact, any "inclusion of elements

---

21. Uspensky, 10.
22. Some of these markers are discussed by Roger Fowler, *Linguistics and the Novel*.
23. Uspensky, *Poetics of Composition*, 17.
24. Uspensky, 20.

of someone else's speech is a basic device of expressing changes of point of view on the level of phraseology."[25]

Uspensky names two ways of reciprocal influence between authorial speech and character speech: the modification of the authorial text under the influence of the speech of the character and the modification of a text belonging to a character under the influence of authorial reworking.[26] One of the most frequent ways to express this influence is the use of quasi-direct discourse.

Spatial and temporal planes manifest themselves when "we may be able to guess the position, defined in spatial or temporal coordinates, from which the narration is conducted."[27] For example, the narrator can assume the spatial position of specific characters. In this case "if the character enters a room, the narrator describes the room; if the character goes out into the street, the narrator describes the street."[28] Merging with the character's spatial position does not immediately require merging in all other planes, although it is possible as well.

The narrator can also assume positions of different characters subsequently and pass the point of view, like a baton, from one character to another.[29] They can also hold the position of detached onlooker who either assumes one spatial position or moves from one place to another or even take a bird's-eye view to observe the whole scene. Likewise, the temporal position of the narrator can concur with the temporal position of one or many characters or they may use their own "authorial time,"[30] for example, speak about events that occurred in distant past.

The psychological plane is distinguished "in those cases where the authorial point of view relies on an individual consciousness (or perception)."[31] In a sense, psychological plane in Uspensky's model equals Genette's idea of zero/external/internal focalization. Consider two following quotations from Uspensky:

---

25. Uspensky, 20.
26. Uspensky, 33.
27. Uspensky, 57.
28. Uspensky, 58.
29. Uspensky, 60.
30. Uspensky, 66.
31. Uspensky, 81.

When an author constructs his narration, he usually has two options open to him: he may structure the events and characters of the narrative through the deliberately subjective viewpoint of some particular individual's (or individuals') consciousness, or he may describe the events as objectively as possible. In other words, he may use the donnees (data) of the perceptions of one consciousness or several, or he may use the facts as they are known to him.[32]

Generally speaking, human behavior may be described in two basically distinct ways. First it may be described from the point of view of an outside observer whose position in the work may be either clearly defined or unspecified, and who describes only the behavior which is visible to an onlooker. Second, behavior may be described from the point of view of the person himself or from the point of view of an omniscient observer who is permitted to penetrate the consciousness of that person.[33]

Structuring events and characters from the subjective point of view of a particular individual (character) corresponds to internally focalized texts. The point of view of an outside observer, which describes only behavior, corresponds to Genette's external focalization. Finally, the point of view of an omniscient observer who is permitted to penetrate the consciousness of characters corresponds to zero focalized texts. However, as I will show later, point of view and focalization are two different ideas that complement each other.

3.2.2. Rimmon-Kenan (1983)

Rimmon-Kenan attempts to merge the typology of Genette with typologies of Bal and Uspensky. She elaborates on Genette's idea of differentiation between perspective and narration but adds to it concepts of focalizer (which Bal calls "focalizor") and considers binary opposition between external and internal types of focalization based on the position of the narrator relative to the story. Rimmon-Kenan, following Bal, draws attention not only to the subjective, but also to the objective nature of focalization and talks about focalized objects

---

32. Uspensky, 81.
33. Uspensky, 83.

that can be seen from without or from within: "In the first case only outward manifestation of objects (persons or things) are presented ... In the second case, the external focalizer (narrator-focalizer) presents the focalized from within, penetrating his feelings and thoughts."[34]

Finally, Rimmon-Kenan undertakes an attempt to join Bal's and Uspensky's typologies with some modification of Uspensky's concept. Instead of having five planes of point of view, Rimmon-Kenan divides the spectrum of focalization into three facets: perceptual, psychological, and ideological. Moreover, the perceptual facet is divided into spatial and temporal components and the psychological facet has cognitive and emotive elements. Yet the most important contribution of Rimmon-Kenan is not the regrouping of the planes, but demonstration of how one can practically discern opposition between external and internal focalization within each component.

For example, the panoramic position or simultaneous view of events happening in different places betrays the external position of focalizer, which is opposite to internal position of limited observer. In the same way the temporal component is either panchronic (internal) or retrospective (external). In regard to the cognitive component, opposition between external and internal focalizers is the opposition between unrestricted and restricted knowledge. The external emotive element is neutral, while the internal will always be colored and involved.

Ideology may also be divided into two components: we can understand the ideological position of the character looking at their behavior or from explicit discussion of it (in direct speech or in interior monologue). Behavior of the external narrator-focalizer is narration, so we can understand their position through the orientation they give to the story. The typology of Rimmon-Kenan can be summarized in the following tables:

Table 1. Subjective and objective nature of focalizations

Subject of focalization		Object of focalization	
External	Internal	Within	Without

---

34. Remarkably, Rimmon-Kenan uses a biblical passage from Genesis 22:3 to illustrate how the external focalizer perceives the object from without: "Abraham is about to sacrifice his son, yet only his external actions are presented, his feelings and thoughts remaining opaque." See Rimmon-Kenan, *Narrative Fiction*, 78.

Table 2. Facets (manifestations) of focalization in respect to subject

		External	Internal
Perceptual	Spatial	Panoramic Simultaneous	Limited Successive
	Temporal	Retrospective	Panchronic
Psychological	Cognitive	Unrestricted	Restricted
	Emotive	Neutral	Colored
Ideological	Behavior	Orientation of the story	Behavior of the character
	Discussion	Author's speech	Direct speech Interior monologue

Trying to elaborate Rimmon-Kenan's typology even further, I made an attempt to create the same kind of table but in respect to the focalized object:

Table 3. Facets (manifestations) of focalization in respect to focalized object

		From within	From without
Perceptual	Spatial	—	—
	Temporal	—	—
Psychological	Cognitive	He thought … He knew …	Apparently … Evidently …
	Emotive	He felt …	As if … It seemed …
Ideological	Behavior	Behavior without implications	Behavior without implications
	Discussion	Interior monologue	Direct speech

After Bal's model, Rimmon-Kenan's typology can be considered as one of the most important refinements of Genette's theory. Compared with Bal's model, it seems better developed and more practical. However, my initial attempt to employ it for analysis of biblical narratives was not satisfactory for two reasons. First, the model of Rimmon-Kenan is more suitable for descriptive narrative texts – something that biblical narratives cannot boast of. But there is the second, deeper reason for this displeasure: it seems that

Rimmon-Kenan is, as much as Bal is, too far from the original ideas of Genette, and this brings into question the kind of phenomena this model explains. What is the core of focalization?

3.3. Preliminary Conclusions

This leads to the preliminary conclusion about approaches to the problem of narrative perspective. In the course of historical discussion, two different understandings of focalization were proposed. The model of Genette that can be called the classical model sees the narrator (even more simplistically, an author) as the only one real focalizer (or subject of focalization). In this model, the object of focalization is text and only text. For this model, the narrative universe exists only on paper, so the characters cannot speak or act and express their point of view; that is done only by the will of the narrator. This model belongs clearly to the level of discourse. The reader is invited to evaluate the ability of the narrator in selecting and conveying narrative information.

The models of Bal and Rimmon-Kenan describe focalization on the level of the story. The emphasis is on relationships between characters. The reader is invited to recreate the narrative world from the text, imagine all its dimensions, and almost become part of it. Focalization is closer to the idea of the opinion of the character; it is, in fact, determined as relationship and the reader is supposed to discover relationships between vision, the one who sees, and the object of seeing. Since in a majority of narratives characters see each other, focalization is the recovery of relationships between characters and between characters and other objects of the narrative world.

That having been said, according to Jahn, two options are possible: "One of the questions that every narratologist has to decide for himself or herself is whether to stick to Genette's or Bal's model, and whether to use a broad or a narrow conception of facets of focalization."[35] However, there is a third, more holistic approach to the study of focalization that includes both Genette's and Bal's. The rest of this chapter will be committed to the search for such a model. Doing this I will follow the advice of Burkhard Niederhoff, who suggests:

---

35. Jahn, "Focalization," in *Cambridge Companion*, 102.

When narratologists review the work of their predecessors, they usually focus on the gaps and the mistakes. Previous theories are demolished or quarried for the purpose of building a new one. This does not make for a fair appraisal of the critical tradition. Perhaps it is time for a non-partisan history of theories of point of view and related metaphors from James (or earlier) to the present day, preferably by someone who makes a vow not to conclude the study with a new theory or typology of their own.[36]

With this in mind, I want to present a short overview of narratological works that explore the notion of focalization since 1991. Strange as it may seem, most of the material in these works still focuses on the questions of the definition of focalization and a comparison between models of Genette and Bal. But the chief value of these works for my research is the attempt to demonstrate how focalization can be employed for practical analysis of narrative texts. My second objective will be to demonstrate the evolution of the notion of perspective from its initial state of separation between point of view and focalization (after the debate of Genette and Bal) to the point of their conjunction. The last two models – of Wolf Schmid and Valeri Tjupa – have formed the basis for my methodology in studying the book of Ruth because these models meet desired criteria better than other typologies.

3.4. Minor Development of the Concept of Focalization in 1990s and 2000s

In the 1990s and 2000s attempts were made to develop or revise existing typologies of focalization with a desire to resolve issues and problems around this concept. Three main directions in these attempts were clearly formulated by Uri Margolin:

> (1) expansion of the domain of application of focalization theory to other media, with the necessary theoretical modifications (2) reconfiguration (add, delete, replace, rearrange) of the systems of categories and distinctions currently available and (3) a reconceptualization of the whole theory by placing it within a

---

36. Niederhoff, "Perspective," Paragraph 30.

more fundamental theoretical framework, be it fictional world semantics or cognitive linguistics, both of which are ultimately semantic theories.[37]

In this brief overview, my attention will be given to the second and the third direction of the evolution of the focalization concept. The works on these matters share several common features. They usually start with exposition of the theories of Genette, Bal, and sometimes Rimmon-Kenan. Often such exposition ends up explaining the core of the theory better than it is done in original texts, though retelling almost never leads to considerable reformulation. The purposes of the works, besides explaining existing theories, are to show points of connection between the theory of Bal and Genette and to elaborate on the theory of Bal.

3.4.1. William F. Edmiston (1991)

Edmiston argues that Uspensky's study actually "prefigure[s] both Genette and Bal" in that its spatio-temporal plane reflects the position of the focalizer in Bal's concept, and the psychological plane is similar to Genette's internal/external opposition, which "refers not to a space relative to the described action but to the characters' mental activity."[38]

The attempt to show the points of connection between Bal and Genette leads to William Edmiston's thoughs, presented in the following table.[39]

Table 4. Points of connection between Bal and Genette

Type	Subject coincides with character	Locus relative to diegesis (spatial)	Access to minds of characters (psychological)
zero	no	outside (unlimited)	inside (unlimited)
internal	yes	inside (limited)	inside own/outside others
external	no (spectator)	inside (limited)	outside (limited)

---

37. Margolin, "Focalization," 41.
38. Edmiston, *Hindsight*, 156n7.
39. Edmiston, 155.

Edmiston then presents the work of Pier Vitoux, which he calls "an admirable synthesis of the theories of Genette and Bal."[40] Vitoux introduces the idea of focalizing the subject, which can be of two kinds: focalizing subject that is outside of the story world and as such has unrestricted access to the minds of characters and focalizing subject (FS) which stays inside the story world to whom FS delegates his responsibility (FS-d). From Genette's theory, Vitoux utilizes the idea of internal and external focalization. He distinguishes between objects of focalization that are focalized internally (FO-int) and objects of focalization that are focalized externally (FO-ext).

3.4.2. Patrick O'Neill (1994)

Patrick O'Neill is particularly interesting for the present research because in his book that is largely based on Bal's and Rimmon-Kenan's conclusions, he, at the same time, develops formulas of focalization that are intended to clearly reflect processes of focalization that take place in narrative texts. In this chapter my goal is to explain how these narratological formulas developed, as well as to analyze pros and cons of using them and to demonstrate their use on the example of one passage from the book of Ruth.

After a brief introduction (with sufficient clarity) of basic ideas of Bal and Rimmon-Kenan, O'Neill moves to the discussion of aspects of focalization. He clarifies that,

> the focalizer is not a "person," not even an agent in the same way that the narrator or implied author is a narrative agent, but rather a chosen point, the point from which the narrative is perceived as being presented at any given moment.[41]

As regards to the story world, he also distinguishes between external focalizer (EF), which generally coincides with narrator and thus called narrator-focalizer (NF) and internal focalizer (IF), which generally coincides with character and thus is called character-focalizer (CF). From here O'Neill makes the important observation that like narration focalization can also be embedded, which means that the same focalization can be at the same time external

---

40. Edmiston, 157.
41. O'Neill, *Fictions of Discourse*, 86.

and internal (in case of embedded stories, for example). The whole narrative is always externally focalized because it is presented by the narrator who is outside of the narrative world by definition. But the narrator who tells the story within the story is internal for the first one and external for the second.

Focalizers (NF and CF) perceive focalized objects that can be character-objects (CO) or any other objects of the narrative world, but only characters can be focalized from within as much as from without. This typology creates "a whole series of new perspectives" such as simple, compound, and complex focalizations. Simple focalization is focalization with a single focalizer like in the sentence: "John watched Mary." The formula in this case would be

$$F = NF(CF_{John}(CO_{Mary}))$$

where John is character-focalizer (CF), Mary is nontransparent character-object (CO) and the whole scene is focalized by external narrator-focalizer (NF).

In the case of a compound focalizer, one focalization is contained within another: "John watched Mary, who looked at the sky." In this case the formula of focalization looks different:

$$F = NF(CF_{John}(CF_{Mary}(CO_{sky})))$$

This formula can be enriched by including the facet of focalization under consideration (psychological, ideological, or patio-temporal). For example, if John knew about Mary who looked at the sky, the formula could look like this:

$$F = NF(CF_{John/cognitive}(CF_{Mary/spatial}(CO_{sky})))$$

In order to examine the feasibility of this method, I attempted to implement it for the passage from the book of Ruth. But it turns out that the method is too subjective and too complicated for practical application.

3.4.3. Ruth Ronen (1994)

One further step in the understanding of focalization can be found in the book of Ruth Ronen[42] where she discusses the way fictional worlds are created. According to Ronen, fictional worlds are created in three steps: selection of narrative information, composition and, finally, verbalization (or

---

42. Ronen, *Possible Worlds*.

textualization) of the material that has been selected and composed. On each step there is a principle that the narrator uses in order to make decisions. It is this principle that Ronen calls focalization.

Therefore, on the level of selection of information, focalization, according to Ronen, is "a principle according to which elements of the fictional world are arranged from a certain perspective or from a specific position."[43] But the narrator has to follow certain principles not only on the level of selection but on the level of composition of the selected material, which means that focalization stipulates both "selection and combination of fictional world-components." Moreover, there is even the principle "according to which elements are textualized in particular manners of expression carried out from a narrating stance."[44] This means that, in a sense, some principle (i.e. focalization) is at work on all three levels of narrative constitution.

3.4.4. Manfred Jahn (1996, 1999, 2005)

Manfred Jahn, in the article "Windows of Focalization," carries out an extensive analysis of "mainstream focalization theory" by which he means largely the theories of Genette, Bal, and Rimmon-Kenan. He points out twelve "problematic distinctions, overt or covert ambiguities, and paradoxes" of focalization theory. He takes first of all Genette's theory and states that:

1. The question "Who perceives?" is not broad enough to cover all facets of focalization.
2. The issue of optionality of focalization remains unaddressed.
3. In contrast to Genette's own words, the narrator is not conferred with the power of focalization.
4. Theory is inoperative in epistolary and homodiegetic narratives.
5. The idea of "speaking" accommodates many meanings and as such is an ill-advised term.
6. "Narratological status of interior monologues remains puzzling and controversial."

---

43. Ronen, 179. Ronen does not describe the perspective of a specific position as point of view. Integration of these concepts will be done by Wolf Schmid.
44. Ronen, *Possible Worlds*, 179.

7. The story told by a character ("subjective analepses") has the same problem with status as interior monologue.
8. The improvement of the idea of focal character is questionable for it does not improve Genette's theory.
9. Ambiguous understanding of the phrase "focalization sur X."
10. The boundaries between three categories of Genette's model are not clear.
11. The idea of completeness of information is not clarified.
12. Zero focalization is still a focalization.[45]

Based on the above list, Jahn criticizes the strict distinction between voice and mood and considers that post-Genettian theories made a step in the right direction when they introduced narrator-focalizer and thus blurred the lines of the earlier account. Taking the next step on in this direction, Jahn[46] proposes his own model that starts from optical metaphor that he later extends to all kinds of mental processes that are involved in focalization. He states that "Mainstream focalization theory largely denies narrators and readers their share as well as their power of imaginary perception."[47] Therefore, in his model Jahn merges James's idea of narrative windows with core intuitions of the concept of focalization. Jahn represents "reading oriented theory of mental imagery" which implies that,

> A passage that presents objects and events as seen, perceived, or conceptualized from a specific focus . . . will, naturally and automatically, invoke a reader's adoption of (or transposition to) this point of view and open a window defined by the perceptual, evaluative, and affective parameters that characterize the agent providing the focus . . .[48]

The second publication of Jahn[49] continues to develop the ideas of windows of focalization. Here one finds a new definition of focalization which

---

45. Jahn, "Windows."
46. Jahn, 250–58.
47. Jahn, 258.
48. Jahn, 256.
49. Jahn, "More Aspects."

is "a matter of providing and managing windows into the narrative world, and of regulating (guiding, manipulating) readerly imaginary perception."[50] Jahn shows that his model of focalization is holistic enough to include all existing models. For example, two focuses that are part of the model illustrate well subjective and objective characteristics of focalization. Criticizing narrowness of existing terms ("seeing" and "perceiving"), he provides the list of aspects of focalization that orient narrative text. The list consists of (a) affect (fear, pity, joy, revulsion, etc.); (b) perception (vision, audition, touch, smell, taste, bodily sensation) and imaginary perception (recollection, imagination, dream, hallucination, etc.); and, finally, he lists (c) conceptualization (thought, voice, ideation, style, modality, deixis, etc.).[51] The main variable of this model is conceptualization, which increases from (a) to (c). Besides all above refinements, Jahn proposes that there should be a scale of focalization from non-focalized passages to strict focalization with weak and ambivalent focalization staying in-between.[52]

As can be seen from this brief review of Jahn's works, attempts to include all the nuances of focalization from different narrative texts lead to complication of the model (like in the case with focalization formulas). However, such complicated models seem difficult to implement.

3.4.5. Essays on Fiction and Perspective (2004)

Two articles from the collection titled *Essays on Fiction and Perspective* seem to be of high importance for this study because they clearly show the difference between the notion of focalization and the notion of point of view.

3.4.5.1. Eva Broman

Eva Broman[53] states that the most important criterion of Genette's model is not who perceives, but what (or how much) is perceived. Internal, external, and zero focalization are no more than the names for specific (limiting)

---

50. Jahn, 91.
51. Jahn, 89.
52. Jahn, 97.
53. Broman, "Narratological Focalization."

techniques of writing for presenting the story.⁵⁴ Therefore, each type of focalization describes certain types of narratives without going into detail. Internal focalization, thus, represents a large group of narratives where narrative information is registered by one of the characters of the story. In narratives with external focalization, registration of dialogues, objects, and different kinds of actions are entrusted to the registering device (not the character) which is situated within the fictive world. Finally, zero focalization "simply denotes specific types of narratives, in which the point of view does not coincide with any characters."⁵⁵

Broman concludes that Genette's theory "lacks of explicit linguistic criteria for determining the various types of focalization" and is "mainly intended to classify various types of texts on the basis of certain properties that only become evident if one considers the text as a whole."⁵⁶ She also states that interpretation of the passage is not determined only by the amount of information about the fictional world (while this is also often important), but by "the manner in which the information is conveyed." In analysis of focalization she calls to pay attention to "small-scale linguistic choices such as indications of spatial deixis, psychological sequencing, or the presence of various linguistic features that reveal the attitudes, emotions, beliefs or judgment of an experiencer within the fictional world."⁵⁷ By saying this, Broman makes a small step toward merging focalization with point of view theory and paying attention to linguistic details (or "detailization" that I am going to talk about, presenting the model of Tjupa).

Analyzing Bal's model and comparing it with Genette's typology, Broman insists that the differences in these models are the result of Bal's misunderstanding of Genette's ideas which lead to creation of a completely new theory, outside of the scope of the original discussion. On the basis of Broman's analysis, the following chart can be formed:

---

54. Broman, 64.
55. Broman, 75.
56. Broman, 71.
57. Broman, 70.

Bal's model	Genette's model
Concern with shorter passages and shifts in point of view between passages and even within the same sentence.	Concern the text's overall composition.
Narrator's point of view always prevailed, but the powers of focalization can be "delegated" to the character.	Narrator's point of view prevails only in zero focalized passages. There are narratives where narrator plays minor role.
Focalization is an *activity* of focalizer that indicates various viewpoints and relationships within the fictional world such as seeing, observing, thinking, deliberating, judging, and remembering.	Focalization is an artistic device in the hand of narrator (or author) which is built on the *restriction* (or concealment) of narrative information that leads to establishing various aesthetic effects.

Bal, Broman concludes, "seems to have forgotten that the text she is analyzing is a text of fiction, created by an author, and that we need not presuppose that someone has seen or experienced the fictional events before they were put into print."[58]

3.4.5.2. Lars-Åke Skalin

Reflecting on Genette's work, Skalin comes to the conclusion that focalization means restriction of field that can be interpreted in at least two ways, both of which are encompassed by Genette's model. First, focalization is "*the amount of information* given to the reader in relation to the whole of relevant information possible." Second, focalization is "*the choice* of information-giving devices in relation to the whole spectrum of relevant techniques available."[59] Skalin considers that these applications of the term "focalization" are fundamentally different, for the first deals with the question of horizon, while the second is about narrative style.

The first type of focalization – restriction of field – can be found in the stories where information is presented from the point of view of one of the

---

58. Broman, 78.
59. Skalin, "Focalization as Restriction," 232.

characters of the story. Restricted horizon of that character is presented consistently in order to produce the desired aesthetical effect. Skalin finds this example in the story of Winnie-the-Pooh. As I will show in the later chapters, many of such examples can be found in the book of Ruth as well.

The second type of focalization is different from the first in that the narrator does not use the horizon of any characters in order to restrict information in relation to completeness, but simply shows the narrative world by the eyes of one of the characters. Of course, theoretically, this approach also leads to the restriction of information, but the restriction is not the purpose here, for the intentions of the narrator are purely aesthetic. Compared with the first type of focalization, which situates on the level of the story, the second type relates only to the narrator and his motivation. If the character's eyes are used to describe the story worlds, it is "vision with, but not restriction of field." Skalin concludes:

> ... we have to admit that sometimes focalization is just motivation in the hands of the literary artist to give a special kind of elegant solution to the problem of constructing the "what is" in the story ... what normally had been given from the storyteller's own voice now has been substituted of a fictional quasi-motif, the reflector perceiving what the storyteller will tell. Since this will imply a substitution of one narrative instrument for another, it indicates that we are not dealing with a matter of *content* but of *style*.[60]

It seems, that the second type of focalization is traditionally understood as point of view – which is a narrative technique that is employed by the narrator for aesthetic effect. Therefore, Skalin makes a clear separation between focalization and point of view which echoes the conclusions of Tatiana Jesch and Maile Stain (see § 3.4.6.2 of this work). Yet, after separating point of view and focalization, Skalin is not trying to find any connection between them.

3.4.6. Point of View, Perspective, Focalization (2009)

In the collections of the articles that were brought together into the book *Point of View, Perspective, Focalization* two articles are of particular importance

---

60. Skalin, 251.

for this project, one written by Uri Margolin and another by Tatiana Jesch and Maile Stain.

3.4.6.1. Uri Margolin

In the article with the catchy heading "Focalization, Where Do We go from Here?" Uri Margolin aims to contribute to reconfiguration and reconceptualization of the notion of focalization. After giving a brief list of reasons that explain why the notion of focalization is worthy of study, he immediately continues with the definition:

> Focalization in narrative involves the textual representation of specific (pre)existing sensory elements of the text's story world as perceived and registered (recorded, represented, encoded, modeled and stored) by some mind or recording device which is a member of this world. In other words, focalization involves at least the internal inscription of external data.[61]

This rather evasive definition becomes clearer when Margolin speaks about five factors of focalization: focalized object, focalizing agent, activity of perceiving, the product of perceiving, and textualization. What must be noted here is that Margolin does not try to allocate only one level for focalization, but rather to spread focalization to all narrative levels – a tendency that will be fully realized in Schmid's genetic model of narrative constitution.

3.4.6.2. Tatiana Jesch and Maile Stain

Tatiana Jesch and Maile Stain consider that Genette's model of focalization is actually "an amalgamation of two wholly independent elements."[62] After comparing works of Genette (*Narrative Discourse* and *Narrative Discourse Revisited*), they come to the conclusion that Genette's own understanding of the term migrates. While in the first volume focalization is closer to the idea of "perspectivization," the second volume strongly adheres to focalization as "the regulation of narrative information within the communication between author and reader."[63] Or as they clarify this thought later in this

---

61. Margolin, "Focalization," 42.
62. Jesch and Stain, "Perspecitivisation," 59.
63. Jesch and Stain, 59.

article: focalization is "the author's temporary or definitive withholding of information from the reader" while perspectivization is "representation of something from the subjective view of a fictive entity (narrator or character)."[64]

There is a point of intersection between perspectivization and focalization. Text can be focalized by means of perspectivization, but perspective can be created without focalization. Therefore, there are four types of passages that can be discerned in the narrative texts:

- focalization through perspectivization,
- perspectivization without focalization,
- focalization without perspectivization,
- and neither focalization nor perspectivization.

As I understand it, what Jesch and Stein call "perspective" is what is usually called "point of view." So, the article actually designates the relationship between focalization and point of view in a fictional text and gradually leads us to the final stage of evolution of the idea of focalization.

Part of the article also addresses the question of "complete knowledge." Each action of the narrative is presented as consisting of four elements: cause, intention, actualization, and result. If the reader is aware of all four elements of the action, his knowledge is considered to be complete. However, "if the corresponding information (in relation to the events presented up to this point) is not communicated to the reader, he is dealing with focalization."[65]

Yet the authors do not advise researchers to follow this schema rigorously and isolate every element for each action of the text in order to find out if the text if focalized. Most of the actions of the text are self-explanatory and it is better to implement the scheme for difficult and disputable passages.[66]

3.4.7. Living Book of Narratology (2011)

Three recent articles from the internet resource "The Living Book of Narratology" are sufficient to bring us to the concluding step of the evolution of the focalization concept.

---

64. Jesch and Stain, 65.
65. Jesch and Stain, 67.
66. Jesch and Stain, 68.

3.4.7.1. Burchard Niederhoff (2001, 2009)

Articles of Burchard Niederhoff are highly important for our study, for the author strongly maintains the opinion of focalization being the restriction of field while it gives space to the idea of point of view. In the first article titled "Fokalisation und Perspektive. Ein Plädoyer für friedliche Koexistenz,"[67] he compares meanings of the terms "focalization" and "point of view" and shows how these concepts can peacefully coexist. In the same vein, he continues his reasoning in the second article "Focalization."[68] He considers that the difference between point of view and focalization is that the point of view is "the more powerful metaphor . . . to render the subjective experience of a character," while focalization is used to create such effects as suspense, mystery, puzzlement, etc.

He concludes his review by this powerful statement that encourages further investigation on the subject: "If focalization theory is to make any progress, an awareness of the differences between the two terms and of their respective strengths and weaknesses is indispensable."[69]

3.4.7.2. Tobias Klauk and Tilmann Köppe (2013)

With the article of Kaluk and Köppe "Puzzles and Problems for the Theory of Focalization,"[70] I finish the review of the evolution of the focalization concept. The article is well suited as the concluding article not only because it was first published in 2009 and then reviewed in 2011, but also because it raises the questions that remain unanswered by the scholars up until today. Here is the list of issues raised in the article:

1. What is the core of the phenomenon?
2. How can the phenomenon/phenomena be cast in definitions?
3. Is focalization a gradual phenomenon?
4. What is the domain of definition?
5. What does a comprehensive taxonomy of types of focalization look like?

---

67. Niederhoff, "Fokalisation," 1–21.
68. Niederhoff.
69. Niederhoff, paragraph 18.
70. Klauk and Köppe, "Puzzles and Problems."

6. Is there a linguistic basis to focalization, and how is the relation between the linguistic basis and focalization to be understood?
7. What about psychological uptake?
8. Can Narrators focalize?

Dealing with these questions, Klauk and Köppe sometimes give possible solutions but never come to the one universal answer. Yet, when one starts to employ the concept (as I am going to employ focalization theory for narratological analysis of the book of Ruth), it is important to have one simple, practical, and yet well-elaborated theory. It is also good for the theory to be comprehensive enough. In my study I come to the conclusion that models of focalization proposed by Schmid and Tjupa fit these criteria well.

3.5. Wolf Schmid (2005, 2010)

With works of Wolf Schmid and Valeri Tjupa I finish my survey of focalization models. The works of these German and Russian scholars were chosen as a basis for my methodology because it seems that both Schmid and Tjupa take into account the accomplishments of previous generations of narratologists yet do not simply merge different models. Rather they find for each classical idea its own place in the overall scheme and provide opportunity for practical application of the narratological concept of focalization.

Schmid's genetic model of narrative constitution was initially proposed in the book *Нарратология* ("Narratology") published in Russian in 2003.[71] Later it was translated and published in German in 2005 under the title "Elemente der narratalogie"[72] and finally in English in 2010 under the title "Introduction to Narratology."[73] From the first glance, Schmid's model compared with other taxonomies does not contain any groundbreaking ideas. What Schmid says has already been said by other scholars in some form.

---

71. Schmid, *Нарратология* (2003). A new edition of this book was published in Russian in 2008. See: Schmid, *Нарратология* (2008).
72. Schmid, *Elemente der Narratologie*.
73. Schmid, *Narratology*. Russian and English publications were not merely translations but new editions of the book. This means that some materials that are found in the Russian edition may not be included in German or English editions and in this research I had to use all three editions in order to absorb all the possible information. Besides, such comparison from time to time brought a better understanding of specific terms.

However, it seems that Schmid could show a logical connection between point of view and narrative constitution.[74]

According to Schmid, the constitution of any narrative starts with the process of selecting narrative information from happenings which he defines as "amorphous entirety of situations, characters and actions explicitly or implicitly represented, or logically implied, in the narrative work."[75] Selection from the unlimited body of happenings results in forming the story, limited and meaningful. The narrator who is responsible for this selection chooses from elements (situations, characters, and actions) and from properties or characteristics of those elements. Any elements that are not included into this list (even those that the reader is supposed to imagine and add to the story intuitively) are regarded as non-selected.

Selected elements are then supposed to be arranged in one line because written text, due to its nature, cannot present two events simultaneously. This process is called composition which, according to Schmid, is done by "*linearization* of things occurring simultaneously in the story" and by "*reorganization* of the segments of the story."[76]

The final and the only layer of the narrative that is "accessible for empirical observation" is presentation, which in case of literary narration is carried out through verbalization. In our case the narrative is presented through the Hebrew text of the book of Ruth.

It is important to note that Schmid himself does not consider this model to be a presentation of focalization taxonomy. Diagrams represent a process of narrative constitution. But, in fact, focalization can be found at work in every layer of this model. The transition from happenings to story is accompanied by selection of narrative information which is focalization, according to Genette's classical definition. The second and the third transformations – composition and presentation – are the ways the chosen information is channeled to the reader. Therefore, Schmid's model correctly describes the whole process of selecting and channeling narrative information (i.e. focalization).

---

74. Besides, Schmid could find a very convenient way to present his idea in the form of graphic diagram. See Schmid, *Narratology*, 193.

75. Schmid, *Narratology*, 190.

76. Schmid, 191.

It is remarkable that the idea of point of view is an integral part of this model and plays its subsidiary role. Focalization is the whole process of selection and channeling narrative information, while point of view is the instrument or means of that selection. Schmid traditionally differentiates perceptual, ideological, spatial, temporal, and linguistic points of view. However, according to Schmid,[77] with each next tier of narrative constitution, the number of possible types of point of view changes. Thus, on the level of selection, all points of view (perceptual, ideological, spatial, temporal, and linguistic) are present.[78] However, on the level of linearization, the use of perceptual and linguistic point of view is not applicable (there is no way how, for example, linguistic point of view can affect ordering narrative events). But linearization reflects only temporal, spatial and ideological positions of the narrator. Finally, in verbalization linguistic point of view takes its rightful place on the par with ideological position.

Besides purely theoretical ideas, Schmid suggests several practical steps to explore narrative constitution. Thus, one of the key issues which is related to Schmid's model and to the issue of focalization is the search for logic of selectivity. For a better understanding of this question, it is worthwhile to make some clarifications about what Schmid means by a narratological event. According to Schmid, life consists of a lot of happenings, but not every one of them can be designated as a narratological event and consequently not all of them are included into narrative text.

> In all three languages, English, German, and Russian, an event is a special occurrence, something which is not part of everyday routine. We shall highlight the importance of exceptionality in our strict interpretation of the event concept: every event is a change of state, but not every change of state constitutes an event. The event, therefore, has to be defined as a change of state that fulfills certain conditions.[79]

Then Schmid names two basic requirements of the event. First, the event should be *factual* or *real*. In other word, changes of state in the framework

---

77. See diagram "Ideal genetic model of the point of view," in Schmid, *Narratology*, 210.
78. For some reason, Schmid leaves linguistic point of view in the brackets.
79. Schmid, "Narrativity and Eventfulness," 24.

of the narrative world should be real, not just wished, imagined, or dreamed. Second, the change of state can be treated as an event only when it meets the requirement of *resultativity*.

> *Resultativity*, the second requirement of the event, is a correlate of the event's reality. The change of state that constitutes an event is neither inchoative (begun) nor conative (attempted) nor durative (confined to an ongoing process). Rather, it must be resultative in that it reaches completion in the narrative world of the text.[80]

This analysis will help to see why these and not other events were selected for the narrative and why they are so important, unique, or unusual. It will help to distinguish framing and embedded events and eventually clarify the logic of selectivity.

However, not each event has equal weight in the course of the plot. Some events are more eventful than the others. Hence, the events of the book will be examined according to their degree of eventfulness. This will demonstrate that the degree of eventfulness tends to change within one framing event. It will help to understand structure of the plot and distribution of events on the fabric of the narrative by identifying central and secondary events.

According to criteria proposed by Schmid, degree of eventfulness depends on the following parameters. First, it depends on its relevancy or significance "in terms of axioms which underline the storyworld."[81] Of course, the same event can be more or less significant depending on the point of view. Second, it depends on its unpredictability. The event should deviate from the generally expected in a storyworld. It should break with expectations: the less expected the change is, the more eventful is the event. And again, unpredictability is in many ways a relative idea. "Relevance and unpredictability are the primary criteria underlying the continuum of eventfulness. A change of state must meet both of these requirements to a minimum degree, if not more, if it is to be perceived as an event."[82]

---

80. Schmid, 24.
81. Schmid, *Narratology*, 9.
82. Schmid, 11.

Schmidt also lists three "less crucial requirements": persistence, irreversibility, and non-iterativity. By persistence Schmid means the impact of the event, "consequences for the thought and action" of the characters. Greater impact leads to the higher degree of eventfulness. However, the absence of impact can be interpreted as the ideological message of the narrator. Irreversibility suggests that the original condition cannot be restored. However, irreversibility relates not only to outward reality, but, for example, to the thinking of the character. The event is irreversible if the character cannot go back to the old way of thinking. Finally, even a significant event, when it recurs, becomes anti-eventful and predictable.

Schmid's work also provides brief guidance for studying narrative on the level of composition and the level of presentation. Composition is the placing of selected information; it is the beginning of the process of channeling narrative information. It consists of two types of activity: linearization and rearrangement of information. Composition is an inevitable step when the narrative plot contains two or more events that happen simultaneously. Apparently, the narrator cannot describe them at the same time due to the nature of narrative (written or speaking) – he has to write/speak about the first event and only then turn to the second.

> The linearization of the actions occurring simultaneously in the story into a narrative sequence, which is an obligatory device in literature, and the reorganization of the sequences following one another in chronological order, which is facultative, bring the parts of the story into a meaningful sequence. In the composition of the narrative, a meaning is formed, which actualizes and modifies the potential meaning contained in the story. As a result, the evaluative position of the narrator, his or her ideological standpoint, is also constituted via the devices of composition.[83]

The other activity – rearrangement – is the instrument by which the narrator can bring to the readers their ideological point of view by creating a certain type of focalization. For example, by placing the most important

---

83. Schmid, 207. The linear nature of narratives (and biblical narratives as well) was also recognized by Berlin, *Poetics and Interpretation*, 98.

event in the narrative at the beginning of the narrative, the narrator can give to the readers more information than any given character has. At the same time, the most relevant information that was known to the characters from the beginning can be revealed by the end of the narrative. By this step the narrator creates narrative intrigue.

Schmidt recognizes that composition is always the subject of different points of view. In his genetic model, he points out that at the linearization step, three points of view are at work: ideological, temporal, and spatial. Indeed, when two simultaneous events are placed one after another, the narrator expresses their (or someone else's) temporal point of view. The same thing is true about spatial position – the same events can be viewed at the same time from different spatial perspective but described in the narrative at different places. The placement of description often plays an ideological role. The simplest example of it is narrative where the act of the same person is described twice: in the beginning by one of the characters negatively and by the end by the omniscient narrator positively.

Describing his genetic model, Schmid, however, does not pay attention to the issue of focalization. But it is quite clear that focalization (restriction of narrative information) is at hand whenever there is a point of view because point of view always restricts horizon, and the matter of the analysis of focalization on this step is to find out which point of view is used in order to restrict the horizon of the reader. Therefore, focalization is also present on the level of linearization, which means that the study of linearization is relevant to the study of focalization.

The third step of narrative constitution is called presentation of narrative. As soon as events are selected and arranged in a certain order, the time comes for actual presentation. According to Schmid, presentation "occurs through verbalization."[84] He lists two kinds of instruments the narrator uses in order to verbalize his narrative. First, it is "purely exegetical textual units" such as "evaluations, generalizations, commentaries, reflections, meta-narrative comments by the narrator" and various linguistic styles:

> [The narrator] can use lexical units and syntactic structures that correspond to his or her own style (i.e., take up a narratorial

---

84. Schmid, *Narratology*, 208.

standpoint) or – as far as his or her linguistic competence allows – align him or herself on the stylistic world of the happenings, and present the narrative in the language of one or more characters (i.e., with figural perspectivization).[85]

By using different styles and giving commentaries in the course of narration, the narrator can further restrict or expand narrative information that the readers receive. Therefore, focalization as manipulation of narrative information is present on the level of presentation as well.

Schmid's model, therefore, helps to comprehend selection and channeling of information in the narrative on different levels of narrative constitution. One can start the study of focalization by considering what events are selected, turning then to the way they are arranged and finally examining what linguistic features the narrator uses in order to focalize narrative information.

3.6. Valeri Tjupa (2016)

Tjupa echoes Schmid by saying that the narrator is not able to provide the reader with all the details of narrated events and is forced to break the continuous flow of life (that is to select information) and then tie them into the storyline (linearize). Therefore, the purpose of narrative analysis consists of identifying separate episodes and finding connections between them.[86] However, Tjupa differs from Schmid in several aspects. First of all, he provides several practical approaches to determine the boundaries of episodes. He considers that the boundaries of each episode can be defined on the basis of three factors: time gap, shift in space, and change in the group of characters (appearance or disappearance of the character).[87]

It has to be considered that episodes can be of different length: some will be more extensive and pictorial while others are limited to brief report. Besides, within the borders of one episode, narration can develop unevenly; the time of narration can numerously speed up and slow down.[88]

---

85. Schmid, 208.
86. Tjupa, Введение, 20.
87. Tjupa, 21.
88. Tjupa, 22–23.

According to Tjupa, analysis can be advanced by assigning each episode into so-called "shots of mental vision:"

> Any statement of narrative text, even the most trivial one, is perceived by the reader as more or less intense shot of "inner" or more precisely "mental vision" ... The meaning of the shot consists of only those details that are named in the text, and not all that the reader/listener is able or desire to imagine.[89]

The borders of the shot are determined with the same three factors as the borders of episode – by place, time, and system of characters. Shots, compared with episodes, are relatively short and more static. For example, in order to perceive a close-up picture, one has to pay attention to the beginning and, specifically, to the end of the phrase. In shots, the narrator picks up several details from the continuous flow of life, which then are tied by the reader to a single picture.[90]

Second, Tjupa also refines the position of Schmid regarding the criteria of eventfulness,[91] and names three (instead of five) essential characteristics of any real narratological event.

A) *Singularity.* The narratological event should be unique, unitary, unprecedented, and unparalleled. Several facts of the story in this matter are highlighted from the inevitable life course and common social rituals.

B) *Fractality.* The narratological event should describe a strictly limited segment of life, marked by the beginning and the end. Without this feature the event can easily dissolve in the course of existence and as a result lose its significance.

C) *Intentionality.* The narratological event should be always associated with a certain consciousness. The significance and the role of the event is formed in the mind of the character. This mind is the one that, in fact, imposes the measure of the singularity and fractality of the event.

---

89. "Всякая повествовательная фраза, даже самая тривиальная в общеязыковом отношении, задана восприятию как более или менее насыщенный деталями кадр «внутреннего зрения», или, точнее нарративный кадр ме́нтального видения ... В смыслообразный состав такого «кадра» входит лишь поименованное в тексте, а не все, что может или пожелает представить себе слушатель/читатель." Tjupa, *Введение*, 23, translated by the author.

90. Tjupa, *Введение*, 24.

91. Tjupa, 24.

While the first two characteristics are easy to comprehend, the last one requires additional explanation. Tjupa considers it as determining because it determines the measure of singularity and fractality of the event[92] (i.e. it determines the first two characteristics). While Schmid proposes to determine the degree of eventfulness by evaluating the event, Tjupa suggests to estimate the measure of intentionality or to evaluate the one who made a selection. He questions, whose mind stands behind this selection? Or what point of view is used in selection of narrative information? Is it possible to find in the narrative characters that saw the importance of the events described, who can allocate a period of life, a particular day or particular night, that very morning and this very hour, and unite them into one story? This kind of mind can be found inside or outside of the story. Intentionality is the characteristic of evaluating mind.

The reason for this approach is that narratological events should be always associated with certain consciousness. The significance and the role of the event are both formed in someone's (character's or narrator's) mind. This mind is the one that imposes the measure of the uniqueness[93] and fractality[94] of the event. In order to explain the need in evaluating mind, Tjupa invokes the reasoning of Bakhtin, who considers that acts of the characters and elements of narrative world become different (obtain the status of the event) only when they find reflection in the mind, which Bakhtin calls "the witness and the judge" of the event:

> Even the sun, while physically remaining the same, becomes different because it began to be understood ... found reflecting in the mind of the other (the witness and the judge). Because

---

92. Tjupa, 17.

93. Tjupa defines the uniqueness of event as singularity. He considers that the narratological event should be unique, unitary, unprecedented, unparalleled. Several facts of the story in this matter are highlighted from inevitable life course and common social rituals. See Tjupa, Введение, 15–16.

94. Fractality is another term introduced by Tjupa. It implies that narratological event should describe a strictly limited segment of life, marked by the beginning and the end. Without this feature, the event can easily dissolve in the course of existence and as a result lose its significance. See Tjupa, Введение, 15–16.

of this manipulation, the sun has been changed completely, has been enriched, has been transformed (*translation mine*).⁹⁵

Therefore the event is the interaction of two realities, the reality of the narrative world and the reality of the reflecting mind. Without this reflection (evaluation) or without intentionality, the group of happenings risks being lost in the steady flow of life.

While Schmid's approach to evaluate the degree of eventfulness should be essential for determining the degree of eventfulness on the level of discourse, Tjupa's criteria seem to be useful to see the selected events on the level of the story. While Schmid answer the question of what is selected, Tjupa considers the evaluating or reflecting mind that made the selection.

The reflecting mind always has a point of view, perspective, or modality. These are the terms that are closely connected with the idea of focalization. However, Tjupa clarifies that there is a difference between these terms as well:

> Explaining the term "focalization," Genette ... refers to the degree of the narrator's awareness and the extent to which his knowledge is restricted. However, the narrator does not always represent knowledge: medieval Christian narrators, for instance, were guided by sacred conviction and tended to ignore or transform empirical facts.⁹⁶

The statement above turns out to be very important for studying focalization in the book of Ruth and, I suppose, for any Old Testament narrative. The point is that Genette's model is cognitive in its nature and as such it is designed to study texts with a great number of descriptive texts where the category of knowledge is the most important. Biblical narratives do operate with knowledge but on the level of composition (as will be demonstrated in chapter 5 of this work). However, on the level of selection, Genette's categories have to be reconsidered in order to become applicable to biblical prose.

In order to determine intentionality in the narrative, Tjupa proposes to consider four narrative world pictures and four corresponding narrative

---

95. "И солнце, оставаясь физически тем же самым, стало другим, потому что стало осознаваться [...] отразилось в осознании другого (свидетеля и судии): этим оно в корне изменилось, обогатилось, преобразилось." Michail Bakhtin, Собр. соч.: в 7 т. Том 6, Moscow, 2002, 396 quoted in Tjupa, *Введение*, 16.

96. Tjupa, "Narrative Strategies," Paragraph 6.

modalities.[97] (1) Modality of neutral knowledge and corresponding precedental world picture; (2) modality of an unreliable narrator's personal opinion and corresponding occasional world picture; (3) modality of understanding and corresponding probabilistic world picture; and (4) modality of authoritative conviction that does not need approval and imperative world picture.

Out of four modalities and world pictures, the narrators of the Old Testament narratives operate in the scope of imperative world picture because, according to Tjupa, compared with other world pictures the imperative world picture

> presupposes an unquestionable axiological system of the world order in which a character always has freedom of choice, even though this choice is objectively assessed in terms of good and evil; an event consists of fulfilling or failing to fulfill a duty, of observing the moral law of the world or of breaching it.[98]

The corresponding modality that creates such a world picture is the modality of conviction which creates "the narrative of conviction" that is "subjective in terms of values (the narrator is not only a witness but also explicitly judges what goes on) . . ."[99] This judgment comes not necessarily from the mouth of the narrator but from the speeches of his characters (as it happens in the book of Ruth).

The concept of intentionality proposed by Tjupa helps to answer one of the most important questions of this work: how do the direct speeches of the characters relate to focalization, and how does the narrator select the very words of the characters? Schmid only points out that

> . . . the characters' (outer and inner) discourses and narratives also belong to the happenings . . . The only difference is

---

97. A similar attempt to differentiate roles was made by Sasson who supplies Propp's categories of the personae (Villain, Provider, Helper, Sought-for person or its father, Dispatcher, Hero [seeker or victim] and False Hero) to the characters of the book of Ruth. Sasson comes to the conclusion that Naomi assumes the role of Dispatcher, Ruth is the Heroine of the book, Boaz is both Provider, New Hero and hero's Helper, Obed is Sought-for person, and the closer relative is False Hero. Sasson, *Ruth*, 202. The other attempt to differentiate roles of Naomi and Ruth is made by Brenner, who sees the book of Ruth as a combination of two stories, of Naomi and of Ruth. See Brenner, "Naomi and Ruth," 385–97.

98. Tjupa, "Narrative Strategies," paragraph 13.

99. Tjupa, paragraph 9.

that these discourses and secondary narratives are "already" complete "before" (to express it in temporal metaphors again) the narrator "cuts" them out of the happenings, along with the characters' perspectives realized in them, in order to narrate the story.[100]

Does this mean that the texts of the dialogues are not selected and thus are out of the scope of focalization problem? If this would be a true analysis of focalization, it would relate to only 15 percent of the text of the book of Ruth. Yet Schmid continues his thought by naming three reasons for which the narrator uses the direct speeches of the characters. First is to present the characters' point of view. In this case the narrator presents to the readers different perspectives on the same events. The second reason is to manage the plot of the story by outlining future events. And the third reason is to demonstrate thier own perspective on the events by selective representation of characters' speeches.[101] The second and the third reasons will be useful in the following chapters of this work.

Indeed, in the same work Schmid seems to come close to this idea. That is when he considers that the narrator selects events according to certain points of view, which can be perceptual, spatial, temporal, ideological, and linguistic. He exemplifies selection of elements by examining a textual extract taken from the beginning of Chekhov's tale "Rothschild's Fiddle." There he comes to the conclusion that "selection and combination of elements are oriented on the spatial and ideological perspective of the protagonist . . . Yakov Ivanov."[102] Moreover, this reasoning is helpful for analysis of "purely narratorial rendering" like this part of "Rothschild's Fiddle." But what about dialogic narratives like the book of Ruth?

The ideas of Tjupa seem to address this question because the selection of narrative information for direct speeches of the characters should always be connected with degree of intentionality or, in other words, with event expectancy. In essence, the character speaks about things that are connected with the routine of life or about things that have made or will make life different (i.e. eventful acts).

---

100. Schmid, *Narratology*, 208.
101. Schmid, *Нарратология*, 189–90.
102. Schmid, *Narratology*, 197–98.

Therefore, Schmid's model and Tjupa's model are complimentary and can be used in combination. They provide a systematic and fairly simple method to examine focalization and give helpful insights to study focalization in the Old Testament narratives.

3.7. Methodology of Studying Focalization in Old Testament Narratives

Ongoing refinements of Genette's theory during last few decades and the simultaneous intense study of the concept have made known to us new dimensions of focalization that cannot be ignored in the study of the subject. On the basis of the material presented in this chapter, it seems necessary to update Genette's initial typology and create a methodology that would be appropriate to study focalization in biblical narratives.

3.7.1. From Genette to Schmid

After considering a number of developments of Genette's notion of focalization, I came to the following conclusions that form the bases of my methodology. First, in order to stay in tune with Genette's original theory, I will resort to Jahn's understanding of focalization as "regulating, selecting and channeling narrative information."[103] The purpose of studying focalization then is to be able to answer the questions of what information was selected by the narrator and given to the reader and how this information is channeled to them. Knowing what was selected helps to assess the amount of information that the narrator shares with the readers or helps to assess the horizon of the readers. Horizon (of the readers and of the characters), therefore, becomes the key term in examining focalization in this work.

This brings inevitable changes to the initial typology of Genette. Instead of comparing what the narrator says with what the characters know, I will operate with the horizon of the readers in relation to the horizons of the characters, implying that the horizon of an omniscient narrator is always wider than the horizon of both the readers and characters. This step refines the definition of different types of focalization. I will consider the text as zero focalized (or non-focalized) when the readers know more than the characters (i.e. the

---

103. Jahn, "Focalization," in *Routledge Encyclopedia*, 173.

horizon of the readers is wider than the horizon of the characters). When the readers know less than the characters (i.e. the horizon of the readers is narrower than the horizon of the characters), the text is externally focalized. Cases when the readers know as much as the characters will be considered as internally focalized.

Finally, the answer to these questions "what" and "how" will be incomplete without answering the question "why," for one can truly understand what information was selected for the narrative and how it was channeled only by knowing the intentions of the narrator or logic of selectivity, and the technical choices of the narrator as they creates their narrative.

Since the process of creation of the narrative is well described by Schmid's model of narrative constitution, I will use Schmid's model with some modifications. Schmid identifies three steps in narrative constitution and shows that on each step the form of the narrative is affected by the chosen points of view. On the initial step of selection, the narrator uses perceptual, spatial, temporal, ideological, and sometimes linguistic points of view. Then on the second step of linearization, the number of points of view reduced to spatial, temporal, and ideological. Finally, on the level of verbalization, the narrator is guided only by ideological and linguistic points of view. I proposed that since the point of view and focalization are just two sides of the same coin,[104] it is legitimate to talk about focalization on each step of narrative constitution. Indeed, on the step of selection, the information is restricted (focalized) according to the spatial, temporal, ideological, and perceptual point of view. On the step of linearization, the information is further restricted according to ideological, spatial, and temporal points of view. The arrangement of information is also related to channeling. Finally, on the step of verbalization, the narrator still has to make some choices (for example, what kind of word forms to use).

Therefore, Schmid's model of narrative constitution (1) creates a structure for methodology of studying narrative from the very beginning of its constitution to the very choice of words and (2) allows the reader to track

---

[104]. According to the opinion of Tjupa expressed during discussion on conference "Belyie Chtenia" in State University of Humanity of Moscow, there is the following line of connection between point of view and focalization: "Narrative is always written with point of view; the point of view intends to reflect someone's horizon; and horizon means that this someone obtain a restricted (focalized) amount of information."

focalization on each level of narrative constitution. Accordingly, the study of the book of Ruth will be guided by three steps of Schmid's model: (1) selection of narrative events, (2) composition of narrative, and (3) presentation of narration. This leads to the following outline of the research.

3.7.2. The Outline of the Research

Chapter 4 of this work will be devoted to the analysis of narratological events of the book of Ruth. Each separate scene of the book will be examined in respect of its degree of eventfulness first according to Schmid's criteria and then according to the criteria of Tjupa. This should help to clarify the logic of selectivity of the narrator or the principle of focalization (i.e. selection of narrative information).

In chapter 5 I will consider the problem of composition of selected events, which consists of the problem of reorganization and linearization of narrative information. The question of this chapter is why the events in the book of Ruth appear in chronological order and how the narrator manages narrative information. Here my purpose will be to show that while the events of the book of Ruth are ordered chronologically, the narrator, nevertheless, purposefully withholds from the readers or shares with the readers certain information, creating a fascinating play of horizons between readers and characters and between characters.

Finally, in chapter 6 I will consider the problem of focalization on the level of presentation of the narrative. However, the elements that are traditionally considered on this level (such as style of speeches, the narrator's comments, etc.) will not be addressed in this work because they have been repeatedly treated in existing commentaries. Instead, chapter 6 will be committed to the study of correlation between *qatal* forms of the Hebrew verb and internal focalization – a correlation that has been identified heuristically. In this final portion of the work, I will attempt to find the theoretical background to the connection that was established empirically.

Therefore, with this work I will attempt to make an original contribution in three related fields of studies. First, it will be the area of general narratology. Staying with Genette's initial understanding of focalization as restriction of narrative information, I will propose to use Schmid's model of narrative constitution as the basis to examine focalization on the level of selection of narrative information, composition of narrative events, and presentation of the narrative.

Second, I will seek to make an original contribution to the field of Old Testament narratology by applying Schmid's model of narrative constitution as regard to focalization to the text of the book of Ruth. This will include (1) an examination of events selected by the narrator of the book with the view of their eventfulness (according to Schmid) and intentionality (according to Tjupa); (2) a demonstration of the play of horizons in the book of Ruth as a specific case of focalization through rearrangement of narrative information.

Finally, I intend to make a modest contribution to the area of Hebrew syntax. Examining the book of Ruth on the level of narrative presentation, I will demonstrate a strong correlation between passages with internal focalization and the use of *qatal* forms of the Hebrew verbs.

CHAPTER 4

Focalization on the Level of Selection of Narrative Information

In the previous chapter, focalization was defined as the selection of narrative information with respect to its completeness. The narrator selects certain episodes from the endless continuum of happenings and then ties them together to create a narrative. The process of selection, therefore, manifests the essential nature of the narrative: to divide the continuous flow of life into discrete units (events) and to tie them together by a certain ideological purpose.[1] Therefore, selectiveness of information inevitably creates lacunas in the story. The process of reading, however, is completely opposite. The readers following their natural desire to try to fill those lacunas and paint the complete picture in their imagination. Thus, they eliminate the fundamental mismatch between human experience, which is holistic and continual, and its inevitably discrete semiotic representation.[2] Commentaries are written exactly for this purpose: they help the readers to reconstruct the whole story from its narrative representation. However, this work presents narratological analysis, which, in contrast to commentaries, aims not to fill the gaps but to emphasize discreteness of the narrative as part of its cognitive organization.

This chapter is devoted to the selection of narrative information in the book of Ruth. The key question is: what are the principles the narrator uses in order to select narrative information? In other words, what is the logic of selectivity in the book of Ruth? In order to answer this question, three

---

1. See Tjupa, *Введение*, 20–21.
2. Tjupa, 19.

steps have to be taken. First, it is necessary to allocate episodes the narrator selects for the narrative. This fairly simple step will help to define the borders of the episodes. Second, the episodes have to be analyzed with a view of intentionality according to the guidelines proposed by Tjupa. This step will help to give a rough estimate of eventfulness and to understand what acts of the story should be considered as narratological events. Finally, third, in order to refine the conclusions made on previous step, it is helpful to evaluate each episode of the book with the view of the degree of eventfulness as it is proposed by Schmid.

4.1. Allocation of Episodes in the Book of Ruth

The first step of analysis of selected events is allocation of episodes of the narrative. According to Tjupa, in order to allocate episode from a narrative text, one has to monitor the change of at least one of three elements.

> ... the chain of imaginary events is manifested in the system of episodes that are put together into a solid chain of textual units that are characterized by cohesion of three elements: a) place, b) time, and c) action – the group of participants (actors or forces). In other words, the border between two adjacent episodes is marked by the shift in space, time lag or change in the group of participants.[3]

The dialogic nature of the book of Ruth also helps in allocation of episodes. As Thomas asserts,

> Dialogue novels are often explicitly organized around set-piece scenes where conversation is central to the ongoing action – for example, highly formalized and structured speech events such as the interview or the interrogation. In the latter case, what characters say and what they are doing while they speak are

---

3. Tjupa, *Анализ художественного текста*, 41.
  ... цепь воображаемых событий манифестируется системой эпизодов, которые слагаются в сплошную цепь участков текста, характеризующихся тройственным единством: а) места, б) времени и в) действия, точнее – состава актантов (действующих лиц или сил). Иначе говоря, граница двух соседних эпизодов знаменуется переносом в пространстве, разрывом во времени или переменой в составе персонажей." Translated by the author.

crucial in terms of the outcome of the "event" in which they are participating, that is, whether they get the job, give away crucial secrets, and so forth.[4]

Tjupa echoes this consideration by pointing out that each performative (character's utterance in the dialogues) is in essence a micro-event because it irreversibly changes the relationship between communicants.

> After a word of affection or hatred, after the word of insult, or admiration, accusation, threat, or concern etc., communicants cannot maintain their former relationship. Even the most active reversal of one's previous statement is incapable of eliminating it from the communicating situation.[5]

Following these principles makes it relatively easy to allocate the following episodes of the book of Ruth:[6]

Initial historical reference: In the days when the judges ruled (1:1a)
Prologue: Elimelech, Mahlon, and Chilion died (1:1b–5)
1) On the way to return to the land of Judah . . . (1:6–14)
2) See, your sister-in-law has gone . . . (1:15–18)
3) When they came to Bethlehem . . . (1:19–21)
   Intrusion: Summary of return (1:22)
   Intrusion: Introduction of Boaz (2:1)
4) At home: and Ruth said to Naomi . . . (2:2)
   Intrusion: Summary of Ruth's gleaning before meeting with Boaz
5) Behold, Boaz came from Bethlehem . . . (2:4)
6) Then Boaz said to his young man . . . (2:5–7)
7) Then Boaz said to Ruth . . . (2:8–13)
8) At mealtime . . . (2:14)

---

4. Thomas, *Fictional Dialogue*, Kindle locations 1052–1057.

5. Tjupa, *Введение*, 10, translated by the author. "После признания в любви или ненависти, после высказанного оскорбления, восхищения, обвинения, угрозы, опасения и т.п. коммуниканты уже не могут в полной мере сохранять неизменным прежнее состояние своих взаимоотношений. Никакой сколь угодно энергичный отказ от своего предыдущего высказывания не способен вполне устранить его из сложившейся коммуникативной ситуации."

6. The names of episodes above emphasize the markers of segmentation in the beginning of each episode. Sometimes a new episode is marked by the change of place and time (like "When they came to Bethlehem . . ." in episode 3) and, sometimes by the change of the group of participants (like "Then Boaz said to the elders and all the people" in episode 16).

9) When she rose to glean . . . (2:15–17)
10) And she went into the city . . . (2:18–22)
   Intrusion: Summary of Ruth's gleaning after meeting with Boaz
11) He is winnowing barley tonight . . . (3:1–5)
   Intrusion: Summary of Ruth's action before meeting with Boaz.
12) At midnight . . . (3:8–13)
13) In the morning . . . (3:14–15a)
   Intrusion: Then she went into the city (3:15b)
14) And when she came to her mother-in-law . . . (3:16–18)
15) Now Boaz had gone up to the gate . . . (4:1–8)
16) Then Boaz said to the elders and all the people . . . (4:9–12)

Epilogue: And she bore a son . . . (4:13–17a)

Final historical reference: He was the father of Jesse, the father of David (1:17b–22)

Apparently, the book consists of the story proper or the core narrative summarized in sixteen episodes (1:6–4:12) and bracketed by outer and inner frames. The outer frame comprises the initial and final historical references that link the story to a specific historical time period (1:1a and 1:17b–22). The inner frame of the story proper is represented by the prologue (1:1b–5) and the epilogue (4:13–17a). The story proper, which is going to be for us of particular interest, covers the period of about two months.[7]

4.2. Intentionality of Events

The next step of analysis involves the allocation of the events of the narrative. According to Tjupa, this includes (1) identification of eventful intentions that lead to full-fledged narratological events and (2) the search for the witness and the judge of each events.[8] Since Tjupa (following Lotman) defines the

---

7. This time period can be identified on the basis of two narrator's remarks: (1) וְהֵ֙מָּה֙ בָּ֤אוּ בֵ֣ית לֶ֔חֶם בִּתְחִלַּ֖ת קְצִ֥יר שְׂעֹרִֽים – "And they [Naomi and Ruth] came to Bethlehem at the beginning of barley harvest" (1:22), and (2) וַתִּדְבַּ֞ק בְּנַעֲר֥וֹת בֹּ֙עַז֙ לְלַקֵּ֔ט עַד־כְּל֥וֹת קְצִֽיר־הַשְּׂעֹרִ֖ים וּקְצִ֣יר הַחִטִּ֑ים וַתֵּ֖שֶׁב אֶת־חֲמוֹתָֽהּ – "So she [Ruth] kept close to the young women of Boaz, gleaning until the end of the barley and wheat harvests. And she lived with her mother-in-law." See Chisholm Jr., *Judges and Ruth*, 641.

8. Case studies proposed by Schmid and Tjupa show that under "event" they usually consider not a lengthy period of time, but a relatively short critical moment, the turning point of the narrative. For example, among the events named by Tjupa are the birth of kittens, the

event as a deviation from the norm, it is important to determine from the beginning what is the norm of the narrative, or, using terminology of Tjupa, what is the narrative world picture and the modality of the narrator of the story? As we will see in the next section, these questions emerge at the very outset of the study.

4.2.1. The Imperatives and the Convictions of the Narrator of the Book of Ruth

The study of the prologue of the book leads to hot debates over the question of the interpretation of the deaths of Elimelech and his sons: should the readers take their deaths as an act of divine judgment over the family for moving to Moab and marrying foreign wives?

There is no uniform agreement among the commentators on this matter. Campbell gives an example of early Jewish exegesis, which interprets this passage on the basis of sin and retribution. Therefore, the death of father and sons is attributed either to the sin of leaving Bethlehem and going to Moab and thus forsaking their God's people in the time of famine or to the sin of marring foreign women. However, Campbell himself favors an idea that the story of Naomi is parallel to the story of Job, for in both stories there is no "final answer to the question 'Why?' And, as in Job, there is going to be some forthright complaining done before the resolution begins to take shape."[9]

Block points to five features of the account that emphasize the possible dependence of the tragedy on the move to Moab and intercultural marriage.[10] Berman also agrees that the deaths of Elimelech, Machlon, and Chilion are "reflective of sin and attendant divine punishment" for which he gives

---

death of son, and the moment of butterfly coming out of cocoon. Only one example names the whole evening as separate event. See Tjupa, Введение, 31.

9. Campbell, *Ruth*, 58–59.

10. Among Block's arguments are: (1) the negative connotation of the phrase "took wives"; (2) Deuteronomic prohibition of marrying pagans; (3) curse that related to marriage to foreigners in the Deuteronomic covenant; (4) the childlessness of Naomi's sons and the barrenness of Ruth and Orpah; and (5) Naomi's loneliness. Block, *Judges, Ruth*, 628–29.

four reasons.¹¹ However, Chisholm, after studying the reasons of Block and Berman, suggests his counter-arguments¹² that lead him to conclude that

> . . . the tragic deaths of Elimelech and his sons should not be interpreted as acts of divine judgment because there is not enough evidence in the immediate context or in the broader context of the Old Testament to sustain such a theory. On the contrary, it would seem that their deaths, like the famine and their move to Moab, are incidental details that set the stage for the story to follow, rather than main themes that should drive one's interpretation of the story.¹³

Schipper comes to the same conclusion, calling attribution of the deaths to divine punishment as speculative because "YHWH does not punish or show disfavor toward anyone in the Book of Ruth."¹⁴

It is true that the prologue of the book does not link the deaths of the men with divine judgment. However, it is structured to raise such a reflection in the mind of some readers. Putting together the sojourn to Moab and the death of Elimelech, the marriage, the childlessness, and the death of Machlon and Chilion, the narrator inevitably calls the readers to find the connection between these events. This implicit ambiguity is very important for the beginning of the story, for it implies different plot lines and the story appears far from being trivial, which, according to McKeown, "is one of the strengths of the story because it relates well to life as we know it."¹⁵

Nevertheless, some life imperatives and convictions of the story world are easily identifiable from the text of the book.¹⁶ Among them one can name the imperative of God being the Lord of the universe and the Lord over his

---

11. Berman, "Ancient Hermeneutics," 22–38. Berman interprets the phrase "and they remained there" as the decision of the family to settle down in Moab. He considers that the use of "also" in 1:5 in relation to Elimelech's sons confirms the idea of retaliation for the sins of the father and the sons. He also emphasizes that Naomi attributes the deaths of her husband and sons to God and that the book in general pictures God as ultimate cause of all.

12. Chisholm Jr., *Judges and Ruth*, 595–98.

13. Chisholm Jr., 599.

14. Schipper, *Ruth*, 88.

15. McKeown, *Ruth*, 18.

16. As Tjupa notes, biblical narrators traditionally operate in the scope of an imperative world picture and modality of conviction. See Tjupa, *Введение*, 82, 91.

people,[17] which also includes the concept of retribution: YHWH rewards both good and bad people according to their behavior.[18] There are also imperatives that relate to practical issues of life. For example, the imperative about levirate marriage that implies that the brother of a deceased husband should marry the widow to save the name of his brother,[19] or the general conviction that the widow has to return to her family.[20] One of the most important imperatives of the book of Ruth is a general negative attitude toward Moabites.[21] These and other imperatives constitute the norms or the imperatives and convictions of the narrative world of the book of Ruth. The narrator uses them as a background to picture the events of the story that are presented as violations from the norm, the incidents that do not conform to the accepted standards.

4.2.2. The First Event of the Book of Ruth

The first act of the story proper begins in 1:6 when the narrator informs the reader about the decision of Naomi to return to her motherland. To this information the narrator adds the reason of Naomi's move: "She heard . . . that the LORD visited his people and given them food" (1:6). This description of Naomi's mind becomes the first step in building the imperatives of the story world. YHWH, who is God of Israel, blesses his people in their land, not in the land of Moab. This gives a delicate hint to the reason of Naomi's tragedy and explains her desire to return to Bethlehem.

The text attributes three verbs (קוּם "to arise," שׁוּב "to return," and שָׁמַע "to hear") to Naomi for they all have feminine singular forms while the subject of the sentence is plural – "she and her daughters-in-law." Because of this inconsistency, as Schipper points out, "several versions smooth out the syntax of this verse. For example, LXX[B] read the second and third verbs as feminine plurals ('they returned' and 'they heard'), and the Syr. reads the third verb as a feminine plural."[22]

---

17. Hubbard, *Book of Ruth*, 69.
18. LaCocque, *Ruth*, 72.
19. Schipper, *Ruth*, 103–04.
20. Bush, *Ruth/Esther*, 75.
21. Schipper, *Ruth*, 38–44. In the section "Exogamy and Ethnicity" Schipper considers that one can read the book of Ruth with the view of a negative as well as a positive assessment of Moabites. See discussion of this topic by Neil Glover, "Your People," 293–313.
22. Schipper, *Ruth*, 85.

However, the use of feminine singular is quite understandable because Naomi is the only one of three women who, being a part of God's people, has a hope for his blessings. This creates the first eventful intention in the book that starts when the readers learn that Naomi goes to Bethlehem not alone but in the company of two Moabite daughters-in-law. This should look surprising to the readers. Even if there is no direct connection between the family tragedy and the sojourn in Moab, it is still obvious that the God of Israel blesses only his people in their land; verse 6 says nothing about foreigners. Grievance and discontent would have had to stop daughters-in-law from going to the country the God of which did not provide their husbands, Machlon and Chilion, with offspring. Nevertheless, they go against the tide and accompany Naomi to Bethlehem.

The imperative world picture and the modality of conviction force Naomi to move the situation back to its normal course. Therefore, she tries to convince her daughters-in-law to return to Moab, to the house of their mothers:

וַתֹּאמֶר נָעֳמִי לִשְׁתֵּי כַלֹּתֶיהָ לֵכְנָה שֹׁבְנָה אִשָּׁה לְבֵית אִמָּהּ
יַעֲשֶׂה יהוה עִמָּכֶם חֶסֶד כַּאֲשֶׁר עֲשִׂיתֶם עִם־הַמֵּתִים וְעִמָּדִי׃
יִתֵּן יהוה לָכֶם וּמְצֶאןָ מְנוּחָה אִשָּׁה בֵּית אִישָׁהּ

> But Naomi said to her two daughters-in-law, "Go, return each of you to her mother's house. May the LORD deal kindly with you, as you have dealt with the dead and with me. The LORD grant that you may find rest, each of you in the house of her husband!" (1:8–9a)

In three stages in Naomi's commands to her daughters-in-law Baylis recognizes Naomi's "common reasoning,"[23] which reflects modality of conviction and imperative world picture. When Naomi urges Ruth and Orpah to return to their own mothers, to find husbands from their own people and then bear their own children, she suggests for them to use this last chance and make a fresh start. She does not see how they can get married according to the levirate marriage law in Deuteronomy 25 and, therefore, concludes that Ruth and Orpah do not have opportunity to marry legally in Israel. Therefore, in the narrator's imperative narrative world picture, the only hope for Naomi's daughters-in-law can be found outside the restrictive laws of Israel's God.

---

23. Baylis, "Naomi," 413–31.

Consequently, in the final address Naomi openly calls Ruth to "return (שׁוּב) after her sister-in-law."

The verb שׁוּב is highly ideological in this context. In Deuteronomy 30:1–10 it is used in order to call Israel to return to Yahweh, but Naomi uses this verb to insist that Ruth return to Moab and Moabite gods which corresponds to the imperative world picture.

The fact that she blesses her daughters-in-law and wishes that YHWH would give them mercy makes some readers of the book puzzled. How is it that an Israelite woman blesses foreigners with YHWH blessing? In fact, Naomi does not deviate from imperative world picture, but rather confirms it. In her mind the God of Israel is the God of all nations, and punishment that she deserves does not actually apply to her daughters-in-law, because they acted with kindness toward her sons. Therefore, all the words of Naomi in her first address to her daughters-in-law absolutely fit into imperative world picture.

But, what about the daughters-in-law? Their answer consists of further eventful intentions. They do not simply follow Naomi for some sentimental reasons but want to return with her to her people. If they would stop at saying that they just want to return with Naomi and omit "to your people," together with the report about them crying and weeping, one could put their desire to simple loyalty or affection. But the little detail that they want to return to the people of Israel makes a big change in the reflection of the narrative. This is the first attempt to transform the normal flow of life into a narratological event. However, the attempt is feeble in comparison to Naomi's persistent and reasoned address. Therefore, by verse 10 the event has not occurred yet, and the narrator is still preparing the readers for it.

Naomi, therefore, returns to her task with her second address. The second speech of Naomi is longer and has a slight narrative element in it. However, as regards to the content of the narrative, it continues to demonstrate an imperative world picture and the same modality of conviction. Naomi wants her daughters to return because there is no way they can benefit from the old tradition of levirate marriage.[24] Several imperatives are encountered here.

---

24. This tradition is certainly in view here because by the end of the book the elders in their blessing wish Boaz to have the family like Judah and Tamar. It becomes especially clear taking into consideration the fact that Tamar had to wait when Shelah, the youngest son of Judah, grows up.

First, the imperative that an old woman cannot get pregnant. Even Sarah, who was not the subject of God's wrath, needed God's miracle to get pregnant – to say nothing of Naomi, for she had YHWH going out against her. In the given situation, according to the imperatives of Naomi, there is no way she and her daughters-in-law can overcome these limits, which means (from a narratological point of view) no event can happen at this stage of the narrative. The narrator shows this by picturing the women crying with loud voices and weeping, reaffirming the uneventfulness of the moment.

Nevertheless, verse 14 makes another step toward a true narratological event. While Orpah decides to stay within imperative limits, Ruth crosses social boundaries. Ruth's decision is not emphasized yet, for it is not supplied with appropriate persuasion. But the whole construction of the phrase points toward the seriousness of Ruth's intention.

Berquist, looking at Ruth's decision from the sociological position, emphasizes that by making her decision to cling to Naomi, Ruth, in contrast to Orpah, *deviates* not only from her mother-in-law's command but also from *standard* expectations for young widows. The very verb "to cling" used in this context underlines deviation from the norm:

> The Hebrew word "cling, cleave" (דָּבַק) is a moderately common term, occurring 40 times in the G stem. The most frequent Hebrew Bible use of this term is in the phrase "to cling to God." There are only eight references to clinging between humans, and four of these appear in Ruth. Of the other references, perhaps the best known is Gen. 2.24: "a man leaves his father and his mother and clings to his wife, and they become one flesh." This clinging between a man and a woman relates to love, to marriage, and/or to intimate sexual relations. Furthermore, דָּבַק refers to the male role in initiating marriage. Outside of Ruth, the term "cling" never describes a woman's act. This makes Ruth 1:14 all the more striking. When Ruth clings to Naomi, Ruth takes the male role in initiating a relationship of formal commitment, similar to marriage.[25]

---

25. Berquist, "Role Dedifferentiation," 23–37.

The bold move of Ruth demonstrates another eventful intention in the book. According to McKeown,

> Ruth's choice is remarkable because it is out of the ordinary and represents a most unusual step of loyalty and bravery. Ruth's commitment is all the more remarkable because of the lack of encouragement that she received from Naomi. Ruth's decision to care for her mother-in-law was not only a selfless decision but also, at least at this stage, a thankless one.[26]

Berquist points that she "remain[s] in the female role of daughter-in-law even though there is no longer any basis for that role" and takes the male role of clinging to Naomi as a husband might be forced to do. It was not a trivial step, which Berquist defines not as role replacement, but as "role addition."[27]

The last attempt of Naomi to put Ruth to the straightway starts with the important particle הִנֵּה "behold," which will play a significant role here and in the whole book. Here, it seems the particle further awakened eventful intentions in the mind of Ruth. From down-to-earth topics, Naomi now turns to the ideological idea of identity – she calls Ruth to follow the example of her sister-in-law to return to the homeland and home gods which, again, corresponds to the traditional imperative world picture and the modality of conviction.

The most eventful scene of the first chapter, then, is verses 16–17 – the moment when Ruth verbalizes the decision that she made in verse 14. Several elements lead to this conclusion. Ruth's speech starts from the phrase with jussive verb אַל־תִּפְגְּעִי־בִי, which means in this context "do not press me" and reflects an attempt to deviate from normal behavior. Ruth does not simply refuse to comply with general expectations but affirms her decision with several phrases that demonstrate her eventful intentions. What she says stands in contrast to the narrator's imperative world picture. So, when Ruth says that she will go wherever Naomi will go, she uses the verb הָלַךְ "to go" which contradicts Naomi's repeated שׁוּב "go back."[28] Then with the choice of the

---

26. McKeown, *Ruth*, 31.
27. Berquist, "Role Dedifferentiation," 27.
28. Hubbard, *Ruth*, 117.

verb לוּן "lodge" instead of common verbs יָשַׁב or שָׁכַן "to dwell" or "to live" the narrator "highlights Ruth's lifelong commitment."[29]

Bush shows that Ruth's speech has chiastic structure with the nominal sentence pair "your people will be my people and your God, my God" staying in the center of the chiasm reflecting the crux of the whole statement.[30] With words "your people will be my people" Ruth again crosses a cultural boundary and shows that her choice differs from the choice of Orpah.

Smith discusses three approaches to interpret Ruth's words: (1) as an expression of conversion of judaization, (2) as expressions of cementing bonds, and (3) as making a treaty or a covenant. He criticizes the first two and supports the last approach. The first view is rejected because of the "relatively minor role that religious observance and belief play in the text." The second view, "does not address the larger conceptual framework" of Ruth's speech. The third view, to the contrary, is supported and developed. According to Smith,

> ... with her words Ruth establishes a family relationship with Naomi that transcends the death of the male who had connected them, and in fact this relationship represents a family tie closer than that expressed by the formal status of former in-laws.[31]

The final phrase of Ruth's utterance is also highly eventful because it reflects her commitment in its extreme for it goes even beyond the death line. In fact, Ruth's answer is so straightforward, detailed, and convincing that Naomi does not even know what to say to that and finally concedes.[32] Naomi's reaction to Ruth's commitment emphasizes the status of eventfulness of the moment. Against the background of the problems launched by Naomi, Ruth's speech does elevate the conversation on the way from Bethlehem to Moab to the level of a true narratological event.

In the final verses of chapter 1 (19–22) the narrative flow returns to its usual framework. The event that happened on the way to Bethlehem is masked by the following passages. First, during the scene of entering Bethlehem Naomi continues to operate within the imperative world picture. Answering the

---

29. Hubbard, *Ruth*, 117.
30. Bush, *Ruth/Esther*, 74.
31. Hyman, "Questions and Changing," 189–201.
32. Hyman, 198.

question of the women of Bethlehem, she presents the God of Israel as the Lord of the universe who determines all the events of life. She is convinced that he makes decisions independently of her efforts and apparently sees the tragedy of her family as inevitable destiny, the act of God's own hand.

The chosen naming for God – שַׁדַּי translated in the ESV as "Almighty" – reflects Naomi's modality of conviction. Baylis points that this name of God is used in Old Testament forty-eight times, thirty-one of which are used in the book of Job. This brings him to the following conclusion:

> Job often used this name to point out the all-powerful nature of God in contrast to his own helpless state. Naomi used it here in the same sense. She felt that this all-powerful God had cursed a poor, helpless widow without a cause.[33]

Previous hardships forced Naomi to see life as the stage with God being the singular real player who acts independently without any obvious reasons, where the acts of people cannot change the situation for better or for worse. Therefore, she continues to stay within the scope of imperative world picture and adapts to the new situation by changing her name and identity.[34]

4.2.3. The Second Event of the Book of Ruth

New eventful intentions start to appear after the return to Bethlehem. In 1:22 after stating the fact of Naomi and Ruth's[35] return, the narrator informs the reader that they "came to Bethlehem at the beginning of barley harvest." This statement stands in contrast with the information about famine in the beginning of the book and breaks an established atmosphere of despair that the readers may feel after the stressful farewell scene.

The reference to Boaz in 2:1 creates the same effect. At this moment in the plot, it points to the coming narratological event because it introduces a new figure to the plot and emphasizes one characteristic of Boaz that distinguishes him from other male characters of the book. Namely, Boaz is called אִישׁ גִּבּוֹר

---

33. Baylis, "Naomi," 426n436.
34. Hyman, "Questions and Changing," 193.
35. One possible reason for Ruth being designated by the long name can be attributed to the desire of the narrator to mask the eventfulness of Ruth's declaration and return the reader to the imperative world picture that the people of Bethlehem reflect. Thus the narrator designates Ruth from the point of view of people of Bethlehem.

חַיִל "a worthy man." According to Schipper, this highly ambiguous definition among others may mean wealthy landholder, a powerful, influential or competent person, a mighty warrior, and a person with honor or high character. Schipper then concludes that "with the exception of a mighty warrior, all of these meanings could describe Boaz at various points in the story."[36] But what also unites these sets of meaning is the distinctiveness of Boaz's figure to which the narrator attempts to refer. It reflects eventful intention for it stands in contrast to other depersonalized male characters of the story.

The eventful intentions continue to grow in the following scene (2:2). Ruth is pictured within the scope of the imperative world picture; any deviation from the norm for her becomes an event. Therefore, the plan to go to the field and glean should not be taken as something extraordinary, but as expected behavior of Ruth, who decided to shoulder the burden of taking care of her elderly mother-in-law.

וַתֹּאמֶר רוּת הַמּוֹאֲבִיָּה אֶל־נָעֳמִי אֵלְכָה־נָּא הַשָּׂדֶה וַאֲלַקֳטָה בַּשִּׁבֳּלִים אַחַר אֲשֶׁר אֶמְצָא־חֵן בְּעֵינָיו

And Ruth the Moabite said to Naomi, "Let me go to the field and glean among the ears of grain after him in whose sight I shall find favor." (2:2a)

The purpose of this introductory dialogue is not to "make subtle reference" back to Moab and not to pick up on the theme of the barley harvest, as Linafelt suggests,[37] but to create the eventful intention that will help to emphasize the event when it comes. Understanding the initial scene as the reflection of the narrator's imperative world picture helps to form the opinion about the legality of Ruth's action. Indeed, there are a number of commentaries that pay attention to the plans of Ruth to ask permission before she starts to glean. In an attempt to explain why she had to ask permission, some suggest that Ruth simply did not have rights to glean because as a Moabite woman she was not under the protection of the Torah.[38] According to another opinion, Ruth had all legal rights to glean but either did not know this or was too shy

---

36. Schipper, *Ruth*, 112.
37. Linafelt and Beal, *Ruth and Esther*, 26.
38. LaCocque, *Ruth*, 62–63.

to realize them.³⁹ Still another opinion says that the reason Ruth was going to seek for favor is because "she wanted to gather among the sheaves and not just pick up the grains that had fallen on the ground," which was more than the law entitled.⁴⁰

Whatever the regulations of the law were, according to the narrator's imperative world picture, Ruth should put her legal rights below her ethnicity and see herself as being on the lowest level of society.⁴¹ She does not have any intention to violate the law or to do anything that would go outside the regular legal or religious practice of Israel. That is why she is so surprised by Boaz's generosity because his actions look very eventful on the background of her imperative world picture.

Ruth does not simply go out to glean in the field but hopes to find someone who would give her favor and, therefore, would bring changes to her life. The expectation of someone is in essence the expectation of an event that would break the routine of life and change the established practice. This expectation of the event is further heightened with reference to Ruth's occasional crossing of the border of the field of Elimelech. This happening is called accidental in the text (וַיִּקֶר מִקְרֶהָ) because coincidence always breaks the normal flow of life.

Let us not forget that all this information (the beginning of barley harvest, the figure of Boaz, the short conversation between Ruth and Naomi, and the report about the crossing of the border of Elimelech's field) does not present the narratological event, but only envisages one. In everything else it stays within the scope of the imperative world picture that the narrator posed in the beginning of the book. The beginning of harvest season, clan structure of the Israel society, a daughter-in-law who is asking permission of her mother-in-law to go out of the house, foreigners/sojourners and widows at the field of the Judah – all these reflect imperative world pictures of an ordinary way of life. Even the following scenes (the arrival of Boaz and the conversation between Boaz and the foreman) do not change cultural imperatives, though they continue to prepare the reader for the central event of the chapter.

---

39. Chisholm Jr., *Judges and Ruth*, 628n644.
40. See Chisholm Jr., *Judges and Ruth*, 628n644, reffering to Lim, "Book of Ruth," 261–82.
41. Schipper, *Ruth*, 115. Schipper considers that Ruth had special status as "household of Naomi." However, it is obvious that she does not take advantage of it. It may be that Naomi had first to approve Ruth's status publicly before her daughter-in-law could exercise her legal rights.

The arrival of Boaz and the following scene reflect the imperative world picture which sees YHWH as the giver of all blessings of life. Then, in the following conversation between Boaz and the foreman, the foreman's derogatory feedback about Ruth reflects the traditional negative attitude toward Moabites. This stands in contrast to Boaz's interest in a young Moabite woman who comes to glean in his field.

Describing the first words of Boaz after his visual contact with Ruth, the narrator does not indicate what was the motivation (or intention) behind Boaz's question. There are three views on Boaz's motives: (1) desire to help to the stranger, (2) sexual desire for a young woman, and (3) desire to rebuke the foreman for letting a stranger glean in his field. The last version, which is, according to LaCocque, supported by an anonymous rabbi in *Ruth Rabbah*, who says: "It is as if he reproached [his foreman] for allowing gleaning,"[42] seems interesting in light of the narrator's imperative world picture. For it is not clear if Boaz would help Ruth if she were not connected with Elimelech's family. However, the narrator does not share with the readers such gentle nuances of the character's traits. Instead, he pays more attention to the actions of Boaz after he realized who Ruth is.

The meeting with Boaz itself does not consist of anything abnormal. But a simple happening becomes an event when the readers find out the attitude of Boaz toward Ruth. It seems that Boaz clearly understands Ruth's situation and, therefore, jumps directly to the matter that is the most important for Ruth at this moment – namely how to stay attached to one particular field and one particular field owner.[43] This nuance is subtly noted by Nielsen, who considers that verse 7 denotes that Ruth is taking a short break in the work which "indirectly raises the question, Where is Ruth to continue, here or elsewhere? Boaz *anticipates* the question by asking her to stay in his field."[44]

Therefore, the meeting itself was not an event, but the attitude of Boaz toward Ruth makes this meeting eventful. There were three obstacles that could prevent Ruth from gleaning on in the field of Boaz. First, if the fields

---

42. Bos, "Out of the Shadows," 37–67.

43. This need was announced by Ruth in the beginning of the chapter when she shares with Naomi the desire to find someone "in whose sight I shall find favor" (2:2).

44. Nielsen, *Ruth*, 58. Emphasis added.

have not been fenced off, she could easily cross the border and be in the field that belongs to someone else. Therefore, Boaz admonishes Ruth:

וַיֹּאמֶר בֹּעַז אֶל־רוּת הֲלוֹא שָׁמַעַתְּ בִּתִּי אַל־תֵּלְכִי לִלְקֹט בְּשָׂדֶה אַחֵר וְגַם לֹא תַעֲבוּרִי מִזֶּה וְכֹה תִדְבָּקִין עִם־נַעֲרֹתָי: עֵינַיִךְ בַּשָּׂדֶה אֲשֶׁר־יִקְצֹרוּן וְהָלַכְתְּ אַחֲרֵיהֶן

> Then Boaz said to Ruth, "Now, listen, my daughter, do not go to glean in another field or leave this one, but keep close to my young women. Let your eyes be on the field that they are reaping, and go after them." (2:8–9a)

The second need was to make sure that הַנְּעָרִים "male workers" would not remove her from the field:

הֲלוֹא צִוִּיתִי אֶת־הַנְּעָרִים לְבִלְתִּי נָגְעֵךְ

> Have I not charged the young men not to touch you? (2:9b)

Chisholm considers on this matter,

> Perhaps the workers typically "roughed up" anyone who tried to mix in with the bundlers without being granted permission to do so. Apparently, Boaz's male workers served as a security force, making sure only authorized personnel were in the field . . .[45]

Then, the third obstacle that could prevent Ruth from gleaning in Boaz's field was the need for water supply.

וְצָמִת וְהָלַכְתְּ אֶל־הַכֵּלִים וְשָׁתִית מֵאֲשֶׁר יִשְׁאֲבוּן הַנְּעָרִים:

> And when you are thirsty, go to the vessels and drink what the young men have drawn. (2:9c)

The intensity of Boaz's first address shows that Boaz decided to make the most of this meeting. As Holmstedt puts it, "we do not know the extent of his plan; but we do know that Boaz conceives of it quickly and implements it immediately. Boaz wastes no time telling Ruth what to do in the future."[46] But it is not the generosity, understanding, courtesy or tenderness of Boaz that

---

45. Chisholm Jr., *Judges and Ruth*, 630. Another opinion that Chisholm argues with belongs to Nielsen who suggests that the word נָגַע "to touch" has in view "sexual attack." See Nielsen, *Ruth*, 58n90. According to Chisholm "this view seems far-fetched in this context."

46. Holmstedt, *Ruth*, 127.

surprise Ruth, but the generosity, understanding, courtesy and tenderness toward a Moabite woman. His actions look very eventful on the background of Ruth's imperative world picture:

וַתִּפֹּל עַל־פָּנֶיהָ וַתִּשְׁתַּחוּ אָרְצָה וַתֹּאמֶר אֵלָיו מַדּוּעַ מָצָאתִי חֵן בְּעֵינֶיךָ לְהַכִּירֵנִי וְאָנֹכִי נָכְרִיָּה׃

Then she fell on her face, bowing to the ground, and said to him, "Why have I found favor in your eyes, that you should take notice of me, since I am a foreigner?" (2:10)

According to Schipper, the word נָכְרִיָּה translated by ESV as "foreigner" "conveys the multiple nuances" and terms like "resident alien" or even "Moabite" do not adequately reflect its meaning.[47] But this ambiguity does not prevent the readers from understanding that what Boaz is doing goes against Ruth's understanding of the norm and greatly exceeds her expectations.

The first words of Boaz toward Ruth go beyond the limits of an imperative world picture and therefore start the second event of the book. In the following scenes that are placed one after another without any delay, while the eventful status of the meeting only grows.

It shouldn't be hard to answer this question because Ruth explicitly enquires of Boaz about his motivation and Boaz, in turn, does not conceal the true reasons for his actions:

וַיַּעַן בֹּעַז וַיֹּאמֶר לָהּ הֻגֵּד הֻגַּד לִי כֹּל אֲשֶׁר־עָשִׂית אֶת־חֲמוֹתֵךְ אַחֲרֵי מוֹת אִישֵׁךְ וַתַּעַזְבִי אָבִיךְ וְאִמֵּךְ וְאֶרֶץ מוֹלַדְתֵּךְ וַתֵּלְכִי אֶל־עַם אֲשֶׁר לֹא־יָדַעַתְּ תְּמוֹל שִׁלְשׁוֹם׃
יְשַׁלֵּם יהוה פָּעֳלֵךְ וּתְהִי מַשְׂכֻּרְתֵּךְ שְׁלֵמָה מֵעִם יהוה אֱלֹהֵי יִשְׂרָאֵל אֲשֶׁר־בָּאת לַחֲסוֹת תַּחַת־כְּנָפָיו׃

But Boaz answered her, "All that you have done for your mother-in-law since the death of your husband has been fully told to me, and how you left your father and mother and your native land and came to a people that you did not know before. The LORD repay you for what you have done, and a full reward be

---

47. Schipper, *Ruth*, 123. To traditional understandings of the term Schipper adds one more variant of interpretation. By calling herself נָכְרִיָּה "Ruth may be identifying herself as another man's wife or as part of another household or clan."

given you by the LORD, the God of Israel, under whose wings you have come to take refuge!" (2:11–13)

Note, that in answering Ruth's question, Boaz signifies the relevancy of her decision to follow Naomi – something that Naomi did not recognize. Boaz, in contrast, points to the event as a remarkable decision and therefore witnesses that Ruth's decision to follow Naomi was a true event against the background of an imperative world picture. Boaz favors Ruth because of the good deeds she has done for Naomi, not because she is part of Elimelech's clan.[48]

All his speech is designed to stress Ruth's decision as an important event in the story. Ziegler pays attention to the way Boaz's speech is introduced. The combination of two separate verbs – עָנָה "to answer" and אָמַר "to say" – has "the force of an official pronouncement, rather than a private communication."[49] Therefore Boaz witnesses for Ruth's decision as an event worthy of admiration in contrast to the foreman whose speech starts with the same combination of verbs but stays as anti-eventful opposition to Boaz's opinion.

The initial clause – הֻגֵּד הֻגַּד לִי "[it] has been fully told to me" – shows that the people of Bethlehem already knew the incident all along. According to Holmstedt, the infinitive absolute here functions "as an open-ended adverb" which is used to emphasize the way it modifies the verb and has "open-ended semantics." This means that the readers can "insert the most contextually appropriate modifier." Holmstedt suggests several ways of translation and leaves the text to the "reader to come up with other, perhaps equally appropriate, options."[50] If the modifier is actually open-ended, one of the possible translations of the infinitive הֻגֵּד is "certainly" – the modifier then points to the relevance of Ruth's decision in the eyes of Boaz. He could not miss what she did for her mother-in-law.

---

48. LaCocque, *Ruth*, 65.

49. Ziegler, *Ruth*, Kindle Locations 4296–4297. Ziegler gives some examples where these verbs are paired: Gen 24:50; 27:37; 31:43; 40:18; Exodus 4:1; 24:3; Number 11:28. It seems that whenever this combination is used, the speaking character plays a role of witness and judge and emphasizes the high degree of eventfulness of the action they are talking about.

50. Holmstedt suggests two possible translations: (1) with manner modification: "it has been thoroughly reported to me," which means "I know everything relevant about you"; and (2) with temporal modification: "it was just recently reported to me." See Hyman, "Questions and Changing," 197.

Some commentaries point to the unusual collocation of the verb עָשָׂה "to do" with the following preposition אֶת. In two other passages of the book (1:8 and 2:19) the verb is used with the preposition עִם.[51] Holmsteadt sees in it a "subtle cue distinguishing Boaz linguistically."[52] But consideration of the eventfulness provides an additional instrument for interpretation of this phrase. In 1:8 and 2:19 the verb עָשָׂה is used by Naomi in relation to the long periods of time. In 1:8 Naomi is talking about the period of ten years during which her daughters-in-law demonstrated kindness toward her sons and her husband. In 2:19 the same combination of verb and preposition עִם appears twice with slight variations as part of Ruth's answer. Again Ruth refers to the whole day of gleaning. In contrast, Boaz in 2:11 points not to the period of time but to Ruth's decision underlining the eventfulness of the moment, focusing on the specific decision of Ruth.

Hawk emphasizes the distinctiveness of Ruth's act in the eyes of Boaz by indicating that Boaz "draws attention to two actions that have come to his attention":

> First, he [Boaz] knows that Ruth has remained loyal to Naomi, even though she could have gone back to her own people after the death of her husband. Secondly, he knows that she has left her own people and native land in order to settle with a new people in a new place.[53]

In the rest of the utterance, Boaz underlines the significance of Ruth's act by comparing it with the decision of Abraham to migrate to the promise land. According to Trible, Ruth's decision seems even more radical than the decision of Abraham, who in contrast to Ruth had wife and possessions, calling and promises of God. Therefore, Trible concludes, "not even Abraham's leap of faith surpasses this decision of Ruth's."[54]

---

51. See, for example, Schipper, *Ruth*, 123.
52. Holmstedt, *Ruth*, 127.
53. Hawk, *Ruth*, 81.
54. Trible, *God and the Rhetoric*, 173. Trible goes on to say that Ruth's decision "has also reversed sexual allegiance" because she committed herself to the old woman instead of looking for a husband. Whether or not Boaz as a character had all these in mind, it may well reflect the narrator's point of view and certainly does not escape the attention of the readers.

Therefore, in this episode Boaz plays the role of the witness and the judge who recognizes Ruth's act as an event. Ruth, from her part, recognizes the act of Boaz as outstanding as she affirms in the following statement:

וַתֹּאמֶר אֶמְצָא־חֵן בְּעֵינֶיךָ אֲדֹנִי כִּי נִחַמְתָּנִי וְכִי דִבַּרְתָּ עַל־לֵב
שִׁפְחָתֶךָ וְאָנֹכִי לֹא אֶהְיֶה כְּאַחַת שִׁפְחֹתֶיךָ׃

> Then she said, "I have found favor in your eyes, my lord, for you have comforted me and spoken kindly to your servant, though I am not one of your servants." (2:13)

The eventful status of this episode is emphasized in the phrase אֶמְצָא־חֵן "find favor," which Ruth repeats three times in verses 2, 10, and 13. Schipper compares Ruth's words with similar expression of Ziba, who thanked David for granting him all of Mephibosheth's land (2 Sam 16:4). Since both Ruth and Ziba speak after they have been shown favor, Schipper, with reference to Callaham, comes to the conclusion that their words reflect "epistemic modality," in which "speakers express their judgments about the factual status of a proposition":

> Ruth makes her *judgment* through a deduction based on Boaz's words just as Ziba makes his *judgment* through a deduction based on David's words. Unlike Ruth, Ziba does not state the evidence for his deduction.[55]

Besides, Ruth underlines the extraordinary status of this meeting by referring to Boaz as "the lord" and to herself as "maidservant," thus acknowledging, from one side, the big distance between her and Boaz, and, from another side, the enormous generosity of Boaz toward her.[56]

This distance tends to reduce even more in the episode of mealtime:

וַיֹּאמֶר לָה בֹעַז לְעֵת הָאֹכֶל גֹּשִׁי הֲלֹם וְאָכַלְתְּ מִן־הַלֶּחֶם וְטָבַלְתְּ
פִּתֵּךְ בַּחֹמֶץ וַתֵּשֶׁב מִצַּד הַקּוֹצְרִים וַיִּצְבָּט־לָהּ קָלִי וַתֹּאכַל
וַתִּשְׂבַּע וַתֹּתַר׃

> And at mealtime Boaz said to her, "Come here and eat some bread and dip your morsel in the wine." So she sat beside the reapers, and he passed to her roasted grain. (2:14)

---

55. Schipper, *Ruth*, 124. Emphasis added.
56. Hawk, *Ruth*, 83.

Several nuances of this verse are discussed in critical commentaries. The first matter is if the clause "And at mealtime" should be interpreted as part of the narrator's discourse or as the beginning of the direct speech attributed to Boaz. Schipper advocates the first option, because LXX^L, Targum, Vulg., and Syr. support interpretation of this clause as the narrator's discourse and only a few other old Greek witnesses read the clause as the beginning of Boaz's dialogue.[57] At the same time, Holmstedt considers this prepositional clause to be part of reported speech because of its unusual placement. Indeed, it would have been quite easy for the narrator to situate the prepositional phrase in the beginning of the sentence.[58]

There are narratological reasons to consider this clause as the words of the narrator. Presented this way, the scene unfolds before the reader as an ordinary lunch break that happens every day. However, the narrator takes this relatively ordinary event of communal meal and converts it into a narratological event. It seems that he does it by contrasting quite ordinary details of the entourage against very eventful actions of Boaz. Indeed, the narrator informs the readers that this scene happens "at the meal time" assuming the ordinary part of the working day. However, according to Linafelt, only so-called "reapers" (the official workers of Boaz) had access to this food. This would exclude "gleaners" and certainly exclude Ruth as a foreigner. But the invitation of Ruth to come and eat turns simple eating into the scene of acceptance.

The bread, the vinegar, and the roasted grain (which Block calls "the staple of Israel's diet, as it was in the broader ancient Near Eastern world"[59]) become special food when it is served by Boaz personally. Moreover, the text uses the verb צָבַט which being *hapax legomenon* may carry more special meaning than simply "to reach" or "to pass." For example, in the given context the idea of Schipper to translate this verb as "to heap up," that is to put together a considerable amount of grain (as in Ruth 2:16 and Gen 41:35, 39), seems very appropriate.[60] Being understood this way it shows that Boaz not simply "passed" the roasted grain, but shared with Ruth a large amount of it so that

---

57. See Schipper, *Ruth*, 125.
58. Holmstedt, *Ruth*, 133.
59. Block, *Judges, Ruth*, 667.
60. Schipper, *Ruth*, 125.

she could not even eat it all. Once again, this act is used to show the eventfulness of the situation. As Block explains,

> Obviously this verse is not simply about feeding the hungry. The narrator hereby shows how Boaz took an ordinary occasion and transformed it into a glorious demonstration of compassion, generosity and acceptance – in short, the biblical understanding of *hesed*.[61]

In the next scene that comes immediately after the mealtime, the level of eventfulness reaches its maximum. Boaz first explains to his workers how they should relate to Ruth:

וַתָּקָם לְלַקֵּט וַיְצַו בֹּעַז אֶת־נְעָרָיו לֵאמֹר גַּם בֵּין הָעֳמָרִים תְּלַקֵּט וְלֹא תַכְלִימוּהָ׃
וְגַם שֹׁל־תָּשֹׁלּוּ לָהּ מִן־הַצְּבָתִים וַעֲזַבְתֶּם וְלִקְּטָה וְלֹא תִגְעֲרוּ־בָהּ׃

> When she rose to glean, Boaz instructed his young men, saying, "Let her glean even among the sheaves, and do not reproach her. And also pull out some from the bundles for her and leave it for her to glean, and do not rebuke her." (2:15–16)

Besides earlier comments, there is one more feature of Boaz's speech in this final episode that is important in relation to Boaz as the witness and the judge of the day of gleaning. Hubbard shows that the whole utterance of Boaz is emphatic by listing six reasons: (1) the emphatic particle גַּם as the command first word; (2) the initial, emphatic position of בֵּין הָעֳמָרִים and מִן־הַצְּבָתִים; (3) the alliteration of t and l sounds in תַכְלִימוּהָ and שֹׁל־תָּשֹׁלּוּ; (4) the imperfect with the sense תְּלַקֵּט "to be able to glean"; (5) the prohibitions with emotionally weighty words וְלֹא תִגְעֲרוּ and וְלֹא תַכְלִימוּהָ ; and (6) emphatic infinitive absolute שֹׁל after the emphatic וְגַם opening.[62]

The importance of these emphases for present study is that out of all other actions of Boaz during this day of gleaning, this last one seems to be the most eventful according to the narrator's imperative world picture which is demonstrated in Boaz's emphatic address. With these words Boaz goes beyond the

---

61. Block, *Judges, Ruth*, 667.
62. Hubbard, *Ruth*, 176n130.

convictions of society or as Bush puts it, "Boaz's magnanimity is significantly extended and expanded, almost as if to give concrete reality to the blessing he has just voiced."63 The other witness and the judge of this second event of the book appears to be Naomi when Ruth after a day of gleaning returns home with a significant quantity of grain and food. Of course, Naomi cannot point to the pivotal moment of the day, for she was not there physically, but she can allocate the whole day as important because she witnesses with surprise six measures of barley that Ruth gleaned and the food that was left from the dinner.

וַתֹּאמֶר לָהּ חֲמוֹתָהּ אֵיפֹה לִקַּטְתְּ הַיּוֹם וְאָנָה עָשִׂית

> And her mother-in-law said to her, "Where did you glean today?
> And where have you worked? (2:19a)

Meanwhile, the day itself started for Naomi without any eventful intentions. In her short answer to Ruth – לְכִי בִתִּי "Go, my daughter" – some commentators detect a note of hopelessness: "The brevity of the permission given to Ruth here expresses her despondency: the two women had arrived at the bitter end—at subsistence. They have nothing more to lose."64 The answer also indicates that the chance has not come along yet. In contrast, when luck is smiling at Naomi, her eventful intentions change to the opposite. The day in the eyes of Naomi becomes even more eventful when she finds out that Ruth happened to work on the field of their relative Boaz, who is qualified to be their גֹּאֵל "redeemer."

וַתֹּאמֶר נָעֳמִי לְכַלָּתָהּ בָּרוּךְ הוּא לַיהוה אֲשֶׁר לֹא־עָזַב חַסְדּוֹ
אֶת־הַחַיִּים וְאֶת־הַמֵּתִים וַתֹּאמֶר לָהּ נָעֳמִי קָרוֹב לָנוּ הָאִישׁ
מִגֹּאֲלֵנוּ הוּא:

> And Naomi said to her daughter-in-law, "May he be blessed by the LORD, whose kindness has not forsaken the living or the dead!" Naomi also said to her, "The man is a close relative of ours, one of our redeemers." (2:20)

Naomi clearly attests to the time of the second event of the story. This helps to solve the seeming ambiguity in the words of Naomi for it is unclear

---

63. See Bush, *Ruth/Esther*, 128.
64. LaCocque, *Ruth*, 63.

from Hebrew syntax whether she blesses Boaz or YHWH for the kindness. According to Collins, while

> Naomi herself meant either the Lord or Boaz as the referent of אֲשֶׁר, but in the haste of ordinary conversation (as opposed to the careful language of literary craft), she framed the clause ambiguously. The narrator found this useful in conveying his message.[65]

However, if Naomi plays a role of the witness and the judge in this event, she, perhaps, should mean the participants of the event. Therefore, in this passage it is more likely that she refers to Boaz rather than the Lord. This pattern repeats next time when Naomi is given the word in the narrative.

4.2.4. The Third Event of the Book of Ruth

The third event of the book is the visit to the threshing floor. Unlike the previous event, this one was carefully planned by Naomi and therefore was singled out from the continuum of life. Naomi clearly states the time (הַלַּיְלָה "this night"), the place (גֹּרֶן "threshing floor") and, what's more important, the reason for it (to seek מָנוֹחַ, "rest" for Ruth).

וַתֹּאמֶר לָהּ נָעֳמִי חֲמוֹתָהּ בִּתִּי הֲלֹא אֲבַקֶּשׁ־לָךְ מָנוֹחַ אֲשֶׁר יִיטַב־לָךְ:
וְעַתָּה הֲלֹא בֹעַז מֹדַעְתָּנוּ אֲשֶׁר הָיִית אֶת־נַעֲרוֹתָיו הִנֵּה־הוּא זֹרֶה אֶת־גֹּרֶן הַשְּׂעֹרִים הַלָּיְלָה:
וְרָחַצְתְּ וָסַכְתְּ וְשַׂמְתְּ שִׂמְלֹתֵךְ עָלַיִךְ וְיָרַדְתִּי הַגֹּרֶן אַל־תִּוָּדְעִי לָאִישׁ עַד כַּלֹּתוֹ לֶאֱכֹל וְלִשְׁתּוֹת:
וִיהִי בְשָׁכְבוֹ וְיָדַעַתְּ אֶת־הַמָּקוֹם אֲשֶׁר יִשְׁכַּב־שָׁם וּבָאת וְגִלִּית מַרְגְּלֹתָיו וְשָׁכָבְתִּי וְהוּא יַגִּיד לָךְ אֵת אֲשֶׁר תַּעֲשִׂין:

> Then Naomi her mother-in-law said to her, "My daughter, should I not seek rest for you, that it may be well with you? Is not Boaz our relative, with whose young women you were? See, he is winnowing barley tonight at the threshing floor. Wash therefore and anoint yourself, and put on your cloak and go down to the threshing floor, but do not make yourself known to the man until he has finished eating and drinking. But when he

---

65. Collins, "Ambiguity," 97–102.

lies down, observe the place where he lies. Then go and uncover his feet and lie down, and he will tell you what to do." (3:1–4)

Let us start from the point of the story that precedes any eventful intentions. This point can be found in the last verse of chapter 2, which describes the routine life of Ruth during several weeks of the harvest. The verse also clearly points to the reason of Naomi's concern in the beginning of chapter 3. According to Bush,

> with the concluding verse of this scene, our narrator brings the whole forward thrust of the narrative suddenly and completely to a halt. "So she gleaned close to Boaz's young women," he tells us, "until the barley and wheat harvests were finished" – a period of some seven weeks! – "and then she lived at home with her mother-in-law"! Once again they exist in much the same state as when they first returned home from Moab, for the end of the harvest season must ultimately mean for them the return of famine and emptiness.[66]

Therefore, the problem of two women was, first of all, the source of the food after the harvest is over. During the harvest season Ruth was gleaning in the field of Boaz, enjoying the rights of sojourner and Boaz's generosity and, therefore, had no need to develop any further relationship. However, after the harvest was over it was necessary to find the way to maintain the relationship with Boaz simply to have food on the table.

There were two possible options for a widow: redemption of the field or levirate marriage. Bewer, on the basis of the article of McKane,[67] convincingly shows the requirement to marry Ruth has no basis in law. However, it would, of course, be ideal if both options go together: the same person would purchase the field and marry the widow. The question of the field was manageable for Naomi who, being the widow of Elimelech, could approach Boaz or any closer relative and ask him to redeem the field. In fact, Boaz starts the legal procedure with this very question. However, there is an obvious problem related to the second question: because of her age Naomi could not have

---

66. Bush, *Ruth/Esther*, 142.
67. Bewer, "Goël in Ruth," 202–06.

children, which abolishes the whole idea of levirate marriage. Redemption of the field and thus provision of some maintenance was the only option left to her.

However, Naomi indicated from the beginning that her main concern is Ruth's wellbeing. From the conversation at the threshing floor, it becomes clear that Ruth could marry outside of the clan of Elimelech. But in this case, she probably would be left without her portion of Elimelech's field and Naomi would certainly be left without the offspring. In contrast, marriage with the redeemer could solve all the problems of the widows: Ruth naturalizes in a foreign country, Naomi is taken care of financially, and the line of Elimelech does not disappear.

Therefore, Naomi conspires to make a move that will help Ruth "to find rest" and not to worry any more about protection and provision. Since the same word מְנוּחָה "resting place" is used in 1:9 in relation to marriage, it is logical to conclude that Naomi means the marriage of Ruth. Obviously, Boaz was the most suitable candidate for this role since he already effectively acted as the redeemer while the closer relative never appears on the scene. The marriage of Ruth and Boaz was the easiest solution for Naomi. Elimelech's field would stay within the possession of the clan and the marriage could lead to the birth of the heir who ultimately could support Naomi in her old age.

By looking at Naomi's plan from this perspective, one can say that preparations (washing, anointing, and putting on the cloak) that Ruth had to undertake are very natural things to do when one goes for a special visit. And a marriage proposal is undoubtedly one of those special moments that goes beyond the routine of life. However, it is not the marriage proposal that deviates from the imperative world picture but the unusual procedure of the proposal, which already contains deviation from the norm for of two reasons.

The first reason is related to the unusual time and place of the marriage proposal: midnight at the threshing floor is not the best place for such activity. The second reason consists of the most unusual part of the proposal: the command to uncover Boaz's feet and lie down (3:4). The reason for such an extravagant method of matchmaking that Naomi chose is not easy to explain because of lack of background information. What is clear is that this extravagancy raises the eventfulness of the moment.

These specifics of the plan already make the preparation to the event highly intentional. However, it would not be so intentional without three other important details. First, Ruth is a Moabite woman. Her visit to the threshing floor happens on the background of the previous meeting with Boaz in the field. There Ruth launched the most difficult question about her life in Judea, "Why have I found favor in your eyes, that you should take notice of me, since I am a foreigner?" (2:10). Very recently this Moabite woman could not even think about being noticed by an Israelite man and now she comes to him with a marriage proposal.

Another detail that one should consider in relation to eventfulness is Ruth's own interests. For she may not be interested in Boaz as husband because of the age difference. Therefore, it was up to Ruth to decide whether to act in her own interests or to put the interests of her former family first. Earlier she promised to Naomi that only death parts them; now the moment of truth has arrived – would Ruth follow her commitment?

The third detail that creates eventful intention is related to the uncertainty of the result of the visit. The words of Naomi, "And he will tell you what to do" create the fear of the unknown. No one guarantees that Boaz will want to redeem Naomi and Ruth and to marry Ruth.

Therefore, by the end of Naomi's speech it becomes clear that something outstanding will happen this night on the threshing floor. However, the planning itself does not constitute the event but only reflects eventful intentions. The following description of Ruth's acts only fosters the interest of the readers and increases the degree of intentionality. Two other nuances help in this process.

First, it is the use of "sexually suggestive"[68] verbs that forced some commentators to think that Naomi simply wants Ruth to seduce Boaz.[69] However, seduction would be a very risky plan for the Moabite woman and it is unclear how one can find rest and security by engaging in compromising situations. Besides, the following characterization of Ruth as a worthy woman runs contrary to this conclusion. This makes other commentators to perceive the

---

68. Schipper, *Ruth*, 157. See also Sakenfeld, *Ruth*, 54.

69. This view is shared by LaCocque, *Ruth*, 91, and Danna Nolan Fewell and David M. Gunn, "Son Is Born," 99–108. See also Halton, "Indecent Proposal," 30–43. Halton suggests that Naomi's plan should be interpreted as "an attempt at sexual entrapment," which Ruth "subtly departs from."

sexually charged atmosphere only as background that helps to underscore the moral virtues of Boaz and Ruth.[70]

Another nuance is related to the very acts of Ruth. Looking at them rigorously, some interpreters[71] see deviation from the norm in that Ruth first promised to act according to the plan (3:5) but, in reality, did not follow the instructions of her mother-in-law. For example, she first went to the threshing floor and only then dressed up. Similarly, instead of coming to Boaz right after the supper, she waits until he falls asleep and only then comes to his feet. Therefore, according to this view, the first eventful intentions appear when Ruth disrupts Naomi's plan by changing the sequence of actions and waiting too long letting Boaz fall asleep.

However, Bos questions these conclusions, considering that the only difference between Naomi's instructions and Ruth's action is in the adding the phrase בַּלָּט "in secrecy" or "quietly" to the verb בּוֹא.

> One may assume on the basis of this word and the sequel, that Ruth deliberately hides from Boaz until he wakes up and notices her. It is not entirely clear whether Naomi's instructions are followed here or whether Ruth introduces a variation in the plot.[72]

To these may be added that this deviation from the norm is not evidenced as anything important by the narrator or any character. Besides, this kind of event would qualitatively differ from two previous events that had to do with deep commitment and serious decisions of the characters. What truly shifts this marriage proposal from ordinary happening to narratological event is the bold decision of Ruth to go to the threshing floor because, like in the first chapter, it means that she again rejects her own interests in favor of Naomi's.

וַיֹּאמֶר מִי־אָתְּ וַתֹּאמֶר אָנֹכִי רוּת אֲמָתֶךָ וּפָרַשְׂתָּ כְנָפֶךָ עַל־אֲמָתְךָ כִּי גֹאֵל אָתָּה:
וַיֹּאמֶר בְּרוּכָה אַתְּ לַיהוה בִּתִּי הֵיטַבְתְּ חַסְדֵּךְ הָאַחֲרוֹן מִן־הָרִאשׁוֹן לְבִלְתִּי־לֶכֶת אַחֲרֵי הַבַּחוּרִים אִם־דַּל וְאִם־עָשִׁיר:

---

70. Bush, *Ruth/Esther*, 155. To these interpretations one must add the view that whole idea is simply an invention of the narrator for the sake of "good narrative art." See Sakenfeld, *Ruth*, 56.

71. Campbell, *Ruth*, 121.

72. Bos, "Out of the Shadows," 61.

וְעַתָּה בִּתִּי אַל־תִּירְאִי כֹּל אֲשֶׁר־תֹּאמְרִי אֶעֱשֶׂה־לָּךְ כִּי יוֹדֵעַ כָּל־שַׁעַר עַמִּי כִּי אֵשֶׁת חַיִל אָתְּ:

> He said, "Who are you?" And she answered, "I am Ruth, your servant. Spread your wings over your servant, for you are a redeemer." And he said, "May you be blessed by the LORD, my daughter. You have made this last kindness greater than the first in that you have not gone after young men, whether poor or rich. And now, my daughter, do not fear. I will do for you all that you ask, for all my fellow townsmen know that you are a worthy woman . . ." (3:9–11)

Ruth clearly proposes marriage to Boaz, which is obvious from his words that follow her answer. And yet by calling him גֹּאֵל "the redeemer" she subtly touches the problem of her mother-in-law to whom Ruth is committed for a lifetime. Now she asks Boaz to solve this problem for her, and the only way he can do it is by taking Ruth as a wife and, at the same time, redeeming the field of Elimelech for Naomi.

One of the critical questions regarding this passage is which later act of kindness Boaz means, for he does not specify it.[73] Several answers to this question have been proposed. First, and the most obvious answer, is that Boaz deciphers this word in the following statement: "in that you have not gone after young men, whether poor or rich." But this means that the act of kindness is the proposal of marriage, which seems unlikely. Bush, after applying criteria of חֶסֶד proposed by Sakenfeld, comes to the conclusion that Boaz's comparison "does indeed seem incongruous."[74] He then concludes that to solve this problem one has to understand Ruth's reference to Boaz as redeemer to be the request to fulfill the duty of levirate marriage in order to raise an heir for the line of Elimelech and Mahlon.

> Therefore, the last חֶסֶד of Ruth is to be understood as Ruth's faithfulness to her dead husband in the continuance of his name and family, rather than pursuing her own desires and fortunes in a marriage to a younger man.[75]

---

73. Schipper, *Ruth*, 154.
74. Bush, *Ruth/Esther*, 170.
75. Bush, 171.

In this episode, Boaz becomes the witness and the judge of the event. The evaluative nature of Boaz's speech was noted by Chisholm, who considered that "having Boaz extol Ruth's value is more effective than if the narrator did so directly."[76] At the same paragraph he recalls Berlin who, in fact, explains the reason for selecting Boaz as the witness and the judge of the event:

> The narrator does not tell us how wonderful Ruth's loyalty to Naomi is; he has Boaz tell us in 2:11. And later at the threshing-floor Boaz tells Ruth that her second kindness is better than her first, and that everyone knows she is an אשת חיל ("worthy woman" – 3:10–11) . . . This internal or embedded evaluation is more authentic and more dramatic than a narrator's comment.[77]

Therefore, the eventfulness of the threshing floor visit is based upon Boaz's conviction which implies that the foreign woman is not burdened with any obligation to her mother-in-law. On this background, the decision of Ruth to choose Boaz out of many other more attractive (physically and financially) candidates looks like an event that deviates from the norm. For him this step was the most unexpected because the decision of Ruth extended beyond the norms as he understands them. If there is any event that happens during the threshing floor meeting, it is the event of Ruth's endless commitment to Naomi and her deceased husband. Boaz, therefore, becomes the witness and the judge of two events in the story of Ruth: one is the decision of Ruth to come to Bethlehem with Naomi and the other is the visit to the threshing floor to propose for Boaz to marry her and redeem her mother-in-law.

4.2.5. The Fourth Event of the Book of Ruth

Ruth's visit gives rise to the final narratological event of the book of Ruth, that is the legal procedure at the city gate. It is witnessed and recognized as an event by Boaz and by people of Bethlehem. Like the visit to the threshing floor, this event is scheduled first and then evaluated immediately thereafter. Let me consider the scheduling first.

Eventful intentions in Boaz's mind start to grow as soon as he realizes that he has to make another turn in his life and somehow to force the closer relative

---

76. Chisholm Jr., *Judges and Ruth*, 659n650.
77. Berlin, *Poetics and Interpretation*, 105.

to make the required decision not to redeem Ruth. This is how LaCocque characterizes Boaz's circumstances in this episode: "Boaz is in the uncomfortable situation of sitting between two chairs, one might say. On one hand, he is not first on the list of 'redeemers'; but on the other hand, he intends to marry Ruth."[78] Therefore Boaz says,

וְעַתָּה כִּי אָמְנָם כִּי אִם גֹּאֵל אָנֹכִי וְגַם יֵשׁ גֹּאֵל קָרוֹב מִמֶּנִּי:
לִינִי הַלַּיְלָה וְהָיָה בַבֹּקֶר אִם־יִגְאָלֵךְ טוֹב יִגְאָל וְאִם־לֹא יַחְפֹּץ
לְגָאֳלֵךְ וּגְאַלְתִּיךְ אָנֹכִי חַי־יְהוָה שִׁכְבִי עַד־הַבֹּקֶר:

> "And now it is true that I am a redeemer. Yet there is a redeemer nearer than I. Remain tonight, and in the morning, if he will redeem you, good; let him do it. But if he is not willing to redeem you, then, as the LORD lives, I will redeem you. Lie down until the morning." (3:12–13)

Boaz's speech shows that upcoming meeting with another relative is considered by Boaz as an eventful act on the background of life convictions. First, he attempts to consider possible results of the court according to the generally accepted procedure of redemption: closest relative first. But then he expresses the overarching idea of YHWH's control over the whole situation by using the formula "as the Lord lives." This insertion betrays the hope that the request of Ruth will be met by the favor of YHWH and despite all legal norms.

In the morning Boaz gives to Ruth an "unspecified but clearly ample amount of barley,"[79] which also reflects his eventful intentions. There is a view that the gift of grain is to be interpreted as the security of the fulfillment of Boaz's obligations. Interpreting this act, Chisholm calls it "a further act of kindness and a guarantee that he [Boaz] would seek her [Ruth's] best interests."[80] Campbell considers it "the clear evidence of Boaz's determination to care for these two widows"[81] and Aschkenasy in artistic style says, "her bulging apron serves as evidence and promise of things to come."[82] The

---

78. LaCocque, *Ruth*, 102. This guards the words of Boaz from any sexual misinterpretation.

79. Linafelt and Beal, *Ruth and Esther*, 59. The issue of the exact amount of grain that Boaz gave to Ruth is not in the scope of this study.

80. Chisholm Jr., *Judges and Ruth*, 660.

81. Campbell, *Ruth*, 138.

82. Kates and Reimer, *Reading Ruth*, 111.

gift would not be necessary if Boaz would not think that the outcome of the meeting will differ from what is expected.

Eventful intentions continue to manifest in the procedure of the gathering of the elders and closer relative. The decision should be made in the presence of the elders and all townspeople, which enhances the degree of eventfulness of the coming event. Boaz wants the elders to be the witnesses and the judges of this moment together with him. The eventful status of the legal procedure becomes evident when right at the beginning of the meeting Boaz appeals to the closer relative, explaining the situation and putting the question bluntly:

וַיֹּאמֶר לַגֹּאֵל חֶלְקַת הַשָּׂדֶה אֲשֶׁר לְאָחִינוּ לֶאֱלִימֶלֶךְ מָכְרָה
נָעֳמִי הַשָּׁבָה מִשְּׂדֵה מוֹאָב:
וַאֲנִי אָמַרְתִּי אֶגְלֶה אָזְנְךָ לֵאמֹר קְנֵה נֶגֶד הַיֹּשְׁבִים וְנֶגֶד זִקְנֵי עַמִּי
אִם־תִּגְאַל גְּאָל וְאִם־לֹא יִגְאַל הַגִּידָה לִּי וְאֵדַע כִּי אֵין זוּלָתְךָ
לִגְאוֹל וְאָנֹכִי אַחֲרֶיךָ

> Then he said to the redeemer, "Naomi, who has come back from the country of Moab, is selling the parcel of land that belonged to our relative Elimelech. So I thought I would tell you of it and say, 'Buy it in the presence of those sitting here and in the presence of the elders of my people.' If you will redeem it, redeem it. But if you will not, tell me, that I may know, for there is no one besides you to redeem it, and I come after you." (4:3–4a)

Boaz's initial address to the relative is based on imperative norms of society. Therefore, it does not come as a surprise and does not pose any difficulties to answer. After the closer relative makes his choice and gets ready to redeem the field, Boaz adds the further condition that changes the whole deal:

וַיֹּאמֶר בֹּעַז בְּיוֹם־קְנוֹתְךָ הַשָּׂדֶה מִיַּד נָעֳמִי וּמֵאֵת רוּת הַמּוֹאֲבִיָּה
אֵשֶׁת־הַמֵּת קָנִיתִי לְהָקִים שֵׁם־הַמֵּת עַל־נַחֲלָתוֹ:

> Then Boaz said, "The day you buy the field from the hand of Naomi, you also acquire Ruth the Moabite, the widow of the dead, in order to perpetuate the name of the dead in his inheritance." (4:5)

This additional condition must infer situation from its default status. In the words of Boaz there was something unexpected, something that the closer relative could not accept because he was guided by the imperative world picture and the modality of convictions.

According to the ESV translation (which follows *Qere* reading), in 4:5 Boaz imposes on the redeemer the legal duty to marry Ruth if he redeems Naomi's possession. But it was already noted the requirement to marry Ruth has no basis in the law and Boaz could not impose it upon the redeemer.[83] Indeed, if these legal acts were related, Boaz would become dependent upon the decision of the redeemer, which contradicts Boaz's promise to Ruth and creates, according to Beattie, an inconceivable situation by all the laws of storytelling: "It would be very strange to find one man informing another of his duty to marry the woman with whom he has himself slept on the previous night, yet this situation occurs if the *Qere* is followed."[84]

According to the *Ketiv* reading, Boaz informs the relative that he is going to marry Ruth, which means that the relative purchase the land of Elimelech only to give it to the son of Ruth and Boaz, whom they possibly have. This reading clearly turns this situation into the category of narratological event, for Boaz presents to the closer relative the news that the relative does not anticipate and which, according to Boaz's understanding of the situation, has to force the relative to abandon his privileges. Therefore, Boaz puts the relative into the position in which, according to Beattie, the one "has no choice but to do what Boaz wants him to do."[85]

Finally, Boaz declares his decision before the elders of the town and all the people at the gate. The form of oath underlines the eventfulness of the moment:

וַיֹּאמֶר בֹּעַז לַזְּקֵנִים וְכָל־הָעָם עֵדִים אַתֶּם הַיּוֹם כִּי קָנִיתִי אֶת־כָּל־אֲשֶׁר לֶאֱלִימֶלֶךְ וְאֵת כָּל־אֲשֶׁר לְכִלְיוֹן וּמַחְלוֹן מִיַּד נָעֳמִי: וְגַם אֶת־רוּת הַמֹּאֲבִיָּה אֵשֶׁת מַחְלוֹן קָנִיתִי לִי לְאִשָּׁה לְהָקִים שֵׁם־הַמֵּת עַל־נַחֲלָתוֹ וְלֹא־יִכָּרֵת שֵׁם־הַמֵּת מֵעִם אֶחָיו וּמִשַּׁעַר מְקוֹמוֹ עֵדִים אַתֶּם הַיּוֹם:

Then Boaz said to the elders and all the people, "You are witnesses this day that I have bought from the hand of Naomi all

---

83. McKane, "Ruth and Boaz," 38.
84. Beattie, "Kethibh and Qere," 490–94.
85. Beattie, 493.

that belonged to Elimelech and all that belonged to Chilion and to Mahlon. Also Ruth the Moabite, the widow of Mahlon, I have bought to be my wife, to perpetuate the name of the dead in his inheritance, that the name of the dead may not be cut off from among his brothers and from the gate of his native place. You are witnesses this day." (4:9–10)

Twice during this final speech Boaz calls the elders and the people to witness this day as a special day in his life and in the whole story. The act that deviates from the social norm and recorded in this story as a true narratological event becomes a fateful decision that will affect future generations, for he does not simply redeem the wife of the dead relative, but perpetuates the name of the relative forever.

4.2.6. Conclusion

The analysis of intentionality indicates that sixteen episodes of the book of Ruth constitute four narratological events that can be allocated according to the time and place and according the testimony of the witnesses and judges. These events stand in sharp contrast to the uneventful routine of life by a high degree of intentionality. Routine of life is characterized by an imperative world picture and the modality of conviction of the narrator and the characters. The eventfulness, thus, constitutes deviation from these norms, the extraordinary acts of the characters against the background of normal dynamics of life.

The first event happened during the conversation between Naomi and Ruth on the way from Moab to Bethlehem. The uneventful scene of breaking up ends with the highly eventful speech of Ruth, which changes the course of the normal flow of life and breaks up the imperative world picture (the existing convictions). The second event of the book – the first encounter of Boaz and Ruth – takes place at the field of Boaz and lasts for about one day. The anticipated wretched existence and hard work of the foreigner is replaced by an unexpected flow of generous gifts. During this meeting Boaz learns about the first event of the book, while Naomi becomes the witness and the judge of the second event.

The third event happens at the threshing floor and describes the last (in the scope of the narrative) encounter of Boaz and Ruth. It lasts for one night. What transforms this meeting into a narratological event is the decision of

Ruth to fulfill Naomi's plan and thus to affirm the decision to stay with Naomi regardless of circumstances. This decision is again witnessed by Boaz.

The final, fourth, event of the book happens on the background of standard legal procedure of the redemption of the field. Boaz first follows the norms of the society, but then presents the extraordinary decision to marry a Moabite woman, which forces the closer relative to withdraw from the transaction. The event is witnessed by the elders and the people of Bethlehem.

The analysis also shows that intentionality grows with eventfulness of the episodes. Within each event one can find more or less intentional and, therefore, more or less eventful episodes. The most eventful episodes are the pivotal, most memorable, most compelling moments of the story. According to the preceding analysis, each event of the book has the following pivotal moments:

1. The moment when Ruth declares her commitment to Naomi (1:16–17) (episode 2)
2. The moment when Boaz instructs his workers to support Ruth with gleaning (2:11–12) (episode 9)
3. The moment when Boaz promises Ruth to marry her (3:11) (episode 12)
4. The moment when Boaz announces his decision to marry Ruth (4:10) (episode 16)

These episodes are respectively preceded and followed by less eventful episodes that form the background of the narrative. They are less intentional and therefore less eventful, but they enhance the eventfulness of the pivotal moments.

The rest of the chapter will be committed to the confirmation of this conclusion with the more formal method proposed by Schmid. Tjupa's method of allocation of narratological events that is based on eventful intentions and the search of the witness and the judge certainly helps to identify the events of the narrative and explain why the narrator selected these events out of an infinite number of other happenings of life. However, this method is largely based on the intuition of the interpreter and gives only a general idea about the narrator's logic of selectivity. In contrast, Schmid's method is more formal and based on the measuring of the degree of eventfulness of each episode of the book according to five characteristics of eventfulness.[86]

However, prior to the analysis of the main story, I would like to devote some time to the analysis of eventfulness of the prologue and the denouement of the story. These parts of the book extend beyond the main story but the analyses of these passages according to Schmid's criteria help in better comprehension of the book.

4.3. The Eventfulness of the Prologue and the Denouement of the Story

4.3.1. Prologue – the Event Preceding the Story Proper

Technically, the prologue consists of several happenings that separately could be developed into full-fledged events. However, they are reduced by the narrator to simple facts and only together present the event that can be defined as a family tragedy. Naomi plays a unifying role in this section because the passage is presented through the prism of Naomi's identity. Initially she is called the wife of Elimelech, then Naomi, and finally "the woman." Not to say that the passage is presented from the point of view of Naomi, but that the narrator uses the character of Naomi as a unifying element of the prologue.

How eventful is this chain of happenings? The deaths of Elimelech and his sons are extremely irreversible events. This irreversibility is actually the reason for Naomi's grief and hopelessness (Ruth 1:12–13). The deaths are not only irreversible but also persistent. They "leave a trail" (using Bakhtin's term) in the entire fabric of narrative. Not only does Naomi grieve about this tragedy, but each of the following events somehow reflects on this tragedy. Finally, death cannot be repeated (unless we are talking about some modern novel with fantastic storyline). Therefore, the death of Elimelech and his sons is non-iterative.

Yet irreversibility and persistence and non-iterativity are only secondary measures of the degree of eventfulness. What about two essential features of eventfulness – relevance and unpredictability? Within the axioms of the narrative world, a death of husband or father was certainly one of the greatest

---

86. The five characteristics are relevance, unpredictability, persistence, irreversibility, and non-iterativity.

tragedies for the whole family. However, this general convention cannot be left without the proof from the text. According to Block, the seriousness of the situation that the women faced is reflected in "the amount of space devoted to describing the response of the women to the death of their husbands."[87]

The unpredictability of introductory events may, at first, seem questionable. Indeed, when three deaths follow one after another, they risk becoming trivial.[88] In order to avoid this situation, the narrator of Ruth (1) introduces marriage after the death of Elimelech and before the death of the sons, (2) informs the reader that their marriage lasted "about ten years," and (3) gives an impression that both Machlon and Chilion died at the same time. By doing this, the narrator achieves the effect of unpredictability.

Finally, the death of Elimelech and his sons greatly influenced the pattern of behavior of both Naomi and her daughters-in-law. If earlier they all were under the security of their husbands, now they have to make their own hard decisions: to stay together or to break up, to remain in Moab or to return to Bethlehem?[89]

It can be concluded then, that Naomi's loss of Elimelech and his sons is an event of the book of Ruth that has a very high degree of eventfulness. This is the very reason why the narrator groups these happenings together into one event and focuses the readers' attention on them. By doing this, the narrator states the main problem of the story, which Bush defines as "the death and emptiness that have afflicted the life of Naomi."[90]

Nevertheless, the prologue only introduces readers to the story proper, and the main interest of the narrator lies in the events that follow this tragedy.[91] Let me now turn to the denouement of the story and likewise analyze it with the view of eventfulness.

---

87. Block, *Judges, Ruth*, 629–30. Bush agrees with this saying that the significance of the problem is underlined by the fact that "after the statement of the problem (1:3–5), he [the narrator] devotes the next two scenes primarily to depicting the affective dimensions of this problem – the bitterness, anger, and despair that Naomi feels . . ." See Bush, *Ruth/Esther*, 51.

88. That is what happened in the story of Judah and Tamar – after the deaths of Er and Onan, the reader (as much as protagonist) expects the death of Shelah.

89. Hawk, *Ruth*, 56.

90. Bush, *Ruth/Esther*, 51.

91. Perhaps it is the main reason why the prologue is given in the scope of external (least detailed) focalization.

4.3.2. The Eventfulness of the Denouement

The birth of a child as well as the death of men have a very high degree of eventfulness. First of all, it is very relevant (or significant) for all the participants of story world and for Naomi in particular. Since the main problem of the story is linked to Naomi, the narrator demonstrates the significance of the resolution through constant reference to Naomi:

> Though a son born to Ruth and Boaz is mentioned (4:13), his significance relates entirely to Naomi. Yahweh is not celebrated by the female chorus because he has not left the line of Elimelech without an heir but because he has not left Naomi without a "redeemer" to restore her to life and provide for her old age (4:14–15). Nor do they celebrate his identity by the cry "A son has been born to Elimelech" but rather by "A son has been born to Naomi" (4:17).[92]

However, if the birth of a child would be the only result of the story, this event, being significant, would not be very unexpected since the birth of the child after marriage reflects the natural flow of life. This gap is being filled with the epilogue of the story: the birth of David is the most unpredictable and the most significant statement of the narrator. It must be noted, though, that it is unpredictable only for the readers of the story because none of the participants of the narrative world could ever imagine that two generations later this marriage will eventually lead to the birth of great King David. Therefore, relevance and unpredictability of the concluding part of the story is based on its significance on both the level of the story and the level of discourse. As Bush puts it:

> This outcome expresses the significance of the story, for the resolution has meaning by virtue of all that the son of Ruth and Boaz meant for Naomi (and Ruth) and also by virtue of the fact that it provided an integral link in the family line that led to David.[93]

One can see here other characteristics of eventfulness as well. The fact that David became a descendant of Obed makes the event very consecutive on the level of discourse. It should have impressed both the thinking of the

---

92. Bush, *Ruth/Esther*, 51.
93. Bush, 52.

original Israelite reader as well as the thinking of the modern readers, which is reflected in the final genealogy. What genealogy is saying to the readers is that David, the greatest king of Israel, has Moabite blood in his veins.[94]

Such is the impact (or persistence) of the event in Israel's history and on the reader of the book. But let's not forget the impact of this event within the story world. The birth of Obed completes the process of evolution of the mind of Naomi that was gradually changing throughout the story. While she is not giving explicit ideological appraisal of this birth, her acts – "Then Naomi took the child and laid him on her lap and became his nurse" (Ruth 4:16) – become an answer to the women's blessing. It should be noted that there is a reason why this reply is given in the scope of external focalization. External focalization always carries the connotation of a riddle – the conclusion about Naomi's attitude is only just a guess (while a very credible guess). It seems that the narrator, focalizing the reaction of Naomi externally, wants to focus the attention of the reader on the more important impact of the story – that the line of Obed leads to David, the fact that is, of course, both irreversible and non-iterative.

The prologue and the denouement of the story, therefore, consist of two full-fledged events – the deaths of three men and the birth of the child. Together they constitute the problem and the solution. However, between these events there is the whole story proper with all its tension, pathos, and excitement that draws the readers to read it.[95] The intentionality and the eventfulness of the main story has been partially explored. The following section aims to confirm those conclusions using Schmid's criteria of eventfulness.

4.4. The Eventfulness of the Episodes of the Main Story

Thus far, the prologue and the denouement of the story were being considered in relation to all five criteria of eventfulness. For all practical reasons, the main story will be analyzed differently. I will take each criterion separately and show the transformation of this criterion throughout the whole book.

---

94. Different positions on the integrated nature of the genealogy will be discussed in the last chapter.

95. Campbell, "Hebrew Short Story," 95.

This approach will help to see the dynamic of transformation of eventfulness according to each characteristic.

Let me recall that according to previous analysis, the main story comprises four narratological events (one event for each chapter of the book) and that each event has one pivotal (most eventful) episode. These conclusions can be presented in the following table:

Event	Pivotal episode
The decision on the way to Bethlehem (1:6–22)	The moment when Ruth declares her commitment to Naomi (1:16–17) (episode 2)
First encounter of Boaz and Ruth (2:1–23)	The moment when Boaz instructs his workers to support Ruth with gleaning (2:11–12) (episode 9)
The last encounter of Boaz and Ruth (3:1–18)	The moment when Boaz promises Ruth to marry her (3:11) (episode 12)
The decision at the gate of Bethlehem (4:1–12)	The moment when Boaz announces his decision to marry Ruth (4:10) (episode 16)

4.4.1. Relevance

Against the background of preceding and subsequent episodes, the pivotal moments chosen above demonstrate a much higher degree of relevance. Preceding and subsequent episodes are more trivial; without these critical moments, they are left unimportant. It is first of all reflected in the fact that preceding events do not change situations in any considerable way. They by themselves do not bring the characters closer to resolution of the problem.

Naomi, for example, discusses with herself the possibility of having more sons that would become husbands to her daughters-in-law. While it is debatable whether or not Naomi refers to the custom of levirate marriage, the truth is that the right answer to this question does not change much to the story for Naomi, as Schipper comments, "dismisses it [levirate marriage] as irrelevant to this particular situation" and "an unrealistic solution to the issue of finding rest or security for her daughters-in-law."[96] Sending Orpah and Ruth back to their families is unlikely to offer much help to either of them or Naomi. The decision of Orpah closes her chapter in the story, while Ruth's decision

---

96. Schipper, *Ruth*, 103–04.

continues to affect the rest of the story. In short, without Ruth's commitment the story would never happen.

One can come to the same kind of conclusion looking at the episodes around Boaz's first meeting with Ruth. Ruth's initial efforts to glean before her meeting with Boaz seems unsuccessful: reference to "an ephah of barley" in 2:17 points to the futility of her morning work. The arrival of Boaz and the greeting of the reapers are also anti-eventful, for the language used in greeting reflects a "formulaic blessing" used in other parts of the Bible (cf. 2 Kgs 4:29; 10:15) and in Hebrew inscriptions.[97] Therefore, the greeting and even the conversation with the foreman are part of the daily routine for Boaz. But in the narrative they create the necessary background to help the reader to allocate the most important moment of the day. The pivotal episode is not the initial desire of Boaz to help Ruth, while it looks like an unexpected blessing for Ruth. The event happens only when two characters reach mutual understanding.[98] Therefore, the actual event happens only when Boaz gives orders to his workers to assist Ruth in her gleaning, which later resulted in the amount of barley she brought home after a day of work.

The plot of Naomi, who felt herself obligated to "seek rest" (3:1) for her daughter-in-law, remains only wishful thinking unless implemented. Measures taken by Boaz in order to gather the assembly are also difficult to call relevant, for they are preparatory in nature, and are part of any legal process. The most important and relevant moment of legal procedure is still ahead.

Criteria of relevancy applied to the episodes following the pivotal moments of the story named above brings similar results. These concluding episodes usually play roles of consequence or assessment of the significant episode that happened earlier. For example, when Ruth returns from the threshing floor, the affirmative actions of Naomi seem to stop: she suggests for Ruth to wait "until you learn how the matter turns out." By the end of chapter 4, assessment takes the form of a wish – people of Bethlehem wish Boaz and Ruth a great future, similar to the life of their ancestors. In this context, the

---

97. Schipper, 118.

98. Etymologically the Russian word for "event" (событие, "sobitye") reflects coexistence ("со-бытие") of two beings at the same time at the same place and consequently their mutual understanding. See Tjupa, *Введение*, 10.

concluding scene of chapter 1 where Naomi gives a negative evaluation of her previous life and the closing scene of chapter 3 where Naomi tells Ruth to wait "until you learn how the matter turns out" (3:18) stay apart. It seems that explicit evaluative statements in both cases would only crumple the intrigue of the story.

Unlike preceding and subsequent episodes, central episodes are very relevant to the story. Their significance is reflected in the fact that they bring fundamental changes in the story world and continue to influence the situation even when the event already came to pass. For example, the decision of Ruth to follow Naomi is discussed in the second, third, and even fourth chapter. The lucky day came when Ruth met with Boaz, while he was feeding both her and Naomi for the entire period of gleaning "until the end of the barley and wheat harvests" (2:23). This provided an opportunity to appeal to Boaz with a marriage proposal: "Is not Boaz our relative with whose young women you were?" (3:2).

The scene that describes meeting with Boaz at the threshing floor is relevant to the story world, because (1) it depicts the moment of truth – Boaz finally has to decide if he is ready to take Ruth as his wife – and (2) new relevant information surfaces that for some reason evaded Naomi. In this sense even the second part of the threshing floor meeting (3:14–15) is less relevant. Finally, Boaz foresees the relevance of the legal procedure at the city gate when he concludes, appealing to the name of the Lord: "if he will redeem you, good; let him do it. But if he is not willing to redeem you, then, as the LORD lives, I will redeem you" (3:13). Its relevance is also underlined by the blessing of the people of Bethlehem, who compared the marriage of Boaz and Ruth with marriages of highly respected Israel's ancestors.

4.4.2. Unpredictability

Application of the second criteria – unpredictability – to the episodes of the story also shows that the four pivotal moments of the narrative are the most unpredictable, while preceding and subsequent episodes are more predictable.

Preceding episodes reveal the element of planning. Naomi in the first chapter unfolds possible scenarios just as bad or worse. In fact, the whole conversation between Naomi and her daughters-in-law seems to serve one function: to prepare the readers informatively about Ruth's commitment, which looks specifically unexpected after one finds out that Naomi is too old to have children and that she considers that her losses are the result of God's intervention in her life. The decision of Orpah also serves to highlight Ruth's commitment as more eventful. For Orpah's leaving is a "reasonable course of action and it is Ruth that does the unreasonable."[99]

> Orpah did what one expects. In the face of Naomi's logic, she said goodbye and went home. But Ruth's love for Naomi caused her to stay with her mother-in-law, even when such devotion seemed illogical and downright foolish. Orpah was not a bad person; on the contrary, she was a good daughter-in-law who had treated Naomi well . . . But Ruth was beyond good; her love for Naomi transcended the norm. The contrast between the two girls should not be expressed as a polarity (bad versus good) but in terms of degree (good versus great). The narrator's purpose in mentioning and describing Orpah is not to criticize her, but to highlight Ruth.[100]

Ruth, before going to the fields, announces that her plans include looking for someone "in whose sight I shall find favor" (2:2). Since the chapter starts from the introduction of Boaz, the readers expect the meeting with him. This mean that the use of particle הִנֵּה "Look!" in 2:4 is not related to the unexpectedness of Boaz's arrival.[101] Boaz's interview with the foreman is quite expected also in contrast to Boaz's first words to Ruth. No one, including Ruth, is expecting such generosity from a stranger. But Boaz's intentions become real only after he gives specific orders that are also unpredictable because they exceed what he said to Ruth in the beginning of the meeting.

The plot of Naomi in the beginning of chapter 3 is another attempt to curb their fate.[102] The flow of her thought is predictable, which is evidenced by the use of the word מְנוּחָה "rest" that she already has used in 1:9. Finally, Boaz acts predictably, going to the city gates for a legal procedure because the city gate was the place where traditionally all legal meetings were held. He

---

99. Linafelt and Beal, *Ruth and Esther*, 15.
100. Chisholm Jr., *Judges and Ruth*, 605.
101. Schipper, *Ruth*, 118.
102. Each chapter begins with a plan being formulated (by Ruth in chapter 2, by Naomi in chapter 3). Boaz then shows favor to Ruth and each chapter concludes with Naomi and Ruth evaluating what has happened. See Chisholm Jr., *Judges and Ruth*, 558.

summons not only another relative but also ten elders of the city to legitimize the decision.

Subsequent episodes are also more predictable than pivotal episodes. The first three concluding episodes are basically Naomi's assessment of the pivotal moments. The first concluding episode is predictable because Naomi has already made a similar statement in her address to her daughters-in-law (compare "the hand of the LORD has gone out against me" [1:13] and "the LORD has testified against me and the Almighty has brought calamity upon me" [1:21]). The only strange and to some degree unpredictable element in her speech is that she does not even mention Ruth. In the second chapter Naomi surprises Ruth with the fact that Boaz is one of their redeemers, but it is not a surprise for her nor for the reader, who is aware about Boaz since the beginning of chapter 2. In the concluding episode of chapter 3 Naomi also does not say anything unpredictable, for she and Ruth (and implicitly the readers) do not have any choice but to wait for the next event. The episode that follows the legal procedure is also predictable because the birth of the child after marriage is part of the natural flow of life (as was already said). In other words, because of predictability concluding episodes work as interim denouement of the story.

As for pivotal episodes, their unpredictability is beyond doubt. Ruth's impressive address is so unpredictable to Naomi that she does not even make any comments on it. The first meeting of Ruth and Boaz is unpredictable for both of them. Besides, Boaz's behavior becomes more and more unpredictable during this meeting. First, he gave her the status of a servant by permitting her to work alongside his female workers; then at mealtime he again demonstrated his kindness by inviting her to share a meal with him and his reapers. Finally, when Ruth finished her meal, Boaz extended even further kindness to her by letting her gather grain among the bundles and ordering his male workers to remove some of the grain from the bundles for Ruth to pick up.[103] The pivotal episode in chapter 3 is unpredictable both for characters and for readers because of its enigmatic atmosphere. The most unpredictable moments are the willingness of Boaz to marry Ruth and the news about the closer relative. Finally, the central episode of chapter 4 that depicts the legal procedure at the city gate has a very high degree of unpredictability

---

103. Chisholm Jr., *Judges and Ruth*, 632–33.

because the decision of the closer relative remains uncertain until the very last moment of the procedure.

4.4.3. Persistence

Pivotal episodes represent dialogues during which one of the characters announces his decision that leads to inevitable results and moves the plot. Without them there would not be any story. Preceding scenes, in contrast, are preparatory in nature and by themselves do not change much. In other words, they do not have a quality of persistence. They certainly help to maximize the effect of pivotal episodes, but by themselves they do not affect the rest of the story.

To be sure, Naomi's farewell speech in chapter 1 does influence Orpah's decision but only for Orpah to leave the story world; Naomi's reasoning does not change Ruth's decision. The same is true for several introductory episodes in chapter 2. No decisions are made during Ruth's fruitless gleaning, greetings, or the conversation of Boaz with his foreman. The course of the story is changed only after Ruth's conversation with Boaz, not when Naomi sends Ruth to the threshing floor. Finally, gathering the court of the elders is standard procedure for any legal business, but the particular decision of the closer relative and the willingness of Boaz to take his opportunity affect the flow of history.

The closing episodes by themselves do not have durative quality, but indicate the durative effect of pivotal episodes. Naomi comes to Bethlehem with Ruth, and Boaz happens to be the relative of Naomi so Ruth could keep "gleaning until the end of the barley and wheat harvests." The visit to the threshing floor has resulted in long and anxious waiting, and the birth of Obed and the restoration of Naomi were the only consequences of the pivotal event – Boaz's victory in the court. Therefore, the pivotal episodes of the story prove to be more persistent than preceding and subsequent episodes.

4.4.4. Irreversibility

As was already said, the only true irreversible events in the book of Ruth are the deaths of Elimelech and his sons and the birth of Obed. All other events, including their pivotal scenes, are technically reversible. However, compared with pivotal and closing episodes, introductory episodes are more reversible because in them characters do not confront fateful decisions. Let's take the example of Orpah. After the first address of Naomi, she and Ruth are willing to follow Naomi and live among her people. However, after Naomi's second persuasive speech, Orpah changes her decision. Was this decision fateful? Not at all. If Orpah for some reason would change her mind, catch up and join Naomi and Ruth, no one, including readers, would consider it to be shameful or illogical. With Ruth's decision it is entirely a different matter. By promising Naomi that "anything but death parts" them, she burned her bridges and could not return to Moab anymore. Her decisiveness is demonstrated, first, phraseologically with the use of short unambiguous phrases, and second, psychologically by presenting the point of view of Naomi who saw that Ruth "was determined to go with her" (1:18).

The meeting of Ruth and Boaz could never have happened if Ruth had not been in the field of Boaz or if Boaz had not come on time or if the foreman would not allow Ruth to stay and wait for Boaz or if Boaz would not hear about Ruth's decision. All these short episodes are very unstable, shaky, and undetermined. Depicting the conversation between Ruth and Naomi in which Naomi shares her plan with Ruth, the narrator points out that Ruth replied, "All that you say I will do." Then the narrator even adds, "So she went down to the threshing floor and did just as her mother-in-law had commanded her" (3:6). However, at any stage of the task Ruth, theoretically, could turn back, which was impossible after Boaz's awakening. Boaz could win the case only because of the happy occasion (or participation of God, speaking theologically). But only after the relative "drew off his sandal," the situation became truly irreversible.

As with persistence, irreversibility remains in the closing episodes just because they are the outcomes of the pivotal episodes.

4.4.5. Non-Iterativity

Central episodes are non-iterative by their nature. Ruth did not have to renew her decision on a regular basis. The meeting of Boaz and Ruth on the field is special because it is first and thus distinctive. If Ruth would go to threshing floor every night, a sexual aspect would be the first assumption. It is impossible to conceive that the closer relative comes to the city gate with an appeal concerning a previous decision.

Preceding and closing episodes are quite another matter altogether. Naomi addresses her daughters-in-law twice – and these are only the recorded speeches. One can assume that in reality she spent a considerable amount of time to convince them to return. Ruth should be gleaning for a long time before she meets with Boaz. Boaz greeted his workers every day and probably with the same words, the same way he asked his foreman about new workers. To gather the legal assembly, one had to go through the same routine procedure. The only exception is Naomi's plot – something that does not happen every day. But the intentions that motivated Naomi to send Ruth to the threshing floor have always been part of Naomi's character. The characteristic of non-iterativity reflects the atmosphere of anti-eventfulness that precedes all true narratological events.

The reasoning would not be complete without mentioning that closing episodes are iterative as well. They either depict the routine of life – "they returned," "she lived with her mother-in-law," she "became his nurse" – or the routine of anticipation: "Wait, my daughter, until you learn how the matter turns out."

4.4.6. Conclusion

The analysis of the episodes of the book of Ruth according to Schmid's characteristics of eventfulness confirms the findings of the previous analysis of intentionality. The prologue and the epilogue, being the most eventful episodes of the book, however, stay outside of the story proper. As for the four events of the book, they include episodes with different degrees of eventfulness. Central pivotal episodes of each event (episodes 2, 9, 12 and 16) are preceded and followed by the less eventful episodes. These four episodes play a central role in the narrative because at these relevant, unpredictable, persistent, irreversible, and non-iterative moments the characters make crucial decisions that change the course of the plot. Decision-making moments are therefore integrated into the thread running through the whole book. This unity that is based upon the thread of the narrative is well described by Campbell:

> What now happens at the threshing floor is as essential to the story-teller's purpose as what happened on the Moabite highway between Ruth and Naomi, or what happened in the harvest scene when Boaz praised an impoverished widow who was gleaning, or what will happen in the solemn civil hearing at the city gate. At each of these points in the story, a moment of

choice is presented to both actors and audience, and at each of these points the choice is made in favor of what righteous living calls for.[104]

4.5. Conclusion of Chapter 4

This chapter consists of an original contribution to general as well as to Old Testament narratology. In the field of general narratology, it shows how the ideas of Tjupa and Schmid were for the first time combined together for the analysis of selectivity (which is in essence the analysis of focalization). Consideration of intentionality and eventfulness of each episode of the narrative helps to identify the narrator's logic of selectivity and therefore understand the principle by which the narrator focalizes narrative information on the first level of narrative constitution. The chapter shows that the ideas of Tjupa and Schmid are complimentary and have to be applied in the sequence proposed in this chapter.

There is also the contribution to methodology of studying focalization in narratives. The chapter shows how focalization, being understood as selection of narrative information, can be analyzed according to Schmid's genetic model narrative constitution.

Although the analysis of eventfulness is traditionally applied to contemporary fiction, this chapter attempts to apply these methods to the Old Testament book of Ruth. The analysis clearly shows that the narrator of the book of Ruth builds the story upon four narratological events: (1) conversation on the way to Bethlehem; (2) first encounter of Ruth and Boaz; (3) last encounter of Ruth and Boaz; (4) legal procedure at the gate of Bethlehem. None of these events were selected at random. They are characterized by a high degree of intentionality, and they are witnessed and judged by the characters of the story. Besides, each event has the most pivotal episode that is distinct by a high degree of relevance, unpredictability, persistence, irreversibility, and non-iterativity.

---

104. Campbell, *Ruth*, 132.

CHAPTER 5

Focalization on the Level of Composition

In previous chapters focalization was defined as the restriction of narrative information as it regards to unrestricted knowledge of an omniscient narrator. This restriction is achieved through selection and channeling of narrative information on different stages of the narrative constitution. Following this definition in the previous chapter, we have explored the events of the story that were selected by the narrator from the continuum of life. As a result, it has been determined that the book of Ruth consists of episodes with different degrees of eventfulness. Some of those episodes can be definitely described as full-fledged narratological events (they were called the central events of the story), and some episodes play a role of introductory and concluding events in relation to the central events.

In this chapter, my purpose is to show how the narrator focalizes the story on the level of its composition. As was explained in chapter 3 of this work, composition in its essence is reorganization of the flow of narrative information with the purpose of creating spectacular narrative and conveying an ideological point of view. But reorganization can be achieved in several ways. Schmid[1] gives an example of the simplest case of composition: rearrangement of events in the literal sense of the word. However, one encounters a problem when considering composition in the book of Ruth, because the episodes of the book of Ruth are placed in simple chronological order. There are no episodes that happen simultaneously, and there are also no occasions when

---

1. Schmid, *Narratology*, 191.

the same episode is recapitulated from different perspectives.[2] However, this does not mean that composition is not applied to the book of Ruth, but that the text of the book of Ruth is composed in a more subtle way.

Instead of mere replacement of events of the book of Ruth, the narrator rearranges the flow and the amount of information in relation to his omniscience. What has happened with the flow of information in the book of Ruth is exactly what Genette means when he speaks about distribution of narrative information relatively to the issue of omniscience,

> So by focalization I certainly mean a restriction of "field" – actually, that is, a selection of narrative information with respect to what was traditionally called omniscience. In pure fiction that term is, literally, absurd (the author has nothing to "know," since he invents everything), and we would be better off replacing it with completeness of information – which, when supplied to a reader, makes him "omniscient."[3]

In the book of Ruth, the narrator who possesses all the information about the story world, nevertheless, is not in a hurry to share it with the readers, but gives it in small portions in different stages of the narrative. Moreover, sometimes new information comes to the readers from the narrator in narratorial intrusions, and sometimes it comes from the mouth of the characters. In the former case, therefore, the readers get more information and become as informed as the narrator, and in the latter case they become less informed than the characters and, therefore, their horizon becomes narrower than the horizon of the narrator. This relationship between horizons of different participants of the discourse (the narrator, the characters, and the readers) seems to be the main way of distribution of narrative information in the book of Ruth. Thereafter it will be called "the play of horizons" and will imply the comparison of the horizon of the readers with the horizons of the characters.

Consequently, the passages where the readers' horizon exceeds the horizons of the characters will be called zero focalized. The passages where the horizon of the readers equals the horizon of the character(s) will be called internally focalized. In contrast, the passages where the readers' horizon is

---

2. One possible exception from this rule will be considered later when I look at chapter 4 of the book of Ruth.

3. Genette, *Narrative Discourse Revisited*, 74.

narrower than the horizon of the character(s) will be regarded as externally focalized. In individual cases when the readers' horizon exceeds the horizon of one of the characters but is the same or narrower than the horizon of another character, the passage will be considered zero focalized in relation to the first character and internally focalized in relation to another character.

As will be shown in a relevant section, the narrator of the book of Ruth expands the horizon of the readers at least twice (in 2:1 and 4:17). There are also two points of the narrative when the readers' horizon is expanded by the characters of the story (in 2:20 and 3:12) but with the opposite effect: focalization from zero changes to external. The readers may know more than they knew before, but less than the characters. Each time the change of horizon forces the readers to re-evaluate their perception of a previous portion of the text.

The book of Ruth also consists of a lot of examples of focalization on the level of the story. It becomes obvious when the narrator brings together characters that possess different amounts of information, which results in the play of horizons on the level of the story. The key role in this process belongs to dialogues. The characters of the book of Ruth constantly picture future or recall past events and give or withhold information. The play of horizons both on the level of discourse and on the level of the story is discussed in this chapter.

As for linearization of the events of the book of Ruth, it is not present in this story in actual terms because the account of the events is never literally repeated from different points of view. However, the characters of the book constantly recall the same events and tend to give appraisal of the same event. By doing so, they in essence repeat some of its elements and technically recapitulate the same event from their points of view. This again proves that linearization is closely related to focalization because it is built upon the point of view of the character. Among those "linearized" events are:

(1) Sojourn in Moab (1:1–5; 1:8; 1:20–21)
(2) The departure of Orpah (1:14; 1:15)
(3) Ruth's decision to follow Naomi (1:16–17; 2:10–12)
(4) Ruth is gleaning in the fields (2:3, 2:6–7)
(5) Ruth's visit to the threshing floor (3:1–4; 3:5–7)
(6) Boaz's gift (3:15, 3:17)

(7) Legal procedure (3:13, 4:3–8)
(8) Blessing of the family (4:11–12; 4:14–15; 4:17–22)

In the following sections of this chapter, I will analyze focalization of the text of the book of Ruth as it is manifested in reorganization and linearization of narrative information.

5.1. The Woman Was Left Alone (1:1–22)

From the beginning of the book, the narrator sets the horizon of the readers in such a way that the readers happen to know less than the characters of the story. This is achieved through several narratorial intrusions. The largest intrusion is found in the prologue to the story (1:1–5) where the narrator situates the story in the historical period of Judges. At the same intrusion, by means of precise and colorful words and expressions, the narrator helps the readers to see the situation through the eyes of Naomi and her daughters-in-law, preparing them to perceive opinions of the characters with the right attitude. Then in the middle of the dialogue the narrator makes two short but vivid statements (in 1:9 and 1:14) that help the readers to see the tragedy of the moment from inside of the story. One more time the narrator describes the reaction of the city of Bethlehem to the arrival of Naomi (in 1:19) with the purpose to emphasize once again the hopelessness of the situation. Finally, the passage ends with designation of Ruth as a Moabite woman (1:22) that in relation to Naomi's evaluation of her destiny completes the description of formidable challenges that the women met after arrival in Bethlehem.

5.1.1. Historical Perspective in the Prologue (1:1)

The prologue to the book of Ruth does not only introduce the narrative proper, but also makes sure the readers assume the right initial position in relation to the narrative world. The readers, according to the concept of the narrator, should enter the narrative proper thinking first of all about the historical period of Judges when the story took place.

Consider that all one knows about the book of Ruth is just the story of two widows that could survive due to the care of one of their relatives. This kind of story could potentially happen in any historical period. But by adding historical remarks and mentioning specific historical figures, the narrator could add ideological value to an otherwise simple folk-wisdom story.

Canonical analysis of Moore[4] shows that the book of Ruth is a "well-crafted, entertaining story, but in its context is something much more."[5] This "something much more" is the ideological message of the book, which is given in the narrator's remarks throughout the book. For example, Moore suggests reading the book of Ruth in the context of Judges 17–21 and looking at the characters and event of the book through three lenses. First, he sees the contrast between three wanderers – two Levites (from Judges 17:8 and 19:1) and Elimelech. The first two never come home, while the third one returns (albeit in his name). Then Moore compares the religious and ethical stands of the three main characters of Ruth with the immoral and unethical behavior of characters of the book of Judges. In fact, he finds here the greatest contrast between the book of Ruth and the book of Judges: "In place of Micah's hollow religiosity stands Boaz's solid integrity. In place of the tribal elders' divination stands Naomi's Yahwistic faith. In place of the Danites' hypocrisy stands Ruth's compassion."[6] Finally, Moore compares two parallel terms for "kindness" and shows that they have completely different origins. While kindness in Judges results from "awkward imposition," the kindness of Ruth is "a gift . . . rooted in the promises of Yahweh."[7]

However, all Moore's conclusions are based on one single phrase in the beginning of the book: וַיְהִי בִּימֵי שְׁפֹט הַשֹּׁפְטִים. One would not be able to come to these insights if the narrator had not highlighted a particular historical period. The phrase "in the days of" does not only refer to the time of the story but reveals the background that helps the narrator to reveal his ideology. Therefore, commentaries can legitimately contrast the story of Ruth with general trends in the period of Judges:

> This was a dark period in Israel's history, when most people followed their own moral and ethical code, rather than the Lord's standards . . . The heading provides a dark backdrop for the inspiring story that follows. During a time when people were

---

4. Moore, "To King or Not," 27–42.
5. Moore, 35.
6. Moore, 38.
7. Moore, 40.

selfish and refused to follow the moral compass God had provided them, this story tells of a woman (a non-Israelite at that!) who demonstrated genuine love for her mother-in-law and her deceased husband. Her actions stand in sharp contrast to the moral chaos that characterized this period.[8]

Considering importance of the initial phrase of the book, scholars have different views. Campbell, for example, sees the initial sentence as important because he considers that the beginning of the book shows "unique syntax." According to Campbell, the combination of וַיְהִי following by very general (not absolute) time reference and "cognate relationship of an infinitive construct and a plural noun" can be found only here and in Genesis 36:31.[9] Holmstedt does not support this insight of Campbell and calls not to "make too much of the uniqueness of the initial clause" because the phrase could occur elsewhere, if we would have broader corpus of books on Biblical Hebrew.[10] Wilch comes to the same conclusion, but because "the entire opening clause (וַיְהִי בִּימֵי שְׁפֹט הַשֹּׁפְטִים) is a temporal modifier of the following clause (וַיְהִי רָעָב בָּאָרֶץ), which is the first main clause in the narrative."[11]

However, according to the narratological approach, this clause is of great importance because it belongs to the narrator and as such is ideologically motivated.[12] Another thing is that its only function is to make sure that the readers would not miss the historical background of the book, and in this sense Holmstedt is right. On the basis of this reasoning, it is impossible to consider this clause as redundant as did some LXX manuscripts, or to consider it as a later addition,[13] for without this clause the book is deprived of its ideological meaning.

Yet, putting too much emphasis into this phrase would be incorrect. According to McKeown, "[While] those days were characterized by violence

---

8. Chisholm Jr., *Judges and Ruth*, 591–92.

9. Campbell, *Ruth*, 49–50. See also Schipper, *Ruth*, 79.

10. Holmstedt, *Ruth*, 53.

11. Wilch, *Ruth*, 111.

12. Lacocque suggests that the reason to use the verb "to judge" (otherwise unnecessary) is the way to say that it was the period of "real" judges and to orient the narrative "toward the legal interpretation." See LaCocque, *Ruth*, 37. However, Holmstedt makes a note that the verb שָׁפַט "to judge" "rarely arbitrates or otherwise acts judicially; instead, the שׁוֹפֵט leads during military crises and otherwise governs generally." See Holmstedt, *Ruth*, 54.

13. Campbell, *Ruth*, 50.

and lawlessness . . . the story of Ruth is not about violence but about love and commitment: the love of people for each other and the love of God that ignores national boundaries."[14]

5.1.2. Restriction of Perspective in the Prologue

In the prologue the narrator also makes every effort to convince the readers that Naomi and (even more so) her daughters-in-law are left alone after the death of their husbands and do not know anybody who could possibly help them to address their problems. That is why the identity of Naomi changes from wife of Elimelech in verses 1–2 to "Naomi" in verse 3 and simply to "the woman" in verse 5. According to Berlin, it is done "for the emotional effect" for Naomi has "lost all status now."[15]

> From wife to widow, from mother to no-mother, this female is stripped of all identity. The security of husband and children, which a male-dominated culture affords its women, is hers no longer. The definition of worth, by which it values the female, applies to her no more. The blessings of old age, which it gives through progeny, are there no longer. Stranger in a foreign land, this woman is a victim of death – and of life.[16]

The other peculiarity of the text that aims to create the same emotional effect is the use of the word "children" in relation to the adult sons of Naomi. Bush offers possible reasons of this choice: first, because "it forms an inclusion with 4:16," which pictures Naomi holding a baby in her arms. But it seems more plausible that "it expresses the poignancy of the mother's loss."[17]

Thus by the beginning of the story itself, the readers find themselves in the position internal to the story world. This position remains until the beginning of chapter 2 when in Ruth 2:1 the narrator introduces Boaz as the relative/friend of Elimelech. But until that moment the idea of hopelessness of the situation is emphasized.

---

14. McKeown, *Ruth*, 13.
15. Berlin, *Poetics and Interpretation*, 87.
16. Trible, *God and the Rhetoric*, 167–68.
17. Bush, *Ruth/Esther*, 66.

5.1.3. The Beginning of the Journey (1:6–7)

Ruth 1:6–22 reports about the journey of Naomi and Ruth to Bethlehem, but in contrast with the previous section, the narrator starts to open up the internal world of the characters. Thus, the second part of 1:6 informs the readers about the decision of Naomi to return from Moab to Bethlehem. By doing this, the narrator starts to open up the inner world of his characters, and the readers become aware of their attitudes and motives. Therefore, the first part of the following passage is externally focalized and the second part of it is internally focalized since in the second part the horizon of the readers becomes as wide as the horizon of the character (Naomi):

וַתָּקָם הִיא וְכַלֹּתֶיהָ וַתָּשָׁב מִשְּׂדֵי מוֹאָב כִּי שָׁמְעָה בִּשְׂדֵה מוֹאָב
כִּי־פָקַד יהוה אֶת־עַמּוֹ לָתֵת לָהֶם לָחֶם׃

Then she arose with her daughters-in-law to return from the country of Moab, for she had heard in the fields of Moab that the LORD had visited his people and given them food. (Ruth 1:6)

Moreover, the second part of the verse reverts to the past activity of Naomi that was not previously reported. Naomi first made a decision to return to Bethlehem and only then arose and went. As was noticed by van Wolde, the first three clauses are narrator's texts, but the fourth one represents Naomi's observation. Van Wolde identifies "different speaking instances (narrator and character) for the forms and/or contents of the information presented."[18] The narrator explains that Naomi's decision to return was based on her assumption of God's activity. She apparently believed that God was responsible for both lack and abundance of food in Judea. This is an example of how reorganization of narrative information produces the shift from external to internal focalization. The perspective is first of all ideological because it shares how Naomi evaluates the world. Then her evaluation is approved by her decision.

In verse 7, however, the narrator seems to return to the external mode of focalization:

וַתֵּצֵא מִן־הַמָּקוֹם אֲשֶׁר הָיְתָה־שָׁמָּה וּשְׁתֵּי כַלֹּתֶיהָ עִמָּהּ וַתֵּלַכְנָה
בַדֶּרֶךְ לָשׁוּב אֶל־אֶרֶץ יְהוּדָה׃

---

18. van Wolde, "Who Guides Whom?," 623–642.

> So she set out from the place where she was with her two daughters-in-law, and they went on the way to return to the land of Judah. (Ruth 1:7)

Without understanding this shift in focalization, it may appear that the repetition is excessive because verses 6 and 7 both share the same information about Naomi's return. Various attempts have been made to explain this seeming redundancy. Joüon considers that verse 7 adds nothing substantial to the verse 6.[19] Hubbard sees in this verse the report of "actual departure from Moab" but does not bring any further explanation.[20] Consequently, he explains the plural form of the verb הָלַךְ as "three sharing the same fate traveling on the road together."[21] Sasson thinks that the purpose of verse 7 is to "heighten the drama of verses 8–18 by sandwiching it between two verses, the first of which (v. 7) speaks of three people about to leave Moab, while the second (v. 19) speaks of only Ruth and Naomi."[22] According to Chisholm, verse 7 repeats the previous verse, because it "begins a more focused, detailed account of Naomi's return."[23]

However, this repetition can be explained better if the analysis of shifts in focalization is employed. In verses 6 and 7, the narrator uses different types of focalization in relation to different characters. The second part of verse 6 is focalized internally in relation to Naomi, for the readers get to know the reasons that led her to return home. This reflects in the use of the verb קוּם "to arise," which otherwise would be redundant. However, the reasons that led Naomi's daughters-in-law to follow her and her attitude toward their decision is left unexplored. Therefore, in 1:7 the narrator focalizes the departure of women externally and uses another verb יָצָא "to go out," which is more applicable for physical movement (as compared with the verb שׁוּב – "to return" in the general sense). Besides, in 1:7 the narrator points our attention to the details of the trip by mentioning the place of departure with deixis שָׁם "there" and specifying that daughters-in-law were עִמָּה "with her." The readers'

---

19. Joüon, *Ruth*, 35.
20. Hubbard, *Ruth*, 101.
21. Hubbard, 101.
22. Sasson, *Ruth*, 22.
23. Chisholm Jr., *Judges and Ruth*, 585.

horizon, therefore, is narrower than the horizons of her daughters-in-law, which results in external focalization in relation to the daughters-in-law.

To sum up, the analysis of focalization shows that these verses present the same act – the beginning of the journey – but from two different perspectives. In verse 6 the text is focalized internally in relation to Naomi explaining the reason for her decision, while in verse 7 the text is focalized externally in relation to Naomi's daughters-in-law, which opens up the way to the following dialogue.

5.1.4. Dialogue between Naomi and Her Daughters-in-Law (1:8–14)

In 1:8 the distance between the narrator and the narrated events is reduced and the narration reaches the level of the story. The narrator takes the position of detached onlooker acquiring the ability to hear and record the words of the characters.

> וַתֹּאמֶר נָעֳמִי לִשְׁתֵּי כַלֹּתֶיהָ לֵכְנָה שֹּׁבְנָה אִשָּׁה לְבֵית אִמָּהּ
> יַעֲשֶׂה יהוה עִמָּכֶם חֶסֶד כַּאֲשֶׁר עֲשִׂיתֶם עִם־הַמֵּתִים וְעִמָּדִי: יִתֵּן
> יהוה לָכֶם וּמְצֶאןָ מְנוּחָה אִשָּׁה בֵּית אִישָׁהּ וַתִּשַּׁק לָהֶן וַתִּשֶּׂאנָה
> קוֹלָן וַתִּבְכֶּינָה:

> But Naomi said to her two daughters-in-law, "Go, return each of you to her mother's house. May the LORD deal kindly with you, as you have dealt with the dead and with me. The LORD grant that you may find rest, each of you in the house of her husband!" Then she kissed them, and they lifted up their voices and wept. (1:8–9)

In this and the following dialogic passages the primarily source of information for the readers is the characters' speeches. As was said in the previous chapter, direct speech represents a borderline case that has been designated as parallel focalization, which means that the readers know as much or even less than the characters, depending on the depth of the character's speech. If the character's speech consists of feelings, attitudes, motives, etc., the text of the dialogue can be considered internally focalized. Otherwise, the text is externally focalized.

The speech of Naomi starts as externally focalized (verbs in imperative forms usually reflect external mode of focalization). However, the more she explains the reasons of her commands, the more internally focalized the text becomes. One of the signs of internally focalized text of the dialogue is rearrangement of flow of information in a character's speech. The information in the speech of Naomi is rearranged for it rearranges the flow of information by recalling past events that were not reported earlier and by placing possible future events before they really happen. For example, what the readers know about the marriage life of Naomi's daughters-in-law they know primarily from Naomi's perspective. According to Naomi, her daughters-in-law related to her and her sons with חֶסֶד. There are no other assessments about the quality of relationship within their family during the sojourn in Moab – only Naomi's perspective is presented. By saying that daughters-in-law dealt with family members with חֶסֶד, Naomi gives ideological appraisal to their behavior for the idea of חֶסֶד reflects the "general system of viewing of the world conceptually."[24]

Furthermore, out of Naomi's mouth come not only memories but also wishes. She describes not only happy old days when she and her daughters-in-law were one family but also pictures their sorrowful future. This picture of the future is, therefore, also internally focalized for it presents Naomi's point of view. It becomes obvious when one realizes how ignorant she is of the real attitudes of her daughters-in-law. She wrongly assumes that Orpah and Ruth don't have any interest in her anymore and thinks that for them it is better to stay in Moab and go back to their families. She thinks that in their own land among their own people, they would have more chances to get married and have children.

The expression אִשָּׁה לְבֵית אִמָּהּ (lit. "woman to the house of her mother") is unusual. In fact, it is so unusual that LXX and multiple Old Greek manuscripts change it to the more standard "father's house."[25] Bush lists several ways how this deviance can be interpreted. Among them are logical (" . . . the fathers are already dead; mothers are named since they know best how to console; the reference suggests the existence of a matriarchal society"); linguistic ("the words were chosen to achieve parallelism and alliteration"); and cultural ("the mother's house was customary the locus for discussion and planning for marriage").[26] Then Bush proposes his own interpretation. He

---

24. Uspensky, Семиотика искусства, 19.
25. Schipper, *Ruth*, 91.
26. Bush, *Ruth/Esther*, 75

considers that the expression is "singularly appropriate here: it emphasizes the contrast Naomi wishes to make – a widow should return to her mother and not stay with her mother-in-law."[27] The analysis of focalization also helps to see this expression not as anomaly but as purposefully inserted by the narrator in order to demonstrate the horizon of Naomi. In her mind she excludes herself from the future of her daughters-in-law and sees her place to be taken by their mothers.

Until this moment the readers are being immersed into the mind of Naomi, watching the world through her eyes. Then just for a few words the text is focalized externally, thus returning to the question about the attitude of Naomi's daughters-in-law. However, even in this text their attitudes start to gush out through the mimetic description of their behavior:

וַתִּשַּׁק לָהֶן וַתִּשֶּׂאנָה קוֹלָן וַתִּבְכֶּינָה

Then she kissed them, and they lifted up their voices and wept. (1:9b)

The intrusion aims to show the reaction of the women to the hopelessness of the situation. According to Hubbard, the verb נָשַׁק "to kiss" here means "kiss goodbye" as in other places with similar contexts, like Genesis 31:28, 2 Samuel 19:39, and 1 Kings 19:20.[28] The readers still do not possess any additional information about the story world; they comprehend the situation according to Naomi's view, and are not aware of the thoughts of Naomi's daughters-in-law. Therefore, the readers are called to show empathy to the women's impasse. The empathy becomes even greater when they hear the objection of the daughters-in-law. These are the first words of the daughters-in-law and the first attempt to share their inner attitudes.[29]

וַתֹּאמַרְנָה־לָּהּ כִּי־אִתָּךְ נָשׁוּב לְעַמֵּךְ׃

And they said to her, "No, we will return with you to your people." (1:10)

For the readers, who do not possess any external information and cannot assess the situation objectively, the words of the daughters-in-law are yet

---

27. Bush, 75.
28. Hubbard, *Ruth*, 98n14.
29. Edmiston, *Hindsight*, 7. See also Berendsen, "Formal Criteria," 79–94.

another version of how the plot can unfold. For Naomi their attitude may be a surprise. The construction of the utterance is unusual, for it starts with the prepositional phrase כִּי־אִתָּךְ, "with you," which typically follows the verb. According to Holmstead, the adjunct "is raised to assert the daughters-in-law's intention over against Naomi's."[30] But the change in syntax could also be the result of their ideological position. Since their utterance is the answer to Naomi's command, by this phrase they may want to show that Naomi is more important for them than their own future or that they do not see their future without Naomi. The use of the phrase "your people" implies the desire to find husbands among men of Israel instead of returning to Moab. Moreover, the use of "mother's house" appears in new light. Orpah and Ruth do not want to go back to their mothers; they want to stay with Naomi.

In this section, the narrator proposes different versions of the future by using perspectives of different characters. Thus, in the next passage Naomi will be speaking about the future again but now she considers not only her daughters-in-law, but also her own future in relation to them.

וַתֹּאמֶר נָעֳמִי שֹׁבְנָה בְנֹתַי לָמָּה תֵלַכְנָה עִמִּי הַעוֹד־לִי בָנִים
בְּמֵעַי וְהָיוּ לָכֶם לַאֲנָשִׁים:
שֹׁבְנָה בְנֹתַי לֵכְןָ כִּי זָקַנְתִּי מִהְיוֹת לְאִישׁ כִּי אָמַרְתִּי יֶשׁ־לִי תִקְוָה
גַּם הָיִיתִי הַלַּיְלָה לְאִישׁ וְגַם יָלַדְתִּי בָנִים:
הֲלָהֵן ׀ תְּשַׂבֵּרְנָה עַד אֲשֶׁר יִגְדָּלוּ הֲלָהֵן תֵּעָגֵנָה לְבִלְתִּי הֱיוֹת לְאִישׁ
אַל בְּנֹתַי כִּי־מַר־לִי מְאֹד מִכֶּם כִּי־יָצְאָה בִי יַד־יְהוָה:

> But Naomi said, "Turn back, my daughters; why will you go with me? Have I yet sons in my womb that they may become your husbands? Turn back, my daughters; go your way, for I am too old to have a husband. If I should say I have hope, even if I should have a husband this night and should bear sons, would you therefore wait till they were grown? Would you therefore refrain from marrying? No, my daughters, for it is exceedingly bitter to me for your sake that the hand of the LORD has gone out against me." (1:11–13)

The main point of second exchange is the inability of Naomi to provide children who would become husbands for her daughters-in-law. The passage

---

30. Holmstedt, *Ruth*, 77.

helps the readers to explore Naomi's inner world, that is to say that Naomi's speech here is also internally focalized. Some nuances confirm this conclusion. For example, Naomi addresses her daughters-in-law as "my daughters" three times. The address itself "betrayed Naomi's tenderness toward her weeping audience"[31] and reflects Naomi's internal perspective toward her daughters-in-law. Naomi's argument is changing accordingly. She agrees that they are not just two strangers to her, but to accompany her in the present circumstances is pointless.

There is a slight difference between this and the previous speech of Naomi in that this time Naomi addresses her daughters-in-law in narrative form. Her speech sounds like the account of possible events in her daughters-in-law's lives if they decide to go with her. Moreover, in her speech she also tries to look at the world from the perspective of her daughters-in-law. By asking the rhetorical question, "Why will you go with me?" she assumes their point of view. Hubbard gives an example of the same construction from 2 Samuel 15:19.[32] In this example the one who asks the question also suggests for the listener to look at the possible consequences of his choice from his (listener's) point of view. However, as the course of events shows, Naomi's horizon is restricted because she does not know "who is behind the door" (to use the metaphor of Skalin), the minds of her daughters-in-law are not transparent to her, her understanding of their attitudes is only partially correct. And soon she will know how mistaken she is.

Numerous commentaries[33] point to the form הֲלָהֵן as one of the "interpretive cruces of the book."[34] Here is the core of the problem. The form הֲלָהֵן consists of three parts: the interrogative particle הֲ, the preposition לְ "to, for," and third-person feminine plural pronominal suffix הֵן "them." Therefore, the form can be translated as "for them" where "them" is feminine plural. However, "the obvious referents are the potential sons of Naomi could bear," which means that "them" should appear in masculine plural form.[35] To address this issue

---

31. Hubbard, *Ruth*, 108.

32. Hubbard, 108n118. The other examples of the same focalizing constructions are 1 Sam 6:6; 17:8; 20:8; Hab 1:3; 2 Sam 12:23; Mic 4:9.

33. This textual problem is discussed by Bush, *Ruth/Esther*, 79; Hubbard, *Ruth*, 111n131; Hawk, *Ruth*, 48.

34. Holmstedt, *Ruth*, 81.

35. Holmstedt, 81.

three solutions are proposed. The first solution is to see this form as neutral, referring to "things that happened." Therefore, the phrase is translated as "to that would you wait?" The second solution suggests considering the form to be equivalent to Aramaic לָהֵן "therefore" as in Daniel 2:6, 9, 4:24. The third view sees this form as a masculine dual absolute ending in Moabite language. Translation in this case would be: "for them [my hypothetical sons] would you wait?" Finally, it can be simply the misspelled masculine form.[36] Schipper points to 4QRuthb, which also reads הֲלָהֵן.[37] So, is it possible to understand this form on its own rights?

This passage is part of Naomi's speech where she expresses her view of how the story will unfold. Moreover, as I mentioned before, her perspective is complicated, for she also tries to reflect the point of view of her daughters-in-law. In this light, the Hebrew expression הֲלָהֵן תְּשַׂבֵּרְנָה עַד אֲשֶׁר יִגְדָּלוּ "would you therefore wait till they were grown?" should have a feminine element that would reflect the point of view of daughters-in-law. Would it be possible that the form הֲלָהֵן, which "does not occur elsewhere in the Hebrew Bible,"[38] has a special meaning that emphasizes the feminine plural point of view?

By the end of verse 13 two more elements that regard to the play of horizons appear. First, the meaning of the form מִכֶּם, which can be translated in one of three ways: (1) "because my bitterness is more than yours"; (2) "because my bitterness is too much for you (to share)"; or (3) "because my bitterness is on account of you." Holmstedt, who proposed these variants of translation, considers that only the second opinion "makes sense of her obvious warm feelings for Ruth and Orpah, and provides a good reason for the women to leave her."[39] However, if in her previous address Naomi was looking at the situation through the eyes of her daughters-in-law, the third option – "because my bitterness is on account of you" – becomes prevailing. Naomi does not want these women to follow the scenario she just presented.

Therefore, in verses 8 through 13 the text is mainly presented in the form of internal focalization. It reflects the perspective of Naomi toward the situation and partially represents the attitude of Naomi's daughters-in-law. Internal

---

36. All four view are presented in this order by Wilch, *Ruth*, 137.
37. Schipper, *Ruth*, 96.
38. Schipper, 96.
39. Holmstedt, *Ruth*, 84.

focalization is confirmed first of all by minor details such as Naomi's designation of her daughters-in-law as "my daughters," the daughters'-in-law desire to return with Naomi and their telling behavior. But mostly, internal focalization is confirmed by reorganization of the flow of narrative information in Naomi's speech by which she expresses her attitude toward the past and the future. From Naomi's address the readers learn about some aspects of life of the family in Moab, but what is more important, they learn about possible scenarios of the plot.

5.1.5. The Decisions of Orpah and Ruth (1:14)

In 1:14 again for just a few words the characters are presented as focalized from without:

וַתִּשֶּׂנָה קוֹלָן וַתִּבְכֶּינָה עוֹד וַתִּשַּׁק עָרְפָּה לַחֲמוֹתָהּ וְרוּת דָּבְקָה בָּהּ:

Then they lifted up their voices and wept again. And Orpah kissed her mother-in-law, but Ruth clung to her. (1:14)

The text is still written in the scope of internal focalization, because the readers are not yet informed about possible solutions of the problem and are forced to participate with the characters in their tragedy. The first clause repeats 1:9 almost verbatim, but in order to increase the tension, this time the narrator describes the scene of separation with additional word עוֹד "again." The ESV translation is not correct, for the word עוֹד, according to Bush, does not mean "again" but "more" stressing "the idea of continuance,"[40] which raises the emotional tension of the situation.[41]

One more question has to be addressed in relation to two similar intrusions (in verses 9 and 14). From the Hebrew text, it is not clear who does the crying: all three women or only daughters-in-law. Hawk convincingly demonstrates that at least in verse 9 the verbs "they raised" and "they wept" relate to daughters-in-law because they stay in one chain with the following

---

40. Bush, *Ruth/Esther*, 81.

41. Between verses 9 and 14 Hubbard points to stylistic chiasm, which brackets the episode emotionally: in verse 9 the farewell kiss led to weeping, while in verse 14a weeping led to the farewell kiss. Moreover, the reversal in the action (in verse 9 Naomi kisses her daughters-in-law, while in verse 14 Orpah kisses Naomi) demonstrates the formal ends of their relationship. See Hubbard, *Ruth*, 115.

verb "they said," while the first verb in the statement "she kissed" "is set apart grammatically and refers only to Naomi."[42] The analysis of focalization confirms this conclusion. The first time this phrase appears in 1:9 it was said that focalization shifts from internal (in relation to Naomi) to external (in relation to Naomi's daughters-in-law), which means that the act of crying may indeed apply only to Orpah and Ruth.

An important role in this short phrase is played by the construction and the very words used. The construction (the second part of the sentence starts with we+noun) of the sentence opposes the attitudes of Ruth and Orpah, and the verb that is used in order to express the attitude of Ruth דָּבַק "cling," carries a deeper meaning. According to Ziegler,

> this verb characterizes Ruth's persona. Ruth is a *devuka*, a woman who knows how to fasten herself to another person . . . The act of cleaving to another is the very opposite of selfishness. Individualistic behavior entails looking out for oneself, regarding one's own interests as paramount even when it undermines the needs of the Other.[43]

After citing examples from different uses of this verb in the Old Testament, Ziegler comes to the conclusion that this verb

> . . . connotes an all-encompassing connection, a relationship characterized by identification, in which one party embraces the totality of the Other, utterly and completely. There is something illogical in this type of relationship, in which one's own ego, one's I-awareness, is subsumed by concern for the Other. This description accurately depicts Ruth's unusual relationship with Naomi, in which her decision to remain with her mother-in-law undermines her own self-interest.[44]

Therefore, Ruth's reaction to Naomi's words, though presented in the mode of external focalization, demonstrates some elements of internality. Nevertheless,

---

42. Hawk, *Ruth*, 47–48. Campbell comes to the same conclusion but on the basis of manuscript a from Qumran Cave 4, which reads קוֹלָמ instead of קוֹלָן and "may reflect the old feminine dual." See Campbell, *Ruth*, 66.

43. Ziegler, *Ruth*, Kindle locations 3035–3038.

44. Ziegler, Kindle locations 3044–3048.

it should be considered as externally focalized, for the narrator does not want to rush into disclosing his characters' attitudes and the readers should wait for Ruth's monologue in order to confirm their hunch.

5.1.6. Dialogue between Naomi and Ruth (1:15–18)

In verse 15 the narrative returns to dialogic form. The change in the number of the characters designates the beginning of a new scene, resulting in reorganization of the flow of narrative information and new mode of focalization. This time Naomi is not talking about the future but comments on the decision made by Orpah (i.e. return to the past event) and urges Ruth to follow the example of her sister-in-law.

וַתֹּאמֶר הִנֵּה שָׁבָה יְבִמְתֵּךְ אֶל־עַמָּהּ וְאֶל־אֱלֹהֶיהָ שׁוּבִי אַחֲרֵי יְבִמְתֵּךְ:

And she said, "See, your sister-in-law has gone back to her people and to her gods; return after your sister-in-law." (1:15)

In the first part of Naomi's utterance the flow of information is rearranged, for the narrator could have given this theological comment earlier when Orpah was leaving. Instead, the readers were focused on the emotional and practical dimensions of the situation. Now Naomi presents the decision of Orpah in a different light by giving ideological appraisal to Orpah's step – Orpah bid farewell not only to her mother-in-law but to Naomi's people and Naomi's God.

This reasoning forces us to reconsider the traditional interpretation of the particle הִנֵּה "behold," which is usually understood as the marker of the perception of the character distinct from that of the narrator. Thus it is called an "attention getter,"[45] the word that Naomi uses to focus Ruth's attention on the action of Orpah hoping "to get Ruth to follow suit."[46] However, Naomi does not simply underline the action itself, but wants to emphasize a specific view on this action by selecting and channeling narrative information. Therefore, it is another example of internal focalization, in this case with an ideological facet in view.

Until verse 16 the readers have only an approximate portrait of Ruth according to the perspective of Naomi. The desire of Ruth (together with

---

45. Berlin, *Poetics and Interpretation*, 91.
46. VanGemeren, *New International Dictionary*, 910.

Orpah) to stay with her mother-in-law that she expressed in 1:9 and in 1:14 partially reflected her inner attitude. Yet information was quite marginal, which left the readers puzzling about Ruth's true motivation. Only when Ruth opens her mouth and explains her firm decision to go with Naomi do the readers become aware of her true attitude.

Like in Naomi's speech, in Ruth's speech the flow of information is rearranged because she pictures her future. This picture is restricted (i.e. focalized internally) as any picture of the future, because the character is not aware of how the story will turn out and the narrator makes sure that the readers conceptualize the situation the same way. Besides, in her speech Ruth deals with issues that reflect her attitude toward Naomi.

All this demonstrates that the text is also focalized internally in relation to Ruth. Therefore, the characters have not moved yet from the territory of Moab but the readers already have two different scenarios: one after Naomi, and one after Ruth. Thus, using focalization on the level of the story, the narrator is able to create suspense based on different horizons.

Verse 18 is also internally focalized, though it does not consist of direct speech:

וַתֵּרֶא כִּי־מִתְאַמֶּצֶת הִיא לָלֶכֶת אִתָּהּ וַתֶּחְדַּל לְדַבֵּר אֵלֶיהָ׃

And when Naomi saw that she was determined to go with her, she said no more. (1:18)

This time the narrator presents the perspective of Naomi, who "saw" (i.e. realized) that Ruth is not going to change her decision. It seems that Naomi was not expecting this turn and is greatly surprised by what she heard. Otherwise, why she does not say anything in order to challenge or approve Ruth's decision? It is interesting to note that Naomi mentioned past and future but never said anything about the present situation probably because she does not "see" how her daughters-in-law can continue to stay with her.

5.1.7. Arrival to Bethlehem (1:19–21)

In this short intrusion,[47] the narrator describes the reaction of women of Bethlehem (which is indicated by the particle with 3fp suffix אֲלֵיהֶן) to the arrival of Naomi:

וַיְהִי כְּבֹאָנָה בֵּית לֶחֶם וַתֵּהֹם כָּל־הָעִיר עֲלֵיהֶן וַתֹּאמַרְנָה הֲזֹאת נָעֳמִי׃

And when they came to Bethlehem, the whole town was stirred because of them. And the women said, "Is this Naomi?" (1:19)

The reaction is pictured with the verb וַתֵּהֹם, which literary means "to make a noisy hum." The meaning is obviously figurative and depends upon the meaning accorded to the whole episode.

The scene can be understood in two quite different ways. On the one hand the "noisy hum" with which the city responds (expressed by the verb וַתֵּהֹם) and the questions "Is this Naomi?" would both convey consternation and concern, perhaps because of Naomi's aged and careworn condition. On the other hand, the "noisy hum" could express delighted excitement and the rhetorical question astonished and joyful recognition.[48] On the basis of Naomi's answer (and she is talking about her identity), Hawk comes to conclusion that the question, as it is understood by Naomi, expresses women's "surprise and incredulity and . . . evokes the question of identity."[49] And McKeown considers that it "reflects the excitement of those who had not seen Naomi for a decade."[50]

In the scope of internal focalization, the question should be understood as surprise that comes as a result of the inconsistency between the Naomi they knew and the Naomi that arrived to the city. In the next verse their curiosity is satisfied, for Naomi explains what's happened with her and why she is not the same person she used to be.

וַתֹּאמֶר אֲלֵיהֶן אַל־תִּקְרֶאנָה לִי נָעֳמִי קְרֶאןָ לִי מָרָא כִּי־הֵמַר שַׁדַּי לִי מְאֹד׃

---

47. According to McKeown, "The details of long journeys are not usually recorded unless they have a direct bearing on the main story line." McKeown, *Ruth*, 30.

48. Campbell, *Ruth*, 75.

49. Hawk, *Ruth*, 62.

50. McKeown, *Ruth*, 33.

אֲנִי מְלֵאָה הָלַכְתִּי וְרֵיקָם הֱשִׁיבַנִי יהוה לָמָּה תִקְרֶאנָה לִי נָעֳמִי
וַיהוה עָנָה בִי וְשַׁדַּי הֵרַע לִי:

> She said to them, "Do not call me Naomi; call me Mara, for the Almighty has dealt very bitterly with me. I went away full, and the LORD has brought me back empty. Why call me Naomi, when the LORD has testified against me and the Almighty has brought calamity upon me?" (1:20–21)

Naomi's answer is a classical example of internal focalization because naming is considered the most vivid way of expressing the point of view of the characters. According to Uspensky, "In a literary work, one character may be called by several different names or designated by a variety of titles. Frequently, different names are attributed to one and the same person in a single sentence or in closely connected passages in the text."[51] This is exactly what happens in this passage. By describing herself with two different names, Naomi expresses her ideological point of view. Besides, her names refer to two different periods of her life – before the sojourn in Moab and after her return – which once more rearranges narrative information. Another indication of internal focalization is the emotional charge of Naomi's speech. According to Chisholm, the words of Naomi "carry an expressive function" because in them "she vented her emotions, expressing her disappointment and her feeling that she was an enemy of God."[52]

5.1.8. Summary of Return (1:22)

By the end of the chapter in the summary statement the narrator unexpectedly gives a full description of Ruth:

וַתָּשָׁב נָעֳמִי וְרוּת הַמּוֹאֲבִיָּה כַלָּתָהּ עִמָּהּ הַשָּׁבָה מִשְּׂדֵי מוֹאָב
וְהֵמָּה בָּאוּ בֵּית לֶחֶם בִּתְחִלַּת קְצִיר שְׂעֹרִים:

> So Naomi returned, and Ruth the Moabite her daughter-in-law with her, who returned from the country of Moab. And they came to Bethlehem at the beginning of barley harvest. (1:22)

Without involving the concept of focalization, this full description of Ruth looks excessive. LaCocque with great indignation says, "What is this sentence

---

51. Uspensky, *Poetics of Composition*, 25.
52. Chisholm Jr., *Judges and Ruth*, 609.

doing here? 'Ruth the Moabite' rings negatively to Israelite ears."[53] Several attempts have been made in order to explain the reason for such a long description. Hawk considers that the description is a kind of irony, for it points to Ruth's goodness: in spite of her "otherness in ethnicity, family and homeland," she stood with Naomi.[54] Hubbard sees in it the subtle introduction of racial tension.[55] He also sees in Ruth's return the idea of finding true homeland and true identity.[56] All these ideas certainly help to see new insights in the text. But perhaps to them it should be added that this description continues to keep the readers within the scope of internal focalization. By narrator's design, at this stage of the story the readers do not have to see possible solutions of the problem and see things as they are seen from the point of view of Naomi and Ruth.

Nevertheless, a glimpse of hope that appears in the final phrase of the chapter starts to prepare the readers to new narratological event: "And they came to Bethlehem at the beginning of barley harvest."

5.2. Boaz, a Relative (2:1–19)

In this section, the narrator expands the horizon of the readers so that the knowledge of the readers grows beyond the knowledge of the characters. This knowledge is particularly pertinent to recognition: Ruth does not know about the existence of Boaz; Boaz does not know Ruth in person; Ruth does not know that Boaz is the relative of Elimelech. In contrast to the characters, the readers possess all this information. This new privileged position, which is set from the beginning of chapter 2, is reinforced once again in 2:3 and 2:4 where the readers are given information that is unavailable to the characters of the story. Therefore, while the readers cannot predict the direction of the dialogues, they obviously look down at the characters and expect them to obtain the same knowledge. The section ends in 2:19 because in 2:20 Naomi communicates information that exceeds even the horizon of the readers that leads to a new shift in focalization.

---

53. LaCocque, *Ruth*, 58.
54. Hawk, *Ruth*, 63.
55. Hubbard, *Ruth*, 128.
56. Hubbard, 128. See also Bush, *Ruth/Esther*, 96.

5.2.1. Introduction of Boaz (2:1)

In the beginning of chapter 2 the narrator introduces a new character with a null copula sentence:

וּלְנָעֳמִי מְיֻדָּע לְאִישָׁהּ אִישׁ גִּבּוֹר חַיִל מִמִּשְׁפַּחַת אֱלִימֶלֶךְ וּשְׁמוֹ בֹּעַז׃

> Now Naomi had a relative of her husband's, a worthy man of the clan of Elimelech, whose name was Boaz. (2:1)

According to Holmstedt, a null copula clause usually

> ... presents background information, that is, information that does not move the "narrative" time (i.e., the time within the story) forward but does move the "narrated" time (i.e., the time it takes to tell the story) forward and adds to the information that the audience receives.[57]

It seems that the information about Boaz is given at this point of the narrative intentionally. First, it forces the readers to re-evaluate the information that has preceded the events in chapter 1. According to Genette, these kinds of remarks play a very important role in classical narratives, for they are purposefully given so that the readers would reconstitute the order of events. Moreover, the readers

> ... must take into account both that this scene comes after in the narrative and that it is supposed to have come before in the story: each of these, or rather the relationship between them (of contrast or of dissonance), is basic to the narrative text, and suppressing this relationship by eliminating one of its members is not only not sticking to the text, but is quite simply killing it.[58]

Second, this particular information being given in this particular moment of the plot certainly points to Boaz as the possible vehicle that would solve the problems Naomi and Ruth encountered in the first chapter. It changes the horizon and the position of the readers in relation to the narrative world because the narrator shares with them the information that exceeds the

---

57. Holmstedt, *Ruth*, 104.
58. Genette, *Narrative Discourse*, 35.

knowledge of Ruth and Naomi.[59] Therefore, the readers, by knowing more than the characters, look at the situation from a privileged position,[60] and focalization changes from internal to zero.

Third, it affirms that by hiding this information from the readers throughout the first chapter of the book, the narrator helped the readers to grasp the depth of Ruth's experience. According to the note of Auld,

> Young Ruth goes out to take her chance but old Naomi knows someone. This is yet another example of . . . how the Book of Ruth invites us to see things from different perspectives; and another such double perspective runs through chapter 2 as a whole.[61]

Ruth is the only character (besides Orpah) who is even unaware of Boaz.[62] By reducing the horizon of the readers to the horizon of Ruth in the first chapter, the narrator gives to the readers opportunity to participate with Ruth in her ignorance. Thus the narrator convinces the readers of the depth of tragedy and the readers naïvely believe the narrator when they listen to women's loud cry, estimate together with Naomi scant chances of Ruth and Orpah and with astonishment discover Ruth's loyalty. These emotions would not be sincere if information about Boaz was given earlier.

---

59. Ofcourse Naomi could know, but that is when we look at the real world, not the story world. I don't mean that Naomi did not know about Boaz's existence. She certainly was aware of him long ago, for he is introduced as a friend (or relative) of her husband. Ruth also could have heard about him before from her Israelite relatives. So, I am not talking about knowledge as such. More than that, taking into account the logical and prudent reasoning of Naomi in Ruth 1, when she thought through different possibilities for the future of her daughters-in-law, it is logical to assume that both Naomi and Ruth could see in Boaz a suitable candidate for perspective marriage. By the same way they could discuss another candidacy but as the saying goes, man proposes but God disposes. In this case the narrator, who looks at these events retrospectively, knows who exactly is going to redeem Naomi and become the husband of Ruth and strategically chooses to inform the readers about this fact.

60. The horizon of the readers is certainly wider, but it is not wide enough to classify it as zero focalization. This is an obvious example of what Klauk and Köppe call gradual character of focalization.

61. Auld, *Joshua, Judges, and Ruth*, 266–67.

62. Most interpreters would agree that Ruth did not know anything about Boaz until she met him in the field and was not aware about his status as redeemer until Naomi informed her about it (2:20). See Bush, *Ruth/Esther*, 103. However, Sasson considers that 2:1 as the statement of Naomi's knowledge, and translates it differently, "Now, Naomi knew of an acquaintance of her husband . . ." See Sasson, *Ruth*, 38. Bush easily demolishes Sasson's arguments on the basis of verses 19 and 20, "for it is clear that . . . the name of Boaz comes as a surprise to Naomi and that here she informs Ruth who he is for the first time." See Bush, *Ruth/Esther*, 103.

5.2.2. Dialogue between Ruth and Naomi (2:2)

Against the background of the previous verse, the placement of the conversation between Ruth and Naomi in verse 2 seems to have a special reason: to underline the difference between the horizon of the readers and the horizon of the characters. While the readers are already aware of Boaz, the surprise still waits for Ruth and Naomi.

וַתֹּאמֶר רוּת הַמּוֹאֲבִיָּה אֶל־נָעֳמִי אֵלְכָה־נָּא הַשָּׂדֶה וַאֲלַקֳטָה
בַשִּׁבֳּלִים אַחַר אֲשֶׁר אֶמְצָא־חֵן בְּעֵינָיו וַתֹּאמֶר לָהּ לְכִי בִתִּי׃

And Ruth the Moabite said to Naomi, "Let me go to the field and glean among the ears of grain after him in whose sight I shall find favor." And she said to her, "Go, my daughter." (2:2)

Ruth is looking for an abstract figure, someone who will let her glean in his field. Reporting this utterance of Ruth, the narrator helps the readers to see the situation with the eyes of Ruth. Indeed, consideration of details of this verse supports this assumption. First, the narrator designates Ruth as "Ruth the Moabite," which otherwise seems to be redundant, for Ruth has already been designated this way in 1:22.[63] According to Holmstedt, the narrator "is intent on keeping Ruth's foreign status highlighted for the audience,"[64] which becomes even more vivid when Naomi calls Ruth בִתִּי "my daughter" (2:2), while Ruth is still not a part of Israel community.

Second, ignorance of Ruth is also shown by the use of the word הַשָּׂדֶה "the field" with an article, which here must be understood in generic sense "some field" or "any adequate field."[65]

Third, Ruth's words show that she is not thinking about a particular person. The narrator chose to convey the decision of Ruth not in his own words but through direct speech (the words of Ruth herself) exactly because she is unaware about Boaz's existence and from her mouth these words create greater suspense. The same words being spoken by an omniscient narrator wouldn't sound so dramatic.

---

63. These kinds of constructions are examined in Liozov and Jakov, "Синтаксис речи рассказчика в древнееврейской повествовательной прозе."

64. Hubbard, *Ruth*, 137.

65. Holmstedt, *Ruth*, 106, Hawk, *Ruth*, 70.

Fourth, the word עַיִן "eye" used in her speech as an idiom could be a perspectival element for the original readers of the text. Starting from this verse, the readers are waiting for Boaz (or someone else) to notice (to see visually) Ruth. This prepares the spatial point of view that is used in the following episode.

Fifth, the short answer of Naomi – לְכִי בִתִּי "Go, my daughter" – is also based upon the previous verse and creates the perspective for the following scene. While knowing Boaz, Naomi does not send Ruth to his field but permits her to find the right person herself. The brevity of her answer is sometimes considered to be the reflection of Naomi's apathy. But this conclusion would not be so obvious without zero focalization of the whole episode. Even though Naomi knows what the readers know, she is so distressed that she cannot even think about a relative or a friend who could help her.

Sixth, the narrator could leave here just one imperative: "go" but he decided to add "my daughter." This designation adds emotional color to Naomi's speech. Ruth, not being aware of the information the readers have in verse 1, seems to think that Naomi is her only friend in the whole of Judea. However, when Boaz starts to talk to her calling her the same way – "my daughter" – Ruth is going to be surprised as much as the readers.[66]

5.2.3. Intrusion: Summary of Ruth's Gleaning before Meeting with Boaz (2:3)

Verse 3 is unique as regard to focalization for one can find all three types of focalization in it.

וַתֵּלֶךְ וַתָּבוֹא וַתְּלַקֵּט בַּשָּׂדֶה אַחֲרֵי הַקֹּצְרִים וַיִּקֶר מִקְרֶהָ חֶלְקַת הַשָּׂדֶה לְבֹעַז אֲשֶׁר מִמִּשְׁפַּחַת אֱלִימֶלֶךְ׃

So she set out and went and gleaned in the field after the reapers, and she happened to come to the part of the field belonging to Boaz, who was of the clan of Elimelech. (2:3)

---

66. There is, however, the possibility that the designation "my daughter" is simple a "socially coded term that reciprocates Ruth's deferential language ... [and] acknowledges the nature of the social relationship that binds the two women and signifies Naomi's higher status in that relationship." If this is the case, Naomi's words are externally focalized, for the readers are "left in the dark about Naomi's disposition towards Ruth." See Hawk, *Ruth*, 78.

From one side, the first half of this verse – "she set out and went and gleaned in the field after the reapers" – is focalized externally because the readers are informed only about acts of the character and are not given any ideas about the character's thoughts or attitudes. But then the readers are given information that exceeds the horizon of Ruth: while gleaning, Ruth finally comes to the field of Boaz. This information is given in the scope of zero focalization, which continues to expand the horizon of the readers. At the same time, the phrase וַיִּקֶר מִקְרֶהָ "and she happened to come," which literary means "and her chance chanced," shows that "Ruth came to Boaz' field by no knowledge of her own,"[67] and could mean that the narrator looks at the event through Ruth's eyes.[68] Finally this verse together with verse 1 may indicate the hand of God that stays behind the scene and who (like the narrator) is characterized by omniscience.[69] Therefore, the verse demonstrates the difference between the horizon of Ruth and the horizon of the readers, or as McKeown comments, "From Ruth's point of view she has found the right field by chance, but the reader is aware that God is working out his purposes in this situation."[70]

5.2.4. The Arrival of Boaz (2:4)

In 2:4 Boaz for the first time appears on the scene.

וְהִנֵּה־בֹעַז בָּא מִבֵּית לֶחֶם וַיֹּאמֶר לַקּוֹצְרִים יהוה עִמָּכֶם וַיֹּאמְרוּ
לוֹ יְבָרֶכְךָ יהוה:

> And behold, Boaz came from Bethlehem. And he said to the reapers, "The LORD be with you!" And they answered, "The LORD bless you." (2:4)

The particle הִנֵּה "behold" in the beginning of the verse gives neither the horizon of Ruth nor the horizon of the reapers but, according to Berlin, should be translated "as at that point." Berlin considers that in the given context, 2:4 is "information to the reader, representing the reader's perception of Boaz's entrance into the scene, with the explanation of where he had

---

67. Holmstedt, *Ruth*, 110.
68. Block, *Judges, Ruth*, 653.
69. Nielsen, *Ruth*, 55.
70. McKeown, *Ruth*, 40.

been beforehand."[71] Berlin supposes that the particle does not expresses Ruth's perception because (1) it would be more appropriate to use here the term of relationship between Ruth and Boaz instead of personal names, like "behold, the owner of the field . . ." and (2) Ruth could not know where Boaz was arriving from.

Besides Berlin's conclusions, it seems that there is one more, subtle, nuance that this particle attaches to the story. In the context of verses 1, 3, and 4 where the name of Boaz is used, the narrator continually broadens the horizon of the readers in relation to the knowledge of Ruth. Taking into consideration the short dialogue between Ruth and Naomi in 2:2 and short report about Ruth's gleaning in the field (2:3a), one can say that the story is developing in two levels. The first level reflects the horizon (the knowledge) of Ruth, while on the other level the readers' perspective is developed. Therefore, the function of הִנֵּה in this case is used to elicit the readers' surprise.[72]

The simple greeting in 2:4 has been developed by some commentaries into a reflection of Boaz's piety or even ideological formula of YHWH presence. For example, Wilch considers that with his greeting Boaz demonstrates "his interest in the welfare of his workers."[73] According to Hawk, the greeting formula "affirms Yahweh's presence with the people," which puts it in contrast to Naomi's bitter declarations.[74] According to another comment made by Hubbard, the scene draws attention not so much to the piety of the speakers as to "the presence of the one whose name is voiced."[75]

Nevertheless, analysis of focalization shows that the scene of Boaz's arrival is focalized more externally than internally and as such is not ideologically loaded because Boaz does not make any considerable statements that would clearly reflect his attitudes or feelings. Besides, in contrast to the dialogic scenes, the greeting formula does not refer to the past or to the future and, therefore, does not rearrange narrative information but simply reports current actions.

---

71. Berlin, *Poetics and Interpretation*, 94.
72. Gerleman, *Ruth*, 25; Hubbard, *Ruth*, 140–41; Wilch, *Ruth*, 191.
73. Wilch, *Ruth*, 212–13.
74. Hawk, *Ruth*, 78–79.
75. Hubbard, *Ruth*, 144–45.

Nevertheless, there should be the reason for the narrator to include this scene into the story. According to the reasonable note of McKeown, "If the greeting was simply a record of the fact that Boaz said 'Hello' to his workers and they replied 'Hello' to him, then it is very doubtful if the narrator would have bothered to mention this detail."[76] The need in this scene can be explained by rearrangement of the flow of narrative information. In Ruth 2:3–4 the narrator has the task to show how two people simultaneously come to the same point and unexpectedly meet each other. In the film narratives, these kinds of scenes are usually presented by showing close-up so that the viewer could see both of them coming to the point of meeting. A fast change of the shots is used for this purpose as well. The narrator of the written text does not have these instruments at their disposal; therefore, the flow of information in the text has to be rearranged. So, the narrator has to find other means to present simultaneous approximation of two people to the point of an unexpected encounter. In the case of Ruth 2:3–4, the narrator uses short episodes that follow one after another, producing the effect of an accidental encounter. Besides, in the next verse Boaz will come to his foreman with the question about "this young woman." In order to ask this question, he needed to take time and look around. It could be assumed that Boaz took notice of Ruth while he was greeting his workers and only then focused his attention on her.

5.2.5. Dialogue between Boaz and Foreman (2:5–7)

From the words of the foreman the readers get to know what the people of Bethlehem (at least some of them) really thought about Ruth (this information was withheld when the scene of entering Bethlehem was described in 1:19–21). To this the foreman adds his own experience of dealing with Ruth during that day. His speech ends with ideological appraisal (2:7) where some commentators see abrupt language.[77]

---

76. McKeown, *Ruth*, 41.

77. This is the opinion of Hurvitz who considers that "the overseer speaks in an apologetic and confused manner because he is not sure whether the 'boss' will approve of the fact that the overseer has given Ruth his permission to stay . . . inside the house reserved specifically for Boaz's workers." See Hurvitz, "Ruth," 121–23. Carasik takes the same view but for different reasons. He considers that Ruth experienced sexual harassment and "the overseer probably began to explain what had happened, become embarrassed, and tried to make some lame explanation." Carasik, "Ruth," 493–94. According to Beattie, the text זֶה שִׁבְתָּהּ הַבַּיִת מְעָט is "marginal note"

וַיֹּאמֶר בֹּעַז לְנַעֲרוֹ הַנִּצָּב עַל־הַקּוֹצְרִים לְמִי הַנַּעֲרָה הַזֹּאת׃
וַיַּעַן הַנַּעַר הַנִּצָּב עַל־הַקּוֹצְרִים וַיֹּאמַר נַעֲרָה מוֹאֲבִיָּה הִיא
הַשָּׁבָה עִם־נָעֳמִי מִשְּׂדֵה מוֹאָב׃
וַתֹּאמֶר אֲלַקֳטָה־נָּא וְאָסַפְתִּי בָעֳמָרִים אַחֲרֵי הַקּוֹצְרִים וַתָּבוֹא
וַתַּעֲמוֹד מֵאָז הַבֹּקֶר וְעַד־עַתָּה זֶה שִׁבְתָּהּ הַבַּיִת מְעָט׃

Then Boaz said to his young man who was in charge of the reapers, "Whose young woman is this?" And the servant who was in charge of the reapers answered, "She is the young Moabite woman, who came back with Naomi from the country of Moab. She said, 'Please let me glean and gather among the sheaves after the reapers.' So she came, and she has continued from early morning until now, except for a short rest." (2:5–7)

The dialogue starts with the reflection of Boaz's horizon. Since he does not know Ruth in person, he cannot recognize her and for him she is just הַנַּעֲרָה "a young woman." Therefore, unless Boaz speaks to the foreman (2:5–7), his horizon is also restricted. The foreman, on the contrary, knows some details about Ruth's origin and had a chance to see her working in the field during this day, but apparently his view of Ruth is different from Boaz's.

At the same time, the readers can identify both Boaz and Ruth. Therefore, until verse 7 the readers know more than both Boaz and Ruth, or to put it another way, this section is zero focalized in relation to both Boaz and Ruth. The function of the foreman now becomes obvious. He plays an important role in the narrative because he happens to be the character who is also totally aware of the identity of both Boaz and Ruth.

In the course of conversation, the foreman shares with Boaz information about his encounter with Ruth and her request. According to some views, Ruth requested to glean among sheaves and the permission was not given to her:

---

made "by some student of the scriptures, at a time before the Septuagint translation." Beattie, "Midrashic Gloss," 122–24. According to Moore, the text contains a wordplay between on the roots שׁוּב "to return" and יָשַׁב "to dwell" in order to show that this Moabite woman is ready to make this field her dwelling place. Moore, "Two Textual Anomalies," 234–43. However, Min does not agree with these ideas. He suggests to translate the words of the foreman as "She came from the morning and has stood by until now. She was sitting for a while under the shelter." See Min, "Problems in Ruth," 438–41.

According to the harvest overseer, this is what Ruth requested when she arrived at the field to glean. He does not indicate his response, although from her actions (she is still not gleaning when Boaz arrived), it is clear that she was not given permission.[78]

According to this reasoning, the narrator again reorganizes the course of the narrative and informs the readers about the scene that has happened using the reported speech of the character. But not everyone agrees with this explanation. According to Grossman, this interpretation contradicts the content of the narrative. Let's say that Ruth had asked for the foreman's permission to glean among the sheaves. But is it "highly unlikely" that Ruth asked the foreman to give her special permission to gather among the bundled sheaves.[79] Even if she really posed this request, it is unlikely that the foreman granted it. For if Ruth already gleaned among the sheaves, why would Boaz have to give her special permission in verse 15?[80]

Grossman proposes an alternative way of interpretation. He compares the words Ruth addressed to Naomi and the words the foreman ascribed to Ruth in his report. This leads Grossman to the conclusion that Ruth in her request repeated the words she addressed to Naomi earlier, but the foreman, following his or a personal dislike toward Moabite women, tried to vilify her actions before Boaz. Therefore, according to Grossman, the foreman's

> ... remarks to Boaz do not add any detail of which the reader has yet to be informed. The discussion between Ruth and the supervising boy, which researchers thought to recreate in light of the boy's words, never actually occurred.[81]

Obviously, the speech of the foreman reflects his point of view. For him Ruth is just a "young Moabite woman, who came back with Naomi from the country of Moab." The foreman either does not know about Ruth's decision to follow Naomi and YHWH or does not see any value in it. Thus, the speech of the foreman is focalized internally, and the readers listening to his words get to know his attitude toward Ruth. Moreover, the language of the final part of

---

78. Holmstedt, *Ruth*, 116.
79. Grossman, "Gleaning," 703–16.
80. Grossman, 704. Campbell, Sasson, and Hubbard follow this line of reasoning.
81. Grossman, 706.

the foreman's words is confused. According to Holmstedt, "the rough, almost stuttering language at the end of the verse, is a literary device intended to convey a character's (the overseer) state of mind and is therefore not meant to reflect smooth syntax."[82]

Hurvitz considers that one of the reasons for it is the cowardice of the foreman, who was afraid that Boaz would be unhappy with this Moabite woman working at his field.[83] Even though the foreman's opinion of Ruth seems negative, he still plays a positive role in the narrative. After Boaz identifies Ruth, he obtains the same horizon as the readers, while Ruth's horizon is kept restricted until 2:19. Therefore, by the beginning of the dialogue between Boaz and Ruth, the readers still know more than Ruth but lose their privileged position in relation to Boaz.

5.2.6. Dialogue between Boaz and Ruth (2:8–13)

The conversation between Boaz and Ruth has two parts. In the first part (2:8–10) Boaz's attitude remains unclear for the readers and for Ruth; therefore, the difference in horizons on the level of the story gives to the narrative an additional dynamic. In the second part (2:11–13) Boaz explains his motives, which makes the flow of the plot more predictable.

> וַיֹּאמֶר בֹּעַז אֶל־רוּת הֲלוֹא שָׁמַעַתְּ בִּתִּי אַל־תֵּלְכִי לִלְקֹט בְּשָׂדֶה אַחֵר וְגַם לֹא תַעֲבוּרִי מִזֶּה וְכֹה תִדְבָּקִין עִם־נַעֲרֹתָי׃
> עֵינַיִךְ בַּשָּׂדֶה אֲשֶׁר־יִקְצֹרוּן וְהָלַכְתְּ אַחֲרֵיהֶן הֲלוֹא צִוִּיתִי אֶת־הַנְּעָרִים לְבִלְתִּי נָגְעֵךְ וְצָמִת וְהָלַכְתְּ אֶל־הַכֵּלִים וְשָׁתִית מֵאֲשֶׁר יִשְׁאֲבוּן הַנְּעָרִים׃
> וַתִּפֹּל עַל־פָּנֶיהָ וַתִּשְׁתַּחוּ אָרְצָה וַתֹּאמֶר אֵלָיו מַדּוּעַ מָצָאתִי חֵן בְּעֵינֶיךָ לְהַכִּירֵנִי וְאָנֹכִי נָכְרִיָּה׃

Then Boaz said to Ruth, "Now, listen, my daughter, do not go to glean in another field or leave this one, but keep close to my young women. Let your eyes be on the field that they are reaping, and go after them. Have I not charged the young men not to touch you? And when you are thirsty, go to the vessels and drink what the young men have drawn." Then she fell on her

---

82. Holmstedt, *Ruth*, 117.

83. Holmstedt considers that this explanation of Hurvitz "makes the most sense of the text as its stands." See Holmstedt, *Ruth*, 117; Hurvitz, "Ruth," 122.

face, bowing to the ground, and said to him, "Why have I found favor in your eyes, that you should take notice of me, since I am a foreigner?" (2:8–10)

Again, with the use of direct speech the narrator describes a possible future of the character – Boaz strongly recommends for Ruth to stay and work in his field. The authoritative tone of his language is supported by the use of the phrase הֲלוֹא שָׁמַעַתְּ בִּתִּי translated in the ESV as "listen to me" with the parental designation "my daughter," and by repetitions of words and thoughts. From one side these words of Boaz are internally focalized because he draws before Ruth the picture of her life during the weeks of harvest. The picture (as description made by any character) is restricted to what Boaz believes is good for Ruth. In his speech, one finds the attitude of care and attention; he is ready to give to Ruth not only food but provide security and comfortable working conditions. The readers should be surprised with his generous offer no less than Ruth. Hence the question of Ruth is also the question of the readers that seek to find Boaz's attitude. Therefore, the narrator purposefully covers the attitude of Boaz, representing this new character from without in order to increase the suspense of the story.

The statement וְאָנֹכִי נָכְרִיָּה "since I am a foreigner" reflects the then existing negative attitudes that people (like the foreman) had toward her and shows that "the acceptance of a foreigner raised particular questions in the Jewish community."[84] Therefore, Ruth's question to Boaz is ideological in nature. It calls Boaz to shift to ideological issues as well. So, Boaz's second address in 2:11–13 is different in this matter. He praises Ruth's decision to commit her life to Naomi and the people of Israel. In order to explain his attitude, Boaz again paints the picture but now it is the picture of the past giving his appraisal of Ruth's decision.

וַיַּעַן בֹּעַז וַיֹּאמֶר לָהּ הֻגֵּד הֻגַּד לִי כֹּל אֲשֶׁר־עָשִׂית אֶת־חֲמוֹתֵךְ
אַחֲרֵי מוֹת אִישֵׁךְ וַתַּעַזְבִי אָבִיךְ וְאִמֵּךְ וְאֶרֶץ מוֹלַדְתֵּךְ וַתֵּלְכִי
אֶל־עַם אֲשֶׁר לֹא־יָדַעַתְּ תְּמוֹל שִׁלְשׁוֹם׃
יְשַׁלֵּם יהוה פָּעֳלֵךְ וּתְהִי מַשְׂכֻּרְתֵּךְ שְׁלֵמָה מֵעִם יהוה אֱלֹהֵי
יִשְׂרָאֵל אֲשֶׁר־בָּאת לַחֲסוֹת תַּחַת־כְּנָפָיו׃

---

84. McKeown, *Ruth*, 47.

וַתֹּאמֶר אֶמְצָא־חֵן בְּעֵינֶיךָ אֲדֹנִי כִּי נִחַמְתָּנִי וְכִי דִבַּרְתָּ עַל־לֵב
שִׁפְחָתֶךָ וְאָנֹכִי לֹא אֶהְיֶה כְּאַחַת שִׁפְחֹתֶיךָ:

But Boaz answered her, "All that you have done for your mother-in-law since the death of your husband has been fully told to me, and how you left your father and mother and your native land and came to a people that you did not know before. The LORD repay you for what you have done, and a full reward be given you by the LORD, the God of Israel, under whose wings you have come to take refuge!" Then she said, "I have found favor in your eyes, my lord, for you have comforted me and spoken kindly to your servant, though I am not one of your servants." (2:11–13)

Reading Boaz's answer, the readers start to understand that information in the story was rearranged again. Apparently, there were some conversations about Ruth among townspeople that the readers were not informed about previously. The questions that the readers should obviously be interested in – if Naomi ever introduced Ruth to people of Bethlehem and what did they think about her? – are now partially answered. If the narrator would have allowed this information earlier, the tension of the moment would disappear.

The other and more important act of reorganization in this passage is the reminder about events of chapter 1. The importance of this reminder is that it (1) summarizes the whole chapter in just two phrases and (2) it gives ideological appraisal to Ruth's decision by leaving aside some elements of the story and adding others. In other words, this passage is focalized internally from the point of view of Boaz.

Elements of focalization in the text are evident if one compares the description of Boaz with the content of chapter 1. In his rendering, Boaz omits almost all episodes of the story except the moment of Ruth's decision. With this internally focalized text, the narrator is able to concentrate the attention of the readers on Ruth's decision in 1:16–17. The words of Boaz look like a summary, the report about the most important scene of chapter 1. Appended to the story is the ideological evaluation of Ruth's acts as the manifestation of commitment, courage, and faith. The picture of the past is then replaced by the picture of the future where Boaz sees Ruth as the foreigner (or the refugee)[85] who seeks protection of YHWH, the God of Israel.[86]

5.2.7. Mealtime (2:14)

The scene of mealtime (2:14) starts as focalized externally:

וַיֹּאמֶר לָה בֹעַז לְעֵת הָאֹכֶל גֹּשִׁי הֲלֹם וְאָכַלְתְּ מִן־הַלֶּחֶם וְטָבַלְתְּ
פִּתֵּךְ בַּחֹמֶץ וַתֵּשֶׁב מִצַּד הַקֹּצְרִים וַיִּצְבָּט־לָהּ קָלִי וַתֹּאכַל
וַתִּשְׂבַּע וַתֹּתַר:

> And at mealtime Boaz said to her, "Come here and eat some bread and dip your morsel in the wine." So she sat beside the reapers, and he passed to her roasted grain. And she ate until she was satisfied, and she had some left over. (2:14)

Block explains that "in the ancient Near East people did not eat only to satisfy hungry stomachs; eating together also had great symbolic significance."[87] He suggests a list of six possible reasons for a corporate meal at those times: an expression of hospitality, a celebration of special occasions, an agreement between treaty partners climaxed with a covenant meal, an expression of social realities, a meeting of religious group, and having a good time together. In this particular case "with this invitation Boaz treated Ruth not as a lowly servant, but as a member of his own entourage,"[88] and that this is "glorious demonstration of compassion, generosity and acceptance, or shortly speaking of the biblical חֶסֶד."[89]

But why is the narrator so attentive to the details of the meal? Why by the will of the narrator does Boaz spell out to Ruth what she can do while sitting at the dinner table? Why does the narrator allocate the passing of the roasted grain? Why does the text resort to a description of visual details such as bread, morsel, wine, roasted grain, and leftovers?

One of the reasons derives from the nature of close-up scenes. Attention to minor details gives an impression of proximity and can be used to express

---

85. Hawk, *Ruth*, 81–82.
86. Grammatical aspects of internal focalization will be considered in the next chapter of this work.
87. Block, *Judges, Ruth*, 666.
88. Hubbard, *Ruth*, 173.
89. Hubbard, 173.

intimacy in relationships. This is certainly true for filmic narratives that have a lot in common with biblical narrative. According to contemporary novelist and writing coach C. S. Lakin, biblical narratives are quite comparable to films:

> Here's where a novelist can sometimes achieve a stronger effect than a screenwriter or filmmaker. Novelists can evoke smells and sensations in a way a movie can't. Sure, a movie can show a plate of mouthwatering pizza, and that visual can set our stomach growling. Yet, a novelist can express from the character's POV [point of view] how that pizza smells and looks and makes her feel. If done well, our mouths will water as well while we read the passage, and we may even need to get up and raid the refrigerator. If you read the book *Chocolat* by Joanne Harris and you didn't go scrounging the house for something chocolate, something must be wrong with you.[90]

Description of simple food that was served at the picnic after several hours of hard work under the hot sun creates a similar sensation, at least in the mind of the contemporary reader. Besides, by including the meal scene, the narrator clearly shows the change in social relationship between Boaz and Ruth. This important role is played not only by the fact of sharing a meal, but also by continuing motifs of place and scarcity/abundance. Thus, Ruth is invited to approach (הָאֹכֶל גֹּשִׁי) the dinner table where she takes a seat among other reapers as part of the group (וַתֵּשֶׁב מִצַּד הַקּוֹצְרִים) and has more than she can eat by the end of the dinner.

5.2.8. Boaz's Commands to His Servants (2:15–17)

Detailed representation of the meal is then replaced by a very short description of the rest of the day:

וַתָּקָם לְלַקֵּט וַיְצַו בֹּעַז אֶת־נְעָרָיו לֵאמֹר גַּם בֵּין הָעֳמָרִים תְּלַקֵּט
וְלֹא תַכְלִימוּהָ׃
וְגַם שֹׁל־תָּשֹׁלּוּ לָהּ מִן־הַצְּבָתִים וַעֲזַבְתֶּם וְלִקְּטָה וְלֹא תִגְעֲרוּ־
בָהּ׃

---

90. Lakin, "Using Close-Up."

וַתְּלַקֵּט בַּשָּׂדֶה עַד־הָעָרֶב וַתַּחְבֹּט אֵת אֲשֶׁר־לִקֵּטָה וַיְהִי כְּאֵיפָה שְׂעֹרִים:

> When she rose to glean, Boaz instructed his young men, saying, "Let her glean even among the sheaves, and do not reproach her. And also pull out some from the bundles for her and leave it for her to glean, and do not rebuke her." So she gleaned in the field until evening. Then she beat out what she had gleaned, and it was about an ephah of barley. (2:15–17)

Because of selective representation, the readers are never told anything about the actual process of gleaning after mealtime. The commands of Boaz look forward to the gleaning, and the report of the narrator about Ruth's working day shows the results of gleaning. Instead of picturing the routine process of gleaning, the narrator describes it in the words of one of the characters. By doing so, he not only narrates the event, but also continues to describe Boaz's attitude:

> It is interesting in that light to observe that the narrator quickly interrupts the description of Ruth's gleaning with an aside, which continues through v[erse] 16, to report on one further set of instructions Boaz gives to his workers concerning Ruth. The aside contributes to the character profile of Boaz that the narrator has been building for the entire chapter: this fellow is a true mensch.[91]

On the basis of the last two passages, it is possible to track the development of Boaz's attitude toward Ruth. It starts from simple permission to glean on in his field, then turns into the caring attitude (when Boaz allows Ruth to drink water and to eat with his workers and protect her against all offences) and ends with intentional help. During this episode Boaz's horizon is gradually expanding. In the beginning he does not know who Ruth is, but after the conversation with the foreman, his horizon becomes wider than the horizon of Ruth. At the same time, Ruth remains unaware of who is her benefactor. All she knows about him is his name. As for the readers, they will continue to enjoy their privileged position for a little longer.

---

91. Holmstedt, *Ruth*, 134.

5.2.9. Ruth Reports to Naomi about Her Day (2:18–19)

Because in verse 20 the horizon of the readers expands, I decided to divide the scene into two parts. In the first part of the scene (2:18–19), the horizon of Naomi expands – Naomi finds out who was the benefactor of Ruth. In the second part of the scene, the horizons of Ruth and the readers expand. Ruth for the first time finds out that Boaz is not only her benefactor but also the redeemer. Similarly, the readers find out that Boaz is not simply a relative or a friend of Elimelech, but the redeemer of Naomi and Ruth.

So, this part of the scene demonstrates how Naomi's horizon expands.

וַתִּשָּׂא וַתָּבוֹא הָעִיר וַתֵּרֶא חֲמוֹתָהּ אֵת אֲשֶׁר־לִקֵּטָה וַתּוֹצֵא
וַתִּתֶּן־לָהּ אֵת אֲשֶׁר־הוֹתִרָה מִשָּׂבְעָהּ:
וַתֹּאמֶר לָהּ חֲמוֹתָהּ אֵיפֹה לִקַּטְתְּ הַיּוֹם וְאָנָה עָשִׂית יְהִי מַכִּירֵךְ
בָּרוּךְ וַתַּגֵּד לַחֲמוֹתָהּ אֵת אֲשֶׁר־עָשְׂתָה עִמּוֹ וַתֹּאמֶר שֵׁם הָאִישׁ
אֲשֶׁר עָשִׂיתִי עִמּוֹ הַיּוֹם בֹּעַז:

> And she took it up and went into the city. Her mother-in-law saw what she had gleaned. She also brought out and gave her what food she had left over after being satisfied. And her mother-in-law said to her, "Where did you glean today? And where have you worked? Blessed be the man who took notice of you." So she told her mother-in-law with whom she had worked and said, "The man's name with whom I worked today is Boaz." (2:18–19)

The scene starts from showing the results of Ruth's day of gleaning from the point of view of Naomi. But instead of direct description of the details of what Naomi might see, the narrator prefers to drop in Naomi's questions that are full of surprise and excitement. This is apparent from the fact that Naomi asks two questions one after another and blesses the benefactor before Ruth says a word.

The text consists of two details that emphasize the play of horizons on the level of the story. First, Naomi, without knowing the benefactor of Ruth, called him "the man who took notice of you," which is derived from the verb מַכִּיר "to take notice." But this is exactly how Ruth characterized Boaz's action in 2:10.⁹² The readers who were there with Ruth and Boaz cannot miss this coincidence.⁹³

The second detail is the way Ruth answers the question of Naomi. First, Ruth's answer is narrated and then Ruth repeats that statement almost verbatim and finally verbalizes the name of her benefactor. Bush sees this response as "carefully calculated to increase our suspense and interest."⁹⁴ It is difficult to miss this repetition, but it seems interesting to discuss not only the outcome of it (the increase of suspense and interest), but also the way this effect is reached. The point is that the first and second halves of the statement belong to different levels: the first half belongs to the level of the discourse and the second half belongs to the level of the story. On the level of the discourse, the narrator reduces the time of narration so that he does not have to explain to the readers all the details of Ruth's account, especially since she does not know the real identity of Boaz. Therefore, for the readers she remains an unreliable narrator. Consequently, the narrator ignores all the content of her speech, leaving the most important part – the name of the benefactor.

5.3. Boaz, a Redeemer (2:20–3:11)

The whole new perspective on the narrative is given with Naomi's remark about Boaz being not simply the relative of Elimelech, but the redeemer of their family. This information prompts the readers to take a fresh look at the status of Ruth in relation to Boaz (2:21–23). But it also puts the readers into a less privileged position because it turns out that some characters possess more information than the readers. This means that from this time on the story is externally focalized in relation to Naomi (the readers know less than Naomi); it is internally focalized in relation to Ruth (the readers know as much as Ruth); and it is zero focalized in relation to Boaz (at least it seems).

5.3.1. The Horizon of Ruth Expands (2:20–23)

The readers were anticipating this moment for the whole chapter. They knew from 2:1 that Boaz was the relative of Naomi. This means that Naomi had to

---

92. In 2:10 the infinitive form of the same root is used. See Schipper, *Ruth*, 138.
93. Hubbard, *Ruth*, 184.
94. Bush, *Ruth/Esther*, 131.

know about his existence. When Naomi asks Ruth where she worked and who took notice of her, the narrator is not putting a simple answer into the mouth of Ruth, for example, "His name is Boaz" but delays with the answer until the very end. The same effect is used when Naomi informs Ruth about Boaz.

וַתֹּאמֶר נָעֳמִי לְכַלָּתָהּ בָּרוּךְ הוּא לַיהוָה אֲשֶׁר לֹא־עָזַב חַסְדּוֹ אֶת־הַחַיִּים וְאֶת־הַמֵּתִים וַתֹּאמֶר לָהּ נָעֳמִי קָרוֹב לָנוּ הָאִישׁ מִגֹּאֲלֵנוּ הוּא׃

> And Naomi said to her daughter-in-law, "May he be blessed by the LORD, whose kindness has not forsaken the living or the dead!" Naomi also said to her, "The man is a close relative of ours, one of our redeemers." (2:20)

Naomi does not say immediately that Boaz is their redeemer, but thanks God first, then calls Boaz קָרוֹב "close relative" and only then adds the most important piece of information, that Boaz is one of their גֹּאֵל "redeemers." This syntax of Naomi's speech only underlines the existing play of horizons, which Bush calls "delightful irony":

> The whole exchange is fraught with delightful irony, for we, the hearers, realize that each of the women know who Boaz is, while Naomi has no idea that Ruth has worked all day with Boaz, but knows very well who he is![95]

The information Naomi shares with Ruth is very important, because it finally supplies Ruth with the knowledge that levels her horizon with the horizon of the readers so that at the end of the chapter the readers seem to know as much as all three main characters of the story. However, in view of the episode on the threshing floor there is information about another relative that both Boaz and Naomi should know. This piece of information is, nevertheless, hidden from Ruth and from the readers. This means that, in fact, in the beginning of the third chapter the story is focalized the same way as it was in the first chapter: Ruth's horizon is limited as much as the horizon of the readers but the readers are not aware of it yet.

In the last two verses of the conversation, Ruth continues to share her horizon with Naomi by conveying in her own words what Boaz told her:

---

95. Bush, 141.

וַתֹּאמֶר רוּת הַמּוֹאֲבִיָּה גַּם כִּי־אָמַר אֵלַי עִם־הַנְּעָרִים אֲשֶׁר־לִי
תִּדְבָּקִין עַד אִם־כִּלּוּ אֵת כָּל־הַקָּצִיר אֲשֶׁר־לִי:
וַתֹּאמֶר נָעֳמִי אֶל־רוּת כַּלָּתָהּ טוֹב בִּתִּי כִּי תֵצְאִי עִם־נַעֲרוֹתָיו
וְלֹא יִפְגְּעוּ־בָךְ בְּשָׂדֶה אַחֵר:

> And Ruth the Moabite said, "Besides, he said to me, 'You shall keep close by my young men until they have finished all my harvest.'" And Naomi said to Ruth, her daughter-in-law, "It is good, my daughter, that you go out with his young women, lest in another field you be assaulted." (2:21–22)

The point that Ruth's words do not exactly match the words of Boaz demonstrates that the readers are presented with the restricted point of view of the character. Moreover, Ruth mistakenly mentions that Boaz let her glean among his male servants, while Boaz meant female servants (וְכֹה תִדְבָּקִין עִם־נַעֲרֹתָי). According to LaCocque, "Ruth's error is attributed directly to her Moabite origins" because her utterance starts from the introductory "And Ruth the Moabite said . . ."[96] Moreover, the restricted point of view is evident in the way the statement of Ruth starts with emphatic גַּם, in which Chisholm sees the evidence of excitement and LaCocque translates as "even."[97] All these elements demonstrate that the statement of Ruth is internally focalized.

So does the answer of Naomi, which, in turn, betrays her perspective on the situation. One of the markers that emphasizes internal focalization in Naomi's answer is the introductory phrase of the narrator. According to Glover, this is the second place in the book where the narrator designates Ruth by name without mentioning her ethnicity.[98] Glover asserts that this happens every time "whenever her re-situation within Israel has been recognized."[99]

---

96. Linafelt lists four ways of Ruth's misquoting of Boaz: (1) the masculine plural form could simply apply to both male and female servants; (2) Ruth's foreignness; (3) the intentional desire of Ruth to be with men; and (4) hinting at the possibility of separation from Naomi. Linafelt considers the last option being "more plausible and more interesting." However, the last possibility, while it looks interesting indeed, cannot be accepted since Ruth mentions that she repeats the words of Boaz. See Linafelt and Beal, *Ruth and Esther*, 43–44.

97. See Chisholm Jr., *Judges and Ruth*, 640; LaCocque, *Ruth*, 79.

98. Glover, "Your People," 302. Two other places are Ruth 2:8 and 4:13. However, according to Schipper, Old Greek, Old Latin, Vulg., and Syr do not have "the Moabite" in verse 21. See Schipper, *Ruth*, 136.

99. Glover, "Your People," 302.

Besides, Naomi corrects Ruth's mistake by pointing out that it is good for her to stay not with male but with female servants of Boaz. By saying this, Naomi, in contrast to the readers and to Ruth, repeats Boaz's words without knowing about it. She also happens to be in accord with Boaz on the matter of Ruth's safety.[100] The reason for such consensus is probably that "both Naomi and Boaz articulate the dominant cultural message to women: if a young woman goes off alone or with men, something unpleasant will happen to her – or be told about her."[101]

The final verse of the chapter presents the next several weeks of harvest in the scope of external focalization.

וַתִּדְבַּק בְּנַעֲרוֹת בֹּעַז לְלַקֵּט עַד־כְּלוֹת קְצִיר־הַשְּׂעֹרִים וּקְצִיר הַחִטִּים וַתֵּשֶׁב אֶת־חֲמוֹתָהּ׃

> So she kept close to the young women of Boaz, gleaning until the end of the barley and wheat harvests. And she lived with her mother-in-law. (2:23)

The reason to consider this passage as externally focalized is that the readers, after reading it, do not expand their horizon beyond the horizons of any characters. Besides, the readers have already lost the privileged position after they received from Naomi the information about Boaz being not simply the relative of Elimelech, but the redeemer of Naomi and Ruth.

5.3.2. Naomi Suggests a Plan (3:1–5)

Ruth 3 starts with inviting the readers into conspiracy of Naomi and Ruth.

וַתֹּאמֶר לָהּ נָעֳמִי חֲמוֹתָהּ בִּתִּי הֲלֹא אֲבַקֶּשׁ־לָךְ מָנוֹחַ אֲשֶׁר יִיטַב־לָךְ׃
וְעַתָּה הֲלֹא בֹעַז מֹדַעְתָּנוּ אֲשֶׁר הָיִית אֶת־נַעֲרוֹתָיו הִנֵּה־הוּא זֹרֶה אֶת־גֹּרֶן הַשְּׂעֹרִים הַלָּיְלָה׃
וְרָחַצְתְּ וָסַכְתְּ וְשַׂמְתְּ שִׂמְלֹתַיִךְ עָלַיִךְ וְיָרַדְתִּי הַגֹּרֶן אַל־תִּוָּדְעִי לָאִישׁ עַד כַּלֹּתוֹ לֶאֱכֹל וְלִשְׁתּוֹת׃

---

100. According to Schipper, the verb פָּגַע "to meet, to encounter" in this context means "to attack," which corresponds with Boaz's commands to his servants not to touch (v. 9) and not to rebuke (v. 16) Ruth. See Schipper, *Ruth*, 136.

101. Eskenazi and Frymer-Kensky, *Ruth*, 45.

וִיהִי בְשָׁכְבוֹ וְיָדַעַתְּ אֶת־הַמָּקוֹם אֲשֶׁר יִשְׁכַּב־שָׁם וּבָאת וְגִלִּית
מַרְגְּלֹתָיו וְשָׁכָבְתְּ וְהוּא יַגִּיד לָךְ אֵת אֲשֶׁר תַּעֲשִׂין:
וַתֹּאמֶר אֵלֶיהָ כֹּל אֲשֶׁר־תֹּאמְרִי אֶעֱשֶׂה:

> Then Naomi her mother-in-law said to her, "My daughter, should I not seek rest for you, that it may be well with you? Is not Boaz our relative, with whose young women you were? See, he is winnowing barley tonight at the threshing floor. Wash therefore and anoint yourself, and put on your cloak and go down to the threshing floor, but do not make yourself known to the man until he has finished eating and drinking. But when he lies down, observe the place where he lies. Then go and uncover his feet and lie down, and he will tell you what to do." And she replied, "All that you say I will do." (3:1–5)

The plan of Naomi is arranged for Ruth and Boaz: Naomi thinks that the time has come and Ruth should use her acquaintance with Boaz to find מָנוֹחַ "rest." While this is not stated explicitly, the readers understand that Naomi is talking about Ruth's marriage with Boaz on the basis of the words of Naomi in chapter 1. There she had wished that the Lord granted her daughters-in-law to find rest in the house of a husband (1:9), which obviously implies the idea of marriage. Then Naomi informs Ruth about the place Boaz is going to spend the coming night and instructs her how to approach Boaz with a marriage proposal. Ruth agrees with Naomi's plot and, according to the narrator's remark, obediently follows the instructions of her mother-in-law.

The play of horizons is best exemplified in conspiracy because any conspiracy is based upon the difference in the amount of knowledge the characters possess. According to Naomi's plan, Ruth should possess the greater knowledge than Boaz, which makes her appearance before him unexpected. According to Linafelt, the speech of Naomi can be presented rhetorically as chiasm, at the heart of which there are two machinations: Ruth should not make herself known unless Boaz lies down.[102] Therefore, Ruth, compared with Boaz, will be in the privileged position when she visits the threshing floor. Linafelt also draws our attention to multiple uses of the verb יָדַע, which reflects the play of horizons in this conspiracy.

---

102. Linafelt and Beal, *Ruth and Esther*, 48.

> Though Ruth has been instructed not to make herself "known"... to "the man," she is nevertheless to make sure she "knows"... where he is lying down. The plan depends on Ruth having more knowledge than Boaz, who is to be literally and figuratively in the dark.[103]

The readers again find themselves immersed into Naomi's mind. Two components of Naomi's direct speech put it into the mode of internal focalization. First, in her speech she shares her attitude. This is done (1) by the use of a rhetorical question: "should I not seek rest for you,"[104] which implies the point of view of the character, and (2) by the ideological appraisal of Ruth's current situation compared with her possible future benefits. As Holmstedt puts it, "In the context the verb in the relative clause, יִיטַב, has an implicit comparative degree: 'a place of rest that is good for you [versus here]' = 'a place of rest that is better for you [than here].'"[105]

The second component that confirms that the speech of Naomi is internally focalized is rearrangement of the flow of narrative information – the character is speaking about past and future events. Naomi starts by speaking about Ruth's work in the field of Boaz during the past few weeks. That her view of the past is restricted becomes apparent when her evaluation of Ruth's work turns out to be different from the view of omniscient narrator. In 2:23 the narrator describes Ruth's activity by saying וַתִּדְבַּק בְּנַעֲרוֹת בֹּעַז לְלַקֵּט "she kept close to the young women of Boaz, gleaning" (2:23). Here the narrator uses the verb דָּבַק "to cling" that has already been used in Ruth 1:14 where it described the relationship between Ruth and Naomi. Like in 1:14 and 2:23, it seems the narrator demonstrates his omniscience and talks about the attitude of Ruth rather than simple activity. In contrast, Naomi has a restricted view on the same events since for her Ruth was simply among young women: אֲשֶׁר הָיִית אֶת־נַעֲרוֹתָיו "with whose young women you were" (3:2).

Naomi also speaks about a future event, specifically about Ruth's visit to the threshing floor. Her speech takes a form of embedded narrative (much like in the first chapter of the book). In it she mentions very specific details of the visit. With four *qatal* verbs Naomi pictures Ruth's preparation: Ruth

---

103. Linafelt and Beal, 48.
104. Holmstedt, *Ruth*, 148.
105. Holmstedt, 148.

has to (1) wash, (2) anoint herself, (3) put on her cloak, and (4) go down to the threshing floor. Then with another four *qatal* verbs she describes Ruth's activity when she arrives at the threshing floor: Ruth has to (1) observe, (2) go, (3) uncover Boaz's feet, and (4) lie down. Then, according to Naomi's plan, Boaz will have to tell Ruth what to do.

Of course, at the moment of the speech Naomi's plan does not sound like restricted, but its inaccuracy becomes apparent when the real visit starts. For example, Ruth waits too long and Boaz fall asleep before she comes to uncover his feet. In addition, instead of Boaz telling Ruth what to do, Ruth tells Boaz what he has to do. All these show the difference between inaccurate restricted human vision of the future and the actual future.

This reasoning helps to make a choice between *Ketiv* and *Qere* readings that are found in this passage. First, there is a difference between שִׂמְלֹתַיִךְ "your garments" as in *Qere* and שִׂמְלֹתֵךְ "your garment" as in *Ketiv*. According to *Ketiv*, Naomi speaks about a single garment (regular clothing) and thus commands Ruth to get dressed. According to *Qere*, Naomi speaks about clothing (in plural form), which implies a set of nice, new clothing. The second difference is found in verse 4 where Naomi says that either Ruth has to go and lie down וְשָׁכָבְתְּ "you will lie down" (*Qere*) or that Naomi herself will lie down וְשָׁכַבְתִּי "I will lie down" (*Ketiv*). Some scholars explain *Ketiv* by the archaic form of the verb,[106] or by the influence of Aram.[107] Holmstedt suggests that this archaism could be used intentionally to color Naomi's speech. However, Holmstedt admits that his idea may seem inconsistent because the first three verbs in this phrase are regular: וְרָחַצְתְּ וָסַכְתְּ וְשַׂמְתְּ שִׂמְלֹתֵךְ עָלַיִךְ וְיָרַדְתִּי הַגֹּרֶן.

Since in the next verse the same pattern is repeated, Holmstedt suggests that the narrator decided to match with archaic language only the last verb in the sequence in order to prevent "too much interference in the communicative process."[108]

Thus, it is used only on the last verb of a four-verb series, allowing the narrator to throw in a speech distinctive for Naomi without sacrificing clarity (in other words, the first three verbs establish beyond any doubt that all the

---

106. Sasson, *Ruth*, 68–69; Hubbard, *Ruth*, 197n198; Bush, *Ruth/Esther*, 145n143.
107. LaCocque, *Ruth*, 90.
108. Holmstedt, *Ruth*, 153.

verb are 2fs). Note a similar sequence of four modal *qatal* verbs with the last a similar -תי verb in v. 4.[109]

Analysis of focalization helps to bring more clarity to this discussion. First, reported speech always involves some degree of internal focalization. As was said before, the degree of internality depends on the content of the direct speech: the more a character reflects his attitude, the more the speech is internally focalized. The command of Naomi does not reflect her inner attitude. In fact, lack of clarity in her intentions is one of the major difficulties of the text. Therefore, it may well be that the narrator colors part of Naomi's speech with archaic language in order to make it internally focalized.

5.3.3. Ruth Fulfills Naomi's Plan (3:6–7)

The picture of the future is then replaced by the picture of the present with a zero focalized passage:

וַתֵּרֶד הַגֹּרֶן וַתַּעַשׂ כְּכֹל אֲשֶׁר־צִוַּתָּה חֲמוֹתָהּ׃
וַיֹּאכַל בֹּעַז וַיֵּשְׁתְּ וַיִּיטַב לִבּוֹ וַיָּבֹא לִשְׁכַּב בִּקְצֵה הָעֲרֵמָה וַתָּבֹא
בַלָּט וַתְּגַל מַרְגְּלֹתָיו וַתִּשְׁכָּב׃

> So she went down to the threshing floor and did just as her mother-in-law had commanded her. And when Boaz had eaten and drunk, and his heart was merry, he went to lie down at the end of the heap of grain. Then she came softly and uncovered his feet and lay down. (3:6–7)

In verses 6 and 7 the narrator informs the readers about actual events of the story. The readers get to know more than Naomi (who is not present at the moment) and more than Boaz (who is not aware about this plan). But the amount of information exceeds even the horizon of Ruth and the passage becomes zero focalized in relation to any characters because the readers are thoroughly informed about the situation.

First, the narrator apprises how accurate Ruth was in fulfilling Naomi's task. According to the narrator, Ruth "went down to the threshing floor and did just as her mother-in-law had commanded her" (3:6). Second, the narrator reports how Boaz felt after eating and drinking, thus exercising his

---

109. Holmstedt, 153.

omniscience, while Ruth cannot be absolutely sure about the mood of Boaz. Third, the narrator assesses how quietly Ruth approached Boaz.

The above reasoning answers one of the problems with verse 6 that, according to Hubbard, "has long troubled scholars."[110] The verse suggests that Ruth executed Naomi's plan in a different order: she first went to the threshing floor and only then followed the rest of the plan. Hubbard proposes that the narrator

> ... simply skipped the preparations and reported Ruth's compliance with everything else in vv. 3–4. Thus the narrator omitted details about the preparations in order to hurry the audience to the next (and more important) scene (vv. 7–15).[111]

According to Berlin, Ruth did not follow Naomi's commands, and the situation is pictured from Ruth's point of view:

> Now certainly this is not what Naomi had in mind. She wanted Ruth to approach Boaz after he had eaten, when he had just lain down, but before he had actually fallen asleep – just at the time that "his heart was good" and he would be most receptive to Ruth's visit. But Ruth waited too long. She did not realize that her mission was a romantic one, thinking rather that she was there on secret legal business. (The fact that she was a foreigner explains how she could be ignorant of the institution of *ge'ullah* and its workings.) So, although she thought she was carrying out Naomi's directions, in reality she was not. The scene read this way becomes both comic and touching.[112]

The analysis of focalization shows that this scene is not written in the scope of internal focalization and thus does not reflect the point of view of Ruth. Besides, the purpose of the narrator in this verse is not to report the sequence of events, but to assess the actions of Ruth, giving the readers the sense of zero focalization – the readers know more than any character.[113]

---

110. Hubbard, *Ruth*, 206n201.
111. Hubbard, 206n201.
112. Berlin, *Poetics and Interpretation*, 91.
113. Bush does not support Berlin's reasoning as well but on a quite different basis. He considers that (1) "the text gives not the slightest hint that Ruth understood her task and purpose any differently from Naomi's intent," and (2) "Naomi's instructions ... clearly imply

The fact that the characters are limited with their knowledge is underlined by the overall context of the scene. First the scene happens in the darkness of the night. Second, it is considered that the place where Boaz went to sleep – "the end of the heap of grain" – is a technical term familiar to the audience (i.e. the central pile awaiting transport to the city), which guaranteed the privacy of conversation.[114]

5.3.4. Exchange at the Threshing Floor (3:8–13)

Ruth 3:8–10 is the turning point of the story. From this moment the plot aims toward the conclusion, to close all the plot lines.

וַיְהִי בַּחֲצִי הַלַּיְלָה וַיֶּחֱרַד הָאִישׁ וַיִּלָּפֵת וְהִנֵּה אִשָּׁה שֹׁכֶבֶת מַרְגְּלֹתָיו:
וַיֹּאמֶר מִי־אָתְּ וַתֹּאמֶר אָנֹכִי רוּת אֲמָתֶךָ וּפָרַשְׂתָּ כְנָפֶךָ עַל־אֲמָתְךָ כִּי גֹאֵל אָתָּה:

At midnight the man was startled and turned over, and behold, a woman lay at his feet! He said, "Who are you?" And she answered, "I am Ruth, your servant. Spread your wings over your servant, for you are a redeemer." (3:8–9)

Reference to specific time is very important for this scene. According to Hubbard, "elsewhere in the Old Testament 'midnight' was a time of momentous events."[115] Information is given neither in perspective nor in retrospective, but exposes what happens currently. The beginning of the scene is focalized externally; the flow of information is not rearranged. Usually this kind of technique is used in the pivotal moments of the narrative. Besides, the setting of the darkness makes the presentation of the scene even more restrictive (external): it is predetermined that characters may not be able to see all the details.

The awakening of Boaz is also described in the scope of external focalization with two verbs: (1) חָרַד "tremble, be terrified" and (2) לָפַת "twist." The exact meaning of both verbs is not clear. As regard to the first verb, there

---

that she is to wait until he has fallen asleep before approaching, uncovering his legs, and lying down." Bush, *Ruth/Esther*, 162.

114. Hubbard, *Ruth*, 209.

115. Hubbard, 210. Hubbard provides examples from Exod 12:29, Judg 16:3, Job 34:20, Matt 25:1–13.

are two broad options surrounding its meaning. According to the first view, the tremble comes as a result of fear of female night demons.[116] In contrast, according to Hubbard, the first verb חָרַד means simply "to shake, tremble" with no fear implied.[117] The same view is held by Bush, who (after Gerleman, Hertzberg, Rudolph, and Würthwein) translates the verb as "to wake with a shudder or start."[118] Analysis of focalization supports this assumption because fear is an expression of inner feelings of the character, while the present scene is externally focalized.[119]

The meaning of the second verb is also uncertain. Schipper, referring to Sasson, says that לָפַת being a *Niphal* form suggests a reflexive sense and thus can be translated as "turning, groping, or twisting about" and can be understood as "fitful sleep in which Boaz is tossing and turning about."[120] But, again, "fitful sleep" reflects a continuous condition of the character, while here the narrator pictures the key moment of the narrative externally. Bush speaks about another interpretation of the passage given by Lorezt and then followed by Campbell. According to this interpretation, the verb means "to grope" and "Boaz awoke trembling from the cold, felt around with his hand in order to cover himself again, and unintentionally struck against Ruth lying beside him."[121] However, this interpretation also reads into the text the elements of internal feeling: Boaz is cold. It seems, therefore, that the most probable translation that reflects external focalization of the moment is "to turn, twist, bend," which reflect the moment of awakening as the most critical moment of the scene.

Up to this point the horizons of Naomi and Ruth were wider than the horizon of Boaz. But from the moment of awakening Boaz's horizon starts to grow. The first significant change of Boaz's horizon happens when he unexpectedly faces a woman's figure at his feet.

It was Berlin who first pointed to the shift to character's point of view in this verse. This is also a classical example of internal focalization. The phrase

---

116. Sasson, *Ruth*, 74–78.
117. Hubbard, *Ruth*, 210n225. See also Joüon, *Ruth*, 71–72; Campbell, *Ruth*; and Trible, "Two Women," 251–79.
118. Bush, *Ruth/Esther*, 162.
119. Contra to Schipper, *Ruth*, 148.
120. Schipper, *Ruth*, 148.
121. Bush, *Ruth/Esther*, 163.

וְהִנֵּה אִשָּׁה שֹׁכֶבֶת מַרְגְּלֹתָיו "a woman lay at his feet" translates Boaz's restricted horizon at the moment: he is not aware that the woman who lays at his feet is Ruth; the only thing he sees is "a woman."

The spatial aspect of focalization in this scene works together with the cognitive aspect. As it was already said, Boaz sees a woman (not Ruth) due to his restricted field of vision and knowledge. His physical field of vision is restricted because of the darkness of the night. His horizon is restricted because he is unaware of Naomi's plot. In the following moment his physical sight will overtake his knowledge. However, the situation will soon reverse.

In verse 9 there is one more piece of information that comes to the readers' attention. Answering Boaz's question, Ruth calls herself "Ruth, your servant" (אָנֹכִי רוּת אֲמָתֶךָ). It seems that after several weeks of harvesting, the status of Ruth changed and from lower-class שִׁפְחָה "maidservant" she became אָמָה "your handmaid."[122] Schipper notes that the switch "may reflect the conjugal context of this scene."[123] However, he notes that this conclusion is not absolutely reliable because אָמָה has "a conjugal sense more frequently" than שִׁפְחָה. There are biblical examples where שִׁפְחָה also refers to a slave-wife. But since Ruth's answer serves to expand Boaz's horizon and since he clearly understood Ruth's reply, it is possible to come to the conclusion that the designation אָמָה is more than just a synonym of the word שִׁפְחָה. Therefore, the analysis of horizons leads to the conclusion that Ruth no longer considers herself as simple lower-class "servant" but rather "identifies herself among those eligible for marriage or concubinage."[124]

For the readers Ruth's reply sounds unexpected only because Naomi did not instruct her to say anything like this. However, the readers are aware of this information and the perspective of Ruth on Boaz as her redeemer. Therefore, the speech of Ruth is internally focalized because the horizon of the readers equals the horizon of the character.

As regards to the content of Ruth's address, according to Hubbard, the phrase "Spread your wings over your servant" (Ruth 3:9) "probably reflects a

---

122. There is discussion about this word. Some scholars (Hubbard and Sasson) think this is a higher status, and others (Morris, Cambell, and Rudolph) think these words are just synonyms.

123. Schipper, *Ruth*, 149. Bush and Sasson hold the same opinion. See Bush, *Ruth/Esther*, 163; Sasson, *Ruth*, 81.

124. Fruchtenbaum, *Ariel's Bible Commentary*, 328.

marriage custom still attested among Arabs whereby a man symbolically took a wife by throwing a garment-corner over her."[125] But for this study the other aspect of the phrase is more important. This phrase recalls the blessing of Boaz in 2:12 "The LORD repay you for what you have done, and a full reward be given you by the LORD, the God of Israel, under whose wings you have come to take refuge!" Thus, Boaz's covering Ruth with his garment-corner (כָּנָף) implements Yahweh's protective covering of her with his wing.[126] This situation shows that the narrator places the same information twice: one time in the form of prophecy or prayer and another time in the form of its fulfillment. Both sayings could be part of the story but the narrator linearizes information and places these statements in different parts of the story for artistic purposes.

Commenting on verse 9, Bush uses, in essence, the analysis of characters' horizons but does not refer to it as a special approach to interpretation of narrative texts. He points that in MT the word כָּנָף "wing" or "skirt" is defectively written as dual/plural. However, in some Hebrew manuscripts, as well as in LXX and Syr, this word is written in singular form כְּנָפֶךָ like in Deuteronomy 23:1; 27:20; and Ezekiel 16:8 where the singular form of the word is definitely used to understand the expression as a euphemism for the consummation of marriage. But since, continues Bush, " . . . verse 10 demonstrates that Boaz *understood* Ruth's words as a symbolic request for marriage, there seems little doubt, with most commentators . . . that the singular is the correct reading."[127] The request of Ruth poses a problem for interpreters: if Ruth proposes marriage, in what sense does she connect it with the responsibility of the redeemer? This problem is directly connected with the distribution of information in the narrative and, therefore, can be partially addressed by the analysis of horizons. Let me first recall the solutions that are available today.

Beattie suggests that on the threshing floor Ruth offers herself to Boaz but, at the same time, asks for his protection, which implies marriage. However, she does not use the word גֹּאֵל "redeemer" in its technical sense, but considers only the function of גֹּאֵל. Boaz, in contrast, speaks about the legal status of גֹּאֵל and considers opportunities not only to marry Ruth but to keep her

---

125. Hubbard, *Ruth*, 212.
126. Hubbard, 212.
127. Bush, *Ruth/Esther*, 164. Emphasis added.

(and Naomi's) piece of land in the hands of the widows to improve their financial position.

> Through his acting as *go'el* in a technical sense and buying from them the property which had been left to them by Elimelech and Mahlon, while, at the same time, by marrying Ruth, he would be allowing them, in effect, to keep it.[128]

According to Beattie, the reason the other relative did not want to exercise his right to redeem the land is because for him it would be "profitless venture if Boaz were to marry Ruth and claim the land on behalf of their children."[129] According to this view, Boaz's agreement with Ruth was that trump card that was used by Boaz at the right moment.

Bush generally supports Beattie's view, but thinks that by the verb "redeem" Boaz could not mean anything but the act of "marrying the widow of a deceased relative" and only then may use it "with a double entendre."[130]

Chisholm considers that events were unfolding as follows: Naomi suggests for Ruth to approach Boaz with a marriage proposal. However, she prefers not to describe Boaz as גֹּאֵל but simply calls him מֹדַעְתָּנוּ "our relative" in order to give Ruth opportunity to reject her plan. Ruth then proposes marriage to Boaz but goes beyond Naomi's instructions. She understands that as גֹּאֵל Boaz will not simply marry Ruth but provide an heir who will become Naomi's redeemer. Therefore, she states her proposal on the basis of Boaz being a redeemer. But she does not understand all the difficulties that permeate the nuances of legal status of redeemer. However, Boaz praises Ruth for taking this difficult path and continuing to take care for her mother-in-law.[131] Even so, it remains unclear if Boaz was convinced that another relative would refuse to marry Ruth. And if he was not sure, how could he promise to do everything that Ruth asked (כֹּל אֲשֶׁר־צִוְּתָה חֲמוֹתָהּ)?

LaCocque's version of the story is that "unique goal of the whole adventure is to assure the continuation of Elimelek's line."[132] However, levirate law and the law of redemption are two different laws that are combined by the

---

128. Beattie, "Ruth III," 39–48.
129. Beattie, 46.
130. Bush, *Ruth/Esther*, 177.
131. Chisholm Jr., *Judges and Ruth*, 655–60.
132. LaCocque, *Ruth*, 101.

narrator of the book of Ruth. LaCocque also considers that both Naomi and Ruth knew that Boaz was not the nearest redeemer but he was chosen for his "sensitivity."[133] A similar stance is taken by Linafelt, who considers that Boaz was the only one who belatedly realized the import of Ruth's linking the issue of redemption and marriage. By doing both things, Boaz could provide not only for Ruth but also for Naomi.[134]

Obviously, each of the above suggestions has weaknesses of some form. Usually to find logical connection, the commentators have to resort to certain assumptions (not to say speculations). To these assumptions one can attribute, for example, the idea that Ruth and Boaz had a different understanding of the concept of redeemer.

As was said, the problem can be partially addressed by the analysis of horizons. The play of horizons implies that in the result of a collision of different horizons, the narrower horizon tends to grow. (Simply put, characters share their horizons with each other, changing the course of the plot.) This is what could happen in the short conversation between Boaz and Ruth. Ruth expands the horizon of Boaz by blending two ideas: of levirate marriage and redemption. It is not like Boaz never thought of this possibility, but that the possibility was first verbalized by Ruth, and from then on Boaz started to consider it practically.

The reason for such blending is addressed by Hawk who says,

> . . . Ruth's declaration that Boaz is a *gōʾēl* introduces a strategy by which Boaz may claim Ruth in marriage and at the same time defuse the scandal of her Moabite identity. Ruth surely recognizes that her Moabite ethnicity presents an impediment to any prospect of marriage to this eminent and powerful man. The social cost of marriage to a Moabite widow would be prohibitive. How can Ruth find her security with him, even if he is romantically inclined, in the face of this seemingly insurmountable obstacle? Ruth's claim that Boaz is a *gōʾēl* suggests a way that he may marry Ruth and in so doing actually enhance his reputation in the eyes of the community. By stepping into the role of *gōʾēl* in order to marry Ruth, Boaz can cast the marriage

---

133. LaCocque, 100.
134. Linafelt and Beal, *Ruth and Esther*, 59.

as an admirable deed, performed to provide for the widow of a kinsman and preserve the assets of the family. Ruth, in other words, suggests a way to make a potentially scandalous marriage work by drawing on the basic social and moral conventions that define the role of the *gōēl*.[135]

The horizon of Boaz is expanded in two different ways: (1) he is aware that Ruth chose him as her prospective husband and (2) he now sees how to perform this plan without possible adverse effects.

וַיֹּאמֶר בְּרוּכָה אַתְּ לַיהוה בִּתִּי הֵיטַבְתְּ חַסְדֵּךְ הָאַחֲרוֹן מִן־הָרִאשׁוֹן לְבִלְתִּי־לֶכֶת אַחֲרֵי הַבַּחוּרִים אִם־דַּל וְאִם־עָשִׁיר: וְעַתָּה בִּתִּי אַל־תִּירְאִי כֹּל אֲשֶׁר־תֹּאמְרִי אֶעֱשֶׂה־לָּךְ כִּי יוֹדֵעַ כָּל־שַׁעַר עַמִּי כִּי אֵשֶׁת חַיִל אָתְּ:

And he said, "May you be blessed by the LORD, my daughter. You have made this last kindness greater than the first in that you have not gone after young men, whether poor or rich. And now, my daughter, do not fear. I will do for you all that you ask, for all my fellow townsmen know that you are a worthy woman." (3:10–11)

In verses 10 and 11 the information is reorganized in a way that the readers get another piece of new information that they did not know before. From the words of Boaz the readers find out that, first, during the harvest season Ruth gained the reputation of a worthy woman. Second, the relationship between Boaz and Ruth has attained a certain depth because Boaz obviously imagined Ruth as a prospective bride but could not think of her making a choice in his favor. Technically the narrator could share this information with the readers earlier in the narrative but decided to rearrange narrative information and hold this piece of the picture until now. The reason for this withholding of information is the same – the opinion of the townspeople is not important as such but it acquires a meaning only in the mouth of Boaz.

It is clear that the first act of devotion (חֶסֶד) that Boaz mentioned was the decision of Ruth to stay committed to Naomi and return with her to Bethlehem. What was the second act of devotion? Bush spends much ink

---

135. Hawk, *Ruth*, 107.

discussing different views on the second חֶסֶד.¹³⁶ Indeed from one side it is clear that Boaz means Ruth's request to marry him. From another side, how can the request to marry ever be compared with showing mercy (Ruth's first חֶסֶד toward Naomi)? Bush cites the reasoning of Sasson, who does not even connect the first act of חֶסֶד with Ruth's devotion to Naomi. According to Sasson, both acts of חֶסֶד can be found in verse 9. However, Bush rejects this opinion on the basis of Hebrew syntax.

Bush also gives Sakenfeld's definition of חֶסֶד, which

> ... denotes loyal and gracious act that (1) springs from an existing relationship; (2) involves an urgent need on the part of the recipient; (3) is a free act of the one performing it, i.e., an act of moral not legal responsibility; and (4) involves an extraordinary element of mercy or generosity, a "going beyond the call of duty."¹³⁷

Yet Bush sees Ruth's request as the call to fulfill the duty of levirate marriage, which is the act of legal not moral responsibility and eventually rejects the definition of Sakenfeld. Bush ends the discussion of verse 10 with a series of questions and concludes that "the story thus far has given us no sure clue."¹³⁸ Here I will try to find some answers using analysis of reorganization.

The law of levirate marriage in its simplest form implies that a younger brother takes responsibility of redeemer and marries the widow of his older brother. But the book of Ruth obviously demonstrates that the principle was not limited to the brother of the deceased husband, and the widow could get married to any suitable member of the clan. Therefore, Ruth was not obligated to marry someone from the clan of Elimelech and could choose a man of her age from another clan. Nevertheless, she made a decision to marry Boaz, who apparently was in advanced age. Her choice, which Boaz calls חַסְדֵּךְ הָאַחֲרוֹן or "the last act of devotion," was determined by her desire to help Naomi, who apparently could not get married because she exceeded childbearing age and the marriage would be pointless. It seems that Naomi had only one choice to acquire the means of subsistence – by selling her possessions. Ruth,

---

136. Bush, *Ruth/Esther*, 170–72.
137. Bush, 170.
138. Bush, 172.

in contrast, could sell her possessions or get married. The second choice was preferable, but if Ruth's husband were from another clan, Naomi would be left only with money acquired by selling Elimelech's possession. In contrast, if the husband was from the clan of Elimelech, Naomi would become part of a new family and Ruth's children would inherit the land of Elimelech. This explains why another relative first agreed to buy the land from Naomi and then backed out of buying it after Boaz's announcement of his plans to marry Ruth.[139]

5.4. Pelony Almony, a Closer Relative (3:12–4:12)

This is the second time when new information comes from the mouth of one of the characters. This time Boaz mentions that there is another, even closer, relative of Naomi who, therefore, has more rights to redeem Ruth. This means that the readers once again happen to be ignorant of the situation and their horizon is expanded again. Even more than in the previous section, the readers find that their horizon is narrower than the horizon of the characters. Therefore, the readers are forced to follow the legal process as detached observers with the hope that the court will make a decision in favor of Ruth and Naomi. Narratorial intrusion that explains to the readers the meaning of ancient custom (4:7) emphasizes the difference between the horizon of the readers and the horizons of the characters.

5.4.1. The Readers' Horizon is Expanded for the Second Time (3:11–13)

Now it is time for Boaz to share his horizon with Ruth. There is actually another closer relative of Naomi who has more rights to redeem Naomi and Ruth. So Boaz cannot break subordination, but can do everything that is in his power to help Naomi and Ruth. The horizon of the readers is expanded again, and once more new information comes from the mouth of the character, which again makes the readers less informed than the character.

---

139. Considering Ruth 4:5 in the next section I will argue for the *Ketiv* reading: קָנִיתִי.

וְעַתָּה כִּי אָמְנָם כִּי אִם גֹּאֵל אָנֹכִי וְגַם יֵשׁ גֹּאֵל קָרוֹב מִמֶּנִּי׃
לִינִי הַלַּיְלָה וְהָיָה בַבֹּקֶר אִם־יִגְאָלֵךְ טוֹב יִגְאָל וְאִם־לֹא יַחְפֹּץ
לְגָאֳלֵךְ וּגְאַלְתִּיךְ אָנֹכִי חַי־יְהוָה שִׁכְבִי עַד־הַבֹּקֶר׃

"And now it is true that I am a redeemer. Yet there is a redeemer nearer than I. Remain tonight, and in the morning, if he will redeem you, good; let him do it. But if he is not willing to redeem you, then, as the LORD lives, I will redeem you. Lie down until the morning." (3:12–13)

After receiving new information, Boaz contemplates on Ruth's proposal in the rest of his speech. The words of Boaz further complicate one's understanding of the role of the redeemer and its connection with levirate. In the previous section, it was concluded that these traditions are not dependent on each other and that it was Ruth's idea to bring them together. In this case the marriage with a Moabite was socially appropriate and honorable at the same time.[140]

The phrase "And now it is true that I am a redeemer" points out that the horizons of Boaz and Ruth become equal, not only in the sense of knowledge, but also in the ways to achieve the goals. Hawk's reference that the use of אָנֹכִי "I" shows that "Boaz places himself on Ruth's level" and the "two now share equivalent social space."[141] Therefore, it can be concluded that Boaz is thinking aloud about this issue from Ruth's perspective. Boaz's answer then can be interpreted as follows: "We can approach this situation this way. But you should know that I am not the only redeemer. And I can marry you and redeem your property only if the nearer relative will refuse to exercise his rights."

In other words, Boaz admits that Ruth proposes a risky scheme and he is compelled to warn Ruth about possible consequences. But Ruth, probably was aware of those consequences, for according to Wilch,

> What Boaz discussed (3:12–13) was no revelation to Ruth, but including his speech was the narrator's way to divulge it specifically for the first time to the audience. Just when we may think that Naomi and Ruth have issued a proposal to Boaz that

---

140. Hawk, *Ruth*, 111.
141. Hawk, 111.

he surely will accept, surprise: there is a closer redeemer! This complication creates added suspense – not for Naomi and Ruth, but for us, the audience of the master storyteller. The suspense for the two widows was, first, whether Boaz would accept their request, and, second, how he could manage to overcome this barrier to become both their redeemer and Ruth's husband.[142]

5.4.2. Early Wake (3:14–15)

וַתִּשְׁכַּב מַרְגְּלוֹתָו עַד־הַבֹּקֶר וַתָּקָם בְּטֶרוֹם יַכִּיר אִישׁ אֶת־רֵעֵהוּ וַיֹּאמֶר אַל־יִוָּדַע כִּי־בָאָה הָאִשָּׁה הַגֹּרֶן׃
וַיֹּאמֶר הָבִי הַמִּטְפַּחַת אֲשֶׁר־עָלַיִךְ וְאֶחֳזִי־בָהּ וַתֹּאחֶז בָּהּ וַיָּמָד שֵׁשׁ־שְׂעֹרִים וַיָּשֶׁת עָלֶיהָ וַיָּבֹא הָעִיר׃

So she lay at his feet until the morning, but arose before one could recognize another. And he said, "Let it not be known that the woman came to the threshing floor." And he said, "Bring the garment you are wearing and hold it out." So she held it, and he measured out six measures of barley and put it on her. Then she went into the city. (3:14–15)

There are at least two features in this final scene of the meeting that the commentaries pay attention to. The first one is related to the seeming inconsistency that one can find in this passage, for Ruth is the one who wakes early in the morning but Boaz is the one who is concerned about the secrecy of their meeting. Indeed, logic dictates that either the words "Let it not be known that the woman came to the threshing floor" should belong to Ruth, who therefore wakes up early, or, if they belong to Boaz, who has to be the one who wakes up first.

According to Bush, to solve this problem Joüon proposes to read וַיָּקָם ("And he arose") instead of וַתָּקָם ("And she arose") but "there is no textural warrant for such a change."[143] There is no evidence for adding בדברו ("according to his word") as well. Bush then suggests that the verb וַיֹּאמֶר ("said") can also mean "said in the heart." Thus the whole sentence constitutes the indirect discourse of Boaz.

---

142. Wilch, *Ruth*, 296–97.
143. Bush, *Ruth/Esther*, 177.

The other issue of the passage that is raised in the commentaries is related to the amount and the purpose of Boaz's gift. Usually it is understood either literally as Boaz's further kindness and the confirmation of his words[144] or symbolically in terms of marriage and redemption.[145]

However, one purpose of this scene that the commentaries tend to underestimate is to emphasize that the meeting went unknown to anyone in the city. The whole episode from the beginning uses words (like "the man" and "the woman" instead of "Boaz" and "Ruth") that aim to show that what happened during this night was hard to see from the outside. The final scene speaks about it explicitly. Ruth wakes up before anyone (including any occasional bystanders) could recognize what's going on. The words of Boaz do not simply ascertain this fact but are future-oriented. (It seems that information in his words is reorganized.) If it is a command, it is a command that he directs to himself. Therefore, the gift of grain is not only intended to be a wedding present or the symbolic way to assure Boaz's promise, but also the way to conceal Ruth's visit. For ". . . grinding kernels into flour was the first work for a woman in the early morning, [therefore] Ruth's carrying grain would appear natural."[146] Therefore, besides other functions the scene informs the readers about the horizon of the townspeople before the next episode. According to the narrator, the only people who were aware of the visit were Boaz, Ruth, and Naomi.

5.4.3. The Dialogue between Ruth and Naomi (3:16–18)

By the end of Ruth 3 horizons of all main characters and the readers meet.

וַתָּבוֹא אֶל־חֲמוֹתָהּ וַתֹּאמֶר מִי־אַתְּ בִּתִּי וַתַּגֶּד־לָהּ אֵת כָּל־אֲשֶׁר עָשָׂה־לָהּ הָאִישׁ:
וַתֹּאמֶר שֵׁשׁ־הַשְּׂעֹרִים הָאֵלֶּה נָתַן לִי כִּי אָמַר אַל־תָּבוֹאִי רֵיקָם אֶל־חֲמוֹתֵךְ:
וַתֹּאמֶר שְׁבִי בִתִּי עַד אֲשֶׁר תֵּדְעִין אֵיךְ יִפֹּל דָּבָר כִּי לֹא יִשְׁקֹט הָאִישׁ כִּי־אִם־כִּלָּה הַדָּבָר הַיּוֹם:

---

144. Chisholm Jr., *Judges and Ruth*, 660.

145. Green, "Plot of the Biblical," 55–68. According to Bush, "his gift is an earnest of his actions to come – actions that will permanently put an end to their plight." See Bush, *Ruth/Esther*, 183.

146. Wilch, *Ruth*, 298.

> And when she came to her mother-in-law, she said, "How did you fare, my daughter?" Then she told her all that the man had done for her, saying, "These six measures of barley he gave to me, for he said to me, 'You must not go back empty-handed to your mother-in-law.'" She replied, "Wait, my daughter, until you learn how the matter turns out, for the man will not rest but will settle the matter today." (3:16–18)

Verse 16 consists of an enigmatic question of Naomi. Scholars try to figure out why Naomi ever asked Ruth this question: מִי־אַתְּ בִּתִּי "Who are you, my daughter?" Since Naomi designated Ruth as "my daughter," she supposedly recognized her. There are two possible ways to answer this question. (1) it is too dark so that Naomi cannot see who this woman is (besides, she is old enough to call anyone "my daughter"). (2) The door is closed and Naomi is asking this question staying behind the door. But these answers are not satisfactory because such questions would require different answer from Ruth.[147]

Therefore, it was suggested to interpret מִי as accusative of condition and translate the phrase as "as who?" or "in what condition or capacity?"[148] or as in the ESV translation that I use in this work, "How did you fair, my daughter?" In other words, Naomi is interested in what's happened during the visit and the information is given to her in full. In fact, the horizon of Naomi becomes even wider than the horizon of the readers, which again makes the whole episode externally focalized. According to Schipper,

> . . . the narrator states that Ruth provided Naomi with a full report but does not reveal what Ruth told her. Ultimately, Naomi learns more about Ruth's household status than the audience does in v. 16. This narrative technique ensures that the audience still does not know exactly what happened on the threshing

---

147. Consideration of the visual aspect of focalization brings us to one more possibility. Ruth is carrying a sack with six measures of barley so that no one can recognize her. The question of Naomi, therefore, could consist of two parts. First, Naomi sees someone and cannot recognize who it is. So she asks a reasonable question: "Who are you?" מִי־אַתְּ. Then, after Ruth puts down the sack with six measures of barley, Naomi recognizes her with a surprising shout, בִּתִּי "My daughter!" Still another option is possible. The scene starts the same way, but the words "my daughter" is a question (or guessing). But this option is not satisfactory as well and for the same reason.

148. Bush, *Ruth/Esther*, 185.

floor. Ruth's status in relation to either the household of her first marriage or the household of Boaz remains an open question.[149]

Once again, the narrator reorganizes information by not informing the readers about the purpose of Boaz's gift. Therefore, one can only speak about the reason for such reorganization. One of the answers is suggested by Sasson, who considers that the statement is the product of Ruth's own mind. In other words, Boaz never says these words but Ruth, playing an active role in the story, wanted to promote him as the redeemer of her mother-in-law.

Berlin, from another side, suggests that these words represent Ruth's direct speech or interior monologue. But in any case, what the readers hear comes as Ruth's understanding of Boaz's action. "We don't know why Boaz gave Ruth the barley; we know only why Ruth thought Boaz gave it to her."[150]

Campbell echoes Berlin by pointing that the narrator uses literary techniques:

> The story-teller chooses to place the word not in Boaz' mouth while he and Ruth are still at the threshing floor, but in Ruth's mouth as she reports to Naomi a part of the conversation we were not in on earlier.[151]

This technique, according to Campbell, helps to keep the story "free of repetition and gives each scene its own contribution to the developing dramatic effect."[152] According to McKeown, Ruth introduces new information at this point in order to inform Naomi

> that Boaz's concern was not just for her but also for her mother-in-law. Boaz did not want her to return to her mother-in-law empty-handed. His generosity extended not just to Ruth but also to Naomi herself. Naomi complained that she had come home "empty," but now Boaz had taken responsibility to provide for her.[153]

---

149. Schipper, *Ruth*, 160.
150. Berlin, *Poetics and Interpretation*, 97–98.
151. Campbell, *Ruth*, 129.
152. Campbell, 129.
153. McKeown, *Ruth*, 60.

By the end of chapter 3 the horizon of the readers narrows, which is enhanced with the words of Naomi, who suggests for Ruth to wait and see how the matter falls. The idiom "a matter falls" (אֵיךְ יִפֹּל דָּבָר) presupposes that what is going to happen next is not predictable. So the readers are going to take the position of detached onlooker, and focalization in the next scene is going to be mostly external, so the readers will know less then Boaz. With this intrigue in mind, the readers move to the final chapter of the book. However, by the end of the chapter the narrator permits the readers not only to observe resolution of the plot but to share with the readers the knowledge about the distant future, which exceeds the horizon of any character of the story. Hence, by the end of the book the text is again not focalized (not restricted or zero focalized).

5.4.4. Boaz Convenes a Legal Assembly (4:1–2)

The scene at the city gate is externally focalized. The readers are not given the thoughts and plans of Boaz. Boaz, in turn, does not share his attitude even in direct speech, which is understandable: the legal process with its official language and delicacy that was required by the situation prevented him from letting anyone know his real motives. The horizon of Boaz is wider than the horizon of the readers. What the readers do not know is how Boaz is going to act. In this sense, the readers are closer to the elders of the city, whom Boaz invited to witness his conversation with the other relative.

וּבֹעַז עָלָה הַשַּׁעַר וַיֵּשֶׁב שָׁם וְהִנֵּה הַגֹּאֵל עֹבֵר אֲשֶׁר דִּבֶּר־בֹּעַז
וַיֹּאמֶר סוּרָה שְׁבָה־פֹּה פְּלֹנִי אַלְמֹנִי וַיָּסַר וַיֵּשֵׁב:
וַיִּקַּח עֲשָׂרָה אֲנָשִׁים מִזִּקְנֵי הָעִיר וַיֹּאמֶר שְׁבוּ־פֹה וַיֵּשֵׁבוּ:

Now Boaz had gone up to the gate and sat down there. And behold, the redeemer, of whom Boaz had spoken, came by. So Boaz said, "Turn aside, friend; sit down here." And he turned aside and sat down. And he took ten men of the elders of the city and said, "Sit down here." So they sat down. (4:1–2)

According to some commentators, 4:1 – וּבֹעַז עָלָה הַשַּׁעַר וַיֵּשֶׁב שָׁם ("Now Boaz had gone up to the gate and sat down there") – is a continuation of 3:15 – וַיָּבֹא הָעִיר ("Then he went into the city").[154] However, this proposal is not clear

---

154. LaCocque, *Ruth*, 124; Sasson, *Ruth*, 141.

according to other commentators who consider that this scene actually could take place before, during or after the final conversation between Naomi and Ruth (3:16–18).[155] Some are more certain that the scene temporally follows the conversation between Naomi and Ruth. Unusual word order – placement of the subject before the verb – is explained by the desire of the narrator, from one side, to start a new act instead of another scene within the preceding act, and from another side, to show that the scene of a new act immediately follows the preceding scene.[156]

Contrary to this last idea, the text of Ruth shows that the placement of subject before the verb can mean that the scene evolves simultaneously with the previous scene. This is evidenced by the use of the same construction in 2:1 – וּלְנָעֳמִי מוֹדָע לְאִישָׁהּ – "Now Naomi had a relative of her husband's." Needless to say, Naomi had this relative long before and during all the events of chapter 1. However, the information about her relative is linearized and placed at the beginning of chapter 2. It seems that the same kind of approach is used in chapter 4. Therefore, if 4:1 actually advances simultaneously with 3:16–18, then we deal with a classic case of linearization: the narrator, following the nature of written narrative, chose to speak first about Ruth's return and then about Boaz's journey to the city gate. Analysis of events and scenes (in the previous chapter) shows that last scene of chapter 3 had to take place before the scene at the city gate.

By the beginning of chapter 4 the readers, together with all characters, are aware of new information about another relative. However, the readers, as much as Naomi and Ruth, are left in the dark of Boaz's plans. Such distribution of horizons facilitates the external focalization mode. In addition, the final words of Naomi, "Wait, my daughter, until you learn how the matter turns out . . ." create an atmosphere of anticipation and intrigue, which is typically created by the mode of external focalization.

This means that verses 1–3 represent a report of events. The readers are given a position of a detached onlooker who is watching the scene from outside and wonders what exactly Boaz is going to do. Even the name of the relative is not disclosed to the reader, while Boaz and other participants of the story certainly know his name. Instead, the narrator uses the Hebrew

---

155. Hubbard, *Ruth*, 232. See also Holmstedt, *Ruth*, 180.
156. Block, *Judges, Ruth*, 704.

phrase פְּלֹנִי אַלְמֹנִי, which, according to Hawk, "refers to a name known by the characters in the story but not divulged to the reader."[157] Thus the narrator says less than the characters know, which represents a classical case of external focalization.

A great deal has been said about the reason the narrator fails to name the closer relative in such curious manner. Most of the commentators recall and compare other uses of this phrase (in 1 Sam 21:3; 2 Kgs 6:8) and consider that nouns פְּלֹנִי אַלְמֹנִי "do not represent the kindred redeemer's proper name."[158] Therefore the phrase can be translated as "so-and-so." The point is that the narrator, if wanting to, could have done without the naming of the closer relative, for it is perfectly acceptable by Hebrew syntax.[159] And if the narrator decides to mention this name, there is supposed to be a reason for it.

Looking for the reason, some commentators attempt to see the reluctance of the narrator to even mention the name of the man who refused to fulfill his direct duties. So, Bush says,

> Surely such a pointed way of underscoring the namelessness of this man in a narrative that so carefully names the other protagonists (cf. 1:2, 4; 2:1) subtly creates a less than favorable impression of him and prompts us to suspect a pejorative purpose in the choice of the expression . . . One wonders indeed if the Hebrew expression we have translated "So-and-So" was also used euphemistically in place of a stronger epithet, as the English expression is![160]

In contrast, Schipper argues that the nouns are the idioms that do not have a negative connotation elsewhere in the Hebrew Bible. Therefore, "one should not read a negative or dismissive evaluation of the character into Boaz's use of the idiom."[161] According to Schipper,

> For the purposes of the narrative, the use of this idiom helps maintain the focus on this character's role as a potential kindred

---

157. Hawk, *Ruth*, 119.
158. See, for example, Schipper, *Ruth*, 163.
159. Campbell, "Hebrew Short Story," 141.
160. Bush, *Ruth/Esther*, 191.
161. Schipper, *Ruth*, 163.

redeemer similar to the way the rhyming names of Naomi's sons maintain the focus on their roles.[162]

The study of focalization and rearrangement of narrative information suggest another possible view on the matter. Obviously, the first two verses of chapter 4 are written first of all to set the stage for the following legal process. But there seems to be another, more important, reason for this short narrative passage. The passage (4:1–2) pictures Boaz as an influential person in the community (the real אִישׁ גִּבּוֹר חַיִל): not only his workers, but even the elders of the town listen to him. In a couple of verses this influential man is going to resolve a dilemma, and maybe add to the traditional precedents with a new problem and possible solution. The elders of the city (ten of them!) have to be there in order to approve this practice for which the exact name of another party is not so important. This setting does not only prepare the stage for the next scene but forms the point of view, and it gives necessary parameters to make the following procedure legal and acceptable.

5.4.5. Legal Discussion (4:3–8)

Beginning from verse 3 when Boaz starts his appeal, focalization receives an internal element. The external component still remains because of the nature of reported speech. However, if the character expresses his attitude or pictures past or possible future events, the character's internal point of view is shared and an internal component is added to focalization. Of course, the line between external and internal focalization is not sharp but in this particular case there are some grammatical issues that emphasize internal focalization. So, Boaz starts to picture the future by saying:

וַיֹּאמֶר לַגֹּאֵל חֶלְקַת הַשָּׂדֶה אֲשֶׁר לְאָחִינוּ לֶאֱלִימֶלֶךְ מָכְרָה
נָעֳמִי הַשָּׁבָה מִשְּׂדֵה מוֹאָב:
וַאֲנִי אָמַרְתִּי אֶגְלֶה אָזְנְךָ לֵאמֹר קְנֵה נֶגֶד הַיֹּשְׁבִים וְנֶגֶד זִקְנֵי עַמִּי
אִם־תִּגְאַל גְּאָל וְאִם־לֹא יִגְאַל הַגִּידָה לִּי וְאֵדַע כִּי אֵין זוּלָתְךָ
לִגְאוֹל וְאָנֹכִי אַחֲרֶיךָ וַיֹּאמֶר אָנֹכִי אֶגְאָל:

Then he said to the redeemer, "Naomi, who has come back from the country of Moab, is selling the parcel of land that belonged to our relative Elimelech. So I thought I would tell you of it and

---

162. Schipper, 163.

say, 'Buy it in the presence of those sitting here and in the presence of the elders of my people.' If you will redeem it, redeem it. But if you will not, tell me, that I may know, for there is no one besides you to redeem it, and I come after you." And he said, "I will redeem it." (4:3–8)

The horizons in these two verses are distributed as follows. Compared with the other relative and the readers, Boaz has the widest horizon. He knows what he is doing. The readers are less informed – the fact that was indicated by McKeown, "This is new information for the reader. Until now there has been no indication that Naomi had land for sale, and the reader will have assumed that she was destitute and dependent on charity."[163] But since the readers witnessed the scene at the threshing floor, at least they know that the purpose of Boaz is to redeem and marry Ruth. However, the readers are not sure how Boaz is going to do it since he started his conversation from the topic that was not even mentioned during his conversation with Ruth: in contrast to the ESV translation (above) the first words in Boaz's sentence are חֶלְקַת הַשָּׂדֶה "the parcel of land." The most ignorant participant of this discourse is the closer relative. He is unaware of Boaz's plan and is certainly ignorant of the threshing floor conversation. Since Boaz presents the property of Elimelech as the primary topic of the meeting, the audience (elders and people of Bethlehem) should have perceived the meeting as a formal redemption procedure.[164]

Then another portion of the picture is added in verse 4, which starts from the overt subject pronoun אָנֹכִי ("I"). This unusual structure of Hebrew sentence serves to expand the horizon of the relative (as was discussed in other places). In this verse Boaz adds himself into the picture of the possible future.

This is the future that Boaz "pictures" for his relative: the relative can become a happy owner of the land that Naomi sells if he agrees to buy it. The picture comes from the mouth of Boaz and by definition is incomplete (restricted or internally focalized). Boaz does not say anything about Ruth yet and his focalized message is the key element that creates suspense in this scene and makes reading thrilling.

There is yet no hint that the issue under discussion concerns anything other than the land that belonged to their relative Elimelek. Boaz seems to

---

163. McKeown, *Ruth*, 62.
164. Holmstedt, *Ruth*, 184.

be waiting until it is completely necessary to reveal that Naomi and Ruth are somehow involved in the deal.[165]

Only after the positive response, Boaz presents before the relative the second portion of the picture:

> וַיֹּאמֶר בֹּעַז בְּיוֹם־קְנוֹתְךָ הַשָּׂדֶה מִיַּד נָעֳמִי וּמֵאֵת רוּת הַמּוֹאֲבִיָּה אֵשֶׁת־הַמֵּת קָנִיתִי לְהָקִים שֵׁם־הַמֵּת עַל־נַחֲלָתוֹ׃

> Then Boaz said, "The day you buy the field from the hand of Naomi, you also acquire Ruth the Moabite, the widow of the dead, in order to perpetuate the name of the dead in his inheritance." (4:5)

Verse 5 is considered to be very difficult to translate. The problems that one finds in this verse are clearly specified by Hayes:[166]

(1) Whether וּמֵאֵת to emend to וּ + מִן + את?
(2) What form one adopts for קנה (either the *Ketiv*, קָנִיתִי, or *Qere*, קָנִיתָה)?
(3) What is the verb's object?

Hayes then briefly mentions the spectrum of opinions on these questions and speaks out in favor of the view of Holmstedt, who considers that וּמֵאֵת means "also." He follows the *Ketiv* reading of the verb, and considers the phrase "the widow of the dead" as an object of the verb. The result is the following translation:

> On the day you acquire the field from the hand of Naomi and from Ruth the Moabite, the wife of the dead man I shall acquire in order to establish the name of the dead man over his inheritance.[167]

Both scholars consider this phrase to be intentionally ambiguous and is constructed by the narrator for literary or rhetorical purposes.[168] However, as Hayes admits, the translation goes against the Masoretic markings, which considerably undermines this interpretation.

---

165. Holmstedt, *Ruth*, 186.
166. Hayes, "Intentional Ambiguity," 159–82.
167. Holmstedt, *Ruth*, 180.
168. See Hayes, "Intentional Ambiguity," 166.

The analysis of the play of horizons brings some clarity to this problem. First, as was said before, Boaz's horizon is wider than the horizon of the relative. During the legal procedure Boaz's speech is focalized, which means that he shares information in parts and the horizon of the relative increases steadily. First Boaz informs the relative about the fact that Naomi is going to sell her portion of the land; then Boaz expresses his readiness to buy the land if the relative refuses to do so. In his first address Boaz selectively talks about two elements of the matter: the parcel of the land and the priority of the right. He is talking about responsibility toward the property of Elimelech, not about responsibility toward widows of Elimelech's family. According to Hawk, "the information comes at the redeemer with such rapid-fire staccato that he can scarcely take it in, let alone weigh his options."[169]

The last portion of information comes to the relative after the particle וּמֵאֵת "and also." With these words the relative receives the maximum possible information and his horizon becomes as wide as the horizon of Boaz. After taking all the facts into account, he changes his decision to the opposite:

וַיֹּאמֶר הַגֹּאֵל לֹא אוּכַל לִגְאוֹל־לִי פֶּן־אַשְׁחִית אֶת־נַחֲלָתִי גְּאַל־לְךָ אַתָּה אֶת־גְּאֻלָּתִי כִּי לֹא־אוּכַל לִגְאֹל׃

Then the redeemer said, "I cannot redeem it for myself, lest I impair my own inheritance. Take my right of redemption yourself, for I cannot redeem it." (4:6)

The final phase of legal procedure is pictured by the custom of confirmation of the transaction. Since the readers may not be aware of this tradition (which points to the late origin of the book), the narrator provides a comment concerning its background. By definition, the text of this comment can be only zero focalized – the narrator communicates directly to the readers, giving comments on characters' actions. However, the action itself is described with externally focalized text.

וְזֹאת לְפָנִים בְּיִשְׂרָאֵל עַל־הַגְּאוּלָּה וְעַל־הַתְּמוּרָה לְקַיֵּם כָּל־דָּבָר שָׁלַף אִישׁ נַעֲלוֹ וְנָתַן לְרֵעֵהוּ וְזֹאת הַתְּעוּדָה בְּיִשְׂרָאֵל׃
וַיֹּאמֶר הַגֹּאֵל לְבֹעַז קְנֵה־לָךְ וַיִּשְׁלֹף נַעֲלוֹ׃

---

169. Hawk, *Ruth*, 127.

> Now this was the custom in former times in Israel concerning redeeming and exchanging: to confirm a transaction, the one drew off his sandal and gave it to the other, and this was the manner of attesting in Israel. So when the redeemer said to Boaz, "Buy it for yourself," he drew off his sandal. (4:7)

Externally focalized action is a very important addition to the end of the scene. It plays a role of conclusion and describes the final setting of the scene.

5.4.6. Decisions and Blessings (4:9–12)

In verses 9 and 10 Boaz summarizes the progress of the legal process, giving his restricted view of what's happened. He draws a picture of the past event.

> וַיֹּאמֶר בֹּעַז לַזְּקֵנִים וְכָל־הָעָם עֵדִים אַתֶּם הַיּוֹם כִּי קָנִיתִי אֶת־
> כָּל־אֲשֶׁר לֶאֱלִימֶלֶךְ וְאֵת כָּל־אֲשֶׁר לְכִלְיוֹן וּמַחְלוֹן מִיַּד נָעֳמִי:
> וְגַם אֶת־רוּת הַמֹּאֲבִיָּה אֵשֶׁת מַחְלוֹן קָנִיתִי לִי לְאִשָּׁה לְהָקִים
> שֵׁם־הַמֵּת עַל־נַחֲלָתוֹ וְלֹא־יִכָּרֵת שֵׁם־הַמֵּת מֵעִם אֶחָיו וּמִשַּׁעַר
> מְקוֹמוֹ עֵדִים אַתֶּם הַיּוֹם:

> Then Boaz said to the elders and all the people, "You are witnesses this day that I have bought from the hand of Naomi all that belonged to Elimelech and all that belonged to Chilion and to Mahlon. Also Ruth the Moabite, the widow of Mahlon, I have bought to be my wife, to perpetuate the name of the dead in his inheritance, that the name of the dead may not be cut off from among his brothers and from the gate of his native place. You are witnesses this day." (4:9–10)

The narrator could make this conclusion by himself, saying that Boaz "bought from the hand of Naomi all that belonged to Elimelech . . ." but preferred to put these words into the mouth of Boaz. The reason for this decision is the following words of the elders that would not be appropriate if the conclusion is made by omniscient narrator with zero focalization. In contrast, the internally focalized speech of Boaz requires approval from the elders and all the people who were present at this legal procedure.

The speech of Boaz has several features that could not be part of the narrator's report. First, Boaz relates to the elders twice as the witness of this transaction. Second, double use of the phrase "this day" is appropriate only for internally focalized speech of the character; the narrator would not need to mention day at all. Third, syntactically verse 10 emphasizes Ruth by putting her on the first position in the sentence. Finally, Boaz uses legal language in this speech. For example, Ruth is identified by her full name "Ruth the Moabite," which is "appropriate in the public setting of the legal assembly, where full identification is necessary."[170]

In response to Boaz, the people of Bethlehem in the form of blessing draw a picture of his future life. Therefore, in their words, information is linearized for they blueprint the destiny of Boaz and Ruth.

וַיֹּאמְרוּ כָּל־הָעָם אֲשֶׁר־בַּשַּׁעַר וְהַזְּקֵנִים עֵדִים יִתֵּן יהוה אֶת־הָאִשָּׁה הַבָּאָה אֶל־בֵּיתֶךָ כְּרָחֵל וּכְלֵאָה אֲשֶׁר בָּנוּ שְׁתֵּיהֶם אֶת־בֵּית יִשְׂרָאֵל וַעֲשֵׂה־חַיִל בְּאֶפְרָתָה וּקְרָא־שֵׁם בְּבֵית לָחֶם: וִיהִי בֵיתְךָ כְּבֵית פֶּרֶץ אֲשֶׁר־יָלְדָה תָמָר לִיהוּדָה מִן־הַזֶּרַע אֲשֶׁר יִתֵּן יהוה לְךָ מִן־הַנַּעֲרָה הַזֹּאת:

> Then all the people who were at the gate and the elders said, "We are witnesses. May the LORD make the woman, who is coming into your house, like Rachel and Leah, who together built up the house of Israel. May you act worthily in Ephrathah and be renowned in Bethlehem, and may your house be like the house of Perez, whom Tamar bore to Judah, because of the offspring that the LORD will give you by this young woman." (4:11–12)

It should be noted that the blessing is mainly concerned with the marriage of Boaz and completely overlooks legal matters of the land. This makes the marriage of Boaz more important than the land ownership and changes our attitude toward the previous scene, which becomes to be something like a game. Thus, focalization shows what is more important from the point of view of the elders.

Their blessing has three parts:

> The blessing dwells first on the woman and her potential to give offspring as did Rachel and Leah, then on Boaz and his potential for fertility, and finally upon the house which will thereby be

---

170. Bush, *Ruth/Esther*, 238.

brought into existence, that it will be as significant as that of Perez, whom Tamar bore to Judah.[171]

Scholars' interest is with the middle part – "May you act worthily in Ephrathah and be renowned in Bethlehem" – which sounds ambiguous. The problem is with wide variety of meanings of phrases "act worthily" and "renown in Bethlehem." A number of different variants have been suggested:

> Bush: "so that you may flourish in Ephrathah and gain renown in Bethlehem"[172]
>
> Hawk: "Act powerfully in Ephrathah and gain renown in Bethlehem"[173]
>
> Campbell: "And may you show fertility in Ephrathah and (then) bestow a name in Bethlehem."[174]
>
> Hubbard: "So you may prosper in Ephrathah and enjoy fame in Bethlehem."[175]
>
> Holmstedt: "Therefore make sons of character in Ephratha and proclaim a name in Bethlehem."[176]

Employing the notion of reorganization helps to add some clarity to this problem. The elders (or rather the narrator by elders' mouth) picture the future of Boaz and Ruth. By doing this, they compare this future with two famous families of Israel. The second blessing standing in the middle should be read in this context. Mentioning Rachel, Leah, Perez, and Tamar in the blessing formula is unusual if one looks only to the story world. But taking into account the whole discourse and specifically the epilogue of the narrator, one can connect the blessing with genealogy and the figure of David. The narrator linearized information so that the words of the elders that are internally focalized become a sort of prophetic vision, which is zero focalized. In

---

171. Campbell, *Ruth*, 156.
172. Bush, *Ruth/Esther*, 240.
173. Hawk, *Ruth*, 118.
174. Campbell, *Ruth*, 140.
175. Hubbard, *Ruth*, 253.
176. Holmstedt, *Ruth*, 198.

this context the phrase וְעֲשֵׂה־חַיִל is better understood as "become great" and וּקְרָא־שֵׁם as "make your name great," which anticipates the coming of David.

5.5. Obed as Predecessor of David (4:17b–22)

5.5.1. Marriage, Conception and Birth of the Son (4:13)

The verse constitutes the summary of the events that followed the legal process.

וַיִּקַּח בֹּעַז אֶת־רוּת וַתְּהִי־לוֹ לְאִשָּׁה וַיָּבֹא אֵלֶיהָ וַיִּתֵּן יהוה לָהּ
הֵרָיוֹן וַתֵּלֶד בֵּן׃

> So Boaz took Ruth, and she became his wife. And he went in to her, and the LORD gave her conception, and she bore a son. (4:13)

The passage is zero focalized because the narrator informs the readers about the transcendent reason of Ruth's conception – "the LORD gave her conception" – the fact that characters could only assume. Yet the readers without objection take this fact because it has been stated by the omniscient narrator.

5.5.2. Naomi and the Women of Bethlehem (4:14–17a)

This passage is the combination of internal and external focalizations. Internal focalization reflects the view of women of Bethlehem on recent events. Externally focalized passages concern Naomi's actions and two acts of the women: proclaiming significance of the child and naming of the child.

The passage serves as the conclusion for the whole story and consists of a look to the past and to the future that women take. As such, this look is evaluative and predictive. The events of the story are first recalled. Women ascribe the happy ending of the story to the hand of God, which is the ideological appraisal of the past events. Then they take a look to the future.

One of the textual difficulties of this passage is found in 4:17 – the naming of Obed. The problem is that (1) the name is given not by Boaz, Ruth, or Naomi but by women of Bethlehem, and (2) it looks like Obed receives his name twice: "the women of the neighborhood gave him a name," and then again "they named him Obed."

At first, I will briefly look at two solutions that are given to this problem by Hubbard and Bush and then make a suggestion how this problem can be approached considering focalization of the passage. Hubbard[177] does not see any problem with other people announcing the birth and the name of a child. In order to support his view, he cites two passages: one from Jeremiah 20:15 and another from Isaiah 9:5. Therefore, he considers only 4:17a as problematic. He resolves the problem by pointing out that in reality Obed is named only once and the expression קרא שם actually means "to proclaim significance." Therefore, Hubbard sees this verse as "a typical birth announcement formula as a climactic editorial comment on the story's closing scene."[178]

Bush sees in this verse "the play based on meaning" between the phrase "a son has been born to Naomi" and the name "Obed" understood here in the sense of "provider."[179]

Let me show to what kind of conclusion one can come to after considering focalization of the passage. Focalization of the passage is continuously changing. It starts with internally focalized reported speech of the women of Bethlehem:

וַתֹּאמַרְנָה הַנָּשִׁים אֶל־נָעֳמִי בָּרוּךְ יהוה אֲשֶׁר לֹא הִשְׁבִּית לָךְ גֹּאֵל הַיּוֹם וְיִקָּרֵא שְׁמוֹ בְּיִשְׂרָאֵל׃
וְהָיָה לָךְ לְמֵשִׁיב נֶפֶשׁ וּלְכַלְכֵּל אֶת־שֵׂיבָתֵךְ כִּי כַלָּתֵךְ אֲשֶׁר־אֲהֵבַתֶךְ יְלָדַתּוּ אֲשֶׁר־הִיא טוֹבָה לָךְ מִשִּׁבְעָה בָּנִים׃

Then the women said to Naomi, "Blessed be the LORD, who has not left you this day without a redeemer, and may his name be renowned in Israel! He shall be to you a restorer of life and a nourisher of your old age, for your daughter-in-law who loves you, who is more to you than seven sons, has given birth to him." (4:14–15)

Then focalization changes from internal to external:

וַתִּקַּח נָעֳמִי אֶת־הַיֶּלֶד וַתְּשִׁתֵהוּ בְחֵיקָהּ וַתְּהִי־לוֹ לְאֹמֶנֶת׃
וַתִּקְרֶאנָה לוֹ הַשְּׁכֵנוֹת שֵׁם לֵאמֹר יֻלַּד־בֵּן לְנָעֳמִי

Then Naomi took the child and laid him on her lap and became his nurse. And the women of the neighborhood gave him a name, saying, "A son has been born to Naomi." (4:16–17a)

---

177. Hubbard, "Ruth IV," 293–301.
178. Hubbard, 299.
179. Bush, *Ruth/Esther*, 13.

Finally, the end of the passage is zero focalized:

וַתִּקְרֶאנָה שְׁמוֹ עוֹבֵד הוּא אֲבִי־יִשַׁי אֲבִי דָוִד׃

They named him Obed. He was the father of Jesse, the father of David. (4:17b)

Therefore, there is a sequence of focalizations from internal to external and to zero. From a literary point of view, this type of sequence is typical for the end of the story: the situation is first considered through the eyes of one of the characters, then the readers are given the situation externally as it is and they are expected to come to their own conclusions. Finally, the narrator explains to the readers the meaning of the story, suggesting broader zero focalized vision.

5.5.3. Epilogue (4:17–22)

The rest of the book is zero focalized because together with mentioning the name of the child – Obed – the narrator immediately informs the readers that the child happens to be forefather of King David. The following genealogy is obviously zero focalized as well.

וְאֵלֶּה תּוֹלְדוֹת פָּרֶץ פֶּרֶץ הוֹלִיד אֶת־חֶצְרוֹן׃
וְחֶצְרוֹן הוֹלִיד אֶת־רָם וְרָם הוֹלִיד אֶת־עַמִּינָדָב׃
וְעַמִּינָדָב הוֹלִיד אֶת־נַחְשׁוֹן וְנַחְשׁוֹן הוֹלִיד אֶת־שַׂלְמָה׃
וְשַׂלְמוֹן הוֹלִיד אֶת־בֹּעַז וּבֹעַז הוֹלִיד אֶת־עוֹבֵד׃
וְעֹבֵד הוֹלִיד אֶת־יִשַׁי וְיִשַׁי הוֹלִיד אֶת־דָּוִד׃

Now these are the generations of Perez: Perez fathered Hezron, Hezron fathered Ram, Ram fathered Amminadab, Amminadab fathered Nahshon, Nahshon fathered Salmon, Salmon fathered Boaz, Boaz fathered Obed, Obed fathered Jesse, and Jesse fathered David. (4:18–22)

The genealogy expands the horizon of the readers to the maximum extent and gives not only afterword, but also attaches meaning to the story. The placement of genealogy at the end of the book is important for two reasons: (1) ideologically, it places emphasis on the fact that the Moabite woman happened to be the great grandmother of King David, and (2) aesthetically, the narrator can hold the intrigue of the story until the end.

However, according to Schipper, "the general consensus is that this final genealogy is a later addition."[180] For example, according to Campbell's opinion,

> ... verses 18–22 form a genealogical appendix to the Ruth story and are not an original part of it. The goal of the story has been reached in verse 17, and it seems most unlikely that the storyteller would backtrack to trace a line from Perez and Judah, whom he had mentioned in 4:12, to Boaz and his offspring.[181]

Defending his position, Campbell points that "the style of the genealogy is distinctly that of the P tradition of Genesis"[182] but even there he adds that in Genesis genealogy never ends the story, which makes the genealogy of the book of Ruth unique and difficult to explain.

More recent commentaries, however, hold a different view, giving reasons why genealogy can be considered as integral and even the most important part of the book. For example, according to Hawk, it "complements the narrative" in three ways.[183] (1) It echoes the naming of father and sons that begins the book (1:1-3); (2) it extends the story's focus on Boaz rather than Elimelech; and (3) it casts the whole book as an ancestral narrative on a par with those of Abraham and Jacob. Therefore, Hawk concludes:

> The genealogy that concludes Ruth, therefore, is an integral part of the book, functioning as the narrative precursor to David in much the same way that the stories of the patriarchs in Genesis serve as the narrative precursor of Moses.[184]

Without going to extremes, it is possible to consider verse 17 (where the name of David is mentioned) and the genealogy (4:18–22) separately. The introduction of David in 4:17 helps to see all the elements of the story in a new ideological light. To start with, a story that ends with women's blessing would

---

180. Schipper, *Ruth*, 186. Shipper names Campbell, Gray, Gerleman, Hertzberg, Joüon, Nielsen, Rudolph, Sasson, Würthwein, and Zenger among those scholars who support this view. Among those who consider the genealogy as an integral part of the book, Shipper mentions Hubbard, Bush, and Fischer. LaCocque, who also holds this view, adds to this list a few names as "notable exceptions" from the general position. See LaCocque, *Ruth*, 148n100. To this list we can also add the commentaries of Hawk, Wilch, and Chisholm.
181. Campbell, *Ruth*, 172.
182. Campbell, 172.
183. Hawk, *Ruth*, 136.
184. Hawk, 136.

not have a chance to survive. For, according to Linafelt, "for a story to really 'count,' to be worth preserving, it must finally have to do with a great man."[185]

According to LaCocque, the mentioning of the name of David shows the importance of the role played by "the sociopsychological community" in Israel's history. LaCocque traces the activity of the women of Bethlehem from the beginning of the story and shows that it is due to their wisdom Naomi and Ruth could finally succeed. For it is the community of Bethlehem (not the elders of the town) "that welcomes Naomi and, cautiously, does not mention Ruth" and, consequently, "suspends all judgment on the foreigner" until the legal process and only then expresses its attitude toward Ruth publicly. Therefore, with the mentioning of David, it turns out that "a member of a loathed people sets in motion the history of the messianic dynasty."[186]

The reference to David as descendant of a Moabite woman helps to subvert xenophobic laws[187] like the one found in Deuteronomy 23:4: "No Ammonite or Moabite shall be admitted to the assembly of the LORD." Therefore, the Israel community gets permission to transcend (but not to violate) some laws. In particular, "creative use of the laws and legal conventions" becomes a standard way to "welcome a faithful foreigner into the covenant community."[188]

Consideration of the concept of focalization brings additional insights to the above reasoning. According to one of the narratological axioms, the last paragraph, sentence, and even the last word of the narrative should be considered as the most important.[189] In the case of the book of Ruth, the story proper ends with the name of David. This information goes beyond the fabric of the narrative and thus makes the final clause of the story zero focalized because the readers know more than any given character in the story. This information, therefore, raises the book to a considerably different level. Indeed, if

---

185. Linafelt and Beal, *Ruth and Esther*, 79. This, however, does not necessarily mean that the second part of verse 17 is a later addition. Contrary to this, Wilch, referring to Witzenrath and Sasson, demonstrates that Hebrew text of 4:17b has normal wording, where the personal name "Obed" immediately precedes the formula of fathering. On the basis of this reasoning, Wilch (following Witzenrath) comes to the conclusion that the clause "He was the father of Jesse, the father of David" is not a later addition but an integral part of the story.

186. LaCocque, *Ruth*, 145.

187. As it is called by Linafelt and Beal, *Ruth and Esther*, 79.

188. Hawk, *Ruth*, 139.

189. According to Brooks, "The sense of a beginning, then, must in some important way be determined by the sense of an ending." See Brooks, *Reading for the Plot*, 94.

the narrator would not inform the readers about Obed's lineage, and if the book of Ruth would end with the words: "Then Naomi took the child and laid him on her lap and became his nurse" (4:16), the story would certainly remain exciting and intriguing, it would constitute resolution of the initial conflict and bring the narrative to the logical end, but the main ideological message of the book would be missed. Without the epilogue, the theological message of the book, according to Chisholm, could be formulated as follows:

> God cares for needy people like Naomi and Ruth; he is their ally in this chaotic world. He richly rewards people like Ruth and Boaz who demonstrate sacrificial love and in so doing become his instruments in helping the needy.[190]

However, the previous conclusion does not count the contribution of genealogy; therefore, Chisholm adds:

> The genealogy contributes to this message in a significant way for it shows that God's rewards for those who sacrificially love others sometimes exceed their wildest imagination and transcend their lifetime. God's blessing upon Ruth and Boaz extended beyond their lifetime and immediate family, for their descendant, David, became the greatest of Israel's kings, and his descendant, Jesus the Messiah, will rule over the entire earth in the kingdom to come.[191]

The phrases like "exceed their wildest imagination," and "transcend their lifetime" very well reflect the idea behind zero focalization – for while what is "wildest imagination" for the characters of the story is known to the narrator of the story, it goes beyond the horizon of the characters.

If the name of David closes the narrative proper, the genealogy can be considered as a footnote to the whole story.[192] However, a footnote is also part of the story and as such it should also carry a certain distinct meaning. While the genealogy is also zero focalized, one can find a slight difference between zero focalization of genealogy and zero focalization of verse 17. Verse 17 connects the lineage with Naomi and therefore the horizon of the

---

190. Chisholm Jr., *Judges and Ruth*, 682–83.
191. Chisholm Jr., 683.
192. Hawk, *Ruth*, 135.

narrator is compared with the horizon of Naomi.[193] In contrast, in the genealogy David and Obed are presented as descendants of Boaz; thus the horizon of the narrator is compared with the horizon of Boaz.

What is more, the genealogy is very selective – a fact that always took a great interest of scholars. Schipper suggests that the "the genealogy is telescoped for some rhetorical purpose."[194] He lists several views of such selectivity including (1) rhyme with the names of Naomi's sons; (2) impossibility to alter the order of genealogy that was already fixed by the time the book was written; (3) connection with genealogy of Genesis 38; (4) the order of names;[195] (5) popular etymology of Perez's name; and (6) connection with blessings in Ruth 4:12.

As for the limits of genealogy (it starts from Perez instead of Judah and ends with David), Sasson, based on Malamat's hypothesis, links it with two periods of Israel history:

> This listing of David's pedigree is divisible into two equal segments: the first of which covers the period between the Eisodus and Exodus (Perez-Nahshon); the second of which witnesses the settlement and the early days of Irael's nationhood.[196]

Therefore, it can be concluded that the genealogy of David in the book of Ruth was restricted to ten members for ideological purposes. For example, the genealogy starts from Perez obviously because he was the son of Judah and Tamar, whom elders of Bethlehem mentioned in the blessing in 4:12. Judah and Tamar are mentioned in blessing because their story has a common ideological motif with the story of Ruth. This motif is that the woman, who

---

193. Chisholm says that the verse connects David with Elimelech, which is "implied by the reference to Obed as Naomi's child" (Chisholm Jr., *Judges and Ruth*, 683), which may be significant theologically, but since Elimelech has been dead for a long time, it is more appropriate to compare the horizon of the narrator with the horizon of Naomi.

194. Schipper, *Ruth*, 187.

195. Following Sasson, many scholars emphasize first, seventh, and tenth names in genealogy as the most important. Chisholm, for example, says that Boaz's name "appears in the symbolically significant seventh position, highlighting his prominence in his family's line and in the nation's history." Chisholm Jr., *Judges and Ruth*, 683.

196. Sasson, *Ruth*, 184.

by all legal reasons cannot be included into Israel's society, ends up playing a key role in Israel history due to her righteousness.[197]

The analysis of focalization of the text in the beginning and in the end of the story leads to the following conclusion.

5.6. Conclusion: Narrative Strategy of the Book of Ruth

The preceding analysis of the composition of the book of Ruth shows that the plot of the book is built primarily upon the instrument of focalization. Focalization as the selection of narrative information was already considered in chapter 4 in regard to the story events. This is, so to say, focalization in the broad sense. As was demonstrated in this chapter, focalization (or selection of narrative information) on the level of composition is reflected in reorganization and linearization of narrative information. Further, it was also demonstrated that reorganization of events in the book of Ruth (as dialogic narrative) assumes the form of the play of horizons on the level of the discourse and on the level of the story.

On the level of the story, restricted horizons of the characters interact with each other, which results in the development of the plot. Most of the time the readers get to know about the horizon of the character through direct speech. However, the narrator uses other means of channeling this information as well (for example, reporting the thoughts or telling acts of the characters). One of the most common ways to demonstrate the focalized nature of the character's view is to report what the character speaks or thinks about the future or the past, and the narrator of the book of Ruth uses this instrument very often.

The characters of the book constantly recall and evaluate the past and the present and picture the future. Recollection of the past explains characters' attitudes, gives the background for ideas concerning the solution of their problems, and helps to fill in gaps that have arisen in the course of narration. The picture of the future directs the narrative and verbalizes possible resolutions of the plot. Evaluation of the present connects the past and the future events, helps the characters to express a current view on themselves, on other

---

197. Comp. Ruth 3:10–11 and Gen 38:25. There are other minor motives that are common for these stories. Besides, genealogies in Genesis 1–11 also have ten generations.

characters, and on the details of the narrative world. With this presentation of information, the narrator is able to update the readers' concept of the narrative world, without literal reorganization of the events.

The play of horizons (and hence focalization) also performed on the level of discourse. This level includes the characters of the story as well as the readers and the narrator. Analysis of focalization on this level demonstrated that some portions of the text of the book of Ruth are zero focalized. This happens primarily when the narrator communicates information that is unknown to the characters of the story, which expands the readers' horizon in relation to the horizon of one of several characters. There are a number of passages where the horizon of the readers does not exceed the horizon of the characters. Sometimes it is only a seeming perception because after all, the character(s) turn out to know more. Every time it makes the readers re-evaluate the perception of a previous portion of the text. Finally, there are passages with external focalization – when the readers realize that they do not have sufficient information to judge the acts of the characters.

This is how focalization is distributed throughout the book of Ruth. After an externally focalized prologue, the text of the first chapter is focalized internally, which means that the narrator does not communicate to the readers information that would exceed the knowledge of the characters. Internal focalization, therefore, plays a very important role in the readers' perception of the story. Being unaware of the relative who potentially can solve the problem of the women, the readers find themselves being hostage to the characters' reasoning. The readers get their knowledge about the characters' point of view mainly by listening to dialogues, where the characters share their positions and try to prove their points.

For example, Naomi, on the basis of her past experience, suggests that her daughters-in-law better return to their families. The daughters-in-law, on the other hand, do not agree with her and suggest their own plan – to go with Naomi and become part of her people. On the basis of her perspective on life, Naomi explains why she does not agree with the plan of her daughters-in-law. In order to do that, she creates the picture of what would happen if the daughters-in-law stay with her. Therefore, the readers become involved in this discussion in which they see the narrative world according to the perspectives of the characters. Internal focalization helps the readers to understand the character's arguments with deep empathy but does not suggest resolution of the problem. To address the problem, one has to view the circumstances from a different (wider) perspective, which presupposes greater knowledge or shift in focalization. This shift happens in the beginning of chapter 2.

On the level of the story, the characters have identical horizons. At least it seems so until in 2:20 when the readers find that Naomi, in fact, was aware of Boaz but for some reason did not inform Ruth about him.

In the very first verse of chapter 2 a new figure is introduced into the plot. The readers find out that in Bethlehem there is a man named Boaz. Boaz is called "relative" or "friend" of Elimelech, the husband of Naomi. Intuitively the readers may assume that Boaz can potentially solve the problem of the widows. But in the first reading of the text one does not necessarily get this impression because relative or friend does not mean redeemer. The horizon of the readers grows only in a sense that now they are aware that the narrative world besides Naomi, Ruth, and the women of Bethlehem has a man, and not simply a man but a man of substance.

On the level of the story the rest of the chapter is built upon the difference in the horizons of the characters. Ruth is the character with the most limited horizon. She identifies who Boaz is only in 2:20 after Naomi's explanation. Boaz also has not met Ruth and until 2:7 his horizon is also limited. But in 2:11 it appears that, while he did not meet Ruth in person, he heard about her and is aware of her proper conduct. Therefore, when Boaz starts to offer his goodwill to Ruth, she was very surprised by this generosity.

On the level of discourse, however, the picture is somewhat different. The information about Boaz certainly affects the way the readers view the following events. It immediately lifts the readers to a higher level as regard to knowledge and perspective. The readers become more knowledgeable than any character of the story and the text becomes zero focalized. It is related to the horizon of Ruth as well as to the horizon of Boaz. However, when Boaz recognizes that this young Moabite is, in fact, the same woman who came with Naomi from the field of Moab, his horizon expands and becomes as wide as the horizon of the readers.

Therefore, in the rest of the chapter Boaz and the readers know more than Ruth, while she remains ignorant of the situation. However, her focalized position becomes the most intriguing and it is Ruth's perception that the narrator is most interested in. This conclusion can be made on the grounds of two facts. First, Ruth is the last person in the chapter who finds out who

Boaz really is. However, and it will be the second fact, together with Ruth the readers get to know about Boaz something that was hidden from them throughout the chapter.

Boaz is not only a man of substance and the friend/relative of Elimelech. He is also potential redeemer (גֹּאֵל) of Elimelech's family. This piece of information changes focalization mode once again; the readers' horizon expands but the information comes not from the narrator, but from one of the characters. Therefore, even though the horizon of the readers expands, focalization shifts towards internal since the readers lose their privileged position in relation to any character of the story.

The information about Boaz as a potential redeemer that comes from Naomi forces the readers to reassess the perception of the previous part of the story. It seems in the whole preceding chapter Naomi also possessed this information but for some reasons remained silent. This means that in reality in the previous chapter Naomi always had more knowledge than Ruth, Orpah, and the readers but preferred to stay quiet or simply did not see Boaz as a possible solution.

In chapter 3 the characters switch roles as regard to the amount of knowledge they possess. If in the previous chapter Boaz possessed greater knowledge than Ruth, here the involvement in conspiracy results in Ruth having greater knowledge than Boaz. Naomi, from whom the idea of visiting the threshing floor originated, is also placed in a more advantageous position. The horizon of the readers is also wider than the horizon of Boaz, for they are aware of Naomi's conspiracy. The readers' zero focalization in relation to Boaz becomes particularly evident when Ruth approaches Boaz: the readers know that the woman beside Boaz is Ruth while Boaz is not aware of this, and his perspective is limited.

However, soon Boaz gets to recognize Ruth and finds out the purpose of her visit. So it seems that for a few moments the horizons of Boaz, Ruth, and the readers meet. However, the information about a closer relative who has a preferential right to redeem Elimelech's property expands the horizon of Ruth and the horizon of the readers, which leads to a new turn in the story.

For the third time the readers are compelled to re-evaluate their perspective. In the beginning of the chapter 3 they thought they possessed greater knowledge then Boaz and their interest was in how Boaz would perceive Ruth's visit. But the appearance of the figure of a closer relative places Boaz in a privileged position and the readers understand that their horizon in previous chapters was even more limited than they thought. Once again the readers wonder about Naomi: did she know about another relative?

But being aware of Boaz's attitude, the readers are not sure about the exact plans of Boaz, which makes Boaz's horizon wider than the horizons of all other participants of the discourse, including the readers.

Therefore, in chapter 4 the readers assume the position of detached observer. The play of horizons in this chapter is related to Boaz and the closer relative. Boaz possesses greater knowledge than the relative and the purpose of Boaz (in many ways like conspiracy) is to turn the tide to his favor.

For the readers, the text that describes the legal process is focalized externally. This is evident by short inconsequential brief sentences that Boaz uses in order to bring together the legal assembly. Another detail that indicates external focalization is the naming of the closer relative. Boaz never designates him by name, which shuts out the opportunity for the readers to know anything about this man. The only certain thing that one can tell about him is that he is unaware of Boaz's plans.

When Boaz articulates the problem to the relative, the readers (that know about the threshing floor visit) are supposed to be surprised because they expect Boaz to talk about Ruth and marriage, but he raises quite a different question of selling of the piece of land that belongs to Naomi. It once again confirms that the passage is written in the scope of external focalization, for Boaz (the character) knows more than the readers. The following dialogue between Boaz and his relative is also focalized externally, for the readers are left wondering (1) why another relative had to take Ruth as his wife if he redeems Naomi's land and (2) how the marriage with Ruth can "impair" his inheritance.

The blessing of the elders and the following episode are both written in the scope of internal focalization as a prediction of the future according to a restricted human point of view. In contrast to previous episodes, Naomi is silent, probably because her previous "predictions" never worked and the present is too good to be true. However, in the end of the chapter, when the narrator informs the readers that the marriage of Boaz and Ruth indeed turned out to be one of the greatest in the history of Israel because from these loins comes the greatest king of Israel, focalization changes from internal to zero.

This chapter makes an original contribution in both general and biblical narratology. In the field of general narratology, it shows how focalization works on the second level of Schmid's model, the level of composition. It also reinterprets reorganization of narrative events into the play of horizons, which has never been interpreted this way. However, this kind of interpretation enables one to apply the model of Wolf Schmid to the biblical narrative of Ruth and explains why the story can remain intriguing and thrilling without rearrangement of narrative events. If other biblical narratives share the same characteristic (pursuing the suspense not by rearrangement but by the play of horizons), we can speak about methodology for the whole corpus of biblical narratives.

Another contribution is related to the analysis of the play of horizons and hence focalization on two narrative levels: on the level of discourse and the level of story. The first allowed one to examine focalization in the narratives with a large number of dialogues by treating reported speeches of the characters as restricted (i.e. focalized). Given that most biblical narratives are dialogic narratives, this direction of research was an important contribution to the field of biblical narratology as well.

The analysis of focalization on the level of the story was notable because it emphasizes the continuity between this study of focalization and the classical typology of focalization, which distinguishes among external, internal, and zero focalizations.

As this chapter demonstrates, analysis of focalization can sometimes help in clarifying and even help in solving the problems that arise with reading, understanding, translating, and interpreting the Hebrew text of the book of Ruth. In particular the chapter proposes new ways of looking at the interpretation of the passages that traditionally are considered as difficult. Among them are Ruth 1:6–7; 1:8; 1:13; 1:22; 2:4; 2:5–7; 3:1–5; 3:8–9; 3:10–11; 4:5; and 4:17b–22.

CHAPTER 6

Focalization on the Level of Presentation

In the previous chapter, it has been demonstrated how the book of Ruth is constituted on the level of composition of narrative information. Even though all the events of the book are located chronologically, the narrator still uses, albeit through the play of horizons, the instruments of reorganization and linearization. As for rearrangement, it has been shown that the narrator rearranges not events but the flow of information. The same applies to linearization: there are repetitions of events as such, but there are a number of times when the same event is evaluated from different points of view.

The level of presentation is the last but not the least important in narrative constitution, for according to Schmid, on the previous levels the narrative is "not yet medially manifested."[1] And only at the level of presentation is it "expressed in specific language of an art form."[2] There are many nuances of presentation that could be considered in this chapter. For example, one can examine purely exegetical textual units such as evaluations, generalizations, commentaries, reflections, and meta-narrative comments that are given by the narrator of the text.

The other aspect of presentation is the linguistic point of view in reported speeches of the characters. According to Thomas,

---

1. Schmid, *Narratology*, 208.
2. Schmid, 208.

The speech of fictional characters[3] is often perceived as offering the reader direct, unmediated access to that individual's emotions, desires, habits, and predilections. If a novel does not offer us direct access to a character's thoughts, then speech is the next best thing, providing a "linguistic fingerprint" in the form of an idiolect that is distinctive and unique to that individual.[4]

Characters of the book of Ruth, according to generally accepted opinion, reflect different idiolects as well. For example, Boaz, according to LaCocque, "speaks with the rhythm reflecting an older man. He is also conscious to say unusual things in an exceptional situation. He weighs his words, which sometimes leads him to stammer."[5]

However, even he changes the way of talking in critical moments. For example, Linafelt points out that in Ruth 3:12 Boaz slides into "a curious sort of sputtering speech pattern."[6] Campbell indicates that the beginning of verse 12 has "too many introductory words."[7] Indeed, the information about another relative is preceded by the introductory phrase וְעַתָּה ("and now"), emphatic particle כִּי, introductory word אָמְנָם ("true" or "indeed") and another emphatic phrase כִּי אִם (usually translated as "that") which may indicate confusion of Boaz. The same nuances can be found in the speeches of other characters of the book.

One more aspect of presentation is related to the male and female voices in the book of Ruth. According to Richard Bauckham, there are female and male perspectives in the book of Ruth that are deliberately placed side by side. Female perspective dominates throughout the book except the episode with legal transaction where "in Boaz's legal declaration (4:9–10) and in the people's congratulation of him (4:11–12) we are given the male perspective on his marriage to Ruth."[8] However, in verses 4:14–15, 17 the narrator returns to female perspectives for, "from the women's perspective what has happened

---

3. It's probably worth noting that in OT narrative, the characters are "fiction like" irrespective of their relationship to history.
4. Thomas, *Fictional Dialogue*, Kindle location 696–699.
5. LaCocque, *Ruth*, 68.
6. Linafelt and Beal, *Ruth and Esther*, 56.
7. Campbell, *Ruth*, 125.
8. Bauckham, *Is the Bible Male*, 11.

is not that Boaz has acquired an heir for Elimelech, but that Ruth's devotion to Naomi has secured a son to be Naomi's support in her old age."⁹

Still another aspect of presentation is naming or designation of the characters. The discussion of this element for some reason disappeared from the English edition of Schmid's book but can be found in German and Russian editions:

> Since selection of lexical units and syntactic structures implies various kinds of evaluative nuances, presentation of narration consists of ideological point of view as well. Naming acquires special importance here.¹⁰

Naming is the issue in the book of Ruth that certainly can be addressed as part of presentation. It expresses both ideological and linguistic points of view, focuses reader's attention on specific traits of the characters, and reflects the type of focalization chosen by the narrator.

However, the aspects of the text listed above have been sufficiently examined and addressed in existing commentaries. As for the present work, I would like to concentrate on one nuance of presentation – linguistic. I would like to consider the connection of focalization with grammatical choices of the narrator. More specifically, I would like to demonstrate the results of my heuristic observations that repeatedly point to a correlation between the *qatal* form of Hebrew verbs and internal focalization.

6.1. General Considerations

According to Arnold and Choi,¹¹

> The perfect views a situation from the outside, looking upon it as a complete whole. It may refer to an action or state in the past, present, or future, although it tends to view it as a complete

---

9. Bauckham, 11.

10. "Поскольку отбор лексических единиц и синтаксических структур подразумевает те или иные оценочные оттенки, в презентации наррации осуществляется также идеологическая точка зрения. Особенную значимость здесь приобретает именование." See Schmid, *Нарратология*, 174. Translated by the author.

11. Arnold and Choi, while they introduced innovation in several points, still are most influenced by traditional Hebrew verbal systems described by Waltke and O'Connor, Jouön-Muraoka and Gesenius-Kautzsch-Cowley. See Arnold and Choi, *Guide to Biblical Hebrew*, xi–xii.

situation or action that is temporally undefined (making it similar to the Greek "aorist" tense). Although not required by the morphology, the perfect is frequently used for actions or states reported in the past, often requiring past tense translations. It may also refer to the perfect state, that is, to an event and a state resulting from that event (making the perfect similar to the Greek perfect).[12]

Arnold and Choi then name six semantic categories that help to clarify the meaning of the *qatal*.

(1) Complete – the action or the state as a complete whole;
(2) Stative – a state of affairs or a condition;
(3) Experience – explain the state of mind;
(4) Rhetorical future – vivid future action or situation, which is not yet a reality but considered a certainty from the speaker's rhetorical point of view;
(5) Proverbial – actions, events, or facts that are not time conditioned, and considered to be general truths;
(6) Performative – an action that occurs by means of speaking.

An alternative approach belongs to Rocine,[13] who disagrees with the idea held by most grammarians "that the *qatal* is the simple past tense of Biblical Hebrew, equal in meaning to a *wayyiqtol*."[14] He also finds untenable the position of Waltke and O'Connor that "*qatal* expresses a complete situation as one unanalyzable whole."[15] In contrast, Rocine sees *qatal* as "more reflective of its origin, described variously as nominal, stative, adjectival, attributive"[16] – the position held by Brockelmann, Bergsträsser, and Hetzron. In addition, Niccacci suggests that *qatal* is

... not a narrative form but retrospective, since its function is to introduce the event which comes before the ensuing narrative. It

---

12. Arnold and Choi, *Guide to Biblical Hebrew*, 54. What these authors call "perfect" I will call "*qatal*" because the word "perfect" implicitly points to the temporal dimension and is far from being a satisfactory term.
13. Rocine, *Learning Biblical Hebrew*.
14. Rocine, 21n2.
15. Rocine, 21n2.
16. Rocine, 21n2.

recalls information already given and so resumes the narrative thread which was interrupted. . . . It is a classic example of the literary "reprise."[17]

The study of the relation between *qatal* and internal focalization should complement these positions and may help in further understanding of the meaning of *qatal* in Hebrew prose. The table below demonstrates distribution of different forms of the Hebrew verb in relation to the type of focalization.[18]

Table 5. Distribution of different forms of Hebrew verbs in Ruth in realtion to types of focalization

Verse	Zero	Internal	External	*qatal*	*wayyiqtol*	*yiqtol*
Ruth 1						
1			x		3	
2			x		2	
3			x		2	
4			x		2	
5			x		2	
6		x	x	2	2	
7		x	x	1	2	
8*[19]		x		1	(1)[20]	1
9*		x			3	1
10*		x			(1)	1
11*		x		1	(1)	1
12*		x		4		
13*		x		2		3
14		x	x	1	3	

---

17. Niccacci, *Syntax of the Verb*, 36.

18. The table includes only three forms of the Hebrew verb – *qatal*, *wayyiqtol*, and *yiqtol* – enough to demonstrate that internally focalized texts prefer *qatal* forms. Syntactic constructions with a *qatal* verb (such as X-*qatal*, We-*qatal* and *qatal* as part of dependent clause) will be considered on the close examination of particular passages.

19. Verses with reported speeches are marked with asterisks.

20. *Wayyiqtol* forms that are used for introduction of direct speech are bracketed.

Verse	Zero	Internal	External	qatal	wayyiqtol	yiqtol
Ruth 1						
15*		x		1	(1)	
16*		x			(1)	5
17*		x				6
18		x	x		2	
19		x	x		3 + (1)	
20*		x		1	(1)	1
21*		x		4		1
22			x	2	1	
Ruth 2						
1	x					
2*		x	x		(2)	3
3			x		4	
4*		(x)	x		(2)	1
5*		x			(1)	
6*		x		1	(2)	
7*		x		1	(1) + 2	1
8*		x		1	(1)	3
9*		x		5		2
10*		x	x	1	2 + (1)	
11*		x		3	(2) + 2	
12*		x		1		2
13*		x		2	(1)	2
14*		x	x	2	(1) + 5	
15*		x			1 + (1)	2
16*		x		2		2
17			x	1	3	
18			x	2	5	
19*		x		4	(3)	1
20*		x		1	(2)	

Verse	Zero	Internal	External	qatal	wayyiqtol	yiqtol
Ruth 2						
21*		x		2	(1)	1
22*		x			(1)	2
23			x		2	
Ruth 3						
1*		x			(1)	2
2*		x		1		
3*		x		4		1
4*		x		4		4
5*		x			(1)	2
6			x	1	2	
7			x		7	
8		x	x		3	
9*		x		1	(2)	
10*		x		1	(1)	
11*		x				3
12*		x				
13*		x		2		3
14*		x	x	1	2 + (1)	2
15*			x		(1) + 4	
16*			x	1	1 + (2)	
17*		x		2	(1)	1
18*		x		1	(1)	3
Ruth 4						
1*			x	2	1 + (1) + 2	
2*			x		1 + (1) + 1	
3*			x	2	(1)	
4*		x		1	(1)	5
5*		x		1	(1)	
6*		x			(1)	3

Verse	Zero	Internal	External	qatal	wayyiqtol	yiqtol
Ruth 4						
7		x		2		
8*			x		(1) + 1	
9*		x		1	(1)	
10*		x		1		1
11*		x		1	(1)	1
12*		x		1		2
13			x		5	
14*		x		1	(1)	1
15*		x		3		
16			x		3	
17*	x		x	1	2	
18	x			1		
19	x			2		
20	x			2		
21	x			2		
22	x			2		

The table above shows that the book of Ruth is generally written in the scope of internal focalization which is natural for dialogic narratives. Reported speech is internally focalized by definition because in the dialogues the characters always present their point of view. Skalin calls it "iconic representation of the predicament of earthly beings sharing the condition of not being omniscient."[21] The character sees only part of the picture; therefore only part of the whole is narrated. Using the term employed by van Wolde, in dialogue the reader is introduced to the mental spaces of the characters.

In the central part of the stories a large number of discourses, or direct speeches, are presented, and in such a way that the reader is able to share the feelings, thoughts, or mental spaces of the characters, especially Naomi,

---

21. Skalin, "Focalization as Restriction," 234. Skalin calls it "iconic" because the form illustrates the meaning.

Ruth, and Boaz. These discourses make it possible for the reader to identify with these characters and to participate in their points of view.[22]

However, it has been observed that in reported speeches constructions with *qatal* verbs demonstrate "the mental space" or limits of a character's horizon better than the constructions with other forms of the verb. This happens because constructions with *qatal* verbs tend to expose inner attitudes and worldview of the characters. In contrast, the reported speech, which consists of formal address, wishes and commands, greeting or parting, and short answers, does not give to the reader as many opportunities to see through the character's mind. They leave the readers uninformed about the true attitude of the characters. Without further explanation of the imperative the reported speech risks being left in externally focalized mode. However, if the speech of the character continues with clarifying, descriptive, and evaluative clauses, it becomes more internally focalized depending of the specifics of the commentary.

For example, Ruth 1:8 consists of the wish, which is followed by the background information that clarifies or explains the reason for such wish.

Wish: יַעֲשֶׂה יהוה עִמָּכֶם חֶסֶד – "May the LORD deal kindly with you" (1:8b)

Background: כַּאֲשֶׁר עֲשִׂיתֶם עִם־הַמֵּתִים וְעִמָּדִי – "as you have dealt with the dead and with me." (1:8c)

In the first part of the sentence the readers wonder why Naomi blesses her daughters-in-law, while in the second part, the reason for such blessing is explained and evaluated. It helps the readers to look at the life of the family from Naomi's perspective. In other words, the second part of the sentence is more internally focalized because it better exposes Naomi's mind to the readers. As we can see, the first part of this verse consists of the wish, which is expressed by the *yiqtol* verb. In contrast, the second part, which gives the reason for her wish, consists of the *qatal* form of the verb עָשָׂה.

In the following pages, I will bring the results of the study of the use of *qatal* verbs in the book of Ruth in order to show that the relationship between *qatal* verbs and internal focalization is not limited by one verse, but is fairly consistent throughout the book of Ruth. For this, I will consider each passage

---

22. van Wolde, "Texts in Dialogue," 1–28.

from the book of Ruth where the verbs in *qatal* form are used. The passages with *qatal* verbs will be divided into three groups according to the following parameters.

In the first group, I will include the passages that restrict the horizon by giving specific details of the event. Usually these passages will include the series of *qatal* verbs that explain the episode. In a way, these passages are similar to embedded narratives and fulfill narrative function: they emphasize certain changes in the life of a character. This group will include the following verses: Ruth 1:6, 11–12, 14, 21; 2:9, 14, 16, 21; 3:3–4, 17; 4:3–5, 7, 9–10, 18–22.

In the second group, I will look at the passages with *qatal* verbs that tend to describe the whole event with just one word. In contrast to the previous group, these passages are evaluative in nature. By one word they do not simply describe the event, but give appraisal of the event. The group will include the following passages: Ruth 1:8, 13, 15, 20; 2:10, 12, 13, 20; 3:9, 10.

The third group includes passages that also refer to events of the story, but without trying to evaluate as in the previous group. Their purpose is not so much evaluation, but drawing the attention of the reader to important events of the story; they have referential function. The verses included into this group are Ruth 1:7, 22; 2:6, 7, 17–19; 3:2, 6, 13, 14, 16, 18; 4:1.

6.2. Narrative Function

6.2.1. Ruth 1:11–12

וַתֹּאמֶר נָעֳמִי שֹׁבְנָה בְנֹתַי לָמָּה תֵלַכְנָה עִמִּי הַעוֹד־לִי בָנִים
בְּמֵעַי וְהָיוּ לָכֶם לַאֲנָשִׁים:
שֹׁבְנָה בְנֹתַי לֵכְןָ כִּי זָקַנְתִּי מִהְיוֹת לְאִישׁ כִּי אָמַרְתִּי יֶשׁ־לִי תִקְוָה
גַּם הָיִיתִי הַלַּיְלָה לְאִישׁ וְגַם יָלַדְתִּי בָנִים:

> But Naomi said, "Turn back, my daughters; why will you go with me? Have I yet sons in my womb that they may *become* your husbands? Turn back, my daughters; go your way, for *I am* too *old* to have a husband. If I *should say* I have hope, even if I *should have* a husband this night and *should bear* sons . . ." (1:11–12)

In this passage Naomi expresses her view of the situation by means of picturing present and future. Her speech has elements of embedded narrative. When a character describes a certain period of life (real or hypothetical), they describe it from a certain point of view and the text becomes internally focalized. In verse 12 by using four *qatal* verbs Naomi makes a prognosis about the hypothetical future of her daughters-in-law if they stay with her. The clause in verse 11 וְהָיוּ לָכֶם לַאֲנָשִׁים "that they may *become* your husbands" with a *qatal* verb functions as representative of the whole narrative by expressing the point of the matter: finding rest through marriage.

6.2.2. Ruth 1:20–21

וַתֹּאמֶר אֲלֵיהֶן אַל־תִּקְרֶאנָה לִי נָעֳמִי קְרֶאןָ לִי מָרָא כִּי־הֵמַר שַׁדַּי לִי מְאֹד:
אֲנִי מְלֵאָה הָלַכְתִּי וְרֵיקָם הֱשִׁיבַנִי יהוה לָמָּה תִקְרֶאנָה לִי נָעֳמִי וַיהוה עָנָה בִי וְשַׁדַּי הֵרַע לִי:

She said to them, "Do not call me Naomi; call me Mara, for the Almighty has *dealt* very *bitterly* with me. I *went away* full, and the LORD has *brought me back* empty. Why call me Naomi, when the LORD has *testified* against me and the Almighty has *brought calamity* upon me?" (1:20–21)

Verse 21 can be considered as a type of short embedded narration where Naomi describes her version of her past life, beginning from the time her family left Bethlehem until the time she returned from Moab. This short narrative is formed by four clauses with *qatal* verbs in their bases and central question in the middle: "Why call me Naomi?" The story is very evaluative in nature because it reflects Naomi's point of view on the situation and, therefore, is internally focalized.

The short narrative is preceded by another *qatal* verb מָרַר "to be bitter" that compiles and evaluates what is going to be said in verse 21.

6.2.3. Ruth 2:8–9

וַיֹּאמֶר בֹּעַז אֶל־רוּת הֲלוֹא שָׁמַעַתְּ בִּתִּי אַל־תֵּלְכִי לִלְקֹט בְּשָׂדֶה אַחֵר וְגַם לֹא תַעֲבוּרִי מִזֶּה וְכֹה תִדְבָּקִין עִם־נַעֲרֹתָי:
עֵינַיִךְ בַּשָּׂדֶה אֲשֶׁר־יִקְצֹרוּן וְהָלַכְתְּ אַחֲרֵיהֶן הֲלוֹא צִוִּיתִי אֶת־הַנְּעָרִים לְבִלְתִּי נָגְעֵךְ וְצָמִת וְהָלַכְתְּ אֶל־הַכֵּלִים וְשָׁתִית מֵאֲשֶׁר יִשְׁאֲבוּן הַנְּעָרִים:

Then Boaz said to Ruth, "Now, *listen*, my daughter, do not go to glean in another field or leave this one, but keep close to my young women. Let your eyes be on the field that they are reaping, and *go* after them. Have I not *charged* the young men not to touch you? And when you *are thirsty*, go to the vessels and *drink* what the young men have drawn." (2:8–9)

The speech of Boaz starts from a construction with the *qatal* verb הֲלוֹא שָׁמַעַתְּ which literary means "are you not listening." In the ESV one cannot find a difference in the form of this verb and the following jussive verbs – they are all translated as imperatives. However, the use of the *qatal* form for the first verb does not seem accidental. It plays a focalizing role for the whole utterance (like the verb הָיָה in 1:11). By this verb Boaz seeks to impose his point of view on Ruth.

Moreover, Hubbard provides examples where the verb שָׁמַע "to listen" in certain circumstances can be translated "with the more specific nuance 'understand.'"[23] This reasoning can be further developed by considering that the verb "to understand" expresses the idea of looking at a situation from a certain perspective. The construction הֲלוֹא in this case plays a role of amplifier. Boaz wants to make sure Ruth understands him correctly by looking at the circumstances from his point of view.

Verse 9 is specifically interesting because the first and the last verbs in this verse are used in *yiqtol* form. Between these *yiqtol* verbs there are five *qatal* verbs. The reason for such distribution of forms is that the first and the last verbs in the sentence explain the habitual acts of Boaz's servants. First Boaz relates the fact that his female servants are reaping (יִקְצֹרוּן) and then he mentions that his male servants draw the water to drink (יִשְׁאָבוּן). Both facts are not focalized, for they describe the routine of everyday life. But Ruth's gleaning is not part of daily routine (at least at this moment). Boaz, in his mind, inserts Ruth into the picture of regular life, and of course his perception of the place of Ruth in this life is internally focalized. Thus, he selects three aspects of her working in the field that he considers as the most important: her place (after the female workers), her security, and water supply.[24]

---

23. Hubbard, *Ruth*, 154.

24. The same approach can be applied in three other places where the construction הֲלוֹא is used. In 2:2–3 Naomi wants to express the reasons for her decision to conspire and wants Ruth to pay specific attention to Boaz as the best candidate for marriage. The same construction is used again in 2:9 in order to emphasize Boaz's viewing of the situation.

Holmstedt partially confirms this approach when he explains that, "Boaz's continuation functions as the complement of the verb שמעת: he first tells Ruth where she should glean – in his field and with his servants (v. 8) – and he then tells her how she should glean (v. 9)."[25] While both parts of the speech are internally focalized, the second part, that says how Ruth should do it, describes Boaz's point of view.

6.2.4. Ruth 2:14

וַיֹּאמֶר לָה בֹעַז לְעֵת הָאֹכֶל גֹּשִׁי הֲלֹם וְאָכַלְתְּ מִן־הַלֶּחֶם וְטָבַלְתְּ פִּתֵּךְ בַּחֹמֶץ וַתֵּשֶׁב מִצַּד הַקֹּצְרִים וַיִּצְבָּט־לָהּ קָלִי וַתֹּאכַל וַתִּשְׂבַּע וַתֹּתַר׃

> And at mealtime Boaz said to her, "Come here and *eat* some bread and *dip* your morsel in the wine." So she sat beside the reapers, and he passed to her roasted grain. And she ate until she was satisfied, and she had some left over. (2:14)

Boaz uses two *qatal* verbs to let Ruth know what she can eat sitting at the dinner table with him. While his invitation to the table גֹּשִׁי הֲלֹם "Come here" is not specific and does not reflect any point of view, a concrete list of food that Ruth can have point to Boaz's attitude toward Ruth. He demonstrates his hospitality by letting her know, there is nothing to be embarrassed about.

6.2.5. Ruth 2:16

וְגַם שֹׁל־תָּשֹׁלּוּ לָהּ מִן־הַצְּבָתִים וַעֲזַבְתֶּם וְלִקְּטָה וְלֹא תִגְעֲרוּ־בָהּ׃

> "And also pull out some from the bundles for her and *leave* it for her to *glean*, and do not rebuke her." (2:16)

Considering focalization helps to explain why in this passage four commands of Boaz are expressed by different forms of the verb: two *qatal* verbs in the center are framed by two *yiqtol* verbs. By giving these commands to his workers, Boaz describes how Ruth's gleaning process should appear. The restricted point of view of Boaz is not fully expressed by the *yiqtol* verbs; there is nothing special in pulling out ears of grain and not rebuking other

---

25. Holmstedt, *Ruth*, 118.

gleaners. However, two *qatal* verbs in the center explain the actions that go beyond the norm: the workers should leave the ears behind so that Ruth could glean them. Therefore, the text with two *qatal* verbs is more internally focalized then the other parts of Boaz's speech.

6.2.6. Ruth 2:21

וַתֹּאמֶר רוּת הַמּוֹאֲבִיָּה גַּם כִּי־אָמַר אֵלַי עִם־הַנְּעָרִים אֲשֶׁר־לִי
תִּדְבָּקִין עַד אִם־כִּלּוּ אֵת כָּל־הַקָּצִיר אֲשֶׁר־לִי׃

And Ruth the Moabite said, "Besides, he *said* to me, 'You shall keep close by my young men until they have *finished* all my harvest.'" (2:21)

The first *qatal* verb in Ruth's speech is caused by the fact that Ruth retells to Naomi what's happened to her during the day. This means that her speech should have some features of embedded narrative, which is by nature internally focalized. In her story Ruth does not recall every detail of the day but touches only those things that are the most important from her point of view. For example, she rightly considers that the permission to work until the end of the harvest is important for her and Naomi's wellbeing. Therefore, the text uses the *qatal* form of the verb אָמַר "to say" in order to express this idea. The function of *qatal* in Boaz's speech that Ruth quotes in her account of the day is again to point to the extreme generosity of Boaz, who not only lets Ruth glean in his field but extends his permission until the end of the harvest.

6.2.7. Ruth 3:3–4

In this passage two series of *weqatal* constructions are used in order to present the plan of Naomi:

וְרָחַצְתְּ וָסַכְתְּ וְשַׂמְתְּ שִׂמְלֹתַיִךְ עָלַיִךְ וְיָרַדְתְּ הַגֹּרֶן אַל־תִּוָּדְעִי
לָאִישׁ עַד כַּלֹּתוֹ לֶאֱכֹל וְלִשְׁתּוֹת׃
וִיהִי בְשָׁכְבוֹ וְיָדַעַתְּ אֶת־הַמָּקוֹם אֲשֶׁר יִשְׁכַּב־שָׁם וּבָאת וְגִלִּית
מַרְגְּלֹתָיו וְשָׁכָבְתְּ וְהוּא יַגִּיד לָךְ אֵת אֲשֶׁר תַּעֲשִׂין׃

Wash therefore and *anoint* yourself, and *put on* your cloak and *go down* to the threshing floor, but do not make yourself known to the man until he has finished eating and drinking. But when he lies down, *observe* the place where he lies. Then *go* and *uncover* his feet and *lie* down, and he will tell you what to do." (3:3–4)

Linafelt, following Campbell, indicates that Naomi's speech is framed by two references to Boaz's actions with a negative imperative and an imperfect. She considers that mentioning Boaz in the beginning and in the end of the speech turns him into "the focus of the machinations." The central part of the structure has deceptive action. The first series of four perfect verbs are to prepare for this action; they "move from Ruth's uncovered body (while washing) to her anointed body to her covered body." After this the second series of four perfect verbs move Ruth to the "opposite direction of literal and symbolic '*un*covering.'" Then Linafelt concludes,

> The plan depends on Ruth having more knowledge than Boaz, who is to be literally and figuratively in the dark. But once the scenario turns to its second phase, Naomi assumes that Boaz will be the one with the knowledge – that is, he will tell (or "reveal to," *ngd*) Ruth what to do next.[26]

The passage starts with an externally focalized sentence that informs the reader about Boaz'a activity. Four *qatal* verbs that follow this information are the first part of the conspiracy – while the acts of Ruth are hidden from everyone, the readers are privy to it. Besides they do not simply enumerate the acts of Ruth, but picture the transformation of Ruth from widow to the bride.[27] The same way, the second chain of four *qatal* verbs picture Ruth's state at the moment of meeting with Boaz from Naomi's perspective.[28] By the end, the text returns to external focalization, for the narrator (in the person of Naomi) does not explain what exactly Boaz has to say to Ruth, though Boaz expects to have a wider horizon than Ruth.

---

26. Linafelt and Beal, *Ruth and Esther*, 48.

27. According to Chisholm "Ruth's attire and appearance would communicate that her period of mourning was over and that she was now available for remarriage." Chisholm Jr., *Judges and Ruth*, 650. See also Bush, *Ruth/Esther*, 152.

28. That the reality of the meeting differed from Naomi's perspective becomes clear as the story unfolds.

6.2.8. Ruth 3:17

וַתֹּאמֶר שֵׁשׁ־הַשְּׂעֹרִים הָאֵלֶּה נָתַן לִי כִּי אָמַר אֵלַי־ תָּבוֹאִי רֵיקָם אֶל־חֲמוֹתֵךְ:

saying, "These six measures of barley he *gave* to me, for he *said* to me, 'You must not go back empty-handed to your mother-in-law.'" (3:17)

Like in the previous example, Ruth presents to Naomi her version of the visit. The words that she attributes to Boaz are absent in the narrator's version of the scene. Therefore, Ruth's speech is focalized according to her point of view so the text uses two *qatal* verbs to emphasize internal focalization.

6.2.9. Ruth 4:3–4

וַיֹּאמֶר לַגֹּאֵל חֶלְקַת הַשָּׂדֶה אֲשֶׁר לְאָחִינוּ לֶאֱלִימֶלֶךְ מָכְרָה נָעֳמִי הַשָּׁבָה מִשְּׂדֵה מוֹאָב:
וַאֲנִי אָמַרְתִּי אֶגְלֶה אָזְנְךָ לֵאמֹר קְנֵה נֶגֶד הַיֹּשְׁבִים וְנֶגֶד זִקְנֵי עַמִּי אִם־תִּגְאַל גְּאָל וְאִם־לֹא יִגְאַל הַגִּידָה לִּי וְאֵדְעָ֗ה כִּי אֵין זוּלָתְךָ לִגְאוֹל וְאָנֹכִי אַחֲרֶיךָ וַיֹּאמֶר אָנֹכִי אֶגְאָל:

Then he said to the redeemer, "Naomi, who has *come back* from the country of Moab, is *selling* the parcel of land that belonged to our relative Elimelech. So I *thought* I would tell you of it and say, 'Buy it in the presence of those sitting here and in the presence of the elders of my people.' If you will redeem it, redeem it. But if you will not, tell me, that I may know, for there is no one besides you to redeem it, and I come after you." And he said, "I will redeem it." (4:3–4)

In this passage Boaz presents the case from his point of view and tells his story, presenting the situation from his perspective in order to win the court. McKeown notes that while the *qatal* verb מכר "to sell" literally reads "she has sold," the scene does not imply that Naomi has already sold her piece of land and that there should be another interpretation of it. He suggests:

> The perfect of the verb probably represents the idea that the decision to sell is final. The land has been put up for sale and there is no turning back on that decision. To sell is Naomi's only hope for the future, and therefore the decision to sell is

irrevocable. The next stage is to find someone within the family circle to buy (redeem) it.[29]

Employing the notion of focalization, it is possible to give the reason for the use of *qatal* verb that compliments the suggestion of McKeown. According to Boaz, Naomi *comes* from the field of Moab, now *exposes* for sale Elimelech's piece of land. As soon as Boaz heard about it, he *thought* he should inform his relative about it. The point of view of Boaz (restricted or focalized) is expressed through three constructions with *qatal* verbs.

6.2.10. Ruth 4:7

וְזֹאת לְפָנִים בְּיִשְׂרָאֵל עַל־הַגְּאוּלָּה וְעַל־הַתְּמוּרָה לְקַיֵּם כָּל־דָּבָר שָׁלַף אִישׁ נַעֲלוֹ וְנָתַן לְרֵעֵהוּ וְזֹאת הַתְּעוּדָה בְּיִשְׂרָאֵל׃

Now this was the custom in former times in Israel concerning redeeming and exchanging: to confirm a transaction, the one *drew off* his sandal and *gave* it to the other, and this was the manner of attesting in Israel. (4:7)

In this comment, the narrator describes the ceremony of transfer of ownership. According to the narrator's own words, it is an ancient tradition and, therefore, needs to be explained. The narrator selects those elements of the ceremony that seems most important to him and draws a picture of the ritual according to his restricted view. This makes his explanation internally focalized.

6.3. Evaluative Function

6.3.1. Ruth 1:6

וַתָּקָם הִיא וְכַלֹּתֶיהָ וַתָּשָׁב מִשְּׂדֵי מוֹאָב כִּי שָׁמְעָה בִּשְׂדֵה מוֹאָב כִּי־פָקַד יהוה אֶת־עַמּוֹ לָתֵת לָהֶם לָחֶם׃

Then she arose with her daughters-in-law to return from the country of Moab, for she *had heard* in the fields of Moab that the LORD *had visited* his people and given them food. (1:6)

---

29. McKeown, *Ruth*, 62.

According to the reasoning presented in the previous chapter, the second part of the verse displays the mind of Naomi and has to be considered as internally focalized, while the first part is the report of her actions and as such is externally focalized. The part of the verse that is internally focalized has two *qatal* verbs. The passage is included into this group because in it Naomi gives an ideological appraisal of the end of the famine. According to her view, the Lord has power to manage natural phenomenon.

6.3.2. Ruth 1:8

וַתֹּאמֶר נָעֳמִי לִשְׁתֵּי כַלֹּתֶיהָ לֵכְנָה שֹּׁבְנָה אִשָּׁה לְבֵית אִמָּהּ
יַעֲשֶׂה יהוה עִמָּכֶם חֶסֶד כַּאֲשֶׁר עֲשִׂיתֶם עִם־הַמֵּתִים וְעִמָּדִי:

But Naomi said to her two daughters-in-law, "Go, return each of you to her mother's house. May the LORD deal kindly with you, as you *have dealt* with the dead and with me." (1:8)

In this verse Naomi calls her daughters-in-law to return to their homes and pronounces blessings on them. In addition, the text consists of a short reference to the past life of Naomi's daughters-in-law. Naomi compares their attitude toward her sons with God's חֶסֶד, which means that she evaluates their behavior in the past by using a construction with a *qatal* verb.

6.3.3. Ruth 1:13b

אַל בְּנֹתַי כִּי־מַר־לִי מְאֹד מִכֶּם כִּי־יָצְאָה בִי יַד־יְהוָה:

"No, my daughters, for it is exceedingly *bitter to me* for your sake that the hand of the LORD *has gone out* against me." (1:13b)

Two constructions with *qatal* verbs are used in verse 13 to describe the past of Naomi. In both cases the description is accompanied by ideological evaluation, which means that this passage may as well be placed in the second category.

6.3.4. Ruth 1:14

Verse 14 does not include direct speech and relates the external action of Orpah and, as it may seem from the beginning, the external action of Ruth as well. Nevertheless, describing the action of Orpah, the narrator uses *wayyiqtol* form of the verb while the action of Ruth is pictured with *qatal* form:

וַתִּשֶּׂנָה קוֹלָן וַתִּבְכֶּינָה עוֹד וַתִּשַּׁק עָרְפָּה לַחֲמוֹתָהּ וְרוּת דָּבְקָה
בָּהּ:

> Then they lifted up their voices and wept again. And Orpah kissed her mother-in-law, but Ruth *clung* to her. (1:14)

Holmstedt explains the switch from *wayyiqtol* to a *qatal* form by simultaneity and contrasting of the actions of the daughters-in-law:

> The switch from the *wayyiqtol* clause to a *qatal* verbal clause indicates a departure from the primary sequentiality of the narrative framework and suggests that the actions are simultaneous. This non-sequential clause contrasts the actions of Ruth with those of 'Orpah, i.e., 'Orpah did X, Ruth did Y. The S-V order of this clause is not basic, but reflects Focus-marking on both the subject and the predicate: Ruth (in contrast to Orpah) clung to her mother-in-law (in contrast to leaving her).[30]

However, according to other commentators, the verb דָּבַק carries in itself deeper meaning. Chisholm, for example, considers the clause דבק -בְּ as idiomatic and lists the following definitions of the verb: (1) cling to, stay close to, stick to; (2) be bound to emotionally; (3) be loyal to; and (4) form alliances with.[31] Definitions 2 and 3 are specifically important because they reflect not only a physical hug but emotional connection between people and as such can be treated as the expression of internal view of the character.[32] Definition 4 is also applicable to this scene for, according to Schipper, "Ruth's clinging to Naomi may indicate a desire for a continued kinship relationship or household affiliation,"[33] which also reflects the far-reaching attitude of Ruth more than her physical act. Therefore, the second part of verse 14 expresses Ruth's attitude with internally focalized text.

---

30. Holmstedt, *Ruth*, 86–87.

31. Chisholm Jr., *Judges and Ruth*, 604.

32. To make his point clear Chisholm provides examples of the use of this verb in other books of the Bible. For example, in Genesis 34:3 this verb obviously reflects the inner state of Shechem: "And his soul was drawn to Dinah the daughter of Jacob. He loved the young woman and spoke tenderly to her," even though the narrator uses the *wayyiqtol* form וַתִּדְבַּק. See Chisholm Jr., *Judges and Ruth*, 604.

33. Schipper, *Ruth*, 98.

6.3.5. Ruth 1:15

וַתֹּאמֶר הִנֵּה שָׁבָה יְבִמְתֵּךְ אֶל־עַמָּהּ וְאֶל־אֱלֹהֶיהָ שׁוּבִי אַחֲרֵי יְבִמְתֵּךְ:

> And she said, "See, your sister-in-law *has gone back* to her people and to her gods; return after your sister-in-law." (1:15)

While in 1:14 the departure of Orpah was described in the scope of external focalization, here Naomi gives ideological appraisal of the departure. Orpah, according to Naomi, returned not only to her family, but "to her people and to her gods." The main idea of Naomi's appeal is to call Ruth to return after her sister-in-law, which results in the use of the imperative form of the verb שׁוּב "return." However, before this appeal Naomi recalls Orpah's return (which includes elements of embedded narrative) and gives to it ideological evaluation. The use of *qatal* verbs reflects Naomi's restricted perspective on Orpah's departure.

6.3.6. Ruth 2:10

וַתִּפֹּל עַל־פָּנֶיהָ וַתִּשְׁתַּחוּ אָרְצָה וַתֹּאמֶר אֵלָיו מַדּוּעַ מָצָאתִי חֵן בְּעֵינֶיךָ לְהַכִּירֵנִי וְאָנֹכִי נָכְרִיָּה:

> Then she fell on her face, bowing to the ground, and said to him, "Why have I *found* favor in your eyes, that you should take notice of me, since I am a foreigner?" (2:10)

Ruth characterized Boaz's attention to her as מָצָאתִי חֵן בְּעֵינֶיךָ "I found favor in your eyes." This is undoubtedly an appraisal of what Boaz did for her, while others may look for different motives behind Boaz's gracious offer. Besides, Ruth's description has elements of embedded narrative. In fact, the whole verse is filled with ideology, beginning from the act of bowing to the ground and finishing with Ruth calling herself "a foreigner." But these acts only confirm what is already known to the readers and to the characters, while the appraisal of Boaz's act opens to the readers new information about the inner attitude of Boaz.

6.3.7. Ruth 2:11–12

In this passage Boaz explains that the reason for his generosity is Ruth's character which is evident in her behavior. In his speech, he uses several *qatal* verbs that demonstrate the horizon of his knowledge.

וַיַּעַן בֹּעַז וַיֹּאמֶר לָהּ הֻגֵּד הֻגַּד לִי כֹּל אֲשֶׁר־עָשִׂית אֶת־חֲמוֹתֵךְ
אַחֲרֵי מוֹת אִישֵׁךְ וַתַּעַזְבִי אָבִיךְ וְאִמֵּךְ וְאֶרֶץ מוֹלַדְתֵּךְ וַתֵּלְכִי
אֶל־עַם אֲשֶׁר לֹא־יָדַעַתְּ תְּמוֹל שִׁלְשׁוֹם:
יְשַׁלֵּם יהוה פָּעֳלֵךְ וּתְהִי מַשְׂכֻּרְתֵּךְ שְׁלֵמָה מֵעִם יהוה אֱלֹהֵי
יִשְׂרָאֵל אֲשֶׁר־בָּאת לַחֲסוֹת תַּחַת־כְּנָפָיו:

> But Boaz answered her, "All that you *have done* for your mother-in-law since the death of your husband has been fully *told* to me, and how you left your father and mother and your native land and came to a people that you *did not know* before. The LORD repay you for what you have done, and a full reward be given you by the LORD, the God of Israel, under whose wings you *have come* to take refuge!" (2:11–12)

Boaz uses four *qatal* verbs in this speech. The first verb נָגַד "be conspicuous" is part of the construction הֻגֵּד הֻגַּד translated in the ESV as "fully told." Boaz in his evaluation of Ruth's acts relies upon the opinion of Naomi or some people of Bethlehem who have heard about the set determination of Ruth to follow Naomi. According to this restricted view, Ruth made this decision אֶת־חֲמוֹתֵךְ "for your mother-in-law." What makes this phrase of Boaz internally focalized is that from another perspective the same decision of Ruth and her motives could be explained differently, not as an act of kindness toward her mother-in-law. Indeed, the foreman did not connect Ruth's arrival to Bethlehem with her desire to come under the protection of YHWH.

6.3.8. Ruth 2:13

In 2:13 Ruth gives ideological appraisal to Boaz's acts of kindness using the construction כִּי-*qatal*:

וַתֹּאמֶר אֶמְצָא־חֵן בְּעֵינֶיךָ אֲדֹנִי כִּי נִחַמְתָּנִי וְכִי דִבַּרְתָּ עַל־לֵב
שִׁפְחָתֶךָ וְאָנֹכִי לֹא אֶהְיֶה כְּאַחַת שִׁפְחֹתֶיךָ:

> Then she said, "I have found favor in your eyes, my lord, for you *have comforted* me and *spoken* kindly to your servant, though I am not one of your servants." (2:13)

She characterizes Boaz as the one who encourages and the one who speaks to her heart (speak kindly). Thus the readers get familiar with Ruth's point of view on Boaz's action. The text is internally focalized because in 2:8–9 the motivation of Boaz's decision to help Ruth remains unclear. This, in fact, causes Ruth to call for explanations, which in turn brings the gradual disclosure of her point of view and depiction of her inner feelings expressed in internally focalized text. The verb הָיָה in the phrase וְאָנֹכִי לֹא אֶהְיֶה כְּאַחַת שִׁפְחֹתֶיךָ "though I am not one of your servants" however is used in *yiqtol* form. The reason for using different forms may lie in different types of focalization. The fact that Ruth is not Boaz's servant is objective and therefore is not internally focalized. At the same time, the feelings of Ruth are subjective and therefore are focalized internally.

6.3.9. Ruth 2:20 (with 2:10)

וַתֹּאמֶר נָעֳמִי לְכַלָּתָהּ בָּרוּךְ הוּא לַיהוה אֲשֶׁר לֹא־עָזַב חַסְדּוֹ אֶת־הַחַיִּים וְאֶת־הַמֵּתִים וַתֹּאמֶר לָהּ נָעֳמִי קָרוֹב לָנוּ הָאִישׁ מִגֹּאֲלֵנוּ הוּא:

> And Naomi said to her daughter-in-law, "May he be blessed by the LORD, whose kindness *has not forsaken* the living or the dead!" Naomi also said to her, "The man is a close relative of ours, one of our redeemers." (2:20)

The act of Naomi (the blessing) is followed by the list of reasons. In it, Naomi expresses her view of the incident and ascribes this favor to the mercy of the Lord. The view of Naomi is focalized because theoretically there could be many reasons why Boaz decided to show mercy to Ruth. There is also more than one reason why Ruth happens to be in Boaz's field. For example, she could come there accidentally. However, Naomi definitely ascribes it to the Lord.

6.3.10. Ruth 3:9–10

וַיֹּאמֶר מִי־אָתְּ וַתֹּאמֶר אָנֹכִי רוּת אֲמָתֶךָ וּפָרַשְׂתָּ כְנָפֶךָ עַל־אֲמָתְךָ כִּי גֹאֵל אָתָּה:
וַיֹּאמֶר בְּרוּכָה אַתְּ לַיהוה בִּתִּי הֵיטַבְתְּ חַסְדֵּךְ הָאַחֲרוֹן מִן־הָרִאשׁוֹן לְבִלְתִּי־לֶכֶת אַחֲרֵי הַבַּחוּרִים אִם־דַּל וְאִם־עָשִׁיר:

> He said, "Who are you?" And she answered, "I am Ruth, your servant. *Spread* your wings over your servant, for you are a redeemer." And he said, "May you be blessed by the LORD, my daughter. You have *made* this last kindness *greater* than the

first in that you have not gone after young men, whether poor or rich." (3:9–10)

Vance referring to Joüon explains that the phrase וּפָרַשְׂתָ reflects modal nuance and has to be translated as "and you ought to spread out" because "Ruth declares to Boaz his obligation" as the redeemer.[34] Taking into account the internally focalized ideological force of *qatal* verbs, it is possible to say Ruth evaluates Boaz by calling him a redeemer, but the act Boaz should do in order to comply with his designation is to spread his wings. Responding to Ruth, Boaz uses the construction with a *qatal* verb in order to evaluate Ruth's act from his own internal perspective as greater than other acts she did before.

6.3.11. Ruth 4:9–10

וַיֹּאמֶר בֹּעַז לַזְּקֵנִים וְכָל־הָעָם עֵדִים אַתֶּם הַיּוֹם כִּי קָנִיתִי אֶת־
כָּל־אֲשֶׁר לֶאֱלִימֶלֶךְ וְאֵת כָּל־אֲשֶׁר לְכִלְיוֹן וּמַחְלוֹן מִיַּד נָעֳמִי׃
וְגַם אֶת־רוּת הַמֹּאֲבִיָּה אֵשֶׁת מַחְלוֹן קָנִיתִי לִי לְאִשָּׁה לְהָקִים
שֵׁם־הַמֵּת עַל־נַחֲלָתוֹ וְלֹא־יִכָּרֵת שֵׁם־הַמֵּת מֵעִם אֶחָיו וּמִשַּׁעַר
מְקוֹמוֹ עֵדִים אַתֶּם הַיּוֹם׃

> Then Boaz said to the elders and all the people, "You are witnesses this day that I *have bought* from the hand of Naomi all that belonged to Elimelech and all that belonged to Chilion and to Mahlon. Also Ruth the Moabite, the widow of Mahlon, I *have bought* to be my wife, to perpetuate the name of the dead in his inheritance, that the name of the dead may not be cut off from among his brothers and from the gate of his native place. You are witnesses this day." (4:9–10)

According to Schipper, the *qatal* verb form in 4:9–10 functions as a performative.[35] However, the statements of Boaz have additional nuance – they affirm his new status as owner of the field and husband of Ruth before the witnesses at the city gate. The *qatal*, therefore, may reflect his new identity, and new restricted vision of Boaz as husband and owner of all Elimelech's possession: from גֹּאֵל he now becomes הַגֹּאֵל.[36] This assumption is supported

---

34. Vance, *Hebrew Reader*, 56–57.
35. Schipper, *Ruth*, 169.
36. Block, *Judges, Ruth*, 720.

by Boecker, who points out that besides settlement of disputes Hebrew legal forums "also had to observe a notarial function."[37]

The second *qatal* in verse 10 is preceded by the object of possession, which puts Ruth into emphatic position and makes marital status of Boaz "the heart of the matter."[38] However, the use of the same verb to portray the acquisition of property and the marriage seems unusual as noted by some commentators.[39] Because the verb קָנָה does not refer to marriage anywhere in the Bible, commentators try to find other ways to explain this usage. Eskenazi and Frymer-Kensky, for example, point out that the verb is used this way in extrabiblical sources. They also provide another explanation based on the reasoning of Weiss and Brichto, that the verb should be understood as "acquiring the rights to/for."[40] All these attempts seem to be very close to the idea that the construction with a *qatal* verb plays an evaluative role and reflects the new marital status of Boaz.

6.3.12. Ruth 4:11–12

וַיֹּאמְרוּ כָּל־הָעָם אֲשֶׁר־בַּשַּׁעַר וְהַזְּקֵנִים עֵדִים יִתֵּן יהוה אֶת־הָאִשָּׁה הַבָּאָה אֶל־בֵּיתֶךָ כְּרָחֵל וּכְלֵאָה אֲשֶׁר בָּנוּ שְׁתֵּיהֶם אֶת־בֵּית יִשְׂרָאֵל וַעֲשֵׂה־חַיִל בְּאֶפְרָתָה וּקְרָא־שֵׁם בְּבֵית לָחֶם: וִיהִי בֵיתְךָ כְּבֵית פֶּרֶץ אֲשֶׁר־יָלְדָה תָמָר לִיהוּדָה מִן־הַזֶּרַע אֲשֶׁר יִתֵּן יהוה לְךָ מִן־הַנַּעֲרָה הַזֹּאת:

> Then all the people who were at the gate and the elders said, "We are witnesses. May the LORD make the woman, who is coming into your house, like Rachel and Leah, who together *built up* the house of Israel. May you act worthily in Ephrathah and be renowned in Bethlehem, and may your house be like the house of Perez, whom Tamar *bore* to Judah, because of the offspring that the LORD will give you by this young woman." (4:11–12)

Two constructions אֲשֶׁר-*qatal* play evaluating role in these sentences. The people of Bethlehem and the elders of the city wish that Ruth would be for Boaz like Rachel and Leah were for Jacob and that the house (or the family)

---

37. Qouted in Bush, *Ruth/Esther*, 237.
38. Hubbard, *Ruth*, 255.
39. Eskenazi and Frymer-Kensky, *Ruth*, 81; LaCocque, *Ruth*, 137.
40. Eskenazi and Frymer-Kensky, *Ruth*, 81.

of Boaz would be like the house of Perez. In their blessing, the people of Bethlehem restrict all possible options, referring only to particular aspects of marriage – the ability to bear children. By doing this they clearly depict their mind better than in the scene of greetings when Boaz arrived at his field (2:4).

6.3.13. Ruth 4:14–15

וַתֹּאמַרְנָה הַנָּשִׁים אֶל־נָעֳמִי בָּרוּךְ יהוה אֲשֶׁר לֹא הִשְׁבִּית לָךְ גֹּאֵל הַיּוֹם וְיִקָּרֵא שְׁמוֹ בְּיִשְׂרָאֵל:
וְהָיָה לָךְ לְמֵשִׁיב נֶפֶשׁ וּלְכַלְכֵּל אֶת־שֵׂיבָתֵךְ כִּי כַלָּתֵךְ אֲשֶׁר־אֲהֵבַתֶךְ יְלָדַתּוּ אֲשֶׁר־הִיא טוֹבָה לָךְ מִשִּׁבְעָה בָּנִים:

> Then the women said to Naomi, "Blessed be the LORD, who *has* not *left* you this day without a redeemer, and may his name be renowned in Israel! He *shall be* to you a restorer of life and a nourisher of your old age, for your daughter-in-law who *loves* you, who is more to you than seven sons, has *given birth* to him." (4:14–15)

In verse 14–15 the readers are finally introduced to the point of view of the women of Bethlehem. This group first appeared in the narrative as early as in 1:19. There the women of Bethlehem ask the question that reflects their ignorance of the situation. The readers can determine their perspective only from fragments of the speech of some characters (see Ruth 2:6, 11; 3:11). And only from 4:14–15 the readers receive opportunity to find out how the women of Bethlehem actually evaluate Ruth, her marriage with Boaz and the birth of Obed. The text uses constructions with *qatal* verbs in order to refer to the point of view of the women.

6.4. Referential Function

6.4.1. Ruth 1:7

וַתֵּצֵא מִן־הַמָּקוֹם אֲשֶׁר הָיְתָה־שָׁמָּה וּשְׁתֵּי כַלֹּתֶיהָ עִמָּהּ וַתֵּלַכְנָה בַּדֶּרֶךְ לָשׁוּב אֶל־אֶרֶץ יְהוּדָה:

> So she set out from the place where she *was* with her two daughters-in-law, and they went on the way to return to the land of Judah. (1:7)

The verb הָיָה "to be" is not part of the main clause, which is externally focalized, but is part of the prepositional phrase that defines the noun מָקוֹם "place." Some consider this phrase excessive, but as internally focalized it plays an important role, for it points to the long period in Naomi's life which is now coming to the end and motivating her return. An interesting commentary in this sense is given by LaCocque, who points out that according to Rashi, the narrator mentions "place" because "the place where she had been suddenly had lost all its glory."[41]

6.4.2. Ruth 1:22

Verse 22 obviously begins as externally focalized, however the *wayyiqtol* verb in the beginning is then followed by two *qatal* verbs:

וַתָּשָׁב נָעֳמִי וְרוּת הַמּוֹאֲבִיָּה כַלָּתָהּ עִמָּהּ הַשָּׁבָה מִשְּׂדֵי מוֹאָב וְהֵמָּה בָּאוּ בֵּית לֶחֶם בִּתְחִלַּת קְצִיר שְׂעֹרִים׃

> So Naomi returned, and Ruth the Moabite her daughter-in-law with her, who *returned* from the country of Moab. And they *came* to Bethlehem at the beginning of barley harvest. (1:22)

The use of the verb שׁוב "to return" in *qatal* form is not difficult to explain. According to Vance, who refers to Joüon, though "definite article ... with a perfect is not unheard of, the author probably intended a participle, which requires only shifting the accent to the end of the word."[42] Vance shows that others agree with this conclusion.[43]

The use of a *qatal* verb in the final clause can be explained by the desire of the narrator to focus the attention of the readers on the event of arrival and connect it with the time of arrival. The construction *wN+qatal* here "signals that the narrator is inserting a parenthetical, explanatory comment about the season when the women arrived."[44] Grant also shows the importance of identifying the season of barley harvest for the structure of narrative. He considers that the beginning of chapter 1 introduces "emptiness motif," while the end of the chapter hints to possible resolution by mentioning that "Naomi

---

41. LaCocque, *Ruth*, 44.
42. Vance, *Hebrew Reader*, 23–24.
43. See Joüon and Muraoka, *Grammar of Biblical Hebrew*, §145e; and Waltke and O'Connor, *Introduction to Biblical Hebrew*, §19.17d.
44. Wilch, *Ruth*, 148.

and Ruth emerged from a literal (and figurative) winter of barrenness into a potentially fruitful spring (the barley harvest began about the end of April in Israel)."[45] He then relates barley harvest with three feasts that were celebrated at that time of year: the feasts of Passover, Unleavened Bread, and Firstfruits and views it as the narrator's design. The arrival, therefore, is presented in certain perspective.

6.4.3. Ruth 2:6

וַיַּעַן הַנַּעַר הַנִּצָּב עַל־הַקּוֹצְרִים וַיֹּאמַר נַעֲרָה מוֹאֲבִיָּה הִיא
הַשָּׁבָה עִם־נָעֳמִי מִשְּׂדֵה מוֹאָב:

> And the servant who was in charge of the reapers answered, "She is the young Moabite woman, who *came back* with Naomi from the country of Moab." (2:6)

From the perspective of the foreman, Ruth is simply a Moabite woman who returned with Naomi. His assessment of Ruth is fundamentally different from the perspective of Boaz, who sees in Ruth's return desire to live with God's people under the protection of YHWH. While the foreman does not appreciate Ruth's return as much as Boaz, the reference to the incident of return certainly point to one of the major events of the narrative.

6.4.4. Ruth 2:7

וַתֹּאמֶר אֲלַקֳטָה־נָּא וְאָסַפְתִּי בָעֳמָרִים אַחֲרֵי הַקּוֹצְרִים וַתָּבוֹא
וַתַּעֲמוֹד מֵאָז הַבֹּקֶר וְעַד־עַתָּה זֶה שִׁבְתָּהּ הַבַּיִת מְעָט:

> She said, "Please let me glean and *gather* among the sheaves after the reapers." So she came, and she has continued from early morning until now, except for a short rest. (2:7)

To follow the logic the construction *weqatal* (וְאָסַפְתִּי) has to play a clarifying role. It clarifies the verb לָקַט "to glean" and expresses someone's restricted point of view. Two ways of interpretation are possible. It is either Ruth's own point of view and she asks the foreman not simply to let her glean but to glean "among the sheaves after the reapers." Another approach is that the situation is represented by the foreman from his perspective.

---

45. Grant, "Literary Structure," 424–41.

6.4.5. Ruth 2:17–18

וַתְּלַקֵּט בַּשָּׂדֶה עַד־הָעָרֶב וַתַּחְבֹּט אֵת אֲשֶׁר־לִקֵּטָה וַיְהִי כְּאֵיפָה שְׂעֹרִים:
וַתִּשָּׂא וַתָּבוֹא הָעִיר וַתֵּרֶא חֲמוֹתָהּ אֵת אֲשֶׁר־לִקֵּטָה וַתּוֹצֵא וַתִּתֶּן־לָהּ אֵת אֲשֶׁר־הוֹתִרָה מִשָּׂבְעָהּ:

> So she gleaned in the field until evening. Then she beat out what she *had gleaned*, and it was about an ephah of barley. And she took it up and went into the city. Her mother-in-law saw what she *had gleaned*. She also brought out and gave her what food she *had left* over after being satisfied. (2:17–18).

The construction אֲשֶׁר-*qatal* in this kind of sentence pictures the perspective on certain results of the work. This is followed by the assessment of the result ("and it was about an ephah of barley"). Similarly, in verse 18 Naomi sees "what she had gleaned." This again describes the perspective of Naomi who also saw "an ephah of barley." In both cases the reference to certain activity in the past brings back memories of the most important events of the narrative.

6.4.6. Ruth 2:19

וַתֹּאמֶר לָהּ חֲמוֹתָהּ אֵיפֹה לִקַּטְתְּ הַיּוֹם וְאָנָה עָשִׂית יְהִי מַכִּירֵךְ בָּרוּךְ וַתַּגֵּד לַחֲמוֹתָהּ אֵת אֲשֶׁר־עָשְׂתָה עִמּוֹ וַתֹּאמֶר שֵׁם הָאִישׁ אֲשֶׁר עָשִׂיתִי עִמּוֹ הַיּוֹם בֹּעַז:

> And her mother-in-law said to her, "Where *did* you *glean* today? And where *have* you *worked*? Blessed be the man who took notice of you." So she told her mother-in-law with whom she *had worked* and said, "The man's name with whom I *worked* today is Boaz." (2:19)

Using constructions with *qatal* verbs, the narrator first demonstrates the mind of Naomi, who obviously knows less than Ruth and the readers but wants to gain this knowledge. Then the narrator demonstrates the mind of Ruth, who has all this information and shares it with Naomi. Between these constructions Naomi with a jussive verb gives ideological appraisal to the act of Boaz.

6.4.7. Ruth 3:2

וְעַתָּה הֲלֹא בֹעַז מֹדַעְתָּנוּ אֲשֶׁר הָיִית אֶת־נַעֲרוֹתָיו הִנֵּה־הוּא זֹרֶה אֶת־גֹּרֶן הַשְּׂעֹרִים הַלָּיְלָה׃

Is not Boaz our relative, with whose young women you *were*?
See, he is winnowing barley tonight at the threshing floor. (3:2)

The verse reminds the readers about the important meeting of Ruth and Boaz in the field and about the whole period of gleaning. While it does not give a transparent ideological assessment of the period, the reference to the young women may serve as a reflection of Naomi's perspective on the period. Later, on the threshing floor Boaz also gives this assessment by praising Ruth's integrity.

6.4.8. Ruth 3:6

וַתֵּרֶד הַגֹּרֶן וַתַּעַשׂ כְּכֹל אֲשֶׁר־צִוַּתָּה חֲמוֹתָהּ׃

So she went down to the threshing floor and did just as her mother-in-law had *commanded* her. (3:6)

The undeniable fact that Ruth went down to the threshing floor is then specified by the internally focalized phrase, "as her mother-in-law had commanded her." That Ruth indeed followed Naomi's instructions is not clear. It was mentioned in the previous chapter the position of some commentators that Ruth in reality deviates from Naomi's plan. If she actually deviates from the plan, the phrase should be read as either the perspective of Ruth or as irony of the narrator.

6.4.9. Ruth 3:13

לִינִי הַלַּיְלָה וְהָיָה בַבֹּקֶר אִם־יִגְאָלֵךְ טוֹב יִגְאָל וְאִם־לֹא יַחְפֹּץ לְגָאֳלֵךְ וּגְאַלְתִּיךְ אָנֹכִי חַי־יהוה שִׁכְבִי עַד־הַבֹּקֶר׃

Remain tonight, and in the morning, if he will redeem you, good; let him do it. But if he is not willing to redeem you, then, as the LORD lives, I *will redeem* you. Lie down until the morning." (3:13)

Boaz shares with Ruth his perspective on the coming legal process. The text uses the clause וְהָיָה which literally means "and it will be" and usually is not translated but used in order to set a scene.⁴⁶ Therefore, it restricts the view of the readers adjusting it to the view of Boaz.

As for the clause וּגְאַלְתִּ֖יךְ אָנֹ֑כִי "I *will redeem* you," according to Holmstead, the use of "an overt pronoun typically marks Topic or Focus."⁴⁷ This consideration can be developed further by pointing that the position of a *qatal* verb in the beginning of the sentence opposes it to previously used *yiqtol* verbs. The construction here in many ways is similar to the one we find in Ruth 1:14, where Ruth's decision to cling to Naomi is opposed to Orpah's departure.

6.4.10. Ruth 3:14

The following verse can be considered as exposition of Boaz's thought:

וַתִּשְׁכַּ֤ב מַרְגְּלוֹתָיו֙ עַד־הַבֹּ֔קֶר וַתָּ֕קָם בִּטְרֹ֛ם יַכִּ֥יר אִ֖ישׁ אֶת־רֵעֵ֑הוּ וַיֹּ֕אמֶר אַל־יִוָּדַ֔ע כִּי־בָ֥אָה הָאִשָּׁ֖ה הַגֹּֽרֶן׃

So she lay at his feet until the morning, but arose before one could recognize another. And he said, "Let it not be known that the woman came to the threshing floor." (3:14)

According to Schipper, it is one of those rare examples when the narrator supplies "Boaz's internal monologue [which] explains the motivation behind Boaz's instructions."⁴⁸ Schipper also draws attention to the fact that Boaz is not concerned about his own reputation as much as the reputation of Ruth. This fact is supported by the definiteness of the word הָאִשָּׁה "woman": "Even Boaz seems aware of the questions surrounding her. His concern is not simply with the possible discovery of any woman with him on the threshing floor, but specifically with 'the woman' . . . which presumably singles out Ruth."⁴⁹

The use of the definite article together with the idea of internal focalization helps to dismiss the proposals that these words (as inner thought or real speech) belonged to Ruth (as in the Syriac version)⁵⁰ or that they were the command of Boaz to his servants (as in Targum *Ruth Rab.* 2:1), or his prayer to God (as in midrash *Ruth Rab.* 7:1), or his address to Ruth (as implied in

---

46. Holmstedt, *Ruth*, 168.
47. Holmstedt, 169.
48. Schipper, *Ruth*, 155.
49. Schipper, 155.
50. See Linafelt and Beal, *Ruth and Esther*, 59.

Old Greek manuscripts and in Vulgate).[51] From this point, further development of the plot is based on the actions of Boaz, therefore his motivation and attitudes become very important for the readers.

6.4.11. Ruth 3:16

וַתָּבוֹא אֶל־חֲמוֹתָהּ וַתֹּאמֶר מִי־אַתְּ בִּתִּי וַתַּגֶּד־לָהּ אֵת כָּל־אֲשֶׁר
עָשָׂה־לָהּ הָאִישׁ׃

> And when she came to her mother-in-law, she said, "How did you fare, my daughter?" Then she told her all that the man had done for her ... (3:16)

The construction אֲשֶׁר-*qatal* in verse 16 is used on the background of the verb נָגַד "declare/tell" specifying what exactly Ruth told Naomi. Of course, in her version of the story Ruth is guided by her point of view on the threshing floor event. While the readers are not informed about the whole answer of Ruth, on the basis of verse 17 it is clear that Ruth selects the facts that the reader is not aware of.

6.4.12. Ruth 3:18

וַתֹּאמֶר שְׁבִי בִתִּי עַד אֲשֶׁר תֵּדְעִין אֵיךְ יִפֹּל דָּבָר כִּי לֹא יִשְׁקֹט
הָאִישׁ כִּי־אִם־כִּלָּה הַדָּבָר הַיּוֹם׃

> She replied, "Wait, my daughter, until you learn how the matter turns out, for the man will not rest but *will settle* the matter today." (3:18)

With the construction כִּי־אִם־כִּלָּה which literally means "unless he will settle," Naomi pictures the portrait of Boaz, who, in contrast to other men, will keep his word.

6.4.13. Ruth 4:1

וּבֹעַז עָלָה הַשַּׁעַר וַיֵּשֶׁב שָׁם וְהִנֵּה הַגֹּאֵל עֹבֵר אֲשֶׁר דִּבֶּר־בֹּעַז
וַיֹּאמֶר סוּרָה שְׁבָה־פֹּה פְּלֹנִי אַלְמֹנִי וַיָּסַר וַיֵּשֵׁב׃

> Now Boaz *had gone* up to the gate and sat down there. And behold, the redeemer, of whom Boaz *had spoken*, came by. So

---

51. See Schipper, *Ruth*, 155.

Boaz said, "Turn aside, friend; sit down here." And he turned aside and sat down. (4:1)

The second *qatal* verb in this verse easily fits into the proposed reasoning. The narrator is clarifying which relative Boaz had met at the city gate. As usual, the construction אֲשֶׁר-*qatal* contains an element of embedded narrative and therefore is presented from the certain restricted point of view.

However, in order to connect the use of the first *qatal* verb with internal focalization, it is necessary to look at the wider context. When the description of the meeting of Boaz and Ruth comes to an end, Boaz "measured out six measures of barley and put it on her" (3:15a). Then the narrator informs the readers וַיָּבֹא הָעִיר. The ESV (as well as majority of modern translations)[52] translates this sentence as "Then she went into the city" (3:15b). However, the phrase undoubtedly speaks about Boaz.[53] Bush provides the following reasons for using the masculine form:

> The main actor in the preceding sequence of clauses has been Boaz, so it is entirely expected that our narrator will finish describing what Boaz did before turning to tell of Ruth's actions. Indeed, without this clause, we would hear nothing about any further actions of Boaz until the opening clause of the next act in 4:1.[54]

This means that the conversation between Ruth and Naomi happened while Boaz was walking to the city. In this, Boaz's departure is presented objectively, as a fact. Having listened to Ruth's version of the meeting, Naomi calls Ruth to not fuss but wait until Boaz fulfills his promise. The next short sentence וּבֹעַז עָלָה הַשַּׁעַר "Now Boaz had gone up to the gate," in contrast to the description of Boaz's departure, has subtle nuance: it is used as confirmation of Naomi's words. The departure of Boaz from the threshing floor is described without much specificity; therefore, the narrator uses the *yiqtol* form of the verb. In 4:1, in order to demonstrate that Boaz is already on track to fulfill his promise, the narrator uses the *qatal* form. This case is a lot like the use of the *qatal* form in Ruth 1:14, with the only difference that in 1:14

---

52. Bush, *Ruth/Esther*, 179.
53. Holmstedt, *Ruth*, 173.
54. Bush, *Ruth/Esther*, 179.

qatal is used in order to demonstrate the contrast, while here *qatal* is used in order to confirm the words of Naomi. Otherwise in both cases the verb in *qatal* form expresses the outer act which implies the inner attitude of the actor, which in turn makes these phrases internally focalized.

It should be noted that, in contrast, the verb in the following phase וַיֵּשֶׁב שָׁם "and sat down there" has *wayyiqtol* form while grammatically both verbs relate to the same period of time. This again shows that the difference between the forms of the verbs is not the matter of grammatical time, but the matter of narratological aspect of focalization. The phrase וּבֹעַז עָלָה הַשַּׁעַר "Now Boaz had gone up to the gate" (4:1a) consists of an element of internal focalization, while the following phrase וַיֵּשֶׁב שָׁם "and sat down there" does not have it.

6.4.14. Ruth 4:5

וַיֹּאמֶר בֹּעַז בְּיוֹם־קְנוֹתְךָ הַשָּׂדֶה מִיַּד נָעֳמִי וּמֵאֵת רוּת הַמּוֹאֲבִיָּה
אֵשֶׁת־הַמֵּת קָנִיתִי לְהָקִים שֵׁם־הַמֵּת עַל־נַחֲלָתוֹ:

> Then Boaz said, "The day you buy the field from the hand of Naomi, you also *acquire* Ruth the Moabite, the widow of the dead, in order to perpetuate the name of the dead in his inheritance." (4:5)

It's been already discussed that there is more logic in *Ketiv*, which reads the verb קָנִיתִי as first-person common singular *qatal*. Boaz pictures before the eyes of the redeemer the perspective of marriage between Boaz and Ruth which, in turn may have negative impact on the inheritance of the closer relative. The fact that Boaz is going to marry Ruth influences the perspective of the closer relative.

6.4.15. Ruth 4:17

וַתִּקְרֶאנָה לוֹ הַשְּׁכֵנוֹת שֵׁם לֵאמֹר יֻלַּד־בֵּן לְנָעֳמִי וַתִּקְרֶאנָה שְׁמוֹ
עוֹבֵד הוּא אֲבִי־יִשַׁי אֲבִי דָוִד:

> And the women of the neighborhood gave him a name, saying, "A son *has been born* to Naomi." They named him Obed. He was the father of Jesse, the father of David. (4:17)

The restricted perspective of the women of Bethlehem in this verse is expressed not in the fact that the child is being born, but in that he was born "to Naomi." The women see in Obed not simply the son of Ruth and Boaz, but Naomi's redeemer in her old age.

6.4.16. Ruth 4:17–22

וַתִּקְרֶאנָה לוֹ הַשְּׁכֵנוֹת שֵׁם לֵאמֹר יֻלַּד־בֵּן לְנָעֳמִי וַתִּקְרֶאנָה שְׁמוֹ
עוֹבֵד הוּא אֲבִי־יִשַׁי אֲבִי דָוִד׃
וְאֵלֶּה תּוֹלְדוֹת פָּרֶץ פֶּרֶץ הוֹלִיד אֶת־חֶצְרוֹן׃
וְחֶצְרוֹן הוֹלִיד אֶת־רָם וְרָם הוֹלִיד אֶת־עַמִּינָדָב׃
וְעַמִּינָדָב הוֹלִיד אֶת־נַחְשׁוֹן וְנַחְשׁוֹן הוֹלִיד אֶת־שַׂלְמָה׃
וְשַׂלְמוֹן הוֹלִיד אֶת־בֹּעַז וּבֹעַז הוֹלִיד אֶת־עוֹבֵד׃
וְעֹבֵד הוֹלִיד אֶת־יִשַׁי וְיִשַׁי הוֹלִיד אֶת־דָּוִד׃

> Now these are the generations of Perez: Perez fathered Hezron, Hezron fathered Ram, Ram fathered Amminadab, Amminadab fathered Nahshon, Nahshon fathered Salmon, Salmon fathered Boaz, Boaz fathered Obed, Obed fathered Jesse, and Jesse fathered David. (4:17–22)

These verses are certainly zero focalized. Nevertheless, the narrator also uses the *qatal* verb יָלַד "fathered" in order to convey information about offspring of Obed. This inconsistency can be explained by the fact that genealogy is zero focalized in relation to the characters of the story. However, as indicated by Schmid, "even an omniscient narrator, whose field of view, in Genette's sense, is not in the least restricted, still narrates with a particular perspective."[55] Indeed, the narrator lists not all the descendants of Obed, but selects only certain names for a certain purpose. Therefore, the use of *qatal* verbs in genealogy is also justified, though the passage is not focalized internally.

6.5. Conclusion

In this chapter I have made an attempt to explain empirically a found connection between the *qatal* form of Hebrew verbs and internal focalization. Surely, this may be the most difficult part of the research mostly because the attempt to explore *qatal* verbs in respect to focalization had never been taken before. Yet, as we can see from the study submitted in this chapter, there is

---

55. Schmid, *Narratology*, 93.

indeed correlation between *qatal* verbs and internal focalization. The connection is most obvious in the dialogic parts of the book.

The finding has one practical application. The constructions with *qatal* verbs, specifically those that are found in reported speech, should clearly draw the attention of the readers, the commentators and the translators because they may reflect the restricted horizon of the character or selective representation of information by the narrator.

It was also demonstrated that there are at least three ways *qatal* verbs are used in order to create an internally focalized view. Sometimes *qatal* verbs occur in a series that have some characteristic of embedded narrative. Usually, the series of *qatal* verbs shows how the character views the events of a certain period of time. Constructions with *qatal* verbs can also have evaluative nature. In these cases with just one verb the character of the narrator may assess the whole event. Finally, *qatal* verbs are used for simple reference to the important event. Usually this reference is lacking any ideological appraisal, but in context even these references can be understood as evaluative.

The correlation between *qatal* verbs and internal focalization demonstrated in this chapter is in no way directed to the removal of existing explanations of syntactic rules of *qatal* verb in biblical Hebrew. However, sometimes understanding of this correlation helps to explain why in the same passage the grammatically similar actions are sometimes expressed by different forms of the Hebrew verb (by *yiqtol* and *qatal* verbs). As the study above shows, with *qatal* verbs the horizon becomes more restricted.

CHAPTER 7

Conclusion

The Results of the Research

The analysis of the concept of focalization in relation to selected Old Testament narratives undertaken in this research shows that the notion has undergone numerous changes since 1972 when it was first proposed by Genette. In order to form an accurate picture of the concept, numerous examples from the works of Genette and other narratologists were analyzed. As a result of this work the concept of focalization was clearly defined as the restriction of narrative information that the narrator conveys to the reader. The more convenient term "horizon" was proposed for ease of reference. As a result, Genette's original triple division into zero, internal and external focalization was reformulated in regard to the horizon of the characters and the horizon of the readers:

Zero focalization: Horizon of the readers > Horizon of the characters

Internal focalization: Horizon of the readers = Horizon of the characters

External focalization: Horizon of the readers < Horizon of the characters

This seemingly simple technical amendment turned out to be quite useful in further steps of the research.

Parallel to the search for the definition of focalization, considerations were given to the development of the concept in the Old Testament narratology. The review of works on the Old Testament narratology showed that for many years the idea of focalization was highly overlooked by most Old Testament scholars. The works that did name the concept used it without due research of the core of the concept, usually as mere substitution of the older term point-of-view. New approaches to focalization that have been developed since first publication of Genette's book in these publications are even rarer.

Consideration of the evolution of the concept of focalization brought several conclusions that formed the bases of the methodology of the research. The definition of the concept was refined and focalization was defined as regulating, selecting, and channeling narrative information, which in turn affected the purpose of studying focalization: to answer the questions of

- *What* information was selected by the narrator?
- *How* is this information channeled to the readers?
- *Why* was information selected and channeled in this particular way?

The answer to the latter question leads to understanding the logic of selectivity and narrative strategy of the book of Ruth.

The need for a methodology for studying focalization brought a thorough consideration of Schmid's ideal genetic model of narrative constitution. Three steps of this model – selection, composition, and presentation – with some modifications formed the basis of the proposed method of studying focalization in the Old Testament narratives in general and in the book of Ruth in particular.

The modification of Schmid's model on the level of selection concerns the method of allocation of the events selected by the narrator. For the initial step of allocating of the events, I proposed to explore the text in respect to Tjupa's characteristic of intentionality, which is easily applicable but not always sufficiently accurate. Therefore, it was proposed to confirm the results by applying more formal characteristics of eventfulness proposed by Schmid: relevance, unpredictability, persistence, irreversibility, and non-iterativity.

The modification on the level of the composition concerns the features of the Old Testament narratives where events are rarely rearranged and linearized, and the development of the plot is primarily done by reported speech and dialogues. Since information in this type of narrative is still rearranged and linearized but indirectly, it was proposed to pay attention to the changes in the amount of information given to different participants of the discourse. For this purpose, I proposed the new characteristic of narrative composition – the play of horizons – to monitor rearrangement and linearization of narrative information on the level of the story and the level of discourse. This, in turn, provided a greater scope of opportunities to identify different types of focalization.

The modification on the level of presentation primarily concerns the specifics of presentation of narratives on biblical Hebrew. The application of the method resulted in the following conclusions regarding the book of Ruth.

On the level of selection, the analysis of the text in respect to Tjupa's characteristic of intentionality revealed that sixteen episodes of the book of Ruth constitute four narratological events that can be allocated according to the time and place and according to the testimony of the witnesses and the judges.

The first event happens during the conversation between Naomi and Ruth on the way from Moab to Bethlehem. The second event of the book – the first encounter of Boaz and Ruth – takes place at the field of Boaz and lasts for about one day. The third event happens at the threshing floor and describes the last (in the scope of the narrative) encounter of Boaz and Ruth. And the final, fourth, event of the book happens on the background of standard legal procedure of the redemption of the field.

The analysis of intentionality also showed that within each event there are more or less intentional and, therefore, more or less eventful episodes. Among other episodes the following four pivotal moments were allocated:

1. Episode 2: The moment when Ruth declares her commitment to Naomi (1:16–17);
2. Episode 9: The moment when Boaz instructs his workers to help Ruth to glean (2:11–12);
3. Episode 12: The moment when Boaz promises Ruth to marry her (3:11);
4. Episode 16: The moment when Boaz announces his decision to marry Ruth (4:10).

These episodes are respectively preceded and followed by less eventful episodes that form the background of the narrative. They are less intentional and therefore less eventful, but they enhance the eventfulness of the pivotal moments. These initial approximate conclusions were then confirmed by applying more formal characteristics of relevance, unpredictability, persistence, irreversibility, and non-iterativity proposed by Schmid. It has been shown that the prologue and the epilogue of the book, being the most eventful episodes, however, stay outside of the story proper.

The analysis of the level of composition was based on the analysis of the play of horizons, which happens on the level of the story as well as on the level of discourse. On the level of the story, the play of horizons becomes the primary means of reorganization and linearization of narrative information in the book of Ruth. The characters of the book constantly recall and evaluate the past and the present, and picture the future. Recollections of the past explain characters' attitudes, give the background for ideas concerning the solution of their problems and help to fill in gaps that have arisen in the course of narration. The picture of the future directs the narrative and verbalizes possible resolutions of the plot. Evaluation of the present connects the past and the future events, helps the characters to express a current view of themselves and other characters, and comment on the details of the narrative world. With this presentation of information, the narrator is able to update the readers' concept of the narrative world without literal reorganization of the events.

The play of horizons is also performed on the level of discourse. This level includes the characters of the story as well as the readers and the narrator. Analysis of focalization on this level demonstrated that some portions of the text of the book of Ruth are zero focalized. This happens primarily when the narrator communicates information that is unknown to the characters of the story, which expands the readers' horizon in relation to the horizon of one of several characters. There are a number of passages where the horizon of the readers does not exceed the horizon of the characters. Sometimes it is only a seeming perception because, after all, the character(s) turn out to know more. Every time it makes the readers re-evaluate the perception of a previous portion of the text. Finally, there are passages with external focalization – when the readers realize that they do not have sufficient information to judge the acts of the characters.

Finally, considering the level of presentation, I have emphasized an empirically found correlation between constructions with the *qatal* form of Hebrew verb and internal focalization. This means that the encounter with a *qatal* verb (specifically in reported speech) should immediately draw the attention of the readers because it may indicate intentional internal focalization. It was demonstrated that there are at least three ways constructions with *qatal* verbs are used in order to create an internally focalized view. In reported speech, the series of *qatal* verbs with some characteristics of embedded narrative may indicate a restricted view of one of the characters on the past or on the future. Besides, constructions with *qatal* verbs often have an evaluative nature. Sometimes with just one qatal verb the character or the narrator might assess the whole event. Finally, constructions with *qatal* verbs are used for simple reference to the important event. Usually this reference lacked any ideological appraisal, but in context even these references can be understood as evaluative. The understanding of this correlation helps to explain why in the same passage the grammatically similar actions are sometimes expressed by different forms of the Hebrew verb.

Original Contribution

As a result, this work attempted to make an original contribution in three related fields of studies. First, it is the area of general narratology. Staying with Genette's initial understanding of focalization as restriction of narrative information, it was proposed to use Schmid's model of narrative constitution as the basis to examine focalization in the narratives. Moreover, Schmid's model was considerably improved on each level.

For the allocation of narrative events on the level of selection, it was proposed to apply the criteria of Tjupa for initial and the criteria of Schmid for further allocation of the events. On the level of composition, the procedure of reorganization of narrative events was reformulated into the play of horizons, which explains why the story can remain intriguing and thrilling without rearrangement of narrative events. Another innovation is related to the analysis of the play of horizons and hence focalization on two narrative levels: on the level of discourse and the level of story. The first allowed one to examine focalization in the narratives with a large number of dialogues by treating reported speeches of the characters as restricted (i.e. internally focalized).

Second, the original contribution was also made to the field of Old Testament narratology by applying Schmid's model of narrative constitution as regard to focalization to the text of the book of Ruth. This included

(1) an examination of events selected by the narrator of the book with the view of their intentionality (according to Tjupa) and eventfulness (according to Schmid); and (2) a demonstration of the play of horizons in the book of Ruth as a specific case of focalization through rearrangement of narrative information.

Third, the contribution was made into an interpretation of the passages that traditionally are considered difficult. Among them are Ruth 1:6–7; 1:8; 1:13; 1:22; 2:4; 2:5–7; 3:1–5; 3:8–9; 3:10–11; 4:5; and 4:17b–22. It has been shown that the analysis of focalization can sometimes help in clarifying and even solving the problems that arise with reading, understanding, translating, and interpreting the Hebrew text of the book of Ruth.

Finally, a modest contribution was made to the area of Hebrew syntax. The last chapter of the work demonstrates a correlation between the constructions with *qatal* forms of the Hebrew verb and the passages with internal focalization, which may point to the constructions with *qatal* verbs as possible markers of internal focalization in the Old Testament narratives.

Doors for Further Study

Because the book of Ruth was in the center of this research, the methodology of analysis of focalization was first of all anchored to this particular narrative. However, many characteristics of focalization that have been found in the book of Ruth can also be traced in other Old Testament narratives. Among them are predominance of dialogues, embedded narratives, evaluative speeches of the characters, restrictions of narrative information on the level of the story and on the level of discourse, and play of horizons. Moreover, unlike the book of Ruth, some Old Testament narratives demonstrate rearrangement and linearization of narrative information more explicitly, which allows one to apply Schmid's model of narrative constitution directly.

Of particular interest are the Old Testament narratives that do not have such clear division of episodes and events as the book of Ruth. Analysis of events and eventfulness will certainly help to clarify their structure and emphasize the most important (for the narrator) episodes of the story and, consequently, to blueprint the thread of the narrative and logic of selectivity.

The narratives with long descriptive passages may lead to new insights if attention is given to the selected details. These passages traditionally are considered more applicable for studying focalization because they usually have a very strong spatial element. Hence, it would be interesting to learn from what perspective the description is given and how it is focalized.

Finally, correlation between constructions with the *qatal* form of Hebrew verb and internal focalization was explored only within the boundaries of the book of Ruth. Whether this connection remains in other Old Testament narratives is one of the questions for future research.

Glossary

Character-focalizer – focalizer internal to the story associated with one of the characters. Can be perceptible or imperceptible depending on its consciousness. Perceptible can be characterized from without or from within.

Composition – the second level of narrative constitution which implies rearrangement and linearization of the events chosen at the level of selection.

Degree of eventfulness – the weight of the event in the plot of the narrative. Degree of eventfulness can be described by one of two sets of characteristics: (1) relevancy, unpredictability, persistence, irreversibility and noniterativity or (2) singularity, fractality, intentionality.

Dialogic narrative – narratives that largely consist of dialogues between characters with minimum narratorial intrusions. Such narratives represent special case with regard to focalization because for the most part they happen to be internally focalized.

Episode – the portion of the narrative for which boundaries can be defined on the basis of three factors: time gap, shift in space and change in the group of characters (appearance or disappearance of the character).

Event (narratological) – unprecedented action of the character which builds the plot of the narrative. Narratological event differs from simple change of state because it departs from the norms of life and crosses certain prohibition boundary. Minimum requirements of narratological event are factuality and resultativity.

Eventfulness – defining feature of narratological event (see degree of eventfulness).

External focalization – narrative situation when the narrator shares with the reader information restricted to a behaviorist report and the reader "sees" the narrative world externally without any additional information about mind or motifs of its inhabitants. The text is accordingly called externally focalized.

External focalizer – focalizer which is placed outside the story world. Usually is bound to the narrator of the story and accordingly called the narrator-focalizer (NF).

Factuality – the first basic requirement of narratological event which implies that the action brought about a real change of state in the narrative world.

Focalization – restriction of narrative information with respect to its completeness according to the chosen point of view.

Focalizer – the concept which was originally introduced by Mieke Bal to indicate the point within or outside the story world from which the elements of the world are described. This point can be placed inside or outside of the story world. If the focalizer is placed inside the story world, it is called internal; if it is placed outside the story, it is called external.

Fractality – one of three characteristics of narratological event (along with singularity and intentionality) that indicates the strictly limited segment of life when the event took place.

Happenings of life – all possible precedents of life that are used by the narrator as raw material for the selection of narrative information with their subsequent transformation into narratological events.

Horizon – the amount of information in the possession of the participant of narrative discourse (the character, the reader or the narrator) as contained in the narrator's or the character's words.

Ideal genetic model of narrative constitution – proposed by Wolf Schmid, a paradigm that demonstrates the process of narrative constitution from initial selection of facts to the actual presentation of the narrative text.

Ideological plane of point of view – the way of evaluating other characters or outer world by one of the characters or the narrator with the aim of building a basic system of worldview in the narrative world.

Imperative world picture – one of four narrative world pictures that "presupposes unquestionable axiological system of the world order in which a character always has freedom of choice, even though this choice is objectively assessed in terms of good and evil; an event consists of fulfilling or failing to fulfil a duty, of observing the moral law of the world or of breaching it."[1]

Intentionality – one of three characteristics of narratological event (along with singularity and fractality) that associates the event with a certain consciousness (i.e. character) which forms the significance and the role of the event in the story.

Internal focalization – narrative situation when the narrator shares with the reader information restricted to the cognition of one of the characters. The reader's horizon, therefore, equals the character's horizon and the reader perceives the narrative world through the mind of this character. Respectively, these texts are called internally focalized. Most dialogues fall within this category.

---

1. See Tjupa, "Narrative Strategies," paragraph 13.

Glossary

Internal focalizer – focalizer which is placed inside the story world. Usually is associated with one of the characters and therefore called the character-focalizer (CF).

Irreversibility – the fourth characteristic of eventfulness that refers to the possibility of returning to the previous state.

Linearization of events – one of two activities of the narrator on the level of composition which implies arranging in sequential order the events that occur in the story simultaneously.

Logic of selectivity – the logic which directs the choice of the narrator in the selection of happenings of life according to the thread of the narrative.

Modality of conviction – medial refraction that implies the imperative world picture based on authoritative convictions that do not need approval.

Narrative agent – the one who actually gives an account of the facts of the narrative.

Narrative discourse – the event of narration that implies interaction between the narrator, the characters, and the readers.

Narrative intrigue – the relevance of the story to the expectation of the readers.

Narrative world picture – sphere of objects relevant to the narration. According to Tjupa, there are four narrative world pictures that can be taken into consideration: imperative, occasional, precedential, and probabilistic. However, biblical narrators usually operate in the scope of only one, imperative world picture.

Narrative modality – rhetorical competency of the subject of speech. According to Tjupa, there are four narrative modalities that correspond to four narrative world pictures: modality of conviction, modality of neutral knowledge, modality of opinion, and modality of understanding.

Narrative strategy – selective configuration of narrative world picture, narrative modality, and narrative intrigue.

Noniterativity – the fifth characteristic of eventfulness that indicates the uniqueness of the event.

Occasional world picture – the world picture that sees the story as the chain of adventurous events. The game of chance is the main feature of eventfulness in such world picture.

Parallel focalization – the term that was invented in the course of this research, which implies a special type of focalization in the texts with reported speech. Focalization is called "parallel" because, from one side, in the text with reported speech the reader assumes the position of detached observer. But since the reported speech is one of the first ways to convey the knowledge and the attitudes of the character, the same text can be equally considered as internally focalized. Therefore, the same portion of the text can be attributed with two types of focalization (external and internal) simultaneously.

Persistence – the third characteristic of eventfulness which measures the impact of the event on the story world.

Phraseologial plane of point of view – the way of describing the characters of the story by imitation of the manner of speech. Usually manifests itself in direct speech and naming.

Pivotal point of the event – the most eventful moment of the event. Usually associated with the moment of decision making or crucial act of the character.

Point of view – the instrument of focalization, the pipe or the principle that guides the narrator in the process of narrative constitution.

Precedential world picture – the world picture that does not leave room for the characters to shy away from their stated purposes. An event in this world picture is related to the idea of destiny.

Presentation – the third and final level of narrative constitution which in case of literary narration is carried out through verbalization.

Probabilistic world picture – the world picture that focuses around the points of bifurcation. An event in such a world picture is the result and the continuation of bifurcation.

Relevancy – the first characteristic of the degree of eventfulness which reflects the significance of the event in the story world.

Reorganization of narrative information – one of two activities of the narrator on the level of composition which entails arbitrary reshuffling of the events with the purpose of better expression of the narrator's purposes.

Resultativity – the second requirement of narratological event that implies that the action reached completion in the narrative world of the text.

Selection – the first level of narrative constitution which implies the process of selecting narrative information from the happenings of life.

Shot of mental vision – the momentous picture of the narrative world or inner state of the character that is perceived by the reader as a result of reading details that are present in the narrative text.

Singularity – one of three characteristics of narratological event (along with fractality and intentionality) The narratological event should be unique, unitary, unprecedented, and unparalleled. Several facts of the story in this matter are highlighted from the inevitable life course and common social rituals.

Spatial and temporal planes of point of view – the way of describing the events of the narrative from certain physical place or point in time.

Story – the narrative that is formed on the second level of narrative constitution when all the events are selected and arranged in certain order ready to be presented in one of many possible languages of presentation (e.g. in the form of prose, poetry, movie, theater, ballet).

The act of narration – the process of transferring the story to the reader which involves the readers into narrative discourse.

The psychological plane of point of view – the way of describing the events of the narrative world through the consciousness or perception of one of the characters.

The witness and the judge of the event – the mind which bestows the happening of life with the measure of the singularity, fractality and intentionality.

Unpredictability – the second characteristic of the degree of eventfulness that signifies deviation of the event from the norms generally expected in a story world.

Zero focalization – narrative situation when the reader obtains information about the narrative world that is not accessible to any character which results in the horizon of the narrator and the reader to be wider than the horizon of the characters. The text in this instance is zero focalized or not focalized (not restricted).

Bibliography

Abbott, H. Porter. *The Cambridge Introduction to Narrative.* Cambridge: Cambridge University Press, 2002.
Aczel, R. "Hearing Voices in Narrative Texts." *New Literary History* 29, no. 3 (1998): 467–500.
———. "Voice." In *Routledge Encyclopedia of Narrative Theory,* edited by David Herman, Manfred Jahn, and Marie-Laure Ryan, xxix, 718. London: Routledge, 2005.
Adelman, Rachel. "Seduction and Recognition in the Story of Judah and Tamar and the Book of Ruth." *Nashim: A Journal of Jewish Women's Studies & Gender Issues,* no. 23 (2012): 87–109.
Aejmelaeus, Anneli. "Function and Interpretation of Ki in Biblical Hebrew." *Journal of Bibilcal Literature* 105, no. 2 (1986): 193–209.
Allen, W. "Narrative Distance, Tone, and Character." In *Theory of the Novel,* edited by John Halperin, 323–37. New York: Oxford University Press, 1974.
Alphen, Ernst van. "The Narrative of Perception and the Perception of Narrative." *Poetics Today* 11, no. 3 (1990): 483–509.
Alter, Robert. *The Art of Biblical Narrative.* New York: Basic Books, 2011.
———. "Biblical Type-Scenes and the Uses of Convention." *Critical Inquiry* 5, no. 2 (1978): 355–68.
———. "The Difference of Literature." *Poetics Today* 9, no. 3 (1988): 573–91.
———. "Sacred History and the Beginnings of Prose Fiction." *Poetics Today* 1, no. 3 (1980): 143–62.
———. *The World of Biblical Literature.* New York: BasicBooks, 1992.
Amit, Yaira. *Reading Biblical Narratives: Literary Criticism and the Hebrew Bible.* Minneapolis: Fortress, 2001.
Amoros, José Antonió Álvarez. "Henry James, Percy Lubbock, and Beyond: A Critique of the Anglo-American Conception of Narrative Point of View." *Studia Neophilologica* 66, no. 1 (1994): 47–57.
Andersen, Francis I. *The Sentence in Biblical Hebrew.* Janua Linguarum Series Practica. The Hague: Mouton, 1974.

———. "Yahweh, the Kind and Sensitive God." In *God Who Is Rich in Mercy: Essays Presented to Dr. D.B. Knox*, edited by D. Broughton Knox, Peter T. O'Brien and David G. Peterson, 41–88. Homebush West: Lancer Books, 1986.

Anderson, A. A. "The Marriage of Ruth." *Journal of Semitic Studies* 23, no. 2 (1978): 171–83.

Andersson, Greger. *Untamable Texts: Literary Studies and Narrative Theory in the Books of Samuel*. Library of Hebrew Bible/Old Testament Studies. New York: T & T Clark, 2009.

Andrew, R. Davis. "The Literary Effect of Gender Discord in the Book of Ruth." *Journal of Biblical Literature* 132, no. 3 (2013): 495–513.

Angel, Hayyim. "A Midrashic View of Ruth: Amidst a Sea of Ambiguity." *Jewish Bible Quarterly* 33, no. 2 (2005): 91–99.

Ap-Thomas, Dafydd R. "The Book of Ruth." *The Expository Times* 79, no. 12 (1968): 369–73.

Arnold, Bill T., and John H. Choi. *A Guide to Biblical Hebrew Syntax*. New York, NY: Cambridge University Press, 2003.

Atkinson, David. *The Message of Ruth: The Wings of Refuge*. Bible Speaks Today. Downers Grove, IL: InterVarsity Press, 1983.

Auerbach, Erich, and Willard R. Trask. *Mimesis: The Representation of Reality in Western Literature*. 50th anniversary ed. Princeton, NJ: Princeton University Press, 2003.

Auld, A. Graeme. *Joshua, Judges, and Ruth*. Daily Study Bible. Philadelphia: Westminster, 1984.

Averincev, Sergey S. "Греческая 'литература' и ближневосточная 'словесность.'" In *Образ античности*, 40–106. Sankt-Peterburg: Azbuka-klassika, 2004.

Baden, J. S. "The Tower of Babel: A Case Study in the Competing Methods of Historical and Modern Literary Criticism." *Journal of Biblical Literature* 128, no. 2 (2009): 209–24.

Bakhtin M. M. "Автор и герой в эстетической деятельности." In *Собрание сочинений*, Том 1, 104–74. Moscow: Russkie slovari. YAzyki slavyanskoj kul'tury, 2003.

———. *Эпос и Роман*. St. Petersburg: Izdatel'stvo "Azbuka," 2000.

Bakhtin, M. M., and Michael Holquist. *The Dialogic Imagination: Four Essays*. University of Texas Press Slavic Series. Austin, TX: University of Texas Press, 1981.

Bal, Mieke. "The Laughing Mice: Or: On Focalization." *Poetics Today* 2, no. 2 (1981): 202–10.

———. *Lethal Love: Feminist Literary Readings of Biblical Love Stories*. Indiana Studies in Biblical Literature. Bloomington: Indiana University Press, 1987.

———. *A Mieke Bal Reader*. Chicago: University of Chicago Press, 2006.

———. "The Narrating and the Focalizing: A Theory of the Agents in Narrative." *Style* 17, no. 2 (1983): 234–69.

———. "Narration and Focalization." In *Narrative Theory: Critical Concepts in Literary and Cultural Studies*, edited by Mieke Bal, 263–96. London; New York: Routledge, 2004.

———. *Narratology: Introduction to the Theory of Narrative*. Toronto: University of Toronto Press, 1985.

———. "Poetics, Today." *Poetics Today* 21, no. 3 (Fall 2000): 479–502.

———. *On Story-Telling: Essays in Narratology*. Edited by David Jobling. Sonoma, CA: Polebridge Press, 1991.

Bal, Mieke, and Christine van Boheemen. *Narratology: Introduction to the Theory of Narrative*. 3rd ed. Toronto: University of Toronto Press, 2009.

Bal, Mieke, and E. Tavor. "Notes on Narrative Embedding." *Poetics Today* 2, no. 2 (1981): 41–59.

Banfield, A. "Narrative Style and the Grammar of Direct and Indirect Speech." *Foundations of Language* 10, no. 1 (1973): 1–39.

Bar-Efrat, Shimon. *Narrative Art in the Bible*. New York: T & T Clark, 2004.

———. "Some Observations on the Analysis of Structure in Biblical Narrative." *Vetus Testamentum* 30, no. 2 (1980): 154–73.

Bauckham, Richard J. *Is the Bible Male?: The Book of Ruth and Biblical Narrative*. Cambridge: Grove Books, 1996.

Baylis, Charles P. "Naomi in the Book of Ruth in Light of the Mosaic Covenant." *Bibliotheca Sacra* 161 (2004): 413–31.

Beattie, Derek R. G. "The Book of Ruth as Evidence for Israelite Legal Practice." *Vetus Testamentum* 24 (1974): 251–67.

———. *Jewish Exegesis of the Book of Ruth*. JSOTSup. Sheffield: University of Sheffield Press, 1977.

———. "Kethibh and Qere in Ruth 4:5." *Vetus Testamentum* 21, no. Fasc. 4 (1971): 490–94.

———. "A Midrashic Gloss in Ruth 2:7." *Zeitschrift für die alttestamentliche Wissenschaft* 89, no. 1 (1977): 122–24.

———. "Redemption in Ruth, and Related Matters: A Response to Jack M. Sasson." *Journal for the Study of the Old Testament* 3, no. 5 (1978): 65–68.

———. "Ruth III." *Journal for the Study of the Old Testament* 3, no. 5 (1978): 39–48.

Berendsen, M. "Formal Criteria of Narrative Embedding." *Journal of Literary Semanitcs* 10, no. 2 (1981): 79–94.

———. "The Teller and the Observer: Narration and Focalization in Narrative Texts." *Style* 18, no. 2 (1984): 140–58.

Bergen, Robert D., ed. *Biblical Hebrew and Discourse Linguistics*. Dallas, TX: Summer Institute of Linguistics, 1994.

Berger, Yitzhak. "Ruth and the David—Bathsheba Story: Allusions and Contrasts." *Journal for the Study of the Old Testament* 33, no. 4 (2009): 433–52.

———. "Ruth and Inner-Biblical Allusion: The Case of 1 Samuel 25." *Journal of Biblical Literature* 128, no. 2 (2009): 253–72.

Berlin, Adele. "Narrative Poetics in the Bible." *Prooftexts* 6, no. 3 (1986): 273–84.

———. *Poetics and Interpretation of Biblical Narrative*. Sheffield: Almond, 1983.

Berman, Joshua. "Ancient Hermeneutics and the Legal Structure of the Book of Ruth." *Zeitschrift für die alttestamentliche Wissenschaft* 119, no. 1 (2007): 22–38.

Bernstein, Moshe J. "Two Multivalent Readings in the Ruth Narrative." *Journal for the Study of the Old Testament* 16, no. 50 (1991): 15–26.

Berquist, Jon L. "Role Dedifferentiation in the Book of Ruth." *Journal for the Study of the Old Testament* 18, no. 57 (1993): 23–37.

Bewer, Julius A. "The Goël in Ruth 4:14, 15." *American Journal of Semitic Languages and Literatures* 20, no. 3 (1904): 202–06.

Beyad, M., and F. Nemati. "Reading Narrative: The Implications of Using Focalization in Narrative Fiction." *Pazhuhesh-e Zabanha-ye Khareji* 27, no. Special Issue (2006): 53–69.

Block, Daniel Isaac. *Judges, Ruth*. New American Commentary. Nashville, TN: Broadman & Holman, 1999.

Booth, Wayne C. "Distance and Point-of-View: An Essay in Classification." *Essays in Criticism* 11, no. 1 (1961): 60–79.

Borowski, Obed. *Agriculture in Iron Age Israel*. Winona Lake: Eisenbrauns, 1987.

Bos, Johanna W. H. "Out of the Shadows: Genesis 38; Judges 4:17–22; Ruth 3." *Semeia* 42 (1988): 37–67.

Brenner, Athalya. "Naomi and Ruth." *Vetus Testamentum* 33, no. 4 (1983): 385–97.

Britt, Brian. "Death, Social Conflict, and the Barley Harvest in the Hebrew Bible." *Journal of Hebrew Scriptures* 5 (2005): 1–28.

Broman, Eva. "Narratological Focalization Models – a Critical Survey." In *Essays on Fiction and Perspective*, edited by Göran Rossholm, 57–89. Bern: Lang, 2004.

Brongers, H. A. "Some Remarks on the Biblical Particle halo." *Oudtestamentische Studien* 21 (1981): 177–89.

Bronzwaer, W. "Mieke Bal's Concept of Focalization: A Critical Note." *Poetics Today* 2, no. 2 (1981): 193–201.

Brooks, Cleanth, and Robert Penn Warren. *Understanding Fiction*. 3rd ed. Englewood Cliffs, NJ: Prentice-Hall, 1979.

Brooks, Peter. *Reading for the Plot: Design and Intention in Narrative*. Cambridge, MA: Harvard University Press, 1992.

Brown, Francis, S. R. Driver, and Charles A. Briggs. *Brown-Driver-Briggs Hebrew and English Lexicon: With an Appendix Containing the Biblical Aramaic*. Peabody, MA: Hendrickson, 2005.

Bush, Frederic William. "Ruth 4:17: A Semantic Wordplay." In *Go to the Land I Will Show You: Studies in Honor of Dwight W. Young Young*, edited by Joseph Coleson and Victor H. Matthews, 3–14. Winona Lake, IN: Eisenbruans, 1996.

———. *Ruth/Esther*. Word Biblical Commentary 9. Nashville, TN: Thomas Nelson, 1996.

Callaham, Scott N. "But Ruth Clung to Her: Textual Constraints on Ambiguity in Ruth 1:14." *Tyndale Bulletin* 63, no. 2 (2012): 179–197.

Campbell, Antony F. "The Storyteller's Role: Reported Story and Biblical Text." *Catholic Biblical Quarterly* 64, no. 3 (2002): 427–41.

Campbell, Edward F. *Ruth: A New Translation with Introduction, Notes, and Commentary*. Anchor Bible. Garden City, NY: Doubleday, 1975.

———. "Ruth Revisited." In *On the Way to Nineveh: Studies in Honor of George M. Landes*, edited by Stephen L. Cook, and S. C. Winter, 54–76. Atlanta, GA: Scholars Press, 1999.

———. "The Hebrew Short Story: A Study of Ruth." In *A Light Unto My Path: Old Testament Studies in Honor of Jacob M. Myers*, edited by Howard N. Bream, Ralph D. Heim, and Carey A. Moore, 83–110. Philadelphia: Temple University Press, 1974.

Carasik, Michael. "Ruth 2,7: Why the Overseer Was Embarrassed." *Zeitschrift für die alttestamentliche Wissenschaft* 107, no. 3 (1995): 493–94.

Carmichael, Calum M. "A Ceremonial Crux: Removing a Man's Sandal as a Female Gesture of Contempt." *Journal of Biblical Literature* 96, no. 3 (1977): 321–36.

———. "'Treading' in the Book of Ruth." *Zeitschrift für die alttestamentliche Wissenschaft* 92 (1980): 248–66.

Chatman, Seymour B. "Characters and Narrators: Filter, Center, Slant, and Interest-Focus." *Poetics Today* 7, no. 2 (1986): 189–204.

———. *Coming to Terms: The Rhetoric of Narrative in Fiction and Film*. Ithaca, NY: Cornell University Press, 1990.

———. *Story and Discourse: Narrative Structure in Fiction and Film*. Cornell University Press, 1980.

———. "What Novels Can Do That Films Can't (and Vice Versa)." *Critical Inquiry* 7, no. 1 (1980): 121–40.

Chatman, Seymour B., and Brian Attebery. *Reading Narrative Fiction*. New York: Macmillan, 1993.

Chisholm, Robert B., Jr. *A Commentary on Judges and Ruth*. Grand Rapids, MI: Kregel, 2013.

———. *From Exegesis to Exposition*. Grand Rapids, MI: Baker Books, 1998.

———. *Interpreting the Historical Books: An Exegetical Handbook*. Handbooks for Old Testament Exegesis. Grand Rapids, MI: Kregel, 2006.

———. "A Rhetorical Use of Point of View in Old Testament Narrative." *Bibliotheca Sacra* 159, no. 636 (2002): 404–14.

———. "Ruth." In *The Bible Knowledge Word Study: Joshua–2 Chronicles*, edited by Eugene H. Merrill, 113–22. Colorado Springs: Victor, 2004.

Coats, George W., ed. *Saga, Legend, Tale, Novella, Fable: Narrative Forms in Old Testament Literature*. JSOTSup 35. Sheffield: JSOT Press, 1985.

Clark, Gordon R. *The Word Hesed in the Hebrew Bible*. JSOTSup 157. Sheffield: Sheffield Academic Press, 1993.

Cohan, Steven, and Linda M. Shires. *Telling Stories: A Theoretical Analysis of Narrative Fiction*. New York: Routledge, 1988.

Cohen, Mordechai. "Hesed: Divine or Human? The Syntactic Ambiguity of Ruth 2:20." In *Hazon Nahum: Studies in Jewish Law, Thought, and History Presented to Dr. Norman Lamm*, edited by Yaakov Elman and Jeffrey S. Gurock, 11–38. Hoboken, NJ: Ktav, 1997.

Cohn, Dorrit. *The Distinction of Fiction*. Baltimore: John Hopkins University Press, 1999.

———. "Narrated Monologue: Definition of a Fictional Style." *Comparative Literature* 18, no. 2 (1966): 97–112.

Collins, C. John. "Ambiguity and Theology in Ruth." *Presbyterion* 19, no. 2 (1993): 97–102.

Cotrozzi, Stefano. *Expect the Unexpected: Aspects of Pragmatic Foregrounding in Old Testament Narratives*. New York: T & T Clark, 2010.

Coxon, Peter W. "Was Naomi a Scold? A Response to Fewell and Gunn." *Journal for the Study of the Old Testament* 45 (1989): 25–37.

Culler, Jonathan. "Fabula and Sjuzhet in the Analysis of Narrative: Some American Discussions." *Poetics Today* 1, no. 3 (1980): 27–37.

Culley, Robert C. *Studies in the Structure of Hebrew Narrative*. Philadelphia: Fortress, 1976.

Culpeper, Jonathan, Mick Short, and Peter Verdonk. *Exploring the Language of Drama: From Text to Context*. New York: Routledge, 1998.

Culpepper, Alan R. *Anatomy of the Fourth Gospel*. Philadelphia: Fortress Press, 1983.

Curtis, John B. "Second Thoughts on the Book of Ruth." *Proceedings, Eastern Great Lakes and Midwest Biblical Societies* 16 (1996): 141–49.

Dauber, Kenneth. "The Bible as Literature: Reading Like the Rabbis." *Semeia* 31 (1985): 27–48.

Davies, Eryl W. "Inheritance Rights and the Hebrew Levirate Marriage." *Vetus Testamentum* 31, no. 2 (1981): 138–44.

———. "Ruth IV 5 and the Duties of the *Gō'ēl*." *Vetus Testamentum* 33 (1983): 231–34.

Dawson, David Allan. *Text-Linguistics and Biblical Hebrew*. Sheffield: Sheffield Academic Press, 1994.

Derby, Josiah. "A Problem in the Book of Ruth." *Jewish Bible Quarterly* 22, no. 3 (1994): 178–85.

Dolezel, Lubomír. "The Typology of the Narrator: Point of View in Fiction." In *To Honor Roman Jakobson: Essays on the Occasion of His Seventieth Birthday*, 541–52. Vol. 1. The Hague: Mouton, 1967.

Edmiston, William F. "Focalization and the First-Person Narrator: A Revision of the Theory." *Poetics Today* 10, no. 4 (1989): 729–44.

———. *Hindsight and Insight: Focalization in Four Eighteenth-Century French Novels*. University Park: Pennsylvania State University Press, 1991.

Eliot, George, and Gregory Maertz. *Middlemarch: A Study of Provincial Life*. Orhcard Park, NY: Broadview Press, 2004.

Eskenazi, Tamara Cohn, and Tikva Simone Frymer-Kensky. *Ruth: The Traditional Hebrew Text with the New JPS Translation*. Philadelphia: Jewish Publication Society, 2011.

Fant, Gene C. *God as Author: A Biblical Approach to Narrative*. Nashville, TN: B & H Academic, 2010.

Fewell, Danna N., and David M. Gunn. "Boaz, Pillar of Society: Measures of Worth in the Book of Ruth." *Journal for the Study of the Old Testament* 14, no. 45 (1989): 45–59.

———. *Compromising Redemption: Relating Characters in the Book of Ruth*. Literary Currents in Biblical Interpretation. Louisville, KY: Westminster John Knox, 1990.

———. "Is Coxon a Scold? On Responding to the Book of Ruth." *Journal for the Study of the Old Testament* 14, no. 45 (1989): 39–43.

———. "'A Son Is Born to Naomi!': Literary Allusions and Interpretation in the Book of Ruth." *Journal for the Study of the Old Testament* 13, no. 40 (1988): 99–108.

Fischer, Irmtraud. "The Book of Ruth: A Feminist Commentary to the Torah?" In *Ruth and Esther*, edited by Athalya Brenner, 24–49. Sheffield: Sheffield Academic, 1999.

Flanagan, J. "Knowing More Than We Can Tell: The Cognitive Structure of Narrative Comprehension." *Partial Answers: Journal of Literature and the History of Ideas* 6, no. 2 (2008): 323–45.

Fludernik, Monika. *The Fictions of Language and the Languages of Fiction*. New York: Routledge, 1993.

———. *An Introduction to Narratology*. New York: Routledge, 2009.

———. "New Wine in Old Bottles? Voice, Focalization and New Writing." *New Literary History* 32, no. 3 (2001): 619–38.

Fokkelman, Jan P. *Reading Biblical Narrative: A Practical Guide*. Louisville, KY: Westminster John Knox, 1999.

Fowler, Roger. "How to See through Language: Perspective in Fiction." *Poetics* 11, no. 3 (1982): 213–35.

———. *Linguistics and the Novel*. London: Methuen, 1977.

———. "Who Is 'The Reader' in Reader Response Criticism?" *Semeia* 31 (1985): 5–23.

Freedman, Amela D. *God as an Absent Character in Biblical Hebrew Narrative: A Literary-Theoretical Study*. New York: Lang, 2005.

———. "Naomi's Experience of God and its Treatment in the Book of Ruth." *Proceedings, Eastern Great Lakes and Midwest Bible Societies* 23 (2003): 29–38.

Fruchtenbaum, Arnold G. *Ariel's Bible Commentary: The Books of Judges & Ruth*. Ariel Ministries, 2006.

Funk, Robert Walter. *The Poetics of Biblical Narrative*. Sonoma, CA: Polebridge Press, 1988.

Genette, Gérard. *Figures III*. Paris: Seuil, 1972.

———. *Narrative Discourse: An Essay in Method*. Translated by Jane E. Lewin. Ithca, NY: Cornell University Press, 1980.

———. *Narrative Discourse Revisited*. Ithaca, NY: Cornell University Press, 1988.

Gerleman, Gillis. *Ruth. Das Hohelied*. Biblischer Kommentar Altes Testament. Neukirchen-Vluyn: Neukirchener Verlag des Erziehungsvereins, 1965.

Glover, Neil. "Your People, My People: An Exploration of Ethnicity in Ruth." *Journal for the Study of the Old Testament* 33, no. 3 (2009): 293–313.

Goldfajn, Tal. *Word Order and Time in Biblical Hebrew Narrative*. Oxford: Clarendon, 1998.

Goldingay, J. "How Far Do Readers Make Sense? Interpreting Biblical Narrative." *Themelios* 18, no. 2 (1994): 5–10.

Goncharova Е.А. "Статус и "Изображенной речи" в Повествовательном Художественном Тексте." In *Немецкая Филология в Санкт-Петербургском Государственном Университете*, edited by Goncharova E. A., Nefyodov S. T. and Novozhilova K. R., 73. St. Petersburg: Sankt-Peterburgskij gosudarstvennyj universitet, 2014.

Gordis, Robert. "Love, Marriage, and Business in the Book of Ruth." In *A Light Unto My Path: Old Testament Studies in Honor of Jacob M. Myers*, edited by Howard N. Bream, Ralph D. Heim, and Carey A. Moore, 241–264. Philadelphia: Temple University Press, 1974.

Goslinga, C. J. *Joshua, Judges, Ruth*. Bible Student's Commentary. Grand Rapids, MI: Regency Reference Library, 1986.

Goulder, Michael. "Ruth: A Homily on Deuteronomy 22–25?" In *Of Prophets' Visions and the Wisdom of the Sages: Essays in Honour of R. Norman Whybray on His Seventieth Birthday*, edited by Heather A. McKay and David J. Clines, 307–19. Sheffield: Sheffield Academic, 1993.

Gow, Murray D. *Book of Ruth: Its Structure, Theme and Purpose*. Leicester: Apollos, 1992.

———. "Ruth Quoque – a Coquette? (Ruth 4:5)." *Tyndale Bulletin* 41, no. 2 (1990): 302–11.

———. 1984. "The Significance of Literary Structure for the Translation of the Book of Ruth." *Bible Translator* 35, no. 3 (1984): 309–20.

Grant, Reg. "Literary Structure in the Book of Ruth." *Bibliotheca Sacra* 148, no. 592 (1991): 424–41.

Gray, John. *Joshua, Judges, Ruth*. Grand Rapids, MI: Eerdmans, 1986.

Green, Barbara. "The Plot of the Biblical Story of Ruth." *Journal for the Study of the Old Testament* 7, no. 23 (1982): 55–68.

Grossman, Jonathan. "'Gleaning among the Ears': 'Gathering among the Sheaves': Characterizing the Image of the Supervising Boy (Ruth 2)." *Journal of Biblical Literature* 126, no. 4 (2007): 703–16.

Gunn, D. M. "New Directions in the Study of Biblical Hebrew Narrative." *Journal for the Study of the Old Testament* 12, no. 39 (1987): 65–75.

Hals, Ronald M. *The Theology of the Book of Ruth*. Facet Books Biblical Series 23. Philadelphia: Fortress, 1969.

Halton, Charles. "An Indecent Proposal: The Theological Core of the Book of Ruth." *Scandinavian Journal of the Old Testament* 26, no. 1 (2012): 30–43.

Hühn, Peter, John Pier, Wolf Schmid, and Jörg Schönert, eds. *Handbook of Narratology*. Berlin: de Gruyter, 2009.

Harm, Harry J. "The Function of Double Entendre in Ruth Three." *Journal of Translation and Textlinguistics* 7, no. 1 (1995): 19–27.

Hawk, Daniel L. *Ruth*. Apollos Old Testament Commentary. Edited by David W. Baker and Gordon J. Wenham. Vol. 7B. Downers Grove, IL: InterVarsity Press, 2015.

Hayes, Jeff. "Intentional Ambiguity in Ruth 4.5: Implications for Interpretation of Ruth." *Journal for the Study of the Old Testament* 41, no. 2 (2016): 159–82.

Hays, J. Daniel. "An Evangelical Approach to Old Testament Narrative Criticism." *Bibliotheca Sacra* 166 (2009): 3–18.

Hemingway, Ernest. *For Whom the Bell Tolls*. New York: Scribner's Sons, 1943.

———. "The Killers." In *The Complete Short Stories of Ernest Hemingway*. New York: Scribner's Sons, 1987.

Herman, David. *Basic Elements of Narrative*. Malden, MA: Wiley-Blackwell, 2009.

———. *The Cambridge Companion to Narrative*. Cambridge Companions to Literature. New York: Cambridge University Press, 2007.

———. "Hypothetical Focalization." *Narrative* 2, no. 3 (1994): 230–53.

Herman, Luc, and Bart Vervaeck. "Focalization between Classical and Postclassical Narratology." In *The Dynamics of Narrative Form: Studies in Anglo-American Narratology*, edited by John Pier, 115–138. Berlin: de Gruyter, 2004.

———. *Handbook of Narrative Analysis*. Translated from the Dutch by the Board of Regents of the University of Nebraska. Lincoln, NE: University of Nebraska Press, 2005.

Holmstedt, Robert D. *Ruth: A Handbook on the Hebrew Text*. Waco, TX: Baylor University Press, 2010.

Hongisto, Leif. "Literary Structure and Theology in the Book of Ruth." *Andrews University Seminary Studies* 23, no. 1 (1985): 19–28.

Hubbard, Robert L. *The Book of Ruth*. The New International Commentary on the Old Testament. Grand Rapids, MI: Eerdmans, 1988.

———. "The Goʾel in Ancient Israel: Theological Reflections on an Israelite Institution." *Bulletin for Biblical Research* 1 (1991): 3–19.

———. "Ruth IV 17: A New Solution." *Vetus Testamentum* 38, no. 3 (1988): 293–301.

Hurvitz, Avi. "Ruth 2.7 – a Midrashic Gloss." *Zeitschrift für die alttestamentliche Wissenschaft* 95, no. 1 (1983): 121–23.

Hyman, Ronald T. "Questions and Changing Identity in the Book of Ruth." *Union Seminary Quarterly Rewview* 39, no. 3 (1984): 189–201.

———. "Questions and the Book of Ruth." *Hebrew Studies* 24 (1983): 17–25.

Irwin, Brian P. "Removing Ruth: *Tiqqune Sopherim* in Ruth 3.3–4?" *Journal for the Study of the Old Testament* 32, no. 3 (2008): 331–38.

Jahn, Manfred, and Allan Nünning. "A Survey of Narratological Models." *Literatur in Wissenschaft und Unterricht* 27, no. 4 (1994): 283–303.

Jahn, Manfred. "Focalization." In *The Cambridge Companion to Narrative*, edited by David Herman, 94–108. New York: Cambridge University Press, 2007.

———. "Focalization." In *Routledge Encyclopedia of Narrative Theory*, edited by David Herman, Manfred Jahn, and Marie-Laure Ryan, 173–77. London: Routledge, 2005.

———. "More Aspects of Focalization: Refinements and Applications." *GRAAT* 21 (1999): 85–110.

———. *Narratology: A Guide to the Theory of Narrative*. Available online. English Department, University of Cologne. Version 2.0. (May 2017). http://www.uni-koeln.de/~ame02/pppn.htm.

———. "Windows of Focalization: Deconstructing and Reconstructing a Narratological Concept." *Style* 30, no. 2 (1996): 241–67.

James, Henry. *The Ambassadors*. London: Harper & Brothers, 1903.

Jesch, Tatiana, and Malie Stain. "Perspectivisation and Focalization: Two Concepts – One Meaning? An Attempt at Conceptual Differentiation." In *Point of View, Perspective, and Focalization: Modeling Mediation in Narrative*, edited by Peter Hühn, Wolf Schmid, and Jörg Schönert, 59–78. Berlin: de Gruyter, 2009.

Joüon, Paul. *Ruth: Commentaire Philologique Et ExéGéTique*. Subsidia Biblica. 2nd ed. Rome: Biblical Institute Press, 1986.
Joüon, Paul, and T. Muraoka. *A Grammar of Biblical Hebrew*. Subsidia Biblica. Roma: Pontificio istituto biblico, 2008.
Joyce, James. *A Portrait of the Artist as a Young Man*. New York: B. W. Huebsch, 1916.
Kates, Judith A., and Gail Twersky Reimer. *Reading Ruth: Contemporary Women Reclaim a Sacred Story*. New York: Ballantine Books, 1996.
Keen, S. "A Theory of Narrative Empathy." *Narrative* 14, no. 3 (2006): 207–36.
Keita, Schadrac, and Janet W. Dyk. "The Scene at the Threshing Floor: Suggestive Readings and Intercultural Considerations." *Bible Translator* 57, no. 1 (2006): 17–32.
King, Greg A. "Ruth 2:1–13." *Interpretation* 52 (1998): 182–184.
Klauk, Tobias, and Tilmann Köppe. "Puzzles and Problems for the Theory of Focalization." In *The Living Handbook of Narratology*, edited by Peter Hühn, Jan Christoph Meister, John Pier, and Wolf Schmid Hamburg: Hamburg University, 2011. Available online http://www.lhn.uni-hamburg.de/discussion/puzzles-and-problems-theory-focalization.
Korpel, Marjo C. A. *The Structure of the Book of Ruth*. Assen: Koninklijke Van Gorcum, 2001.
LaCocque, André. *Ruth: A Continental Commentary*. Continental Commentaries. Minneapolis: Fortress, 2004.
Lakin, C. S. "Using Close-Up Shots to Give Sensory Detail." *C. S. Lakin*, blog post, 3 April 2013. https://www.livewritethrive.com/2013/04/03/using-close-up-shots-to-give-sensory-detail/.
Lanser, Susan Sniader. *The Narrative Act: Point of View in Prose Fiction*. Princeton, NJ: Princeton University Press, 1981.
Lasine, S. "Fiction, Falsehood, and Reality in Hebrew Scripture." *Hebrew Studies* 25 (1984): 24–40.
Leggett, Donald A. *The Levirate and Goel Institutions in the Old Testament: With Special Attention to the Book of Ruth*. Cherry Hill, NJ: Mack Publishing, 1974.
Lim, Timothy H. "The Book of Ruth and Its Literary Voice." In *Reflection and Refraction: Studies in Biblical Historiography in Honour of A. Graeme Auld*, edited by Robert Rezetko, Timothy H. Lim, and W. Brian Aucker, 261–82. Leiden: Brill, 2007.
Linafelt, Tod. "Narrative and Poetic Art in the Book of Ruth." *Interpretation* 64, no. 2 (2010): 117–29.
Linafelt, Tod, and Timothy K. Beal. *Ruth and Esther*. Collegeville, MN: Liturgical Press, 1999.

Liozov, Sergey.V., and Jejdel'kind Jakov. D. "Синтаксис речи рассказчика в древнееврейской повествовательной прозе." In *Библия. Литературные и лингвистические исследования.*, 18–259. Moscow: RGGU, 1999.

Loader, J. A. "Ruth 2:7 – an Old Crux." *Journal for Semitics* 4, no. 2 (1992): 151–59.

Long, Burke O. "Historical Narrative and the Fictionalizing Imagination." *Vetus Testamentum* 35, no. 4 (1985): 405–16.

———. *Images of Man and God: Old Testament Short Stories in Literary Focus*. Sheffield: Almond Press, 1981.

Long, V. P. "Toward a Better Theory and Understanding of Old Testament Narrative." *Presbyterian* 13, no. 2 (1987): 102–09.

Longacre, Robert E. "*Weqatal* Forms in Biblical Hebrew Prose." In *Biblical Hebrew and Discourse Linguistics*, edited by Robert D. Bergen, 50–98. Winona Lake, IN: Summer Institute of Linguistics, 1994.

Loretz, Oswald. "The Theme of the Ruth Story." *Catholic Biblical Quarterly* 22 (1960): 391–99.

Lubbock, Percy. *The Craft of Fiction*. Minneapolis: Filiquarian, 2007.

Magonet, Jonathan. "Character/Author/Reader: The Problem of Perspective in Biblical Narrative." In *Literary Structure and Rhetorical Strategies in the Hebrew Bible*, edited by L. J. de Regt, Jan de Waard, and J. P. Fokkelman, 3–13. Assen: Van Gorcum, 1996.

Manolov, Gueorgui V. "Elements of Narrative Discourse in Selected Short Stories of Ernest Hemingway." PhD dissertation, University of South Florida, 2007. Avilable online, http://scholarcommons.usf.edu/etd/2277.

Margolin, Uri. "Focalization: Where Do We Go from Here?." In *Point of View, Perspective, and Focalization: Modeling Mediation in Narrative*, edited by Peter Hühn, Wolf Schmid, and Jörg Schönert, 41–58. Berlin: de Gruyter, 2009.

Marguerat, Daniel, Marcel Durrer, and Yvan Bourquin. *How to Read Bible Stories: An Introduction to Narrative Criticism*. London: SCM, 1999.

Martin, Wallace. *Recent Theories of Narrative*. Ithaca, NY: Cornell University Press, 1986.

Mathewson, Steven D. *The Art of Preaching Old Testament Narrative*. Grand Rapids, MI: Baker Academic, 2002.

Matthews, Victor H. "The Determination of Social Identity in the Story of Ruth." *Biblical Theology Bulletin* 36, no. 2 (2006): 49–54.

McIntyre, Dan. *Point of View in Plays: A Cognitive Stylistic Approach to Viewpoint in Drama and Other Text-Types*. Philadelphia: J. Benjamins, 2006.

McKane, William. "Ruth and Boaz." *Transactions of the Glasgow University Oriental Society* 19 (1961): 38.

McKeown, James. *Ruth*. Two Horizons Old Testament Commentary. Grand Rapids, MI: Eerdmans, 2015.

Meister, Jan Christoph, and Jörg Shcönert. "The DNS of Mediacy." In *Point of View, Perspective, and Focalization: Modeling Mediation in Narrative*, edited by Peter Hühn, Wolf Schmid, and Jörg Schönert, 11–40. Berlin: de Gruyter, 2009.

Merrill, Eugene H. "The Book of Ruth: Narration and Shared Themes." *BS* 142 (1985): 130–41.

Miall, D.S. "Episode Structures in Literary Narratives." *Journal of Literary Semantics* 33, no. 2 (2004): 111–29.

Miall, David S., and Don Kuiken. "Shifting Perspectives: Readers' Feelings and Literary Response." In *New Perspectives on Narrative Perspective*, edited by Willie van Peer and Seymour Benjamin Chatman, 288–301. Albany: State University of New York Press, 2001.

Michael, Matthew. "The Art of Persuasion and the Book of Ruth: Literary Devices in the Persuasive Speeches of Ruth 1:6–18." *Hebrew Studies* 56 (2015): 145–62.

Michener, James A. *Hawaii*. London: Secker and Warburg, 1976.

Min, Young-Jin. "Problems in Ruth 2.7." *Bible Translation* 40, no. 4 (1989): 438–41.

Moore, Michael S. "To King or Not to King: A Canonical-Historical Approach to Ruth." *Bulletin for Biblical Research* 11, no. 1 (2001):27–42.

———. "Ruth the Moabite and the Blessing of Foreigners." *Catholic Biblical Quarterly* 60, no. 2 (1998): 203–17.

———. "Two Textual Anomalies in Ruth." *Catholic Biblical Quarterly*, no. 59 (1997):234–243.

Mundhenk, Norman, and Jan de Waard. "Missing the Whole Point and What to Do About It – With Special Reference to the Book of Ruth." *Bible Translator* 26, no. 4 (1975): 420–33.

Myers, Jacob Martin. *The Linguistic and Literary Form of the Book of Ruth*. Leiden: Brill, 1955.

Nazarov, Konstantin. "Концепция фокализации в ее историческом развитии." In *Белые чтения: к 85-летию Галины Андреевны Белой: сборник научных статей*. – Moscow: EHditus, 2016.

Nelles, William. "Getting Focalization into Focus." *Poetics Today* 11, no. 2 (1990): 365–82.

———. "Stories within Stores: Narrative Levels and Embedded Narrative." *Studies in the Literary Imagination* 25, no. 1 (1992): 79–96.

Niccacci, Alviero. *The Syntax of the Verb in Classical Hebrew Prose*. Translated by W. G. E. Watson. Sheffield: JSOT Press, 1990.

Niederhoff, Burchard. "Fokalisation Und Perspektive. Ein Plädoyer Für Friedliche Koexistenz." *Poetica* 33, no. 1/2 (2001): 1–21.

———. "Perspective – Point of View." In *The Living Handbook of Narratology*, edited by Peter Hühn, Jan Christoph Meister, John Pier, and Wolf Schmid. Hamburg: Hamburg University, 2011. http://www.lhn.uni-hamburg.de/.

Niehoff, M. "Do Biblical Characters Talk to Themselves? Narrative Modes of Representing Inner Speech in Early Biblical Fiction." *Journal of Biblical Literature* 111, no. 4 (1992): 577–95.

Nielsen, Kirsten. *Ruth: A Commentary*. London: SCM Press, 1997.

Nieragden, Göran. "Focalization and Narration: Theoretical and Terminological Refinements." *Poetics Today* 23, no. 4 (2002): 685–97.

Norkus, Zenonas. "Historical Narratives as Pictures: On Elective Affinities between Verbal and Pictorial Representations." *Journal of Narrative Theory* 34, no. 2 (2004): 173–206.

Nünlist, René. "The Homeric Scholia on Focalization." *Mnemosyne* 56, no. 1 (2003): 61–71.

O'Neill, Patrick. *Fictions of Discourse: Reading Narrative Theory*. Toronto: University of Toronto Press, 1994.

Ostriker, Alicia. "The Book of Ruth and the Love of the Land." *Biblical Interpretation* 10 (2002): 343–59.

Palmer, Alan. *Fictional Minds*. Frontiers of Narrative. Lincoln: University of Nebraska Press, 2004.

Parker, Robert Dale. *How to Interpret Literature: Critical Theory for Literary and Cultural Studies*. New York: Oxford University Press, 2008.

Peer, Willie van, and Seymour B. Chatman, eds. *New Perspectives on Narrative Perspective*. Albany: State University of New York Press, 2001.

Penrod, Lynn Kettler "Focalization without (Too Much) Fuss: Using Narratology to Teach Thérèse Desqueyroux." *Association of Departments of Foreign Languages Bulletin* 6, no. 2 (January 1988): 7–12.

Peter Hühn, Wolf Schmid, and Jörg Schönert, eds. *Point of View, Perspective, and Focalization: Modeling Mediation in Narrative*. Narratologia: Contributions to Narrative Theory. Berlin: de Gruyter, 2009.

Phelan, James, and Peter J. Rabinowitz. *A Companion to Narrative Theory*. Oxford: Blackwell, 2005.

Pier, John, and José Angel García Landa. *Theorizing Narrativity*. Narratologia. Berlin; New York: de Gruyter, 2008.

Pohler, E. M. "Floating in Space and Time: Where and When Is the Story?" *Narrative* 4, no. 3 (1996): 278–86.

Polak, Frank H. "Forms of Talk in Hebrew Biblical Narrative: Negotiations, Interaction, and Sociocultural Context." In *Literary Construction of Identity in the Ancient World: Proceedings of a Conference, Literary Fiction and the Construction of Identity in Ancient Literatures: Options and Limits of Modern Literary Approaches*, edited by Hanna Liss and Manfred Oeming, 167–98. Winona Lake, IN: Eisenbrauns, 2010.

Prince, Gerald. *Narratology: The Form and Functioning of Narrative*. Janua Linguarum Series Maior. New York: de Gruyter, 1982.

Rauber, D. F. "Literary Values in the Bible: The Book of Ruth." *Journal of Biblical Literature* 89, no. 1 (1970): 27–37.

Rebera, Basil Arthur. "The Book of Ruth: Dialogue and Narrative, the Function and Integration of the Two Modes in an Ancient Hebrew Story." PhD dissertation, Macquarie University, Sydney, 1981.

Rendsburg, Gary A. "Confused Language as a Deliberate Literary Device in Biblical Hebrew Narrative." *Journal of Hebrew Scriptures* 2 (1999): article 6. https://journals.library.ualberta.ca/jhs/index.php/jhs/article/view/5995.

"Researchers Needed! The Vast Array of Point-of-View Topics Crying Out For Attention." *PerspectiveCriticism*, blog. https://perspectivecriticism.com/2014/06/12/researchers-needed-the-vast-array-of-point-of-view-topics-crying-out-for-attention/.

Revell, Ernest J. "The Repetition of Introductions to Speech as a Feature of Biblical Hebrew." *Vetus Testamentum* 47, no. 1 (1997): 91–110.

———. "The Two Forms of First Person Singular Pronoun in Biblical Hebrew: Redundancy or Expressive Contrast?" *Journal of Semitic Studies* 40, no. 2 (1995): 199–217.

Richardson, Brian. "Voice and Narration in Postmodern Drama." *New Literary History* 32, no. 3 (2001): 681–94.

Richter, David H. *Narrative/Theory*. White Plains, NY: Longman, 1996.

Rimmon-Kenan, Shlomith. *Narrative Fiction: Contemporary Poetics*. 2nd ed. New York: Routledge, 2002.

Rocine, Bryan M. *Learning Biblical Hebrew: A New Approach Using Discourse Analysis*. Macon, GA: Smyth & Helwys, 2000.

Ronen, Ruth. *Possible Worlds in Literary Theory*. Cambridge: Cambridge University Press, 1994.

Rooke, D. W. "Feminist Criticism of the Old Testament: Why Bother?" *Feminist Theology* 15, no. 2 (2007): 160–174.

Rossholm, Göran. *Essays on Fiction and Perspective*. New York: Lang, 2004.

Rossow, Francis C. "Literary Artistry in the Book of Ruth and its Theological Significance." *Concordia Journal* 17 (1991): 12–19.

Rüsen, Jörn. "Historical Narration: Foundation, Types, Reason." *History and Theory* 26, no. 4 (1987): 87–97.

Sakenfeld, Katharine D. *The Meaning of Hesed in the Hebrew Bible*. HSM 17. Missoula, MT: Scholars Press, 1978.

———. *Ruth*. Interpretation. Louisville, KY: Westminster John Knox, 1999.

———. "Ruth 4, An Image of Eschatological Hope." In *Liberating Eschatology: Essays in Honor of Letty M. Russell*, edited by Margaret A. Farley and Serene Jones, 55–67. Louisville: Westminster John Knox, 1999.

Sasson, Jack M. "Ruth III: A Response." *Journal for the Study of the Old Testament* 3, no. 5 (1978): 49–51.

———. *Ruth: A New Translation with a Philological Commentary and a Formalist-Folklorist Interpretation*. Baltimore: Johns Hopkins University Press, 1979.
Savran, George W. *Telling and Retelling: Quotation in Biblical Literature*. Bloomington: Indiana University Press, 1988.
Saxegaard, Kristin M. *Character Complexity in the Book of Ruth*. Tubingen: Mohr Siebeck, 2010.
———. "'More Than Seven Sons': Ruth as Example of the Good Son." *Scandinavian Journal of the Old Testament* 15, no. 2 (2001): 257–75.
Schipper, Jeremy. *Ruth: A New Translation with Introduction and Commentary*. New Haven, CT: Yale University Press, 2016.
Schmid, Wolf. *Elemente Der Narratologie*. Berlin: De Gruyter, 2005.
———. *Нарратология*. Moscow: YAzyki slavyanskoj kul'tury, 2003.
———. *Нарратология*. Moscow: YAzyki slavyanskoj kul'tury, 2008.
———. "Narrativity and Eventfulness." In *What Is Narratology?: Questions and Answers Regarding the Status of a Theory*, edited by Tom Kindt and Hans-Harald Müller, 17–33. Berlin: de Gruyter, 2003.
———. *Narratology: An Introduction*. Berlin: de Gruyter, 2010.
Scholes, Robert, James Phelan, and Robert L. Kellogg. *The Nature of Narrative*. 40th anniversary ed. Oxford: Oxford University Press, 2006.
Schoors, Antoon. "The Particle *Ki*." In *Remembering All the Way . . .: A Collection of Old Testament Studies Published on the Occasion of the Fortieth Anniversary of the Oudtestamentisch Werkgezelschap in Nederland*, 240–76. Leiden: Brill, 1981.
Schwartz, Regina M. *The Book and the Text: The Bible and Literary Theory*. Cambridge, MA: Blackwell, 1990.
Selden, Raman, Peter Widdowson, and Peter Brooker. *A Reader's Guide to Contemporary Literary Theory*. 5th ed. Harlow: Longman, 2005.
Shen, Dan. "Narrative, Reality, and Narrator as Construct: Reflections on Genette's 'Narrating.'" *Narrative* 9, no. 2 (2001): 123–29.
Shepherd, David. "Violence in the Fields? Translating, Reading, and Revising in Ruth 2." *Catholic Biblical Quarterly* 63, no. 3 (2001): 444–63.
Shklovsky, Viktor B. *О Теории Прозы*. Moscow: Izdatel'stvo "Federaciya," 1929.
Shmaina-Velikanova, Anna. "Книга Руфи как символическая повесть." PhD diss., Rossiĭskyi gosudarstvennyi gumanitarnyi universitet, 2011.
———. *Книга Руфи: перевод, введение в изучение Книги Руфи, комментарий*. Izdatel'skiĭ tsentr Rossiĭskogo gosudarstvennogo gumanitarnogo universiteta, 2011.
Silant'ev, Igor V. *Поэтика мотива*. Moscow: Jazyki slavjanskoj kul'tury, 2004.
Simpson, Paul. *Language, Ideology and Point of View*. London: Routledge, 2003.

Siquans, Agnethe. "Foreignness and Poverty in the Book of Ruth: A legal Way for a Poor Foreign Woman to Be Integrated into Israel." *Journal of Biblical Literature* 128, no. 3 (2009): 443–52.

Ska, Jean Louis. *"Our Fathers Have Told Us": Introduction to the Analysis of Hebrew Narratives*. 2nd ed. Roma: Editrice Pontificio Instituto Biblico, 2000.

Skalin, Lars-Åke. "Focalization as Restriction of Field." In *Essays on Fiction and Perspective*, edited by Göran Rossholm, 223–54. Bern: Lang, 2004.

Smith, Mark S. "'Your People Shall Be My People': Family and Covenant in Ruth 1:16–17." *Catholic Biblical Quarterly* 69 (2007): 242–58.

Stanzel, Franz K. "Teller-Characters and Reflector-Characters in Narrative Theory." *Poetics Today* 2, no. 2 (1981): 5–15.

———. *A Theory of Narrative*. New York: Cambridge University Press, 1984.

Stendhal, Marie-Henri B. *Charterhouse of Parma*. Translated by E. P. Robins. New York: George Richmond, 1895.

———. *The Red and the Black: A Chronicle of the Nineteenth Century*. World's Classics. Oxford: Oxford University Press, 1991.

Sternberg, Meir. *The Poetics of Biblical Narrative: Ideological Literature and the Drama of Reading*. Bloomington: Indiana University Press, 1985.

———. "The World from the Addressee's Viewpoint: Reception as Representation, Dialogue as Monologue in Narrative Poetics." *Style* 20, no. 3 (1986): 295–318.

Sutskover, Talia. "The Themes of Land and Fertility in the Book of Ruth." *Journal for the Study of the Old Testament* 34, no. 3 (2010): 283–94.

Tamarchenko, Natan D., Tjupa Valeri, I., and Broitman Samson N. *Теория художественного дискурса. Теоретическая поэтика*. Edited by Tamarchenko Natan D. 2 vols. Moscow: Izdatel'skiĭ tsentr "Akademiya," 2004.

Thomas, Bronwen. *Fictional Dialogue: Speech and Conversation in the Modern and Postmodern Novel*. Kindle edition. Lincoln: University of Nebraska Press, 2012.

Thompson, Michael E. W. "New Life Amid the Alien Corn: The Book of Ruth." *Evangelical Quarterly* 65, no. 3 (1993): 197–210.

Thompson, Thomas, and Dorothy Thompson. "Some Legal Problems in the Book of Ruth." *Vetus Testamentum* 18, no. 1 (1968): 79–99.

Tjupa, Valeri I. "Драма Как Тип Высказывания." *Novyj filosofskij vestnik* 14, no. 3 (2010): 7–16.

———. "Нарратив и Другие Регистры Говорения." *NARRATORIUM* no. 1–2 (Spring-Autumn 2011). Accessed 3 May 2006, http://narratorium.rggu.ru/article.html?id=2027584.

———. "Что Такое Логос Вербализации?" *OpeNarratology* (2015). Published electronically 28 December 2015. http://www.opennar.com/single-post/2015/12/28/Что-такое-логос-вербализации.

———. *Анализ Художественного Текста*. Moscow: Izdatel'skiĭ tsentr "Akademiya," 2009.

———. "Narrative Strategies." In *The Living Handbook of Narratology*, edited by Peter Hühn, Jan Christoph Meister, John Pier and Wolf Schmid Hamburg: Hamburg University, 2014. http://www.lhn.uni-hamburg.de/article/narrative-strategies.

———. *Анализ Художественного Текста*. Moscow: Izdatel'skiĭ tsentr "Akademiya," 2009.

———. *Введение в сравнительную нарратологию*. Moscow: Intrada, 2016.

Tollers, Vincent L. "Narrative Control in the Book of Ruth." In *Mappings of the Biblical Terrain: The Bible as Text*, edited by Vincent L. Tollers and John Maier, 252–59. Lewisburg: Bucknell University Press, 1990.

Tolmie, D. F. *Narratology and Biblical Narratives: A Practical Guide*. San Francisco: International Scholars Publications, 1998.

Toolan, Michael J. *Narrative: A Critical Linguistic Introduction*. 2nd ed. London: Routledge, 2001.

Trible, Phyllis. *God and the Rhetoric of Sexuality*. Overtures to Biblical Theology. Philadelphia: Fortress, 1978.

———. "Two Women in a Man's World: A Reading of the Book of Ruth." *Soundings: An Interdisciplinary Journal* 59, no. 3 (1976): 251–79.

Uspensky, Boris A. *A Poetics of Composition: The Structure of the Artistic Text and Typology of a Compositional Form*. Translated by Valentina Zavarin and Susan Wittig. Berkeley: University of California Press, 1973.

———. *Поэтика Композиции*. Moscow Iskusstvo, 1970.

———. *Семиотика Искусства. Язык. Семиотика. Культура*. Moscow: SHkola. "YAzyki kul'tury," 1995.

van Wolde, Ellen. *Ruth and Naomi*. Translated by John Bowden. London: SCM, 1997.

———. "Texts in Dialogue with Texts: Intertextuality in the Ruth and Tamar Narratives." *Biblical Interpretation* 5, no. 1 (1997): 1–28.

———. "Who Guides Whom? Embeddedness and Perspective in Biblical Hebrew and in 1 Kings 3:16–28." *Journal of Biblical Literature* 114, no. 4 (1995): 623–42.

Vance, Donald R. *A Hebrew Reader for Ruth*. Peabody, MA: Hendrickson, 2003.

VanGemeren, Willem. *New International Dictionary of Old Testament Theology & Exegesis*. 5 vols. Vol. 1, Grand Rapids, MI: Zondervan, 1997.

Verne, Jules, and William Butcher. *Around the World in Eighty Days: The Extraordinary Journeys*. Oxford: Oxford University Press, 1995.

Vette, Joachim. "Narrative Poetics and Hebrew Narrative: A Survey." In *Literary Construction of Identity in the Ancient World*, edited by Hanna Liss and Manfred Oeming, 19–62. Winona Lake, IN: Eisenbrauns, 2010.

Walsh, Jerome T. *Old Testament Narrative: A Guide to Interpretation*. Louisville, KY: Westminster John Knox Press, 2010.

———. *Style and Structure in Biblical Hebrew Narrative*. Collegeville, MN: Liturgical Press, 2001.

Walsh, Richard. "Who Is the Narrator?" *Poetics Today* 18, no. 4 (1997): 495–513.

Waltke, Bruce K., and Michael Patrick O'Connor. *An Introduction to Biblical Hebrew Syntax*. Winona Lake, IN: Eisenbrauns, 1990.

Wardlaw Jr., Terrance R. "Shaddai, Providence, and the Narrative structure of Ruth." *Journal of the Evangelical Theological Society* 58, no. 1 (March 2015): 31–41.

Weisberg, Dvora E. "The Widow of Our Discontent: Levirate Marriage in the Bible and Ancient Israel." *Journal for the Study of the Old Testament* 28, no. 4 (2004): 403–29.

Weitzman, S. "Before and After the *Art of Biblical Narrative*." *Prooftexts – a Journal of Jewish Literary History* 27, no. 2 (2007): 191–210.

Wendland, Ernst R. "Structural Symmetry and its Significance in the Book of Ruth." In *Issues in Bible Translation*, edited by Philip C. Stine, 30–63. London: United Bible Societies, 1988.

Wilch, John R. *Ruth: A Concordia Hebrew Reader*. St Louis, MO: Concordia Publishing House, 2010.

———. *Ruth*. Concordia Commentary. St. Louis, MO: Concordia Publishing House, 2006.

Womack, Peter. *Dialogue: The New Critical Idiom*. London: Routledge, 2011.

Yamasaki, Gary. *Perspective Criticism: Point of View and Evaluative Guidance in Biblical Narrative*. Eugene, OR: Cascade Books, 2012.

———. *Watching a Biblical Narrative: Point of View in Biblical Exegesis*. New York: T&T Clark, 2007.

Younger, K. Lawson, Jr. "Two Comparative Notes on the Book of Ruth." *Journal of the Ancient Near Eastern Society* 26, no. 1 (1998): 121–32.

———. *Judges and Ruth*. NIV Application Commentary. Grand Rapids, MI: Zondervan, 2002.

Zevit, Ziony. "Dating Ruth: Legal, Linguistic and Historical Observations." *Zeitschrift für die alttestamentliche Wissenschaft* 117, no. 4 (2005): 574–600.

Ziegler, Yael. "'So Shall God Do . . .': Variations of an Oath Formula and its Literary Meaning." *Journal of Biblical Literature* 126, no. 1 (2007): 59–81.

———. *Ruth: From Alienation to Monarchy*. Jerualem: Maggid Books, 2015. Kindle.

Zipfel, Frank. "Non-Fiction Novel." In *Routledge Encyclopedia of Narrative Theory*, edited by David Herman, Manfred Jahn, and Marie-Laure Ryan, London: Routledge, 2005.

Langham Literature, with its publishing work, is a ministry of Langham Partnership.

Langham Partnership is a global fellowship working in pursuit of the vision God entrusted to its founder John Stott –

> *to facilitate the growth of the church in maturity and Christ-likeness through raising the standards of biblical preaching and teaching.*

Our vision is to see churches in the Majority World equipped for mission and growing to maturity in Christ through the ministry of pastors and leaders who believe, teach and live by the word of God.

Our mission is to strengthen the ministry of the word of God through:
- nurturing national movements for biblical preaching
- fostering the creation and distribution of evangelical literature
- enhancing evangelical theological education

especially in countries where churches are under-resourced.

Our ministry

Langham Preaching partners with national leaders to nurture indigenous biblical preaching movements for pastors and lay preachers all around the world. With the support of a team of trainers from many countries, a multi-level programme of seminars provides practical training, and is followed by a programme for training local facilitators. Local preachers' groups and national and regional networks ensure continuity and ongoing development, seeking to build vigorous movements committed to Bible exposition.

Langham Literature provides Majority World preachers, scholars and seminary libraries with evangelical books and electronic resources through publishing and distribution, grants and discounts. The programme also fosters the creation of indigenous evangelical books in many languages, through writer's grants, strengthening local evangelical publishing houses, and investment in major regional literature projects, such as one volume Bible commentaries like the *Africa Bible Commentary* and the *South Asia Bible Commentary*.

Langham Scholars provides financial support for evangelical doctoral students from the Majority World so that, when they return home, they may train pastors and other Christian leaders with sound, biblical and theological teaching. This programme equips those who equip others. Langham Scholars also works in partnership with Majority World seminaries in strengthening evangelical theological education. A growing number of Langham Scholars study in high quality doctoral programmes in the Majority World itself. As well as teaching the next generation of pastors, graduated Langham Scholars exercise significant influence through their writing and leadership.

To learn more about Langham Partnership and the work we do visit **langham.org**